1 WESSEX

A WEST COUNTRY TERRITORIAL ARMY BATTALION
1967 – 1995

The Battalion at Knook Camp, Warminster, Camp 1990

1 WESSEX

A WEST COUNTRY TERRITORIAL ARMY BATTALION 1967 — 1995

Martin Lee-Browne

Chester House Press
Fairford
2009

First published in Great Britain in 2009 by
Chester House Press
Chester House
Fairford
Gloucestershire
GL7 4AD

ISBN 978-0-9560391-0-1

Typeset by Paul Brooks, Design & Print (Oxford)
Printed and bound by
Remous, Wyvern Buildings, Glovers Close, Sherborne, Dorset

DEDICATION

To the wives, girl-friends, and a few husbands, without
whose generous support and understanding 1 Wessex
could never have been what it was.

CONTENTS

PREFACE

by

General Sir John Waters GCB, CBE, JP, DL

This book will be read with pride, pleasure, and nostalgia by soldiers who served in 1 Wessex and the wider regimental family — and sometimes, I suspect, anger, when they discover some of the things that were going on behind the scenes. I hope that it is also read by ex-French Foreign Legionaire XXXX (Chapter 9, first letter)!

That, from time to time, there have been misunderstandings between the Regular Army and the Territorial Army is clearly apparent from the text. This is sad but probably unavoidable. The TA provides amazingly dedicated soldiers. Two examples will suffice. A senior civil servant in Whitehall commuted weekly to Belfast to his drill nights as a junior officer in a gunner regiment and a much more senior one, now a Permanent Under Secretary, did the same from HQ Rhine Army, flying back weekly to London. I think that most regular soldiers thought that they were mad. But this degree of commitment is common in the TA, and it was in 1 Wessex as these immaculately recorded pages demonstrate.

The TA is "different but the same", as I realised when I became Commander-in-Chief, United Kingdom Land Forces and visited TA units throughout the Kingdom, and also when I was the Honorary Colonel of the Royal Wessex Yeomanry. The slogan "One Army", adopted some time ago, is good so far as it goes. But the TA approach their military tasks from a different starting point to the Regular Army. However, the ultimate aim is the same — military excellence and professionalism.

I hope that the readership of this book will be wider than the regimental family. In these socially abrasive days it is heartening to read how an organisation drawn from every background and social group can unite to form a band of brothers.

Martin Lee-Browne's book is obviously a bitter-sweet labour of love. However, I hope that it is some consolation, in the light of what eventually happened to 1 Wessex, that TA soldiers, drawing on the standards established by their forbears, have since served with such courage and distinction in Iraq and Afghanistan.

April 2009

INTRODUCTION

This is not a traditional regimental history, about fiercely fought battles and heroic deeds, but in many ways almost a piece of social history – recounting the endeavours of a minute proportion of the population of the West Country to create and maintain a small part of the British Reserve Army of the finest quality.

It attempts to chronicle the almost unfashionable, and certainly unselfish, efforts of between 500 and 600, mainly young, men, and a small number of young women, to make an organisation 'work', as it were 'for its own sake', with only a modest hope and expectation of personal advancement, and certainly not for any appreciable financial gain. That organisation was a Territorial Army battalion, which started life in 1967 as The Wessex Volunteers, but in 1972 became the 1st Battalion The Wessex Regiment (Rifle Volunteers). The former is generally referred to here as "the Battalion", and the latter as "the Battalion" or, using its official abbreviation, "1 Wessex".

Few, if any, of those men and women joined the Territorial Army [the TA] with the object of becoming a captain or a sergeant, let alone a lieutenant colonel or a warrant officer, and, when it came, promotion was more often than not a stimulating mix of surprise and pleasure. In a period of great social change, for some it was a deliberate, and for others a sub-conscious, move from an unsatisfying job or an aimless lifestyle to doing something worthwhile in a structured environment — perhaps a friend had persuaded them, or they had seen a television advertisement, and soldiering has, of course, always appealed to the romantic side of many people. A substantial proportion of the soldiers, however, would probably have been unable to explain exactly why they took the quite difficult step of walking off a street with which they were probably quite familiar, over the threshold into the totally unknown world of a TA Centre. They almost certainly, though, never did so for the reasons described by the Duke of Wellington in 1831 — but one hopes that the end result was similar:

> People talk of their enlisting from their fine military feelings – all stuff – no such thing. Some of our men enlist from having got bastard children – some for minor offences – and many more for drink; but you can hardly conceive of such a set brought together, and it is really wonderful that we should have made them the fine fellows that they are.

The phrase "Twice a Citizen" was coined to demonstrate the fact that every member of the TA had two jobs – one civilian and the other military

– and was good at both. The civilian ones were as varied as could possibly be imagined: in the Battalion there were accountants and telephone engineers, civil servants and bricklayers, garage mechanics and solicitors, long-distance lorry drivers and postmen — and even a gynaecological surgeon (who was content to remain a private soldier for ever and thus have no responsibilities whatsoever in his military career). Military competence — in equally varied tasks — had to be worked for in addition.

I was once asked, in a committee that included a number of senior Regular officers, to describe the ethos of the TA in one sentence. My reply was: "Whether I go with you or not is my decision – but if I do, then I will go with you the whole way". There have, of course, always been a few who get home from work on a Friday evening, or wake up early on a Saturday morning, with a freezing wind blowing the rain almost horizontally, and say to themselves "I'm not ****** going out in that" and stay at home with the family. The vast majority, however, did go, weekend after weekend, giving their all for the next 36 or 48 hours – and getting home on the Sunday evening almost invariably feeling a sense of achievement, having forgotten the discomfort, the occasional sense of fear and the physical hardship of the training. Had they not done so, of course, they would have 'voted with their feet'. As the writer of the A Company Notes in the Summer 1989 issue of *The Back Badge* (the Journal of The Gloucestershire Regiment) said:

> Members of the TA are in it principally because they enjoy it. They like the training, they like the companionship, and they feel that they are doing something worthwhile. A divisional exercise in BAOR cannot be guaranteed to provide the genuine daily pleasure which a TA private soldier seeks, but each individual will make any effort he can to be there, for it is widely recognised that, if UK training can be fun, the German Camp is what the commitment is all about.

Many Regulars and Volunteers believe that the period covered by this book was the 'golden age' of belonging to the TA. Excellent Camps, both at home and abroad, good equipment, high quality training and decent strengths ensured a real cohesion and robustness for many units, and for the Battalion in particular.

Perhaps curiously, although the basic tasks of the TA during the 28 years covered by this book were extremely serious ones, practised year in and year out, probably very few of its members actually contemplated the possibility of being required to go to war. Although the 'mechanics' of mobilizing complete units were regularly rehearsed, there was in fact never a realistic possibility of their having to do so in earnest. Towards the end of that period, however, because of the dramatic cuts in the size of the Regular Army, an ever-increasing number of individual Volunteers (at the outset, mainly specialists such as doctors and engineers) were called up to reinforce it, albeit (I believe) very few, if any, from 1 Wessex. For some, of course, that was extremely exciting, but most of them – with families, mortgage instalments to be paid, and often a small business to keep running – undoubtedly felt that to be 'singled out' at very short notice, and sent off abroad to a Regular unit where they would know absolutely nobody, would be unacceptable. (That has, of course, now changed. The TA now provides a significant proportion of the Army on active service in Iraq and Afghanistan, and finding Volunteers willing to go there does not seem to be a problem). If, however, the entire Battalion had been required to mobilize and fulfil its war role, the very large proportion of its members would – because of the 'togetherness' of the Companies and the Battalion – unquestionably have gone with it.

No one, however, <u>has</u> to join the TA, and in practice (although not by law) any member of it is free to 'vote with his (or her) feet' and leave at any time. Unfortunately, no records exist of the rate of turnover in the Battalion – the percentage of its official strength that leaves in any given period – but it was probably appreciably lower than that of most of the units of the TA. A low turnover results in a greater feeling of comradeship among all ranks, reduces the repetitiveness of the instruction cycle for the NCOs, enables more ambitious training to be carried out, and is a major factor in maintaining training standards and morale. Another important element in the feeling of 'togetherness' was the fact that, by and large – as has no doubt always been the case across the Reserve Forces generally – there were very few unpleasant or unkind people who just did not fit in and could have made life difficult for the majority.

In one respect, writing the history of a Regular infantry or cavalry regiment has always been relatively easy, in the sense that, although it moves around the country or various parts of the world every few years[1], it basically exists only in and around one barracks, with the officers and other ranks, and their families, normally working and living together, as a compact entity. Furthermore its Regimental Headquarters provides a focus for everything except operational and training matters. From the creation of the Territorial Force in 1908 every county and the biggest cities had their own battalion (indeed sometimes two battalions), with drill halls spread throughout the city, or the county town and other smaller towns, none of which were very far apart – so, there was a sense of 'togetherness' not too different from that in regular battalions, and a Regimental Headquarters to provide some support. The 13 NATO-roled TA battalions formed in 1967, however, covered simply enormous areas, in many cases five or six times the size of those of their predecessors. The shortest distance between any of the Companies of The Wessex Volunteers and Battalion Headquarters was about 100 miles – and, apart from Annual Camp, the 'living-and-working-together' element was entirely absent, and (with occasional 'social' exceptions) the only activity was the soldiering. Furthermore, although somewhat tenuous links with the Regimental Headquarters of the Regular regiments from which the Battalion was formed were retained, it had no equivalent of its own. With no 'real' soldiering to experience (for example, being involved in peace-keeping duties in Northern Ireland), the Battalion's sense of 'togetherness' could only be built up gradually, in the TA Centre bars after training on drill nights, through Dinner and Guest Nights in the Officers' and the WOs & Sergeants' Messes, from the camaraderie of exercises at both battalion and company level, the open-hearted friendship and competition between the Companies, and above all at Camp. It is probably true to say that that spirit, which enabled most members of the Battalion to feel a real sense of belonging, and a fierce loyalty to it, had been achieved by the end of Camp in 1973 and continued until its amalgamation with The 2nd Bn The Wessex Regiment in 1995. The Farewell Parade at Devizes in September that year was as well executed as the Colour Presentation Parade in June 1973, and as moving as that of any Regular infantry regiment.

The Battalion was undoubtedly regarded by the rest of the Army as one of the best – indeed, possibly the best – in the whole TA, and there were two major reasons for that. First, the fact that on its formation in 1967 it was the direct and only TA descendant of six splendid Regular regiments, all of which were united by their 'West Country-ness', and whose TA battalions had in them many excellent soldiers. Secondly, through the tremendous enthusiasm and firm-but-kindly direction of the first two Commanding Officers, Lieutenant Colonel John Sellars and Lieutenant Colonel Paul Freeland, the Battalion started off on the right foot from the very first Annual Camp, and – despite much organisational upheaval from 1986 onwards – it never lost its immense pride, its training standards, or its ability to laugh at itself or difficult situations.

With the benefit of hindsight, one can now see the Battalion's whole existence as a (albeit originally unintended) 'holding operation' until the time should come when the six Regular Regiments from whom it was directly descended, or their successors, would again have their own TA battalions –

thus restoring the true regimental family of Regulars, Volunteers and Cadets. It was completely acceptable and understandable that those regiments should, by fair means, try their utmost to have their own TA battalions again – although, as the result of three amalgamations and the transfer of The Royal Hampshire Regiment out of The Prince of Wales's Division into The Queen's Division, by the time that actually happened there would only be two who achieved it – The Devonshire & Dorset Regiment and The Royal Gloucestershire, Berkshire & Wiltshire Regiment [RGBW].

From the mid-1980s, there were, therefore, two diametrically opposing wishes – the Regular Regiments wished to 'take back' the appropriate parts of 1 Wessex, while 1 Wessex, a proud and highly successful battalion, fervently wanted to stay as it was. It is difficult to argue that either was 'wrong', but – in the light of the Battalion's achievements and high standing – to everyone within it and who had belonged to it at one time or another, as well as to many outside the Regular Regiments, the gradual transfer of Companies to the 4th Battalion The Devon & Dorset Regiment [D & D] was seen as being completely unwarranted and sometimes unfairly achieved. There were also exchanges of Companies between 1 Wessex and the 2nd Battalion The Wessex Regiment [2 Wessex], but, being 'within the family', they were not regarded as major disasters. The possibility of their amalgamating to become the TA Battalion of RGBW was first mooted in 1992, by which time it was accepted that The Wessex Regiment was not going to survive indefinitely. Assuming, with considerable justification, it would retain its unique mobilization role and general standing within the TA as a whole, 1 Wessex was perfectly happy to become the TA Battalion of what was clearly going to be a very fine new Regiment, but 2 Wessex was definitely not. In due course, however, their amalgamation was confirmed – but the way in which it was achieved unfortunately created tremendous anger and frustration in 1 Wessex. As this book shows, in the end it was the Generals who 'won' – but, despite my emotional ties with 1 Wessex, I believe that, dreadful though the achieving of it was, in principal the outcome was the right one.

On a personal note, The Wessex Volunteers and 1 Wessex played a major and fulfilling part in my life for virtually the whole of its existence, and this book is one way of saying thank you to everyone I knew in it, for the sharing of experience, the laughter, the occasional burying of hatchets, and above all for the many friendships which have resulted from my long connection with this marvellous battalion.

Most Volunteers in the TA Infantry would feel that, quite differently from the position in the Regular Army, the Companies (the 'parts') are almost always more important than the 'whole' — the Battalion of which they form part — and that they have much greater significance than just as one of four, five or six 'cogs in a machine'. It would, therefore, have been marvellous to be able to include a chapter on each of the original six Companies, in addition to the general narrative. This book is, however, long enough as it is, and I have therefore very reluctantly decided that it is unrealistic to do so.

The Battalion's achievements would never have been possible without two groups of people. The first was the Permanent Staff – the Regular officers, the Permanent Staff Instructors [PSIs] and latterly the Permanent Staff Administrative Officers [PSAOs] – who were so generous with their extremely effective leadership, administrative and instructional skills, and they served the Battalion quite marvellously. Almost without exception, they quickly came to identify themselves with the Battalion, and to enjoy working with the Volunteers. Not a single Regular CO, Training Major, Adjutant or QM was disliked, and many of them were officers of the very highest quality. In the very early days, one or two of the PSIs were of the 'scream and stamp' school, but otherwise they were all, too, quite excellent representatives of the Regular Army. It is difficult to think of any member of the Permanent Staff who was not an excellent administrator, (in the case of the PSIs) a very high-class instructor, and blessed with a good sense of humour. After the initial very steep 'learning curve' for those who had not served with the TA before, every one of them proved to have been well-chosen to work with the Volunteers – in some cases possibly even better suited to the world of the part-time soldiers than to life in a Regular battalion! The PSIs adapted well to their curious existence in TA Centres that (apart from themselves) were empty for most of the week, and their contribution to the success of the Battalion was beyond praise.

The second group was our spouses and girlfriends. The Battalion – or, indeed, any other unit of the Reserve Forces – could not possibly have existed and succeeded without their quite indescribable, but rarely praised, generosity and selflessness. They endured countless weekends and, from time to time, longer periods for courses and Annual Camps, in probably the majority of cases left alone with the children or just alone, and it is sincerely hoped that very few marriages 'came unstuck' as a result. A TA Centre is not the most suitable place to take one's beloved for a party, but they were the scene of hundreds of evenings of enormous companionship, conviviality and enjoyment. It is to 'The Ladies', therefore, that this book is affectionately dedicated.

———

EDITORIAL NOTES

Between 1967 and 1979 the Territorial Army was officially known as the Territorial & Army Volunteer Reserve, or "TAVR". Nevertheless, for simplicity, except in those places where "TAVR" is clearly appropriate, I have used "TA" throughout this book. The expression "the Battalion", with a capital B, always means The Wessex Volunteers or 1 Wessex; "the TAVRA" refers to Western Wessex TAVR Association (while any other TAVRAs are given their full name); and "the Regular Regiments" means The Devonshire & Dorset Regiment, The Gloucestershire Regiment, The Royal Hampshire Regiment and The Duke of Edinburgh's Royal Regiment collectively. After the first mention of a regiment, it is referred to by its usual Army abbreviation – but I have generally disregarded the standard military practice of putting those particular abbreviations in capital letters, and referred to them instead as one does in speech. I have referred to myself throughout as "the author". Square brackets denote an abbreviation or explain one.

I have unfortunately not had access to as much material for this book as I would have liked. Much of it comes from the "Company Notes" that appeared, almost always, in the half-yearly regimental Journals of the four affiliated Regular Regiments, and I have chosen extracts from them as widely as I thought would help to make 'good reading'. Although my 'roots' in the Battalion were with A Company, and I may therefore be accused of bias, I make no apology at all for the fact that the highest proportion of those quotations come from A Company's Notes in The Gloucestershire Regiment's *The Back Badge* – closely followed by many from *The Royal Hampshire Regiment Journal*. That is simply because they were generally much fuller, more amusing and more interesting than the others. Although there is overall a large amount of material on the Battalion's 27 Annual Camps in the Notes in those Journals and the *Western Wessex TAVRA Newsletters*, as the years went by, with a few honourable exceptions, the reports in them gradually became much shorter and, frankly, less interesting. The reasons for that were almost certainly just increasing pressures on the officers who were the writers or potential writers, both in their TA lives – the demands of the Battalion's in the United Kingdom Mobile Force [UKMF] role, exhausting major Regular Army exercises – and their civilian ones. Life simply got busier and busier – and furthermore, of course, as the Battalion's end drew near, those who normally wrote about its activities were increasingly involved in the very depressing processes of the winding-up and amalgamation.

In the closing-down of Battalion Headquarters, during late 1995, a substantial amount of what could well have been interesting and worthwhile material seems to have been destroyed. My task would have been appreciably easier if I had had a complete, or nearly-complete, set of Part 1 Orders.[2] Most surprisingly of all, the Ministry of Defence Records Offices have been unable to find a single one of the Battalion's Annual 'Unit Historical Records' – the peacetime equivalent of War Diaries. The result of all that is that there are bound to be a considerable number of incorrect facts, omissions or statements throughout this book, and I apologise for them.

In Appendix 2, I have tried to list all the officers and senior NCOs who served in and with the Battalion. I am sure, however, that very regrettably some individuals have been left out – simply because their names and/or details do not appear in any of my material – and in quite a large number of cases it has unfortunately not proved possible to check initials, and whether individuals were awarded an honour, the TD or TEM, and Clasps [bars][3] to them. It would have been marvellous to have been able to mention, or at least list some of the Volunteers who made a great contribution to the life of the Battalion without reaching the rank of Sergeant – for example all those who were awarded bars to their TEM for more loyal service, or received a Lord Lieutenant's Certificate – but sadly the records are incomplete. Wherever possible, Volunteers are shown in the ranks they held at the end of their TA service, and those who served in more than one Company are shown under both, but in some instances they may have fallen through the net. My humble apologies are therefore also offered to everyone who has been omitted, deprived, or whose details are incorrect.

In defiance of convention again, and because I suspect that an appreciable number of readers of this book will have served in the Battalion and therefore known many of the more senior of its members, I have rarely referred to people by their ranks after their first mention – and I hope that will cause no offence. Another good reason for doing so is that, because many members of the Battalion knew each other in 'civilian life' as well as in the TA, the boundaries of formality between officers, NCOs and soldiers were usually happily disregarded away from the TA Centre or training area.

In the numerous quotations from the regimental journals, I have taken the liberty of tidying up some of the punctuation, occasionally altering a word here or there, and removing a few sentences to avoid repetition, in the hope that these very lively pieces of writing flow even better than they did in the originals.

I am very grateful to a number of organisations and people. First, my thanks go to the Regimental Headquarters of the Regular Regiments and

The Royal Gloucestershire, Berkshire & Wiltshire Regiment for giving me access to their libraries, and permission to reproduce numerous extracts from their Journals; then to the Ministry of Defence for permission to reproduce Crown Copyright material; and to Christine Beresford, Michael Grenfell, Robin Grist, Tim May, Andrew Ravenhill and Peter Whiteman for reading and commenting on all or some of my draft Chapters. Nigel Attwood, Robin Heatley, Jim Mitchell, David Ryan, Nick Speakman and Paul Wood have helped with some of the lists in Appendix 2, and Richard Nicholson revealed the secrets of the Permanent Staff Administrative Officers. Adrian Grazebrook and *The British Army Review* have kindly allowed me to reprint an article of his in Chapter 7, and Keith Taylor and Brian Stewart to quote from their *Call to Arms*. Paul Brooks, who typeset my drafts and put up with many requests for amendments, has been a tower of strength, and Remous of Sherborne, who printed and bound this, could not have been more helpful. As they are at Wyvern Buildings there, I had no alternative but to ask them to do the work! Above all, however, I must thank my wife Diana for her constant and devoted encouragement and support – both when I was commanding the Battalion and over the writing of this book – without which the latter would certainly have never happened.

I have tried in good faith to contact the holders (or probable holders) of the copyright in all other material used in this book – including the owner of the amazing, but seemingly now defunct, website www.regiments.org – and to obtain permission to use it. Sometimes, however, I have failed. Any breaches of copyright are unintentional, and I apologise for them.

Finally, anyone who may be interested to look at some of the material on which this book is based (including the two huge scrapbooks) will find it at The Soldiers of Gloucestershire Museum in the old Gloucester Docks, where it will shortly be deposited on permanent loan.

----

[1] This system changed completely in 2004. Now the battalions and regiments remain in one barracks permanently, and, broadly speaking, 'all ranks' and their families may either stay with the unit indefinitely or move to another one – a vast improvement, if only in terms of family life.

[2] A formal, usually daily, 'bulletin' produced by every unit in the Army, setting out all promotions, course results, honours and awards, arrivals and departures of senior ranks and their transfers between the different companies or squadrons, current strength figures, and significant achievements by individuals, the sub-units or the Battalion – although not information on training or operational matters].

[3] The Territorial Decoration (for Officers) and Territorial Efficiency Medal (for other ranks), awarded for 12 years' service, and bars for every further six years.

ILLUSTRATIONS

ABBREVIATIONS

REGIMENTAL:

"the Regular Regiments" means collectively The Devonshire & Dorset Regiment [Devon & Dorsets or D & D], The Gloucestershire Regiment [Glosters], The Royal Hampshire Regiment [Royal Hampshires] and The Duke of Edinburgh's Royal Regiment [Duke of Edinburgh's or DERR].

AAC	The Army Air Corps
AGC	The Adjutant General's Corps
POW (Division)	The Prince of Wales's Division
RA	The Royal Artillery
RAOC	The Royal Army Ordnance Corps
RCT	The Royal Corps of Transport
REME	The Royal Electrical & Mechanical Engineers
RMonRE	The Royal Monmouthshire Royal Engineers (Militia)
RTR	The Royal Tank Regiment
RGH	The Royal Gloucestershire Hussars (TA)
RGBW	The Royal Gloucestershire, Berkshire & Wiltshire Regiment
RGJ	The Royal Green Jackets
RLC	The Royal Logistics Corps
RRF	The Royal Regiment of Fusiliers
RWY	The Royal Wiltshire Yeomanry (TA)
RWxY	The Royal Wessex Yeomanry (Volunteers)
266 Battery	266 (Gloucestershire Volunteer Artillery) Battery (Volunteers), Royal Artillery
37 Signals	37 (Wessex & Welsh) Signal Regiment (Volunteers), Royal Corps of Signals
4 D & D	The 4th Battalion The Devonshire & Dorset Regiment (Volunteers)
6 LI	The 6th Bn The Light Infantry (Volunteers)
245 Squadron	245 (Petroleum) Squadron, Royal Corps of Transport, (Volunteers)

IN THE FOOTNOTES:

D&DJ	The Devonshire & Dorset Regiment Journal
BB	The Back Badge – The Journal of The Gloucestershire Regiment
RHJ	The Journal of The Royal Hampshire Regiment
DERRJ	The Journal of The Duke of Edinburgh's Royal Regiment

GENERAL:

APC	Armoured Personnel Carrier
BAOR	British Army of the Rhine
BEM	British Empire Medal
BFA	Blank Firing Attachment [to make the use of blank ammunition completely safe]
Bn	Battalion
BGTT	Battle Group Tactical Trainer
CB	Commander of The Order of The Bath
CBE	Commander of The Order of The British Empire
CCF	Combined Cadet Force
CINC	Commander-in-Chief
Coy	Company
CPX	Command Post Exercise [for Divisional, Brigade, Battalion and/or Company HQs]
CQMS	Company Quartermaster Sergeant
DSO	Distinguished Service Order
DTA&C	Director Territorial Army & Cadets
FEBA	Forward edge of the battle area
FIBUA	Fighting in built-up areas
FTX	Field Training Exercise
GOC	General Officer Commanding
GPMG	General Purpose Machine Gun [SF = Sustained Fire role]
LMG	Light Machine Gun [Bren]
MBE	Member of The Order of The British Empire
MC	Military Cross
MOD	Ministry of Defence
MTO	Motor Transport Officer
NATO	North Atlantic Treaty Organisation
NBC	Nuclear, Biological, and Chemical [Warfare]
NCO	Non-Commissioned Officer
NRPS	Non-Regular Permanent Staff
OC	Officer Commanding [usually of a Company]
OP	Observation Post
OTC	Officer Training Corps
PSAO	Permanent Staff Administrative Officer
PSI	Permanent Staff Instructor [NCO]
PTA	Primary Training Area

PTI	Physical Training Instructor
QPSI	Quartermaster PSI (NCO)
R & R	Rest and Recreation [a 36-48-hour break from training]
RHQ	Regimental Headquarters
RMAS	The Royal Military Academy, Sandhurst
RAuxAF	Royal Auxilliary Air Force
RMR	Royal Marine reserve
RNR	Royal Naval Reserve
RRTT	Regimental Recruiting (or Recruit Reception) and Training Team
SAAM	Skill at Arms Meeting
SAS	Special Air Service
SNCO	Senior Non-Commissioned Officer
SOPs	Standard Operating Procedures
SPSI	Senior PSI (normally a WO2)
STRATCO	Strategic Reserve Company [attached to a Regular Infantry Battalion]
TASAAM	Territorial Army Skill at Arms Meeting [at Bisley]
TAVRA	Territorial Auxilliary & Volunteer Reserve Association
TD	Territorial Decoration (Officers)] Asterisks denote
TEM	Territorial Efficiency Medal (Other Ranks)] Clasps awarded
2IC	Second-in-Command
UKLF	United Kingdom Land Forces
UKMF	United Kingdom Mobile Force [part of NATO's Allied Rapid Reaction Force]
UOTC	University Officers' Training Corps
WOMBAT	Medium Anti Tank Weapon
WO1 & WO2	Warrant Officers: Class 1 (Regimental Sergeant Majors and Bandmasters); Class 2 (often Company Sergeant Majors)

---

1 WESSEX
CHRONOLOGY

1967 The Wessex Volunteers formed on 1 April, with BAOR support role.

1969 Bn HQ moved from Exeter to Trowbridge, and new HQ Company formed there, substantially based on 4 Wilts (TA);
Former HQ Company in Devonshire became E Company, and re-roled as a rifle company.

1971 2nd Bn The Wessex Volunteers formed in Berkshire, Buckinghamshire & Hampshire;
Titles changed to 1st Bn The Wessex Regiment (Rifle Volunteers) and 2nd Bn The Wessex Regiment (Volunteers).

1973 Presentation of Colours to 1 Wessex at Knook Camp, Heytesbury, Warminster, Wiltshire;
Bn HQ and HQ Company moved to Le Marchant Barracks, Devizes.

1977 D Company (Berkshire) transferred to 2 Wessex, in exchange for 2 Wessex's D Company in Poole.

1982 The Battalion joined 1 Infantry Brigade of 4 Division, part of the NATO-committed United Kingdom Mobile Force (Land).

1986 B Company (Hampshire) transferred to 2 Wessex;
New B Company formed in Swindon (to replace B Company (Hampshire)) became operational.

1987 E Company (Devonshire) transferred to 4th Bn The Devonshire & Dorset Regiment.

1990 C Company (Dorset) transferred to 4 D & D;
New C (originally N) Company raised in Newbury from Platoon of 2 Wessex.

1992 The Battalion taken out of the UKMF while restructuring;
B Company (Swindon) transferred to 2 Wessex;
New B Company formed in Bristol from A Company (Gloucestershire) Platoons;
C Company (Newbury) transferred back to 2 Wessex;
New C Company raised in Cheltenham from A Company Platoon;
D Company (Poole) transferred to 4 D & D;
UKMF disbanded and its role taken over by the ACE Mobile Force (Land);
The Battalion (now 'fit for role' again) becomes part of 1 Mechanised Brigade in the AMF(L).

1995 The Battalion amalgamated with 2 Wessex on 1 October to form 2nd (Volunteer) Battalion The Royal Gloucestershire, Berkshire & Wiltshire Regiment.

CHAPTER 1

THE TERRITORIAL ARMY AND ITS PREDECESSORS: THE 17TH CENTURY TO 1965

When the Boer War ended in 1902 – five years before the story of the TA begins – the reserves of the British Army were the Militia and the Volunteers. The history of the Militia goes back into the early 17th century – for example, in 1625 in Bristol there was:

> ….a voluntary company of gentle, proper, martial and disciplined men who have their arms in a handsome Artillery House, newly built in the Castle yard, where once a year they entertain both earls and lords and a great many knights and gentry of rank and quality.[1]

The Militia, an official part of the Army, and funded from a land tax, was based on the counties. The officers were appointed by the county Lieutenants[2], and the 'rank and file' were chosen by lot from the parishes, to serve for three years. They were part-time soldiers, but could be called up to join a regular regiment, even overseas – and there was probably as much bribery used in getting those who wanted a life of adventure, but who had not been selected, into the system, as there was getting those who had been selected against their wishes out of it. In the 1750s and 1760s:

> England was at war [against the French], and news was good. There was vigorous leadership at the top, and brilliant young commanders were making history in distant parts of the world. They were stirring times, and a healthy feeling of patriotism was abroad, so men joined the Militia. There was also the contributory factor that young men, and old ones too, were not above the vanity of fancying themselves in a scarlet jacket faced with blue and laced with gold.[3]

The Volunteers were, however, for all practical purposes originally private armies, raised on a local basis, mainly for defence as and when some particular threat was perceived, but also to maintain civil law and order. They were neither an official part of the Army, nor generally recognised by the government of the day, but in some cases Volunteer companies were formed as part of Militia regiments. By the early 1790s, Napoleon was rapidly becoming the most powerful individual in Europe, and there were real risks of his French Army invading Britain – so, in 1793, not only were 19,000 Militia mobilised against that threat, but a large force of Volunteers was officially formed to supplement the Militia and the Regular Army. As if, however, anticipating the many reorganisations that would bedevil the British Army at increasingly frequent intervals for the next 200 years and more, right up to the present day, they were disbanded only three years later – but, because the French were growing increasingly powerful, re-formed in 1803. Companies of Volunteers and troops of Yeomanry (who were the mounted element of the Volunteers) were raised in every county on a full-time basis, and they were provided with uniforms and equipment at public expense, rather than, as traditionally, by the Commanding Officer. By 1815, though, the British Army had finally conquered Napoleon, and, although there were periodic (but not serious) threats of invasion by the French in the middle 1840s and twice in the 1850s, major military intervention was not needed to support foreign policy for the next 30 years or so. There were garrisons, ranging in size from the modest to the huge, to maintain law and order in Canada, India, South Africa, the East and West Indies and the Mediterranean, but the Regular Army was well enough recruited to meet those tasks on its own. Reinforcement by the Volunteers was accordingly no longer needed, so in 1816 they were disbanded yet again – although, by and large, the Yeomanry remained in existence, albeit more to carry out a local policing role than anything else. The Militia likewise became less and less active, and in 1831 they too ceased to exist – but only to be re-formed once more in 1852. Fears of France arose again in the late 1850s, resulting in a much stronger Volunteer movement than before, and the formation of Rifle Volunteer Corps (RVCs) throughout the length and breadth of the land. This time, however, the RVCs were to remain in existence for the next 25 years or so.[4]

Between 1868 and 1874, Edward Cardwell (later the 1st Viscount Cardwell), the Secretary of State for War in Gladstone's Liberal Government, initiated the first serious reorganisation of the Army

– "the Cardwell Reforms". Firstly, he abolished long-term service, and made 12 years the maximum period for which recruits could enlist, usually divided into six with the Colours and six with the reserves; the object of that, Cardwell explained to the House of Commons, was the very commendable one of "passing a large number of young men through the Army, learning trades in it, and afterwards returning to civil life to be ornaments and advantages to those around them, and at the same time to be ready to the defence of the country in case of emergency". His next major step, in 1872, under the Military Forces Localization Act 1872, was to divide the country for administration and recruiting purposes into 66 Districts, each of which had under its command two apparently haphazardly selected Regular line regiments, or one that already had two battalions, with two battalions of Militia and whatever Volunteer organisations there were in the area; one of the Regular battalions would serve abroad and the other at home, and they shared a depot. In 1874 the Liberals were ousted by Disraeli's Conservatives, but six years later the Liberals were back in power, again under Gladstone, who appointed a new Secretary of State for War, Hugh Childers. In 1881, Childers took Cardwell's reforms a significant stage further, amalgamating the two line regiments in each district to form new county regiments of two Regular battalions, with their own Militia battalions and RVCs. Some, such as the 44th (East Essex) and the 56th (West Essex) combining to become The Essex Regiment (44th/56th), were obvious pairings, but many of them were seemingly just as haphazardly put together as they had been before, and in very few cases is there any explanation of why and how it was actually done. For example, the 30th (Cambridgeshire) Regiment of Foot and the 59th (2nd Nottinghamshire) Regiment of Foot amalgamated as The East Lancashire Regiment (30th/59th), and the 41st (Welsh) Regiment of Foot and the 69th (South Lincolnshire) Regiment of Foot became The Welsh Regiment (41st). That policy was repeated throughout the Army, and thus there came into being all the famous regiments whose names remained so familiar until the 1960s. In the West of England, there were The Devonshire Regiment (10th Foot); The Dorset Regiment (11th Foot); The Gloucestershire Regiment (28th/61st Foot), formerly the 28th (North Gloucestershire) and 61st

(South Gloucestershire) Regiments; The Royal Hampshire Regiment (37th/67th Foot), formed from the 37th (North) and 67th (South) Hampshire Regiments; The Royal Berkshire Regiment (49th/66th Foot), created by the amalgamation of the 49th (Princess Charlotte of Wales's) (Hertfordshire) Regiment and the 66th (Berkshire) Regiment; and The Wiltshire Regiment (62nd/99th Foot), formerly the 62nd (Wiltshire) Regiment and the 99th Duke of Edinburgh's (Lanarkshire) Regiment.

The Regular battalions of the new regiments were numbered 1st and 2nd; the 3rd was a Militia battalion (and in the case of the Devons and the Glosters, among others, there was a 4th as well); and the 'regimental family' was completed with a 1st and either a 2nd or 4th Volunteer battalion – although the Devons and the Hampshires had 1st, 2nd, 3rd, 4th and 5th Volunteer battalions. Much later, after World War 2, those six regiments became collectively known as "the Wessex regiments".

Those changes did not, however, prevent the performance of the Army in the Boer War from being far from satisfactory, or even lamentable – the *Report of Her Majesty's Commissioners on the War in South Africa* "had harsh words to say on almost every aspect of the Army's organisation, training, administration and its men, from…. the Commander-in-Chief down to the private soldier"[5]. The huge number of troops involved – a total, including colonial forces, of over 448,000 – and the expenditure of over £200 million (a total today of around £13.2 billion) consistently failed to achieve obvious results against only some 30,000–35,000 Boers. Following the end of the War in 1902, public and parliamentary concern forced the Government to carry out what was the first comprehensive review of the entire Army, apart from the regimental system – its organisation, administration, training and equipment. This led to numerous reforms, in their different ways even further-reaching than Cardwell's, including the improvement of recruiting and terms of service, new training methods at all levels, the provision of new weapons, and finally the creation of the General Staff (with its A (Administrative), Q (Quartermaster's) and G (Operations and Training) Branches, which names lasted until the 1980s. Although many thought that a long period of peace would follow the War, a handful of far-seeing politicians had considerable doubts about the likelihood of that – notably Field Marshal Lord Roberts and Lord Haldane, who was the Secretary of State for War from 1905 until 1912. In the face of much apathy, rather than opposition, during 1906 and 1907 Haldane therefore brought about yet another series of developments, of which the most far-reaching in the context of this book was the creation of the Territorial Force under the Territorial & Reserve Forces Act 1907 and it came into being on 1 April 1908.

Under Haldane's plan, most of the Militia battalions were disbanded, but the remainder (usually one per county) became the Special Reserve for supplying trained drafts for the Regular Army. The Territorial Force was raised from the Yeomanry and the Volunteers, to provide 14 cavalry brigades and 14 infantry divisions (including artillery, engineers, medical and veterinary units, and supply services), which would fight alongside the professionals. The battalions became, for the first time, part of their county regiments, Officer Training Corps [OTCs] were formed, and much effort was put into revitalising the volunteer part of the Army – although, because of the general lack of interest in military matters throughout the country, in the next four or five years it never managed to reach its establishment (i.e. full strength). The Territorial Force was organised and trained, and partly equipped, on Regular Army lines, but initially it was only liable to be called out for service within the United Kingdom; if there were to be general mobilization, a six-month training period before active service abroad was envisaged. It was administered and recruited (but not, of course, trained) by Territorial Associations formed in each of the 80 or so counties of England Scotland and Wales under the chairmanship of the Lord Lieutenant, and which were represented at national level by the Council of Territorial Associations. Those Associations were the forerunners of the Territorial Auxilliary & Volunteer Reserve Associations to be set up in 1967, which in turn became the Reserve Forces & Cadets Associations on 1 April 2000.

An astonishing event took place at Windsor Castle on 21 June 1909, when King Edward VII presented stands of Colours to 108 new infantry battalions. Each battalion was represented by the Commanding Officer and 25 men, and in all there were almost 3,000 Territorials, and also (although one wonders why) 3,000 Regular troops, on parade. Among the Colours presented were those for the 4th and 6th (but not the 5th) Glosters and the 4th Royal Berkshires. The 4th Wiltshires (previously the Wiltshire Rifle Volunteers), however, did not get theirs until 1927, when the regiment was at last recognised as a line Regiment.[6]

The name "Wessex" was introduced into military language for the first time in 1908, when all the divisions making up the Territorial Force were given titles. "The Wessex Division" was one of them, and in 1915, when they were numbered as well, it became the 43rd Wessex Division. Made up of battalions of the Devons, the Dorsets, the Hampshires, the Wiltshires and the Somerset Light Infantry (but not the Glosters), it spent the whole of World War 1 in India. Unknown to many, there was also (although only for the duration of the War) a 45th (2nd Wessex) Division, raised as part of the hurried creation of an additional 14 Territorial Divisions in September 1914.

The general apathy towards all things military that was the background to Haldane's reforms certainly extended to Parliament, being reflected in a feeling of helplessness when it came to debate the funding for the Territorial Force in 1913. The Force came in for considerable criticism, and there was concern about maintaining it at a proper strength. For example, in the course of a debate on the Army Estimates, Mr Leo Amery (one of the MPs for Birmingham):

> went on to address himself to the question of home defence when the Expeditionary Force was out of the country……..In such an event, reliance would have to be placed on the Territorial Force, and the Territorial Force, he contended, was not equal in numbers or in training to the task. It was necessary, he said, for men to serve continuously for fifteen or sixteen years if the Territorials were to maintain the nominal establishment of 314,000 men. What was required was in reality a body of 400,000 or 500,000 men…..He did not want to argue the case for national service, though he thought that as to the Territorial Force there was no alternative before the country except compulsion.

while Sir C S Henry (a Liberal representing Wellington) made a comment that is still widely and forcibly heard today, and came up with two novel ideas:

> He was surprised that a more substantial sum was not provided in the
> Estimates for the Territorial Force. It seems to him that the War Office
> were trying to run the Force on the cheap. He suggested that members
> of the Force should be given some preferential treatment under the
> Insurance Act. He also offered the suggestion that the work of the
> County Associations should be transferred to the county and borough
> councils, who should be responsible for supplying a quota of men and
> for their efficiency, any deficiency to be a surcharge on the rates.

Haldane's intention that the Territorials should have six months'
training after a general mobilization went by the board immediately
after the start of World War 1 in August 1914. Indeed, such was the
urgent need to reinforce the Regular Army, that the first Territorial
Force battalion, the London Scottish, found itself in France within a
month, and it was in action two months later. By the end of March
1915, three Territorial Force divisions had crossed the Channel.
Although the Force's role was legally speaking limited to Home
Defence, as soon as war was declared a very large proportion of all
the Territorials across the country volunteered to serve abroad. By
the end of the War, an astonishing total of 692 Territorial Force
battalions had been formed – 35 more than in the "New Army" of
Regulars created by Field Marshal Lord Kitchener (who had become
the Secretary of State in August 1914) – and their contribution,
particularly in France and Belgium, was beyond praise. They suffered
over 577,000 casualties, and won 71 Victoria Crosses. Unfortunately,
however, Kitchener was almost contemptuous of the "weekend" or
"Town Clerks" Army, and little effort was made to put them on an
equal footing with their Regular counterparts who had responded to
the call of his pointed finger in the "England Needs You" poster, by
flocking to the recruiting offices throughout the land. Perhaps he felt
that the Territorials had been inculcated with the wrong attitudes, or
badly trained, by their officers drawn largely from the landed gentry.
He believed that the New Army would prove to be better soldiers, and
there was even a restriction on recruiting by the Associations, so that
the New Army could get the best of the thousands and thousands who

were prepared to leave their civilian jobs and homes to fight for their country. The real, pre-war, Regulars were not interested in training volunteers, and that was therefore largely done by their own, mainly elderly, officers or retired Regulars – but the volunteer battalions were nevertheless expected to go straight into the front line alongside those of the Regular Army. It was accordingly "perhaps inevitable that the special qualities of the Territorials should have been submerged in the mobilization of the entire nation's resources".[7] Furthermore, at the end of the War, despite the fact that it could not possibly have been won without them, there was little or no governmental recognition of the sterling service of the Territorial Force battalions – except that they were permitted to dress exactly as their Regular battalions, and from then on all battalions of a regiment bore the same battle honours on their Colours, whether they had been won by Regulars or Territorials. Thus, for example, the Gloster Territorial battalions started wearing the Back Badge, which they had not done before – and the thread of that drawing together of Regulars and Territorials ran right through to the formation of The Wessex Volunteers nearly 50 years later.

Between 1918 and 1939, against a background in which there was no obvious enemy until the emergence of Adolf Hitler in the early 1930s, the volunteer Army was something of a political football – its fortunes depending on the now so familiar see-saw of the needs for cost-cutting on the one hand, and maintaining adequate reserves on the other. All the battalions of the Territorial Force were disbanded in 1918, only for some of them to be reconstituted two years later as the Territorial Army (TA), and then threatened with substantial reductions only two years after that. Bounties were introduced in 1920, (at £5 a year – the equivalent of about £650 in 2007), but cut to £3 in 1922, and (in an early example of political correctness) renamed "proficiency grants" in 1927. Annual Camps were cancelled at short notice, and little money was available for equipment or training. Things might have been different had the majority of senior Regular generals been supportive, but that was not the case, perhaps because, not for the first or the last time, many of them had their own interests to preserve.

When, in 1935, all the Divisions adopted badges for the first time, the 43rd (Wessex) Division chose the wyvern:

The Wyvern links the Division with the age-old traditions of the Anglo-Saxon kingdom of Wessex, and at the same time provides a symbol which typifies the essentially pagan spirit of the art of war. It recalls deeply buried memories of the old warrior gods, Odin and Thor.[8]

In both the Eastern and Northern mythologies, the dragon is the bringer of death and the serpent the symbol of guile. When the West Saxons landed in the West Country in the fifth century, they bore dragons painted on their shields and carved on the heads of their long ships. Sometime in the Dark Ages, realising that in the grim business of war the will to destroy must be combined with cunning, they blended the snake with the dragon and the wyvern was born. Thus the winged dragon, with two feet like those of an eagle and a serpent-like barbed tail, became the emblem of the Wessex kings. Alfred the Great certainly carried it on his battle standard in his many campaigns in Wessex and Kent in alliance with the Celts of Wales and Cornwall. Harold raised it at Hastings, for it twice appears in the Bayeux Tapestry. Ever since it has been the badge of the fighting men of Wessex, in whose coats of arms it appears time and time again.[9]

The Munich crisis in 1938 led to yet another major reorganisation, resulting in the establishment within the TA of 3 motorised and 9 infantry divisions. The TA became responsible for the anti-aircraft and searchlight defence of the UK, and a number of Yeomanry regiments and Infantry battalions were transferred to The Royal Artillery. In March 1939, all TA units were duplicated, so that there were soon 18 infantry divisions. Then, in September 1939, for the first time since the militiamen of the 18th century, except in World War 1, conscription was introduced – for all males between 18 and 41, who had to serve for six months with the Regular Army and then three-and-a-half years with the TA[10] – and on 1 September the TA was mobilised, becoming in effect part of the Regular Army.

The 43rd (Wessex) Division spent the first four and three-quarter years of World War 2 in England, but it achieved conspicuous and well-merited fame as part of the 21st Army Group, from the D Day landings in June 1944 until the end of the War on the River Elbe in May 1945. A genuine mix of Regular Army and TA, its Infantry battalions included the 4th & 5th Wiltshires (in 129 Brigade), the 7th Royal Hampshires and the 4th & 5th Dorsets (in 130 Brigade), and the 43rd Reconnaissance Regiment, which had been formed from the 5th Glosters. The TA battalions of the Devons and the Royal Berkshires were in other Divisions, and the 4th and 5th Royal Hampshires became parachute battalions. The six 'Wessex regiments' (although they were not yet known as such) together provided over 60 TA battalions between 1939 and 1945.

After the War, in 1947 there were of necessity major changes to the structure of the British Army, both the Regular and Territorial elements. All but a very few of the huge number of wartime Divisions were disbanded, and those that did continue in existence only had TA units under command, primarily with training and quartermastering functions. One of them was the 43rd (Wessex) Division, and, like the others, its name was changed (albeit only marginally) to reflect its new role – the 43rd Wessex Division (TA) – and it had its Headquarters in a large wartime hutted barracks, Sherford Camp, just outside Taunton. In July 1948, a number of Brigades were formed on a geographical basis, becoming responsible for recruit training, and all personnel, posting and regimental matters for Regular and TA battalions alike. The one in the West Country was The Wessex Brigade, made up of the Devonshire, Dorset, Gloucestershire, Royal Hampshire, Royal Berkshire and Wiltshire Regiments, with its Headquarters at Wyvern Barracks, Exeter. At the same time, there was a major reduction in the number of TA battalions across the country, and many were disbanded, but each Regular regiment was allowed to retain one – and within The Wessex Brigade they were the 4th Devons, the 4th Dorsets, the 5th Glosters, the 4/5th Royal Hampshires, the 4/6th Royal Berkshires, and the 4th Wiltshires. All TA battalions had simply a general reserve role, and even in the mid-1950s they were still full of officers and NCOs, and to a lesser extent soldiers, who had served in the War. Whilst those officers enjoyed the undemanding soldiering and the 'club atmosphere' of the TA, many of them had never been near a battlefield or in action, and (sad to say) for some their principal post-war concern seemed to be to retain the social status that they believed went with their rank. In complete contrast to that, it was to become a feature of the post-1967 TA (certainly in the South West of England) that for the most part its successful officers and soldiers were not over-concerned with "what they had on their shoulders". Indeed, in the course of the appreciable number of reorganisations of the 1980s and 1990s covered in this book, many individuals had their units or sub-units, as it were, changed around them, and willingly accepted a lower rank and a new cap-badge – some of them on up to three or four occasions, and occasionally even more than that – if that meant that they could continue their soldiering.

Following the end of the hostilities, Germany was divided and occupied by the four post-war Allied powers – the United States, Britain, France, and the Soviet Union. In 1948, unable to agree on terms for the reunification of Germany, the Western and Soviet leaders began planning to transform their respective occupation zones into two Germanys, one aligned with the democratic West, and the other integrated into the communist East – and the result of that was the Cold War, the long period of fear and mistrust on both sides about the aggressive intentions of the other. To show in no uncertain terms that they were not going to be intimidated, the Western Allies therefore signed the collective defence agreement which created the North American Treaty Organization [NATO] – and a few years later the Russians countered it with the Warsaw Pact, a very similar arrangement between the Soviet Union and most of the Eastern European countries, which in practice was soon to give almost total control to the former.

There therefore arose the need for the Allies to provide occupation forces in Western Germany to counter the threat posed by the Soviet Union and the Warsaw Pact countries that were in effect ruled by it – and in the United Kingdom's case it was the 80,000-strong British Army of the Rhine [BAOR – which had previously been the 21st Army Group, created by General Montgomery in 1943 for the invasion of Europe]. All the conscripted and volunteer troops who had fought in the War needed, of course, to be 'demobbed' – but, quite apart from having to maintain BAOR, there was still a need for a substantial Army to meet Britain's other commitments around the world. National Service was therefore introduced, and by 1951 the Regular Army was almost 415,000 strong – the largest it had ever been in peacetime – and comprised substantially of National Servicemen.

Those National Servicemen who were selected for officer training at the end of their basic training first had to "pass WOSB"[11]. War Office Selection Boards were a two-day test, partly physical, of character, intelligence and leadership qualities – and the successful ones from the infantry regiments (with a few others) then went on to a 16-week, well designed and effective, commissioning course at Eaton Hall Officer Cadet School, near Chester (the seat of the Duke of Westminster). Between 1947 and 1958, some 15,000 young men were turned from (in the very large majority of cases) schoolboys into platoon commanders. "It was a tough apprenticeship, but many former Cadets were conscious that they had been privileged to receive a most excellent training for life, and remembered comradeship, team spirit and accomplishment, as well as pain.....Most of them, with the benefit of hindsight, would agree that it was a memorable and invaluable experience that served them extraordinarily well during their subsequent lives and careers."[12]

From 1950 onwards, the National Servicemen's obligation was two years service with the Regular Army, followed by three year's reserve training with the TA – whose battalions therefore received a perpetual inflow of 20-23 year olds. The majority of those young men were at least reasonably pro- (or at least not anti-) Army, and, certainly in the case of most of the young officers, keen to get as much fun as they could out of the compulsory sequel to, in many cases, a thoroughly enjoyable and worthwhile two years with the colours. Almost all National Servicemen had been born in the 1930s, and brought up during the war, with all its restrictions and shortages. For many, therefore, National Service was a marvellous release – offering postings to exciting faraway places that had only been pink areas in school atlases; new and stimulating companions; and often (in the terms of those days) real adventure. Whilst by its very nature the TA could not match that sort of life, it did provide a social focus for thousands of young men throughout the country – particularly in the

"Club"[13] and the Officers' Mess after training finished at around 9 o'clock on a "drill night". New friendships were forged; social evenings, dances, balls, dinners and even steeplechases, were organised[14]; and sometimes business ventures resulted from those TA contacts.[15] It must be said, though, that for a small minority (almost entirely in the other Arms and Services, rather than the Infantry) National Service varied from the totally boring to a disastrous psychological experience. Many in the Regular Army resented the fact that it had to spend a vast amount of its time and resources in providing training for the conscripts, and in a significant number of cases frustrations were undoubtedly worked out on recruits through "square-bashing", "spud-bashing", doing extra guard duties or tackling the assault course. Very naturally, those who had suffered that then resented having to fulfill their TA commitment, and many others undoubtedly felt that, having done their two years with the Regulars, they had simply 'had enough'. Probably, therefore, only about half those on the strength of any TA unit really enjoyed their compulsory three years with it – as witness the last morning of one of the 5th Glosters' Annual Camps in the late 1950s, when the fleet of coaches to take the battalion home from Penhale failed to arrive on time, and there was an astonishing scene on the square when the Adjutant and the RSM were aggressively and embarrassingly barracked by 300-400 home-hungry soldiers.

To the very considerable relief of not only those young men whose turn had yet to come, but also of the Regular Army – which was freed of the time-consuming task of training, and functioning with, a high proportion of transient and sometimes reluctant soldiery – call-up for National Service finally finished in 1963, and the last of the '2-year men' completed their service with the TA in 1965. That had two effects – the strengths of both the Regular and TA units dropped dramatically, and they gradually became all-volunteer. Relatively few soldiers, but quite a number of National Service officers – mainly those who looked forward to their new 'with-you, but not always of-you' commitment – actually opted to transfer direct into the TA, rather than into the Army Reserve. They had thoroughly enjoyed their regimental service, and the TA offered the opportunity to continue the experience, whilst getting on with their chosen careers – and they

were welcomed in their units because of the first-class training they
had received at Officer Cadet School and in their Regular battalions or
major units in the other Arms and Services. Another reason sometimes
mentioned was the discovery that, although their three years in the
TA was compulsory, if they nevertheless *volunteered* to join it, they
got another four or five shillings over the pay-table at the end of each
month – which was big money in those days! For quite a number
that simple, but worldly, act triggered a commitment that lasted in
some cases for 20 or even 30 years. Gradually the philosophy grew up
that if you 'survived' three Annual Camps, you were 'hooked for life'
– and neither job changes nor marriage would make you readily give
up the almost always companionable and amusing, usually stimulating,
sometimes frustrating, and occasionally frightening, 'second lifestyle',
with its almost ceaseless round of drill nights, weekends, courses and
Camps having to be fitted in around your wife or girl-friend, family and
work.

To a large extent, however – almost entirely because of the TA's
totally vague role as "the reserve", coupled with a near-complete
lack of what could have been stimulating contact with the Regular
battalions – the actual soldiering became increasingly boring. In
particular, there was an "air of stagnation"[16] in both 5 Glosters and 4
Wilts, and they had a very substantial turnover of junior ranks. That
boredom was often reflected in the TA battalions' notes in the pre-
1967 Wessex regimental journals, when reports of Camp merited but
a few lines – such as:

> Camp this year was at Okehampton. It was a fine day when we arrived,
> and fine on the day we left. Enough said!

– and many were written in a dead-pan style which seems to reflect
no great enthusiasm for the training side of the event. Every few
years the entire 43rd Division went to Camp on Salisbury Plain, and
proved beyond any doubt the old adage that, even then, the bigger the
exercise the less there is for everyone except the Directing Staff to do.
Those Camps, on hallowed sites such as Windmill Hill and Tilshead
Down, were still run very much along pre-war lines, with hundreds
of bell tents in long lines, standard army brown marquees for dining

halls, and resplendent white ones provided for the Messes by breweries such as Whitbread, H & G Simmonds and Eldridge Pope. On one celebrated occasion, the GOC rode about during the big exercise on a white charger (wearing, of course, service dress with breeches and highly "bulled" boots, with his gold-oak-leafed and red-banded hat), saying "Good morning – do you know who I am?", and leaping off from time to time to inspect a group of slit trenches full of incredulous soldiery or a trembling Company Headquarters. Nevertheless, despite the fact that the TA had undoubtedly lost its way, there were a good many Camps and weekends that still remain in the memory – those trips to the Channel Islands in an RNVR minesweeper, mid-winter escape-and-evasion exercises, and, for a lucky few in most of the battalions, idyllic summer days spent on country ranges practising for Bisley. The compensation for staying in was that one gradually got promoted, and began to have a hand in planning what actually happened.

So, by the mid-1960s, almost all the old wartime soldiers had gone from the TA, and the large majority of its serving officers, NCOs and soldiers were of much the same ages and backgrounds as their Regular Army counterparts – but much of their energy and enthusiasm was not being channelled in the right ways. It was time for change.

---

[1] *Cap of Honour: The Story of The Gloucestershire Regiment 1694-1950* (3rd Edition, David Scott Daniel and others, ed. Major Claud Rebbeck; Sutton Publishing Ltd, Stroud, 2006, p.25).

[2] The office of County Lieutenant – the Monarch's representative in the counties – was created in Tudor times. Early in the 20th century (at around the time of Haldane's 1907 Act referred to above) "County Lieutenant" became "Lord Lieutenant" – and when two or more of them were gathered together they were unofficially referred to as "Lords Lieutenant". Under the Local Government Act 1972, however, they were (very possibly by accident) re-titled "Lord-Lieutenants". Nevertheless, in this book the much more distinguished 'old plural' is used throughout.

[3] *Ibid.* 1, p.26.

[4] Much of this paragraph is based on Lieutenant Colonel R A Leonard's paper *The Dorset Volunteer Soldier* (obtainable from The Keep Military Museum in Dorchester).

[5] *The Armies of Britain, 1495-1980* (Michael Barthrop - National Army Museum, c.1985).

[6] It has not proved possible to discover when the Devon, Dorset and Royal Hampshire

battalions received theirs.

7   *The Territorial Army 1907-40* (Dr. Peter Dennis - Royal Historical Society, Boydell Press, 1979).

8   *The 43rd Division at War, 1944-1945* (Major-General H. Essame – William Clowes & Sons Ltd, 1952).

9   1 Wessex Fact Sheet 1987 and *The Sphinx & Dragon*, Winter 1994.

10 The Military Service Act 1939 and the National Service (Armed Forces) Act 1939. It was possible to claim exemption from call-up, although some other form of 'public service' (e.g. working down a coal mine) had to be undertaken instead.

11 Pronounced "Wosby".

12 Life at Eaton Hall is vividly described in *Call to Arms – Officer Cadet Training at Eaton Hall 1943-1958* by Keith Taylor and Brian Stewart (Meigle Colour Printers Ltd, 2006) – largely made up reflections on what it did for some of the 15,000 Cadets who went through its gates.

13 The NCO's and soldiers' bar in a TA Centre. Occasionally, in a large TA Centre, the WOs and Sergeants had their own separate Mess, while in a very small one all ranks would share one bar.

14 The last, perhaps needless to say, by the Yeomanry!

15 The author and his original solicitor-partner, Adrian Crazebrook (who became the 2IC of the Battalion, and later a Lieutenant Colonel) first met in the 5th Glosters.

16 *The Sphinx & Dragon*, Winter 1994. *The Sphinx & Dragon* [S & D] was the Regimental Journal of The Royal Gloucestershire, Berkshire & Wiltshire Regiment.

CHAPTER 2

THE FORMATION OF THE TAVR
AND THE WESSEX VOLUNTEERS

"The Battalion disbanded on 1st April – a foolish decision implemented on a "foolish" day – leaving a void in the lives of many Territorial Officers and Soldiers, and sadness in the hearts of members and friends of the Regiment. We feel, however, that it would be wrong to dwell on the macabre, and instead we should bid farewell with good cheer…..it is apparent to all that the spirit of the Battalion has been transferred with the men".[1]

Harold Wilson's Labour Government came to power in October 1964. It badly needed to save money, and to distance itself from the battered Imperialism of the Conservatives, who had been in power since 1951, led successively by Winston Churchill, Anthony Eden and then Harold Macmillan. On the other hand, the continuing Cold War still necessitated the maintenance of a large numbers of troops in the BAOR, and it was realised that the TA could make a real contribution to that. 14 months later, therefore, in December 1965, the Secretary of State for Defence, Denis Healey, presented to Parliament a White Paper titled *Re-organisation of the Army Reserves*[2]. Its Introduction said:

> Despite various measures brought in by the previous Government in recent years – the re-organisation of the Territorial Army in 1960, the [Army Reserve] Act of 1962 which introduced the "Ever Readies", and the [Navy, Army & Air Force Reserves] Act of 1964 which laid the foundation of a long-term reserve for ex-Regulars – the Army Reserves still do not measure up to the operational tasks for which they might be required. There is a general recognition that a further re-organisation of the Army Reserves is now necessary and indeed long overdue. This situation is not the fault of the Reserve Army, for despite deficiencies in their equipment the Territorial Army and Army Emergency Reserve carry out their training with enthusiasm; and many units have achieved a high standard. The Territorial Army

have helped to save the nation in two World Wars. They, and the Army Reserve, have a conspicuous record of service and it is right that tribute should be paid to this. The character and scope of the military operations we must be prepared to undertake have radically changed, and we must shape the re-organisation of the Army Reserves to meet these new circumstances, but the opportunity to express the spirit of voluntary service in the reserve will still remain.

and, not surprisingly, as soon as the initial proposals were announced, they generated immediate and intense criticism – angry debate in Parliament, difficult meetings between senior representatives of the TA and Ministers, furious letters to *The Times* and *The Daily Telegraph* (many of the latter from "Disgusted, Tunbridge Wells"), and intense wringing of hands from one end of the country to the other. There was, of course, equally great concern on the part of the serving Territorials as to what the future might hold for them, and the Drill Halls became hotbeds of rumour.

The changes were planned by two very aptly named senior officers, Major General Michael Carver (later to become Field Marshal Lord Carver), the Director of Army Staff Duties, and Lieutenant General Sir John ("Shan") Hackett, the Deputy Chief of the General Staff. Notwithstanding that when they began work neither of them actually knew anything about the TA, their proposals, whilst very radical, were wise and to a very large extent made good sense – so much so that the principles behind them remain valid to this day. The TA and the Army Emergency Reserve were to be amalgamated and become the Army Volunteer Reserve – although, as the result of considerable pressure on the Government, before the reorganisation actually took effect, the proposed name was changed to Territorial Army & Volunteer Reserve [TAVR – that & was never used in speech]. It would have a total establishment of about 50,800, and the task (jointly with the Regular Reserve) of providing:

(a) Some individuals and a few units who could be called out at any time, and on very short notice, at the discretion of the Secretary for State, to reinforce the Regular Army;
(b) Unit reinforcements for the Regular Army's contribution

to NATO;
and
(c) Reinforcements to support the Regular Army in major
operations outside Europe.

It was abundantly clear from the outset that the re-organization was
going to be completely 'root-and-branch'. It involved the disbandment
of literally all existing TA units, and, in the case of the Infantry,
their replacement by 13 completely new battalions, and three new
battalions of the Parachute Regiment with that NATO reinforcement
role. The Yeomanry, and the Arms and Services – every major and
minor artillery, engineer, signal, transport, medical, supply, electrical
and mechanical engineer, military police and intelligence unit – would
also be completely re-formed, and pools of individual officers for
head (a) above found from many of the disbanded units. Before the
reorganisation actually took effect, however, there were a number
of significant 'second thoughts'. Most importantly, it was decided to
go some considerable way to meeting the enormous groundswell of
concern at the proposed loss of the large number of Infantry battalions
which were not going to contribute to the NATO-roled ones (as well
as many artillery regiments and batteries) by creating 41 new battalions
with a Home Defence role and a lower training commitment.

The TAVR was divided into four categories. TAVR I (originally
intended to be called the "Special Army Volunteer Reserve", but in the
event retaining the name "Ever Readies", which dated from the 1962
Act) consisted of some 7,000 individuals and small specialist units
liable to be called up for any emergency. The "NATO battalions", the
Parachute Regiment battalions, a new Yeomanry regiment, The Royal
Yeomanry (Volunteers), and a number of likewise newly-formed major
and minor units of the Arms and Services with a NATO role were TAVR
II, and given the historic name of "Volunteers". TAVR III comprised
the new Home Defence battalions, which were almost literally 'thrown
together' in an *ad hoc* and unholy mix of the Yeomanry, Infantry and
Royal Artillery units disbanded in the reorganisation. They retained
the name "Territorials", and were given (albeit in brackets) the names
of their predecessor units – for example, there were "The Devonshire

Territorials (Royal Devon Yeomanry/1st Rifle Volunteers)" – and they were very largely manned by those who were not selected to join TAVR II. Lastly, TAVR IV was made up of bands, University OTCs and a few specialist units. The categories also indicated differing individual training obligations. Units would be either "Independent" – the NATO units (organised and administered on a relatively local basis) and the Home Defence battalions – or "Sponsored" (the remainder of the Arms and Services, each administered on a countrywide basis by a Central Volunteer Headquarters [CVHQ], and with most of their members having military jobs related to their specialist civilian skills). Independent units were to be known as TAVR IIA, and Sponsored units TAVR IIB – although those designations were rarely used.

The 1965 White Paper included 'half-suggestions' for names for the new battalions, such as "Lancastrian Battalion" or "Highland Battalion", and when finally agreed, in order of precedence, they were:

> 52nd Lowland Volunteers
> 5th (Volunteer) Bn The Queen's Regiment
> The Lancastrian Volunteers
> The Fusilier Volunteers
> 5th (Volunteer) Bn The Royal Anglian Regiment
> The Wessex Volunteers
> The Light Infantry Volunteers
> The Yorkshire Volunteers
> The Mercian Volunteers
> The Welsh Volunteers
> The North Irish Militia
> 51st Highland Volunteers
> 4th (Volunteer) Bn The Royal Green Jackets
> 4th, 10th & 15th (Volunteer) Bns The Parachute Regiment

The TAVR formally came into being on 1st April 1967 – a very special day in the history of the British Army. It was 86 years since the last new Infantry regiments had been formed (in 1881, as part of the Childers Reforms), other than by a few amalgamations. All the new NATO battalions (except for the three battalions of The Parachute Regiment) were therefore the direct descendants of some of those regiments, and they were linked to the existing regional Regular/TA Brigades. The Wessex Volunteers accordingly became part of The Wessex Brigade, based at Wyvern Barracks, Exeter. In almost every case, the new TAVR battalions were formed by taking a company's worth of officers, NCOs and soldiers from each of four or five 'old' battalions, which in most cases provided 'pools' of between 200 and 400, from which the personnel of the new companies could be chosen.

The 'old' TA battalions from which The Wessex Volunteers were formed, and the Companies they became, were:

> 4th Bn The Devonshire Regiment – Headquarter Company (Devonshire)
> 4th Bn The Dorset Regiment – C Company (Dorset)
> 5th Bn The Gloucestershire Regiment – A Company (Gloucestershire)
> 4th/5th Bn The Royal Hampshire Regiment – B Company (Hampshire)
> 4th/6th Bn The Royal Berkshire Regiment – D Company (Berkshire)

Very disappointingly, however – partly because of its low strength, and partly for geographical reasons – the 4th Bn The Wiltshire Regiment did not initially contribute a company to the new Battalion (although some 40 of its members joined the Gloucestershire Company), but in due course Battalion HQ and Headquarter Company would move into the county. All those 'old' battalions had given very distinguished service in World War 2 – and, in one of those curious and inexplicable ways, without having ever been made particularly conscious of the fact that some 22 years previously "their forebears fought their way gloriously across a continent"[3], The Wessex Volunteers came to adopt the tremendous, 'knowing what it wanted, and determination to achieve it', ethos of the 43rd (Wessex) Division.

The first meeting of the COs of the 'old' TA battalions to discuss the details of the formation of the new one was held (prophetically, as it would eventually turn out) at Le Marchant Barracks, Devizes on 22 February 1966. Chaired by the Brigade Colonel, Denis Harding of the Glosters (who had commanded the 5th Glosters in the late 1950s), the agenda covered basic matters such as the Battalion's name, the titles of the individual Companies, the relationship with the four Regular regiments in The Wessex Brigade [the Regular Regiments][4], Colours and finance. At that stage, there was absolutely no question of a "Let's start with a clean sheet" approach, and the minutes reported that "It was quite clear that COs wished to perpetuate a County, rather than a Regular battalion, regimental link – largely on the grounds that, in the case of amalgamated regiments[5], the regimental sub-unit title would not correctly describe the geographical area of sub-units".[5] A major topic, almost needless to say, was that on which every officer in the Army is an expert – dress. The minutes of the meeting are, of course, entirely factual, but it must be beyond any doubt that that item on the agenda generated more heat, and took up more time, than any other during the day. Some held the view that the Companies should keep the badges and distinctions of their 'old' TA battalions, and the others voted for the adoption of the Wessex Brigade badge and buttons – never anticipating, of course, that only a little more than two years later, in July 1968, the Brigade would cease to exist[6], and that thereafter the badge would be worn only by The Wessex Volunteers. Those questions of dress took many months to resolve – partly, no doubt, because even at that time there was a major concern among the Regular Regiments that they would be forced to follow the then current fashion for "large regiments", and become six battalions of, say, The Royal South-Western Regiment, with The Wessex Volunteers as its TAVR battalion, and all their 'old' badges and insignia being lost. The Regular Regiments were not, however, the only people considering the topic:

> The main concern of all ranks has been over uniform, and our wives have little idea of how much hot air has been expended as [the Companies] try to be as different between each other as possible. Fortunately, however, after a few months we were issued with combat

kit, and that has, at one stroke, covered up many of the wide varieties of mixed dress we could have displayed.[7]

The first Dress Regulations for the Battalion were issued in January 1967, and ran to nearly 20 pages. Each of the new Companies was allowed to keep one or two of their former distinctions, to acknowledge their descent from the Regular Regiments. A Company retained the Back Badge; B Company officers a whistle on the Sam Brown shoulder strap and an extra-wide chin-strap on the SD cap; C Company the Croix de Guerre ribbon at the top of the sleeve; D Company, the red Brandywine flash behind the cap badge; and Headquarter Company a Croix de Guerre red-and-green lanyard. The last four of those distinctions were only worn on the parade uniform – which, for the first few months, was battledress with berets, but subsequently No 2 Dress (the khaki barathea 'suit') with a peaked cap – but A Company had the Back Badge on their berets on both parade and working dress. The Battalion's cap badge was the Wessex Brigade's Wyvern – white metal on berets or gold wire on SD caps for officers, and gilt metal for NCOs and soldiers – and there were Wyvern buttons for everyone. The 'old', pre-1967, curved regimental shoulder flashes (saying, in white on red, for example, "Devon" or "Royal Berkshire") were still worn on battledress, as were the officers' 'old' regimental collar badges (apart from B Company, as The Royal Hampshires did not wear them). After a few months, battledress was replaced by the up-to-date DPM [Disruptive Pattern Material] combat kit – a great morale booster – without the shoulder flashes or collar badges. The Regulations only seem to have needed amending three times – to cover the adoption of a stable belt in 1968; the abandoning by the Companies, during the six years up to 1973, of all those regimental distinctions in the cause of the Battalion's unity; and the adoption of a lanyard in 1973.

In the 'old' TA, there was one event that displayed the magnificence of the British Army's quite amazing variety of uniforms – the annual Divisional Dinner. Sherford Camp, outside Taunton, was still the Headquarters of the 43rd Wessex Division (TA), and it was known to virtually all the officers as (if nothing else) the scene of numerous Study Weekends. The one that had the Dinner on the Saturday evening was a major event in everyone's training calendar. It was held in the huge

Study Centre, and was an astonishing sight – with between 200 and 300 officers 'dressed up to the nines' in scarlet, blue and rifle green, with facings of green, primrose, black, blue and red, gold braid and frogging, 'chain mail' epaulettes, and medals, and the silver of many of the Division's units on the tables. Some of the behaviour was amazing too, for a good many junior officers arrived already bent on pranks of varying degrees of audacity, both during and after dinner. Without fail, however, year after year, they completely disregarded the high risk of being rudely woken up during the Sunday "morning after the night before" cloth-model exercise, from what they hoped would be a quiet 'zizz' in the back rows, to be asked by one of the Divisional Staff – or, horror of horrors, the GOC himself – their opinion on some particular manoeuvre, or what to do with the soldiers' greatcoats during a dawn attack. The final Dinner Night was held in the winter of 1966/67, and, not surprisingly, most of the officers from all the Divisional units were there. The inside of the enormous, bare, hall was (in the standard way) semi-disguised with a lining of old parachutes, and, egged-on by his fellow officers, Lt Tim Lowden of the 4th/5th Royal Hampshires nearly achieved immortality, or at least a court-martial, for doing his best to set them alight with the aid of a candelabra; a lot of water subsequently found its way into the dining room. The Hampshire officers subsequently tried to brazen it out – and the reason given for their antics was very appropriate:

> ….our performance at the Dinner was, we thought, misrepresented. Those who attended were determined that the 4th/5th should go out on the crest of a wave, and therefore practically flooded the dining room to achieve this![8]

Had he succeeded, the conflagration would have been a cataclysmic and aptly symbolic end to an era that began before World War 2. In the Swinging Sixties, new ideas and philosophies abounded throughout the country, and, in military terms, the TAVR was set to reflect them.

It quickly became obvious that, even allowing for the low numbers in a good many of the 'old' TA units, by no means everyone who wanted to do so would be able to transfer to TAVR II. Every serving member of the TA in 1966 (whether officers, NCOs or soldiers) who hoped to get a place in one of the NATO units therefore had to go through an agonising period of waiting to learn of his future or fate. Once, however, the selections had been made and approved, the lucky ones who were offered places in the new units, they were full of enthusiasm and excitement for the prospects ahead – albeit obviously tempered by great disappointment at the passing of their old units. There were, of course, others who had 'had enough' and, perfectly properly, saw the reorganisation as a way of achieving a graceful retirement.

The CO designate of The Wessex Volunteers, Lieutenant Colonel John Sellars of The Duke of Edinburgh's Royal Regiment (then the CO of the 4th/6th Royal Berkshires) approached the task of selecting the first members of the Battalion in what was quickly realised to be his efficient and understanding way. All the intended Company Commanders were required to provide their COs' recommendations, with reasons, as to who should be chosen. That provided, of course, a once-in-a-lifetime opportunity to get rid of much 'dead wood' – the heavily moustached Company Seconds-in-Command, the pear-shaped Colour Sergeants and storemen, and those whose sole motive for remaining in the TA was to get away from their wives. The author, who was the lucky Company Commander in the 5th Glosters selected to command the Gloucestershire Company, vividly remembers sitting in the sunshine outside a Cotswold pub with his CO, Lieutenant Colonel Pat Durant of The Light Infantry, deciding who of the existing active members of the battalion would be proposed to John Sellars as those whom he would like to 'bring' with him – the sparkiest, best trained and most companionable 120 officers, NCOs and soldiers. It was a great privilege, and happily it worked. Unfortunately, however, that was not how things were done in Hampshire, where the 'old and bold', without any reference whatsoever to the new Company Commander, Major John Roberts, selected a lot of other 'old and bold' who were 'good chaps' – but not necessarily the best soldiers. It was a while before he had weeded-out those whose ethos was without question going to remain that of the old TA, rather than their being willing to adopt what was clearly going to be the new, positive, attitude of the TAVR – of which John Roberts was the epitome – and initially he had to make do with quite a number of disgruntled NCOs and soldiers who found the going rather too tough for their liking, but were nevertheless reluctant to leave, whether voluntarily or 'under pressure'. There were the same sort of problems in the Berkshire, Devon and Dorset Companies, but they were not as serious. In due course, all the various merits were weighed, and the choices made – and, the Battalion was initially organised at slightly over its official full strength.

It was, of course, envisaged that there would be strong ongoing links between The Wessex Volunteers and the four Regular Regiments of The Wessex Brigade. Battalion Headquarters and Headquarter Company were therefore to be located in Wyvern Barracks, Exeter, right next to the Brigade Headquarters. In the event, however – luckily before they started moving in – there turned out not to be enough room for them there, and they accordingly took over the 4th Devons' Drill Hall at Butts Road, on the east side of the city. Curiously, however, (and for some apparently unexplained reason), the Regular Regiments did not officially become the "parent regiments" of the Companies, but instead they were "affiliated" to them – although having the Companies affiliated to the Regular Regiments would have been more logical. For that reason and perhaps others, those links were therefore never as strong as the Regular Regiments might have hoped. In retrospect, though, on balance that proved to have been a good thing, as it undoubtedly enabled the Battalion to acquire its own identity and ethos from the outset, and more quickly than might otherwise have been the case,

Sad to say, for a good many years it had seemed that in many counties very little, if any, real interest in the TA battalions had been shown by the Regular Army's regimental headquarters or battalions. The TA battalions did, of course, take part in major regimental events, but that did not usually result in much enduring 'togetherness'. Only a very few Regimental Secretaries, COs of the Regular battalions or Honorary Colonels did more than attend a TA parade or two and a Guest Night in the Officers' Mess each year, and they had little real knowledge of whether 'their' battalion was functioning well or not. Nevertheless, the news of the reorganisation was immediately greeted with universal consternation and condemnation by the 'old and bold' – as much Regular as TA – but (as is so often the case in life) a substantial number of those who complained loudest about the changes probably knew even less about the subject of their indignation than those Regimental Secretaries, Regular COs and Honorary Colonels. An unfortunate attitude of 'disinterest' in the new Companies seemed to pervade at least some of the Regimental Headquarters – for example, the editor of *The Back Badge* seemed to have made up his mind that the successor to the 5th Glosters would not, at least in regimental terms, be looked on with much favour:

> We shall miss the old 5th very much in so many ways which its "successor unit", A Company The Wessex Volunteers, with the best will in the world, will be unable to fulfill.[9]

and although the issue of *The Journal of The Duke of Edinburgh's Royal Regiment* for the spring of 1967 included a page explaining the changes that were going to happen to the TA in Wiltshire (but not in Berkshire), for the next two years there was no mention whatsoever of the new Company that had been formed from the 4th/6th Royal Berkshires.

It was, however, very much to the credit of the various Regimental Headquarters [RHQs] that, when it at last became obvious that there was absolutely no question of retaining the *status quo*, tremendous efforts were made to give the TA battalions a memorable send-off in March 1967. In Berkshire, 12 days before the reorganisation formally took effect, "two Guards from the 4th/6th Battalion, with the Colours and the Battalion's own Band, supported by a large contingent of Old Comrades and dignitaries from all across the county, paraded at Brock Barracks in Reading – and with the marching off of the Colours to *Auld Lang Syne* it was all over, and the last surviving unit of The Royal Berkshire Regiment passed into history".[10] Memorable parades – and, of course, disbandment cocktail parties and balls – for every single unit of the TA, the infantry and the other arms and services alike, were held throughout the country, and that in our whole military history, in such a short space of time, there cannot ever have been such a huge number of farewell events, and such collective deep sadness and sense of loss for the passing of a substantial part of the Army. A major element of local society throughout the country, it had been dearly loved, and in its heyday had performed magnificent feats of arms. There was therefore a heavy burden on the new units everywhere to show that they could become worthy successors.

The first Permanent Staff of Battalion HQ were:

CO	Lieutenant Colonel JA Sellars MBE, DERR
Training Major	Major R Jury MVO, D & D
Adjutant	Captain EG Churcher (D & D)
Quartermaster	Major PE Allen DERR
RSM	WO1 Sutherland D & D

and, with Major Gerry Fulford (from the 4th/5th Royal Hampshires) as the 2IC, they assembled at Butts Road some while before 'formation day' – and together they made a marvellous job of getting the new Battalion up and running.

John Sellars was one of the Army's great characters – military eccentric, genial and caring, a desert navigator by the stars, with an infectious smile, an endearing habit of rubbing his hands together with enthusiasm at any prospect which particularly delighted him, and an avid collector of books, new and second-hand, on military and general history. These filled every Army quarter into which he and his long-suffering wife Lindsay ever moved, from the front door to the attic, and he continually drove her to distraction by buying more and more on at least a weekly, and sometimes almost a daily, basis. His staff-work was as exceptional as his exercise instructions were monumental. He exuded a huge personal warmth, and – with his deep interest in people and a great ability to get the best out of them – a better choice for the first CO of this initially disparate organisation is hard to imagine. Dick Jury was the epitome of an upright and efficient soldier, and Eddie Churcher (who went on to command the 2nd Battalion The Wessex Regiment, which was formed in 1971), very tall and well built, looked down on one somewhat quizzically over an imposing moustache. It is not given to many soldiers to form a new battalion virtually 'from scratch', and doing so must have been as exciting for them as it was for the Volunteers. One of their first major tasks, of course, was to organise the Battalion's first Annual Camp, and something about it will be found in Chapters 3 and 5.

The initial layout of the Battalion was:

Battalion Headquarters	Butts Road, Exeter
Headquarter Company	Butts Road
A Company	Eastern Avenue, Gloucester
	Speedwell, Bristol
B Company	Newburgh House, Winchester
	Newport, Isle of Wight
	Basingstoke
C Company	Poundbury Barracks, Dorchester
	Poole
D Company	Brock Barracks, Reading
	Church Place, Swindon

and, with a few exceptions, all the TA Centres were either post-World War 2 drill halls, or old Victorian barracks which had once been the regimental depots of two of the Regular Regiments. The latter may not have provided the most suitable accommodation, but they were steeped in military history and provided excellent reminders of those regimental links. They were mostly in, or reasonably soon put into, good condition – but the one truly awful place was D Company's accommodation in Brock Barracks. The Company Office was not much more than a big broom cupboard with a telephone; nevertheless, with the new spirit abroad, that had no adverse effects whatsoever on the Company's energetic performance.

In one respect, the Battalion was probably quite unique in the British Army, in that, in addition to its Corps of Drums, for over 20 years it had two Bands – The Devon Band of The Wessex Volunteers (formerly the Band of the 4th Devons), whose home was in Plymouth and which was part of the Battalion's establishment, and the newly formed Hampshire and Isle of Wight Band (TAVR)[11], based in Winchester and administered by, but technically not part of, the Battalion. Both were almost always fully recruited to their full establishment of 36 and a Bandmaster, and many of their members were retired Regulars, from Band Sergeant Majors down to ordinary bandsmen – and they, of course, brought a wealth of experience that gave the Bands a remarkable quality. A high proportion of the Devon Band (which, incidentally, sported a dance band that was in constant demand) were employed in HM Dockyard – and, again perhaps uniquely, it included four brothers, Charles, Dave, Ray and Terry Roberts, all of whom also played football for the TA team in the Plymouth Combination League. On parade, the combined Bands and the Corps of Drums were a magnificent sight, just about 100 strong, and their musicianship was of a very high order indeed. The Bandmasters and Drum Majors are listed in Appendix 2, Part 1.

The original Company Commanders were the author in A; John Roberts with B; the imperturbable Dorset farmer with interests in the world of education, Martin Evans, in C; David Heavens (the Deputy Town Clerk of Abingdon, another of the 'training is all' school) in D; and a solicitor with a great interest in competition shooting, Michael Anstey, running Headquarter Company. All the first Company Sergeant-Majors – Dick Keitley of A Company, Ron Witt in B Company, Ken Gover in C Company, Peter Reader with D Company, and George Crawley in Headquarter Company – had transferred from the 'old' battalions, and every one of them was a real character. They – and, almost without exception, their successors over the next 27 years – all had that traditional combination of fierceness without ever bullying anyone, huge experience, a great sense of humour, and tremendous loyalty:

> [setting] the highest standards of behaviour and bearing, [so that] by their example those serving under them aspired to the same heights. [They were] the epitome of all things good about a Sergeant-Major.[12].

There were, of course, a large number of other 'characters' of all ranks spread over the entire Battalion whom it would be invidious to name here, as it were 'cold', but many of them are mentioned in the following pages.

In addition to the four Regular officers in Battalion HQ, every NATO battalion had a number of senior Regular NCOs posted to it as "Permanent Staff Instructors" [PSI], usually a Warrant Officer Class 2 (the "Senior PSI" [SPSI]), a Colour Sergeant and a Sergeant with each company, as well as three or four specialists in the mysteries and skills of signals and support weapons [anti-tank guns and mortars]. From the outset, the Battalion was incredibly lucky in its PSIs – all of whom came from the Regular Regiments – and the greatest credit is due to their battalions for so unselfishly 'lending' some of their best senior NCOs to 1 Wessex. They dealt with much of the day-to-day administration in Battalion HQ and the Companies; they instructed at both Company and Battalion level, as well as helping with Battalion training generally. That they knew their job inside out went without saying, but most of them were also extremely good psychologists, and so expert at cajoling or frightening the Volunteers, as the occasion demanded, into doing whatever was required of them. Many of them went on to become the Regimental Sergeant Major of their own battalions, and they were such good examples of the best Regular soldiers that the younger (and occasionally older) Volunteers almost involuntarily sought to emulate them – as, indeed, they did the TA Company Sergeant Majors. In the first few months of a PSI's appointment, the learning curve was understandably steep, and relationships were sometimes a little fraught – but thereafter, as they came to appreciate the qualities and varied personalities of the Volunteers, in almost every case they were soon really enjoying their jobs:

> The Permanent Staff never seem to stop laughing and cracking jokes, and we are fortunate that their poor standard of humour bears no relation to the efficiency, cheerfulness, enthusiasm and drive.[13]

> The PSIs who tried to understand the Volunteers – very few didn't – not only succeeded, but ended up liking and admiring them.[14]

Their great popularity can be judged by the fact that they were mentioned by name in very nearly all the Notes about the Battalion and the various Companies in the Regular Regiments' journals. At

the end of their two to three-year tours of duty with the Battalion,
most PSIs were nearly as sad to go as the Volunteers were to lose them
– as this tribute to the TAVR, written by one of A Company's PSIs,
Colonel Sergeant Heavens of the Glosters, shows:

A TAVR unit is perhaps one of the least looked-for posting for most
senior NCOs, so in the November of 1974 during our tour in Belfast,
it was with a large groan that I found out that this was to be my fate,
beginning in April 1975……..

When the Battalion finally left Minden in early May for sunny
Blackpool, I headed for the hotspots of Gloucester. The title PSI meant
nothing to me then, and apart from RQMS Matthews' comments like
"They're great boozers" and "There's plenty of ale about", I had no
idea what the job was all about. I arrived on a Wednesday morning,
and on the Wednesday afternoon the local law knocked on the door
to inform me that I was required for a Court case in Belfast the next
day; that took five days. On my return the OC, with a smile on his
face, welcomed me to the Company and said how pleased he was that
I would be going to BAOR with them on Saturday. Now my wife is
an understanding sort of woman, but she does tend to get excited
at times. She did get excited that week, but, nevertheless, on the
Saturday morning I stepped off the aircraft at RAF Gütersloh (yet
again)……

I'm not sure what I expected from the unit, because most Regulars
have varying opinions of them, which range from "Poor" to "A right
waste of money". 'A' Company……became the [notional] fourth
Rifle Company of 1 WFR [The Worcestershire & Foresters Regiment]
and acquitted themselves well. In small things they were perhaps
not as expert as their Regular counterparts, and at times they lacked
the polish, but their overall standard was as good as many Regular
companies, and I've seen some 'Regs' who wouldn't get into the TAVR
even after their 18 weeks' training. A thought also to remember is that
men who make up the TAVR are not forced to dig trenches in the rain
on a weekend, or sweat through a section attack, they do it because
they want to, and here lies the TAVR's greatest asset: the soldiers do
not need motivation, they want to do the job correctly. How many
Regulars can claim the same thing? To summarise, whilst I will be very
pleased to return to Bn life, it is with mixed feelings that I will leave
the TAVR. I hope in some small way that I have contributed to the

strong position that 'A' Company now finds itself in. It was a pleasure
to have served with so many nice people, despite some times having
to grit my teeth at some horrible malpractice which they get up to
now and again, or at the constant hammering on the door for keys
or information when on leave. I shall miss most of all the cheerful
outlook on soldiering, and after Drill Nights in the Sphinx Club,
where it seems 90% of TAVR business, if not all, is done. So cheers
to one and all – it was my pleasure.[15]

and there is no doubt that a major factor in creating that pleasure was
that the Battalion included many people who went out of their way to
make the PSIs feel welcome when they arrived, and then, throughout
their tours, showed them how much they were appreciated.

As mentioned in Chapter 1, the Act of 1907 had established a
Territorial Association in each of the counties, responsible for virtually
all aspects of the life of the Territorial Force except "training or actual
military service, or when embodied". That meant recruiting; "the
provision of rifle ranges, buildings, magazines and the sites of camps";
"facilitating the provision of areas to be used for manœuvres"; "the
provision of horses for the peace requirements of the Territorial Force",
and "the registration in conjunction with the military authorities of
horses for any of His Majesty's forces"; "arranging with employers of
labour as to holidays for training, and ascertaining the times of training
best suited to the circumstances of civil life"; and finally "the care of
reservists and discharged soldiers".[16]

On 1 April 1967, the Associations (then, including Northern
Ireland, numbering 90) were re-organised on a regional basis, in the
same manner as the Infantry battalions had been, as 13 Territorial,
Auxilliary & Volunteer Reserve Associations [TAVRAs – in practice
the "&" was never used in that abbreviations or speech][17] – and
one of their most important, but unwritten, functions was to act as
'buffers' between the Regular Army and the TA at District and Brigade
levels. Inevitably, following the huge reduction in the number of TA
battalions in 1967 (and hence the fewer opportunities for Regulars
to get a command or become an adjutant), more and more Regulars
appointed to jobs in brigade and divisional and headquarters – and most
importantly, of course, the divisional brigade commanders and their

deputies – had had any previous experience of the TA. Consequently, from time to time a Divisional or a Brigade Commander, or a senior member of their staffs, would make a decision or float a proposal that the Volunteers could have difficulty in accepting. The TAVRAs therefore provided a number of senior officers able to advise the General Officer Commanding [GOC] the District or the Brigade Commander on almost every subject relating to the Volunteers. In every District Headquarters there were two or three TA Colonels – Volunteers promoted after successful tours of command of a major unit, who were members of the TAVRA (or, in 'Wessex', the two TAVRAs) within the District's area – while the TAVRA Secretaries, almost invariably recently retired Brigadiers, had often had a TA posting at some time during their Regular careers. Both were always willing and able to put the TA point of view quite fearlessly at any level, whether within the divisional or brigade Headquarters, or to visiting generals or Defence Ministers. Furthermore, the TA Colonels and the Secretaries could rely not only on the backing of the Association Chairman – who, until the 1990s, was always a retired TA Colonel,[18] and who was by convention able to talk to at least major generals, and often more senior ones, on a Christian name basis after their first meeting – but also, if the problem was a really serious one, on the influence of one or more of the Lords Lieutenant of the counties within the Association's area, who took it in turn to act as its President.

The Western Wessex TAVR Association covered Avon, Cornwall and Somerset (soon to become the recruiting area of the new 6th Bn The Light Infantry[19]), Devon, Gloucestershire and Wiltshire – and was therefore initially responsible for A and HQ Companies, while the Eastern Wessex Association looked after Hampshire, Dorset and Berkshire, and thus B, C and D Companies, as well as Oxfordshire and Buckinghamshire (known to many as 'Green Jacket Country').

To link all the TAVRAs together, there was an 'over-arching' body, the Council of TAVRAs – whose President was also normally one of the Lords Lieutenant[20]. During the period covered by this book, the Chairman was always a distinguished retired senior Regular officer, and its Secretary (i.e. chief executive) a retired Regular major general or brigadier.[21] Its main task was to act as a link between the TAVRAs and the Ministry of Defence at the highest level, and to provide (as the Council's 2006 website had it) "corporate direction" for the TAVRAs – which, in more realistic language, meant ensuring that they were all 'singing from the same hymn-sheet'. One of the more satisfying aspects of becoming a senior TA officer or member of a TAVRA was one's increasing awareness of the quite tremendous contributions to the success of the TA – indeed all the Reserve Forces – made by the Chairmen and Secretaries of the Council. For very understandable reasons, not all Regular soldiers have an instinctive interest in, and empathy with, the 'part-timers', but these were all so friendly, open and realistic, excellent at their jobs, regarding problems in the 'system' as challenges to be met and not to be defeated by, and the sort of people after meeting whom one always felt better. They gave devoted service to the TA, and in recognition of that their names are given in Appendix 7.

Even though the wording of some parts of the 1907 Act had been brought up-to-date, until the 1980s hardly any of the defined purposes of the Associations had been altered – even the reference to horses remained, although now coupled with "mechanical transport".[22] It was therefore still the most important task of the Associations, not the Regular Army or the dreaded and inefficient Property Services Agency, to provide accommodation for all the companies and detached platoons of the TA (and, in due course, units of the other Reserve Forces) in their respective areas – maintaining, improving, altering and enlarging the TA Centres as became necessary from time to time – and they were also responsible for the quite considerable number of shooting ranges that, in the past, had been acquired and built by the original Associations, rather than by the War Office. Although the financial constraints on their work became increasingly severe over the years covered by this book, without exception they ran a marvellously efficient and streamlined system – based on good relationships with local builders, electricians, plumbers and architects – that was the envy of the Regular Forces. They were jointly responsible, with the units themselves, for recruiting and 'Keeping the TA in the Public Eye', and most of the funds provided by the Ministry of Defence for those two tasks was channelled through them. In particular, they allocated money to all the units in their areas towards the cost of advertising and printing recruiting literature; arranged much of the public relations activity; and in later years organised, jointly with a major unit, the weekend-long Executive Stretch Exercises intended to show managers from all walks of life what the leadership training in the TA could do in terms of confidence-building, improving personal man-management skills, and organising their work.[23]

It is often said that the best rank and job in the British Army is being a brigadier commanding a brigade. At that stage in their careers, they have had enormous experience of people and soldiering in general, are still very much in touch with officers, NCOs and soldiers on a daily basis, and have not lost the zest and enthusiasm which stems from having recently commanded a battalion or regiment – and it was therefore an extremely sensible decision on the part of the Ministry of Defence that the TAVRA Secretaries across the whole country should normally be retired brigadiers (or occasionally 'two-star' officers – i.e.major generals). They were there to support the TA – and, despite ever-increasingly heavy work-loads, they did so willingly, efficiently and cheerfully, travelling many thousands of miles each year. They visited all their TA Centres regularly, agreeing alterations and improvements, and planned new ones; they organised and attended a plethora of committee meetings at the TAVRA's headquarters and across their counties, as well as at the Council of TAVR Associations in London; and they were responsible for their Association's finances and staff.[24] They arranged countless receptions, and events to inform employers about the Reserve Forces and to encourage them to persuade their employees to join-up; they dealt with the press at local and national level; and they gave advice on recruiting matters. The list of their doings is endless – and Eastern and Western Wessex (as they were normally known) were particularly well-served by their various Secretaries. The first ones were Lieutenant Colonel George Moss and Colonel "Cat" Halliday, who had already been the Secretaries of the Gloucestershire and Hampshire TA Associations for many years. There will be few who served in the Battalion of the rank of sergeant and above who will not remember with affection one or more of their successors: Lieutenant Colonel Malcolm Carr, Brigadier "Joe" Starling and latterly Brigadier

Bruce Jackman of Western Wessex (whose office was at 2 Beaufort Road, Clifton, Bristol), or Brigadier John Oldfield, Major General Tony Ward-Booth and Brigadier Bob Long of Eastern Wessex (at 30 Carlton Place in Southampton). They were all so very successful because, quite apart from anything else, they really understood the ethos of the Volunteers, they were really interested in what they were doing, and really wanted them to succeed. Rarely was there a major difference of opinion with them.

It was the Lord Lieutenant of Dorset, Colonel Sir Joseph Weld, who was the Battalion's first Honorary Colonel. He was the epitome of everything that one in his position should be – of immense personal charm, with wide interests, able to talk perfectly naturally to anyone, be he a private soldier or the Secretary of State for Defence, and wise – and strongly committed to the Battalion. Following his death, a brief memoir of him appeared in Country Life:

> Colonel Sir Joseph Weld was a great figure in Dorset through much of my life. At Sandhurst with his son, the present owner of Lulworth, I was lucky enough to be roped in occasionally to partner one of his daughters. I particularly remember a dance in the Dorchester barracks when he set about quizzing me, a callow subaltern whose views were not worth tuppence, while doing his kindly best to get me drunk. He had an extraordinary knack of making one feel at the same time both very small and incredibly important. A week or so later, I appeared before him, defending one of my soldiers, at Wareham Magistrates' Court. I cannot believe that anyone who had met the full battery of his charm or met the twinkle of his eye could ever forget Joe Weld.[24]

Very early on, the Battalion adopted "The Farmer's Boy" as its regimental quick march. It had originally 'belonged' to both the Royal Berkshire and Wiltshire Regiments, and also (albeit perhaps unofficially) to the The Royal Hampshires, and it is undeniably one of the best in the British Army – a really good, swinging and eminently singable, traditional English tune that makes one almost automatically stand up straight, and with at least the refrain of the four verses (if not much of the rest) being easy to remember. The words are printed in Appendix 1. Perhaps reflecting its 'Don't waste time on unnecessary activities' approach to life generally, and the fact that TA battalions tended to

have very few formal parades when the Colours were trooped, the
Battalion never had a slow march. John Sellars's researches through his
vast library produced the Battalion's motto – "Their Land to Defend"
– and it was formally adopted early in 1969.

So the scene was set for 27 years of marvellous soldiering:

> The Wessex Volunteers are a new Regiment, carrying on none of the
> traditions of former units, and free from all the bad habits of their
> predecessors! It is not given to all men to have a hand in the formation
> of [one], and it [will be] quite an experience...[25]

-----

[1] The Royal Hampshire Regiment Journal, May 1967. NB: In these footnotes, from here
     on The Royal Hampshire Regiment Journal is referred to by the abbreviation RHRJ.
[2] Cmnd.2855, HMSO.
[3] The 43rd (Wessex) Division at War, 1944-1945 (Major General H Essame, William
     Clowes 1952).
[4] See the Abbreviations pages above.
[5] The Devonshire and Dorset Regiments had amalgamated in 1958, and the Royal
     Berkshires and the Wiltshires had combined to form the Duke of Edinburgh's Royal
     Regiment in 1959.
[6] By absorbtion into the newly created Prince of Wales's Division.
[7] The Devonshire & Dorset Regimental Journal, October 1967. NB: In these footnotes,
     from here on
[8] RHRJ November 1966.
[9] Summer 1967 issue.
[10] The Royal Berkshire Regiment – The Last Twelve Years (Major F Myatt MC).
[11] The Band of the 4th/5th Royal Hampshires in fact provided about half its members.
[12] RHRJ, November 1976.
[13] Ibid, May 1981.
[14] Unattributed.
[15] The Back Badge, Winter 1976. NB: In the footnotes, from here on The Back Badge will
     be referred to by the abbreviation BB.
[16] Territorial & Reserve Forces Act 1907, Section 2.
[17] Highland, Lowland, North of England, Yorkshire & Humbershire, North West of
     England & Isle of Man, Northern Ireland, Wales, West Midlands, East Midlands,
     Western Wessex, Eastern Wessex, East Anglia, Greater London and South East.
     Although the Territorial Army was renamed the "Territorial Army Volunteer
     Reserve", the Associations became "Territorial, Auxilliary & Volunteer Reserve
     Associations" because their responsibilities were extended to include certain services
     to the Royal Auxilliary Air Force and the Royal Naval Reserve.
[18] As time went on, however, senior retired members of the other Volunteer Forces became

Chairmen.

[19] The first time that a TA unit (other than The Wessex Volunteers and the two Battalions of The Wessex Regiment) is mentioned, its full title is given, but thereafter its standard Army abbreviation is used – and all those abbreviations are given in the Abbreviations section above.

[20] Although in the late 1970s/early 1980s the very 'Reserve Forces-friendly' retired Under-Secretary of State for Defence, The Rt Hon Roger Freeman, held the office.

[21] Since 2000, however, the Chairmen of the Council have been retired senior Volunteers, and the Secretaries retired senior officers of the Royal Air Force.

[22] Reserve Forces Act 1980, Sections 121–129.

[23] See Chapter 9.

[24] David Edelstein in Country Life, 25th October 2001.

[25] D&DRJ, October 1967.

CHAPTER 3

THE EARLY YEARS: 1967–1973

The Battalion's initial war role, like that of the other NATO Volunteer battalions, was to support the Regular Army's NATO-committed 1 (BR) Corps in Germany or, if necessary, the Regular Army in the United Kingdom. Largely, however, because of the unexplained disappearance from the Ministry of Defence's 'old file stores' of the Battalion's Annual 'Unit Historical Record', briefly mentioned in the Introduction, it has proved impossible to discover anything more specific, save that for the first 15 years of its existence it formed part of 4 Division, and that in the early 1970s it provided protection for 50 Missile Regiment of The Royal Artillery — based at Menden near Dortmund, and armed with American Honest John rockets and 8" howitzers. That task was, though, never actually practised 'on the ground', although there were occasional visits by the CO and two or three other officers from Battalion HQ, and the Battalion as a whole did not go to Camp in BAOR until 1975. The object of all training was, of course, to get and keep the Battalion "fit for role" – and it began as soon as the Companies and Platoons first met in their (sometimes new) TA Centres. Gone were the days when, it used to be said – in jest, but with some justification – that an order was an invitation for a discussion! At first, most people thought that:

> The pattern of life we lead [is] much the same as that to which Territorials have been used, with a fortnights annual camp, weekend exercises roughly once a month, a range course to fire and regular drill nights.[1]

but it quickly became obvious that everyone was going to work – and play – very much harder than that. Two weekends a month (often starting on Friday evenings) – one when the individual Companies trained on their own, and the other when they came together as the Battalion – soon became the norm, and key people were often doing three. New style Battalion exercises involved tasks and skills which had for practical purposes never been heard of, let alone carried out, in the pre-1967 TA – night river crossings, dawn attacks, the occupation of defensive positions, minefield clearance, forced marches, helicopter drills, night defence, operating with armour, bridge demolition guards, house clearing, and on almost *ad infinitum*, covering virtually every aspect of the Army Training Manuals. Most company training was geared either to teaching and improving individual skills, or preparing everyone, individually and collectively, for those exercises. Completely oblivious of the weather, all the Companies, but particularly B and D, took to spending virtually all their weekends out in the field, rather than in training camps, very often working throughout the night, with no one getting more than a few hours sleep snatched in a sodden bivvy [bivouac]. It was all very different from the old TA – and HQ Company was very conscious of the changes:

> We started off with Exercise Welcome Stranger on Dartmoor in April. Certain very senior NCOs were seen cramming twenty years map-reading experience into twenty minutes before leading patrols for the first time in their lives, and we hear of one Sergeant who believed that a back-bearing was something to do with a stretcher.........After using many infantry weapons – in many cases for the first time – and eating beautiful [*sic*] food in beautiful weather, we went home feeling that perhaps the Wessex Volunteers was going to be fun after all.[2]

Another report of an early weekend exercise included a mildly philosophical comment:

> The overriding recollection is of a shivering night spent lying in ambush, waiting for an enemy who never came, a quick change of plan by the directing staff to ensure that some sort of hostilities took place, and another ambush set up – only to discover that by then the opposition had passed by. Perhaps this is no bad thing, however. We may be too used our every exercise being a potted battle, with none of the frustrations and near misses which must characterise a real-life war.[3]

whilst a good example of playing hard was A Company's 1971 Christmas Party:

An excellent cuisine and a well-stocked cellar set the party off in
high spirits. No. 2 Platoon stole the glory by appearing in fancy
dress. Although Lance-Corporal Hamblin closely resembled King
Henry VIII, whose portly figure could be seen behind a mountain
of chicken legs, fruit salad and crazy foam, Catherine Parr and her
five predecessors were absent, unless Private Woodland wearing two
balloons, a ballet skirt and a pair of off-colour white tights, could have
been mistaken for one of them. After the meal the power group were
subjected to a candle-light carol service which can only be described
as a flaming success.[4]

Christmas and Bounty Night parties were the main social events
of the TA year for the Companies – held either at the Company HQ
TA Centre or one of the Platoon locations. The former, although not
so often the latter, were always attended by wives and girlfriends, and
the traditional custom of the officers and senior NCOs serving the
meal was invariably followed. "Bounty" was an annual payment to all
ranks whose training standards and attendance record had qualified
them for it – in 1971 for a trained private soldier it was £75–£80, the
equivalent of approximately £525 in 2005 – and, like all Army pay, it
used to be received in cash "over the pay table" on "Bounty Night".
The party was always planned in advance – and the custom continued
even after the system was changed, and all pay was credited to bank
accounts. Both occasions were the very best of what some would now
call bonding sessions, but that process in fact continued week after
week, all the year round, after Drill Night training had finished. Then,
most of those who had come in for the evening would go to the Club
for a drink; the PSIs were almost invariably there – and so were the
officers, unless they wanted some privacy in their mess. Visitors from
Battalion HQ – who quickly learned that the atmosphere in the Club
was an extremely good indicator of how things were going with the
Company.

The company-versus-battalion conflict of loyalty has always been
an important factor in the life of any Infantry battalion, whether
Regular or Territorial, and it was very evident in both The Wessex
Volunteers and subsequently in 1 Wessex. Indeed, it is not actually
easy to say whether, over the 28 years of the Battalion's existence,

the prime loyalty of the Volunteers was to their Companies or to the Battalion – and the truth is probably that, as in the Regular Army, it depended on the activity of the moment.

In the Company locations, and particularly in the case of the outlying platoons such as Barnstaple and the Isle of Wight, the TA Centre was very much the hub of the military world for most of the Volunteers – indeed, the keen ones spent an appreciable part of all their free time there – and when a Company was training on its own at a weekend they saw that as working for the benefit of the Company, not the Battalion. By 1972, quite apart from Battalion-organised training Camps, major exercises, specialist cadre training and study days, there were nearly 800 separate drill nights or out-of-camp days training (the latter, of course, all at weekends) to be planned and run in fourteen TA Centres spread over six counties. That meant that by far the largest proportion of all training was carried out at local level – and so, with the strong social element mentioned above, the Companies very much tended to become almost semi-private armies. The situation was certainly not helped by the huge geographical spread of the Battalion, which meant that quite a substantial number of the members of, say, D Company in Reading were almost unaware that Headquarter Company was in Exeter – or, in some cases, that there was a Headquarter Company at all – and that when the Companies were working (or playing) on their own, the rest of the Battalion might as well not have existed. Ironically, however, the separation of the Companies – so different from the days when each TA battalion was contained within its own county boundaries, and inter-company postings were common – tended to heighten the rivalry between them, and that in turn resulted in continuously improving training standards.

Battalion weekends (whether for exercises, specialist training or parades) and Annual Camp were therefore the occasions when the hierarchy could try to correct that tendency and weld the Companies together as a single major unit. Those events provided regular opportunities for all ranks not only to see the other Companies and meet some of their members – and almost invariably to make comparisons (usually amusingly invidious) between the state of training, and the general good discipline and military efficiency, of their own Company and that of some or all of the others – but also for discovering that members of other Companies were in fact very nice guys rather than the uncouth dwellers from another region that the dispersal of the Battalion led some people to imagine. Many good friendships between members of different Companies were made in the backs of 4-tonners, over the barrel of a Wombat anti-tank gun or around a radio set. Gradually and almost imperceptibly, therefore, although it did not displace the Company loyalties, there arose a 'Wessex ethos' – a feeling of belonging, and the sense that the Battalion was indeed a corporate whole with a single identity, and not just a collection of disparate, albeit very effective, sub-units. When everyone came together at Annual Camp or for a big parade, by and large Company loyalties were put to one side, and all effort was for the Battalion.

Happily, without exception the regular officers and senior PSIs fully understood that without strong Platoons based on a sort of tribal instinct there could be no strong Companies, and without strong Companies no strong Battalion – and that local loyalties therefore had to be fostered perhaps more than a Battalion one. Sometimes it needed the firm judgement and steadying hand of the CO, the Training Major, the Second-in- Command or the RSM to ensure that, as far as possible, the right balance was maintained. As the success of the Presentation of Colours parade in 1973 was to show very clearly, however, the Battalion's spirit grew and grew as the years went by, and it never waned.

Each Company soon acquired its own and immediately recognisable character – which was undoubtedly a reflection of the personalities of the first Company Commander, the other officers, the Company Sergeant Major and the other senior NCOs. C Company was without question always the most comfortable, cheerful and laid-back, indeed almost happy-go-lucky – a one-off and probably almost unique in the TA. B and D Companies were extremely well-trained, efficient and warlike, never happier than when doing a ten-mile forced march, followed by a sleepless night in the open with nothing more than a groundsheet for shelter, all in pouring rain and howling wind.

Many thought that B Company were too keen, and D Company were regarded with some suspicion, as the 'townies' of the Battalion. For those reasons, both were somewhat underrated by the other Companies, who (so far as D were concerned) were much more 'country town' based. A Company was, at least in the early stages, somewhere in the middle; one view was that it was run by gentlemen who liked port. E was solid but over-pressed – and HQ was a complete mystery to everyone except themselves.[5]

Despite all the promises by the Ministry of Defence and countless generals of a new future, for the first few months and to some dismay, everyone had to soldier on in their old TA battledress, ammunition boots and "(19)'37 pattern" equipment – and the delays and muddles in issuing the promised up-to-date uniforms and equipment undoubtedly caused some soldiers to leave fairly quickly. There was, though, a funny side to many of the failures:

> ….for some reason known only to the Ministry of Defence, our first issue of extra clothing consisted of a housewife, a pair of braces and a cap comforter – the last of these being promptly withdrawn….

but before long:

> …..the withdrawn cap comforters had been re-issued, together with three pairs of assorted underpants….[6]

Nevertheless, in due course everyone was properly dressed for training like the Regular Army – in combat kit, DMS boots [Boots, Direct Moulded Sole], 'battle bowlers' and "(19)'58 pattern" equipment. The last of those, though, was not issued until just before Camp in 1971, and it was not until the Presentation of Colours in 1973 that everyone had No 2 Dress [parade] uniform and No 1 Dress [all-blue] hats to go with it. So far as weapons were concerned, the initial priorities were learning to shoot and drill with the Self Loading Rifle, and training on support weapons and new radios.

The first Annual Camp[7], for the whole Battalion, was held at East Wretham Camp on the Stanford Primary Training Area in Norfolk, from 1–14 July 1967. 505 Volunteers attended – and, of course, the Permanent Staff, who then numbered about 25. Although the

Companies had been together on a few Battalion training weekends in the previous three months, it understandably took a while for them to get an initial measure of each other, and Company identity ruled supreme. Perhaps the most blatant example of that was in the Officers Mess, where all the china from the old TA battalions was pooled. Although hopefully without making life too difficult for the staff, a number of officers would (in jest) refuse to eat off a plate with the crest of a regiment other than their own – "I was a Royal Berkshire, and I would rather not have my porridge out of a Dorset bowl! Would you mind bringing it back in one of my own, please?" On the more serious side, the whole of the first week was spent firing platoon weapons – although the pace was sufficiently relaxed to allow the officers of A Company, in the few evenings which were not taken-up with social events, to go patrolling among the hotels and pubs of central Norfolk, and find 23 different varieties of brandy. There was a great deal more (soldiering) activity in the second week – the main object of which was perhaps to make clear beyond all doubt the high standards which John Sellars and the rest of his Regular Permanent Staff would expect of everyone in the Battalion. First came an Internal Security exercise, and then three days in the field on the first of what would eventually turn out to be perhaps sixty or eighty demolition bridge guard exercises[8] that the Battalion would eventually carry out over the years. There was, of course, considerable interest on the part of the Regular Army and the Ministry of Defence in how the new TAVR was settling down, and that was reflected in the very large number of VIP visitors during the fortnight, including the Minister for Defence (Administration), the Director of Volunteer Training (Major General JA d'Avigdor-Goldsmith), the GOC South West District (Major General Tom Acton), and the Brigade Colonel of The Wessex Brigade (Colonel Denis Harding) – the last two of whom were particularly supportive of the Battalion in its early days.

When life resumed its normal pattern after Camp, D Company attacked the Isle of Wight in an amphibious assault, with B Company defending it. Legend has it[9] that by far the most interesting event of the weekend was the ramming at 35 knots in heavy fog of a large buoy in the middle of the Solent by a Fast Patrol Boat of the Royal Naval

Reserve, with part of D Company on board. A few weeks later, A Company was out, when:

> a remarkable battle occurred on Salisbury Plain. Exercise Sharp End should have taken place in March, but, as a result of the Great Gas Stoppage, it had been adjourned. It was a sort of calculated fratricide, where the two rifle platoon commanders sat down and devised a plan whereby each could decimate his colleagues ranks. In the end, it is understood that this did not happen, for the warring factions were largely kept apart by some mercenaries from the Mortar Section. Eventually, some judicious umpiring was required to point out to the attacking forces where the defenders might be found, and a clash took place. Whatever the outcome, you will be relieved to know that the parties later appeared fit and well, and that Private Parkes had enjoyed a good nights sleep.[10]

During the autumn and early winter, there were three major Battalion events – a Support Weapons Concentration; the Inter Platoon Competition – which was repeated virtually every year in the future; and finally a night withdrawal exercise on the Plain (with D Company intact):

> perhaps memorable for the nameless Platoon Commander who achieved the feat of leading two platoons and Company Tac HQ off the training area on a compass march. A remark was heard to the effect that it was as well that, unlike the world (which according to mediaeval intellectuals had an edge), Salisbury Plain Training Area has a fence round it.[11]

The second Camp, in 1968, was the first one to be split – John Sellars took most of the Battalion to the Sennybridge Training Area in Wales, but both B Company and the Signal Platoon went, at different times, to spend the fortnight in BAOR with 1 D & D at Osnabrook. Reports can be found in Chapter 5.

As part of a Regular Army reorganisation in 1968–69, what were known as the Divisions of Infantry took over the functions of the administrative Brigades, each embracing several of those Brigades. The Divisions had no operational function, but became responsible for the initial training of all recruits for the Regular battalions, and for all regimental and personnel matters for both the Regular Army and the TA. The Prince of Wales's Division comprised the four Wessex Regiments and The Wessex Volunteers; the Royal Welsh Fusiliers, The Welch Regiment, the South Wales Borderers and The Welsh Volunteers; and the Regular regiments which had been in The Mercian Brigade (the Cheshires, Worcesters, Staffords and Sherwood Foresters) with their TA battalion, The Mercian Volunteers. The Divisional Headquarters were in what had formerly been The Staffordshire Regiment's Depot at Whittington Barracks, Lichfield. Just as the senior officers in the Brigades had had their Brigade Colonels, so each Division had a General as its Colonel Commandant – an appointment, as it turned out from the Battalion's point of view, of some consequence. On 1 January 1969, The Wessex Brigade ceased to exist, and it has never revived as an administrative entity.

Needles to say, there was a simultaneous reorganisation of the TA – but this time, contrary to all expectations, it was 'good news' for the Territorials. In 1967, all had seemed set for a period sufficiently long to let everyone iron out the wrinkles of the reorganisation, and make a good start on acquiring the skills needed in the new roles. Quite astonishingly, however, the TAVR III units were to last for fewer than two years, and early in 1969 they were all reduced to eight-man "Cadres" of three officers and five other ranks, albeit still with TAVR III terms of service. They continued to bear the titles and retained the traditions of their pre-1967 battalions or regiments, and were intended to act as a structure upon which the TA could be enlarged again, should the need for that arise. It did in fact, only another two years later, in the second of the post-1967 reorganisations – and between 1971 and 1975 most of those cadres were expanded to provide the basis of companies for new TAVR II Home Defence battalions – so that, for example, The Humber Regiment, Royal Artillery (Territorials) became a Company in a new battalion of The Yorkshire Volunteers. Officially the remainder of the cadres were completely disbanded and no longer formed part of the Army Order of Battle – but their anger at being disbanded and their spirit was so great that a number of them remained in existence in effect as private clubs, a sort of phantom TA. There is a story of the GOC of one of the Divisions who received an invitation from "The

Commanding Officer and Officers of The........Yeomanry, to Dinner on ...." at their Mess on one of the training areas regularly used for TA Camps. The regiment in question was in fact one of the disbanded units, but, intrigued, he nevertheless accepted. On the evening in question, he drove into the Camp, where he was greeted by a Quarter Guard in full ceremonial uniform, complete with fanfare trumpeters; the Mess turned out to be an immaculate white marquee, and on being taken inside by the PMC to meet "the Colonel" (something of a surprise, as the senior officer of every cadre was a major) he found a complete regiment's-worth of officers, all in mess kit. An extremely pleasant evening was had by all, and the General departed in very good humour without having said a word about training or other military matters – perhaps wiser in the ways of the TA than he had been before dinner.

The 1969 New Year's Honours List was the first to include the name of a member of the Battalion – Sergeant Bert Midson, the MT [Motor Transport] Sergeant in HQ Company was awarded the British Empire Medal:

> It is difficult to explain why we are so pleased about the award without it reading like his obituary, but he has been a very loyal servant of the Queen for many years, and a good friend to a very large number of Terriers and Volunteers. Well done, Bert![12]

Lieutenant Colonel Paul Freeland, of The Devonshire & Dorset Regiment, commanded the Battalion from 1969 to the end of 1970. Tall, elegant, urbane, and very friendly, he was originally a Devon, but had also served with the Wiltshires, the Royal Hampshires and the Duke of Edinburgh's, and as a staff officer at the Wessex Brigade HQ. Furthermore, having been the Adjutant of 4 Devons from 1955 to 1958, on his arrival (like John Sellars before him) he already well understood the ethos of the part-time soldier. Quickly warming, therefore, to the approach of the post-1967 Volunteers, he commanded his far-flung empire, now some 650 strong[13], with very considerable flair and poise. Paul Freeland was a totally unflappable CO, who only very rarely seemed to get angry – indeed, why should he, for things were going extremely well? – and he made a real effort to ensure that everyone in the Battalion felt that what they were doing improved its cohesion and sense of togetherness.

He was well supported by Battalion HQ, which at that time was very much a DERR enclave. The studious and (until his face broke into a smile) somewhat worried-looking Major Robin Wilson (who subsequently retired to run a book and print shop in Westbury, on the edge of the Salisbury Plain PTA) was the Training Major; the Adjutant was the 'bright-eyed and bushy-tailed' Captain Nigel Sutton (very tragically killed in a vehicle accident in Northern Ireland in 1973); and the ruddy-faced, always-smiling and imperturbable Major Jack Price was the Quartermaster. One memorable Exercise which they all planned together was New Look I, testing the Battalion on company advance to contact, patrolling and tank-co-operation with the help of a troop from 3 Royal Tank Regiment.

It soon became very clear that Exeter was the wrong place for Battalion Headquarters, and therefore for Headquarter Company as well. The first reason was an almost psychological one, in that – although, in military terms, there has often been a lot to be said for being well removed from one's headquarters! – Exeter was a very, very long way from the rifle companies (except for C Company), and, as a result, while they thought they were uncared-for, Battalion Headquarters thought that it was not in control. Neither was in fact true, but nevertheless everyone felt it. The second was a physical one, as to go to Exeter for a conference involved a round trip of over 300 miles from Reading, 220 miles from Gloucester, and over 200 from Winchester – which wasted a great deal of both fuel and time. Furthermore, the disbandment of The Wessex Brigade had removed what was perhaps the main reason for Battalion HQ being there – and, although John Sellars stuck it out, in 1970 Paul Freeland grasped the nettle, and the first of a considerable number of changes in the Battalion's layout took place. It was made a great deal easier than it might otherwise have been because, as luck would have it, at the end of 1969, in common with a number of other NATO battalions, 1 Wessex had been directed to raise a fifth rifle company, so that on mobilization it could provide a "Strategic Reserve Company" [Stratco Company][14] for an air-portable Regular battalion in 3 Division. The result was that, in the spring of the following year, Battalion HQ moved to Bythesea Road, Trowbridge (a former Drill Hall of the Royal Wiltshire Yeomanry); A Company was nominated as the Stratco Company; Headquarter Company in Exeter became E Company, the fifth Rifle Company;[15] and a new Headquarter Company was formed, also in Trowbridge.

The return of the TA Infantry to Wiltshire was, of course, a marvellous turn of events, and it provided a double benefit. Firstly, it enabled a good number of 'old' Territorials, most of whom had been in Headquarter Company of the 4th Wiltshires, to join up again, and thus provide a 'flying start' for the new Company. Two of them in particular, RQMS Gordon Sheppard (in due course Captain Sheppard, MBE) and Colour Sergeant Harry Mower (later to become the RQMS), gave truly devoted service to the Battalion for the rest of its existence, as did a number of other former, relatively senior, 4th Wiltshires' NCOs and soldiers. There were also a few NCOs in the Devon-based HQ Company who already lived in various places between Exeter and Trowbridge, and so could continue to serve – but nevertheless a fair proportion of the new Company had to be recruited from scratch. Secondly, because it would have been foolhardy to try to recruit the additional rifle company in west Wiltshire (and there was not, at that time, really anywhere else within the Battalion's area that it could have been done), had Headquarter Company not moved from Exeter, it is unlikely that the Battalion would ever have acquired its fifth Rifle Company – a change which virtually guaranteed it a really challenging role, and enabled it hugely to enhance its standing in the Army as a whole.

Although the transfer of the 'power-house' to Trowbridge brought it physically much closer to all the Companies (but again, except C), and the earlier command difficulties were for practical purposes resolved, because both the buildings and the site had considerable limitations, in the medium and long term it was unlikely to remain an acceptable location – and luckily it quite soon proved to be the 'springboard' from which the eminently satisfactory move to Devizes, covered later in this Chapter, became possible.

Many people have wondered how the name Bythesea came to be

associated with a street in Trowbridge. The Bythesea family originated in the town in the mid-1600s, and owned a number of houses near Stallard Street. In the 1890s, those houses were demolished to make way for a new road, which was presented to the town by Samuel Bythesea. He was either the uncle or great uncle of a Rear Admiral John Bythesea, one of the first holders of the Victoria Cross – which he was awarded during the Crimean War, only a year after it had been instituted, for disguising himself as a Russian peasant and attempting to intercept an important dispatch from the Tsar; he succeeded in doing so, and then forced a group of Russians at pistol point to row him and a fellow sailor back to his ship, the curiously named HMS Arrogant.

Of all the NATO Volunteer Battalions, the Battalion was probably the best placed in relation to ranges, training areas, and many schools and establishments of the Regular Army. They were therefore able to get a tremendous amount of help from the School of Infantry at Warminster, its Support Weapons Wing at Netheravon, and from Regular Army units stationed at Bulford and Tidworth – in later years frequent use was made of the Battle Group Trainer at Bovington in Dorset. That could well have been one of the main reasons why, for almost the whole of its existence, the Battalion retained perhaps the most testing mobilization task of all the NATO battalions, as part of 3 Division. For exercise-planning right across the TA, the extent to which outside help was available very much depended on the 'its whom you know' principle – and the support received by the Battalion over the years well reflects the wide range of friendly contacts which all the COs, Training Majors and Adjutants had throughout the Regular Army.

In the world of not-strictly-training activities, 1970 was a good year. A team from A Company, led by Lieutenant Peter Lintott, came third in the extremely tough Cambrian Marches Competition, open to both the Regular Army and the TA. Then, as is shown in Appendix 6, the Battalion had considerable success at the TA Skill at Arms Meeting at Bisley.

Paul Freeland was followed as the Commanding Officer, in December 1970, by the author, who, after commanding A Company, had become the Battalion 2IC. A former National Servicemen, he began his military career as a rifleman in the King's Royal Rifle Corps (60th Rifles) and in May 1952 was commissioned into the Glosters, a few weeks before they returned from Korea to become the Demonstration Battalion at the School of Infantry. He then transferred to the 5th Glosters, in which his last appointment was OC Headquarter Company. He was one of the first Volunteers to be given command of a NATO infantry battalion, and the appointment undoubtedly caused a certain amount of unease within the Battalion! Some officers and senior NCOs feared that the new CO might well try to be more 'dead-Reg' than a Regular, and others that he might not be up to the job. What was abundantly clear, however, was that, between them, the Permanent Staff would be well able to keep him under control and on the right rails. His two Training Majors (Major Desmond Redding of the DERR, and then Major Robert Jarman of the Glosters), two Adjutants (Captain Mike Tulloch of The Worcestershire & Foresters Regiment – the first officer not in one of the Regular Regiments to serve with the Battalion – who was followed by the Royal Hampshires' Captain James Shrimpton), and the RSM, the extremely smart and efficient WO1 Mick Chappell (also a Gloster) could not have been more supportive, and they were real towers of strength. Major John Roberts, the OC of B Company, became the 2IC so that he could impart some of the 'parachute outlook' for which he was already famous throughout the Battalion.[16]

As the Battalion continued to acquire its own identity, by 1970 all the Companies except A Company had voluntarily abandoned the wearing of items of their affiliated Regular Regiment's insignia. Under pressure from The Gloucestershire Regiment, however, against their impending amalgamation with The Royal Hampshire Regiment, it had been agreed that A Company should retain the Back Badge. The Glosters feared that the new Regiment might not adopt it, and if A Company were to give it up as well, the result would have been the complete loss of one of the most celebrated badges of the British Army. In the event, just over three weeks before the "vesting day", the Conservatives under Edward Heath won the 1970 election from Labour, the amalgamation was called off and the badge was 'saved' – but the Company nevertheless continued to wear "brass before and brass behind"[17]. It has to be said that, having given up their own distinctions, the other Companies resented that, and A Company's relationship with the rest of the Battalion was not helped by the fact that it had held the coveted Stratco role from the outset. This was a classic example of the 'company-versus-battalion' loyalty conflict mentioned at the beginning of this Chapter – it was generally felt that A Company was becoming 'too cocky by half', and the situation detrimental to the growing feeling of unity within the Battalion. As the Presentation of Colours drew closer, the author, having no doubt at all in his own mind that the parade would greatly enhance that unity, in March 1973 therefore directed that the Back Badge would no longer be worn. Not surprisingly, there was an immediate and angry reaction from The Gloucestershire Regiment, and the author was very roughly, and probably rightly, hauled over the coals by the Colonel of the Regiment, Brigadier AJA (Tony) Arengo-Jones, for making the decision without consulting him first – although, strictly speaking, he could not have prevented it. Very understandably, A Company didn't like it at all either, but after vociferous complaints they nevertheless accepted the decision with good grace:

> The 1st Battalion The Wessex Regiment is a regiment with its own identity, and it was quite properly felt that A Company should, in keeping with the other five Companies which make up the Battalion, adopt a uniform dress.[18]

The other Companies all thought (happily with no crowing, and almost a sense of relief) that the decision was the right one – and in fact even by the end of Camp the matter had been largely forgotten by everyone.

There was, however, one really sad, indeed almost tragic, consequence. The CSM of A Company, Dick Keitley, had been the author's CSM in the 5th Glosters, and he was a Gloster through and through. One of the original members of the Battalion, he really wanted it to succeed – but he felt that the order was so wrong, and that his conflict of loyalties was too great to bear, that he resigned his appointment and left the Battalion before Camp and the Parade. It was both one of the saddest happenings in the whole history of 1 Wessex, and possibly the morally bravest decision ever taken by a member of it – particularly as the Parade, in which he would have unquestionably taken part, would have thrilled him to the core. The Battalion and A Company lost a much loved and respected figure who epitomised all that was best about the Volunteers. A well-built, imposing man, he exuded great authority and confidence in all he did; genial, and often with a little twinkle in his eyes, he was a marvellous man-manager – and, like all the best Sergeant Majors, his bark was far worse than his bite. If he had not decided to resign, the Company Commander, Peter Whiteman, having said in effect "You've had your grumble (or worse), so now let's get on and make it work", like everyone else (including the author), he would have simply taken the traditional step of transferring his Back Badges from the outside of his No 1 Dress Hat and beret to the inside. Only once was he lost for words: a new black recruit was given his kit, and told to come back the following drill night wearing it, including his boots – "and you can tell me what DMS stands for." The following Tuesday, the recruit appeared, and, on being asked what DMS meant, gave the unexpected answer: "Dem's Ma Shoes, Sah!" Dick Keitley did, however, 'retain' his Back Badge after all, by becoming the Secretary of the Back Badge Ball Committee of five Branches of The Gloucestershire Regimental Association.

The enlargement of the TA mentioned above began on 1 April 1971, when 19 new battalions, with TAVR II terms of service, were formed for Home Defence from some of the TAVR III 8-man cadres which were all that had survived of the large majority of the pre-1967 TA units. One of the new battalions was created from The Buckinghamshire Regiment RA, The Hampshire & Isle of Wight Territorials, The Royal Berkshire Territorials and The Dorset Territorials, within the area covered by Eastern Wessex TAVRA. Although there is no record of any consultation on the question, the decision was made that it should become another battalion of The Wessex Volunteers – which thus became a proper Regiment, with 1st and 2nd Battalions. Battalion HQ and HQ Company of the 2nd Battalion were established in Brock Barracks at Reading, and there were Companies in Bletchley, Maidenhead, Southampton and Bournemouth. The first, and very successful, CO of the 2nd Battalion was Lieutenant Colonel Tim May (formerly of The Oxfordshire Yeomanry), a Volunteer of very considerable experience, with great physical presence and charisma, as well as a good sense of humour – and he deserves more credit than the author for trying to ensure that the Regiment worked as a whole. In due course, he became Chairman of Eastern Wessex TAVRA. It is probably true to say that the 1st Battalion was unable to decide whether to make a determined effort to establish a friendly rivalry with the 2nd, or to maintain a somewhat stand-offish position as the senior one with a better war role – and although, in the event, there was spasmodic and enjoyable contact between the two Battalions, albeit usually at Company level, more often than not the feeling was that neither rivalry nor unity were seriously on the agendas of either. As will be related in Chapter 12, however, the 2nd Battalion eventually secured an amalgamation with the 1st Battalion on a basis that destroyed the latter.

Another of the new Home Defence major units – in this case officially an Infantry battalion, but in spirit a Yeomanry regiment – was formed from the cadres of the Royal Gloucestershire Hussars [RGH], the Royal Wiltshire Yeomanry [RWY] (which in 1967 had contributed one Squadron to the very widely dispersed Royal Yeomanry, a new TAVR II reconnaissance regiment with its RHQ in London) and The Royal Devon Yeomanry [RDY]. This was The Royal Wessex Yeomanry [RWxY], based in Cirencester, with two Squadrons in Gloucestershire, one in Salisbury and one in Barnstaple. Taking the view that when the time came to expand back into three regiments – as, with a sadly misplaced faith in the 'system', they were convinced that in due course it would[19] (although in the event it did not) – matters would be infinitely simpler if each Squadron had continued to wear its own cap-badge, the yeomen declined to adopt a new regimental one. Many 'old' Territorial Yeomen were able to resume their part-time soldiering careers – and one unexpected result of that expansion was that the long-standing lack of communication between those three Yeomanry regiments and the 'old' TA battalions in the same counties which had existed almost since time immemorial, were forgotten.

1971 was a particularly busy year in terms of Battalion training – perhaps the direct result of having a Volunteer CO! Exercise

State Trust in April was conceived in an excess of lateral thinking by Desmond Redding and the author over a pub lunch on the way to visit one of the Companies. It was an extremely ambitious and realistic mobilization exercise, the first-ever training air-movement of an entire TA battalion. Just over 500 Volunteers turned out to fly from RAF Lyneham or Exeter Airport to RAF Leeming in Yorkshire, and it involved a huge amount of organising and planning by the Training Major, the recently appointed new Adjutant, Captain James Shrimpton and the RSM. A preliminary weekend for many of the officers and senior ranks was spent at the Joint Air Training Establishment at RAF Old Sarum, learning about pax, chalks, dangerous cargos, tie-down drills and the myriad of other aspects of flying a large number of troops and their equipment (although not, in this case, any vehicles) with Royal Air Force Transport Command. A few weeks later, on a Friday evening the Companies assembled in their TA Centres, went through their mobilization procedures – documentation, medicals, kit checks and packing vehicles with all the air freight – and early the following morning set off for the departure airfields. In those days, when mass air travel was only in its infancy, for most people the prospect of flying was very exciting, but on this occasion it was somewhat tempered when it was discovered that we were not to go in elegant, huge and fast VC10s, or even the Hercules, but in Argosys – one of the slowest and, with its cavernous, slug-like, hull slung between two booms, oddest-looking aircraft ever invented. Nevertheless, they all got there, and miraculously the RAF's co-operation did not stop on arrival at Leeming – for, waiting on the tarmac, was a Sioux helicopter, available mainly for the Company Commanders' recces over the whole weekend. After marching straight to the Catterick Training Area, each Company in turn was immediately ambushed by the enemy. The writer of the C Company Notes in *The Devonshire & Dorset Regimental Journal* thought that they were provided by The Lancastrian Volunteers – but the rest of the Battalion were actually fighting 1 DERR! The exercise, in bitterly cold conditions, was fast and furious, involving (needless to say) digging-in, day and night patrolling and finally a dawn battalion attack – which, whether or not it was actually the case, and possibly to keep spirits up towards the end of a thoroughly exhausting weekend,

the Directing Staff decreed that 1 Wessex had won. When the idea
was first floated, it was considered by many to be over-ambitious,
but in the event it proved to be a great success, with much training
value.

After five separate Camps for various elements of the Battalion,
the final Battalion event for 1971 – for which the weather was, again,
unbelievably cold and wet – was the two-day Exercise Wessex Marches
in October:

> …..an inter-platoon competition cunningly designed and conceived
> to exhaust both physically and mentally all 700 members of 1
> Wessex. Tasks included patrolling by both day and night, crossing
> of a minefield, river crossing, house-clearing, street fighting, wood-
> clearing, tank-hunting and the many other incidents with which the
> infantry are expected to cope.[20]

At Westdown Camp on the Plain in January 1972, the mobilisation
exercise – a standard requirement, not a whim of the Training Major
– was:

> ……the most boring and unproductive, albeit necessary, weekend
> of the training year. Our weekend visits to this dreadful training
> centre are so frequent that many members of the company use it as
> an accommodation address. Upon arriving in the correct place at the
> correct time with a company's-worth of military impedimenta, we
> went to bed. The following morning we were medically examined and
> pronounced fit for death, and then followed a series of audiences with
> various knowledgeable persons from Battalion HQ, who explained to
> an enraptured body of soldiers what happened to them on mobilisation,
> and how they are paid, fed and watered. This rather mentally strenuous
> experience was interspersed with physical exercise in the form of yet
> another battle efficiency test.[21]

From the early 1970s onwards, the amount of activity within the
Battalion was without question prodigious, and generally speaking it
increased almost year by year. More and more Battalion training was
taking the form of inter-Company competitions, to test their skills
in an ever-increasing variety of operations, and the description of B
Company's training programme in the summer of 1982 in Chapter

9 and the following well illustrates effort and enthusiasm that the dedicated Volunteer put into to training:

> The post-Camp recruiting figures, and general high spirits in both A and B Companies after their 1971 Camps showed that long, tough exercises were popular with the members of the Battalion. B Company spent a total of eight days in the field (and pouring rain) on the Soltau Training Area, practicing virtually every phase of war likely to be met in BAOR. Despite sodden clothing, compo, blisters, the compulsory abandoning of rifle slings and an almost total lack of sleep, they came out smiling, and B Company are convinced, of course, that they are far and away the best company in the Battalion. To prove that really hard training is popular, we finished up the training year with an Inter-Platoon Tough Training Competition involving a forced march from one end of Salisbury Plain to the other, with various incidents to be dealt with, or techniques to be practiced, on the way.[22]

Whilst training was the be-all and end-all of the Battalion's existence, it could not possibly have flourished without an efficient administrative backing – and the credit for that was unquestionably due to the never-ending behind-the-scenes work of the Adjutants, the Quartermasters, the Regimental Medical Officers, the RSMs and the PSIs, the Orderly Room staff, the Colour Sergeants, Pay staff, storemen, civilian vehicle mechanics, and the clerks in each of the Companies. Sadly, there are far too many of them to mention their names here, and to do so for only a few of them would be invidious – but hopefully all the senior ones are listed in Appendix 2. It was, indeed, very unusual for anyone not to 'pull their weight' in whatever particular 'slot' they occupied. In the old TA days, their work was the subject of the Annual Administrative Inspections – but, if memory serves right, there was (perhaps not surprisingly) no assessment of a unit's ability to carry out its totally vague mobilization role of being just a general reserve for the Regular Army. From 1967, however, all TA units had basically the same yearly Fit For Role Inspection as the Regular Army [FFR] – and it was equally concerned with every aspect of both administration and training. The administration part was perhaps the more exacting one, in that in the end it largely came down to figures and records – the stores checks, the state of all the vehicles, the personal details and achievements of every individual, and so on – and short vehicle inspections. Like many other aspects of Army life:

....the Deputy Commander expressed his satisfaction with all that he saw, and the less said about what he did not see the better.[23]

The training part of the FFR was ultimately, of course, the more important, and in 1972 it took the form of a defence and withdrawal exercise, State Trust II, on Salisbury Plain at the beginning of April. It was the first time that the Battalion had been inspected, rather than just 'being seen', whilst actually in the field – undoubtedly a reflection of the importance of its role:

......four Companies of 1 Wessex deployed on Salisbury Plain. A Company, donning cap comforters in lieu of berets and steel helmets, were instructed to harass and inconvenience [the rest of the Battalion] whilst they employed their military skills. Incidents occurred almost hourly, as sentries were sniped, vehicles ambushed, meals disrupted and sleep disturbed. This was the first occasion in which we were the Bad Guys and we thoroughly enjoyed the experience, sneaking into the Check Point as the Battalion was withdrawing over a river bridge, and attempting to climb into the Medical Officer's ambulance; blowing up the bridge before the Battalion had crossed the river, ambushing the Bridge Demolition Party, and joining on to squads of our enemy as they trekked over the Plain in pitch darkness to try and discover their final positions. When dawn broke ....we were ordered with our troop of Centurions to attack the enemy battalion position. The tanks rumbled forward, using their main armament against the heavy anti-tank emplacements, and, as the range shortened, their coaxial machine guns against the enemy infantry occupying a wood. A Company advanced behind the screen of tanks into the wood, meeting considerable resistance until the umpires deemed we had done our bit and the war was over.[24]

All seemed to go well, and the CO's congratulatory message to the Battalion[25] included the following:

In his General Remarks, the Reporting Officer, Major Gen DL

Lloyd-Owen CB OBE DSO MC, who attended Ex State Trust II, said that, from what he saw on the exercise, he formed the impression of a Battalion carrying out their training in a realistic and workmanlike way. Having spoken to a large number of men and some officers, he found all of them cheerful, interested in their work and as reasonably proficient in their trades as is possible under the circumstances. He judged the Battalion to be effective in its role, and making the best of the facilities available to it.

The GOC South West District, Major General HP Cunningham OBE, stated in his comments that the Battalion has had a successful year, showing a realistic approach to their training, and ensuring that they are efficiently administered. He said that the Battalion was well recruited, which is particularly commendable in view of the fact that two new units have been raised in the area over the last year. He concluded by saying that all ranks were to be congratulated on a good report.

As mentioned at the end of Chapter 2, in 1967 virtually all the new TAVR battalions had adopted "Volunteers" as the generic word of their titles, and at the time it seemed an appropriate description to match the fresh start. Gradually, however, and particularly as the Battalion came to work more and more closely with the Regular Army, it was felt that "The Wessex Volunteers" evoked an image that was a mixture of figures with straw behind their ears who had escaped from one of Thomas Hardy's Dorset novels, and the Home Guard of Dad's Army – and that the Battalion's name ought to reflect the up-to-date, professional image and state of training to which it aspired, and had hopefully achieved. As mentioned above, in April 1971 the 1st and 2nd Battalions The Wessex Volunteers came into being, and so, six months later, with wholehearted support of the GOC South West District, Major General Hugh Cunningham, and the two TAVRAs, the Battalions made a joint application to alter their titles to 1st Battalion The Wessex Regiment (Rifle Volunteers), and 2nd Battalion The Wessex Regiment (Volunteers) – and to everyone's delight that was approved by HM The Queen on 30th March 1972. The word Volunteers was retained, at the direction of the Ministry of Defence, to avoid any misunderstanding that the Regiment was a Regular one, but the 1st Battalion adopted the "(Rifle Volunteers)" to reflect the historically important fact that E Company was the direct successor of the 1st Devonshire Volunteer Rifle Corps, formed in 1852 and then the senior volunteer unit in the United Kingdom. The change was universally welcomed throughout the Battalion – as was the resulting substitution of "1 Wessex" and "2 Wessex" as the official abbreviations of the Battalions' titles, in place of the uninspiring and unattractive "Wessex (V)" or "Wessex Vols" – and it certainly resulted in a new out-with-your-chests-and-up-with-your-heads confidence.

Although Paul Freeland's decision to move Battalion HQ from Exeter to Trowbridge had been an excellent one in command terms, the TA Centre in Bythesea Road was dreadful. It had been unoccupied, except by an Army Cadet Force Detachment, since the RWY were disbanded in 1967, and it was far too small to accommodate both Battalion HQ and Headquarter Company in any sort of comfort. Furthermore, because of its position in a network of back streets, it was virtually impossible to enlarge, or even to find, it; for the most part, the people of Trowbridge certainly never appreciated that there was a major TA unit in the town, and indeed in almost every respect the place was thoroughly unsatisfactory. One day in the spring of 1972, however, the CO and the Training Major, Desmond Redding, were driving through Devizes, and noticed that the imposing red-brick, late-Victorian Barracks, the former Regimental Depot of The Wiltshire Regiment, was standing completely empty.

The Barracks were built in 1898, and named after Major General Sir John Gaspard Le Marchant (1803–1874). He entered the Army at 17, and over the next 12 years reputedly spent £10,000 (at least £650,000 in today's money) in purchasing his way up the ranks; he acquired the colonelcy of the 99th Regiment of Foot in 1839, at the age of 36 and was one of the youngest officers in those days ever to get a command. His father, Major General John Le Marchant was a dashing, some say reckless, cavalryman, and he is famous for both having designed a new cavalry sword, and his development of officer training which led directly to the establishment of what is now The Royal Military Academy, Sandhurst; he was killed at the Battle of Salamanca in 1812. In the Cardwell Reforms of 1881, the 99th became the 2nd Bn The

Wiltshire Regiment.

With surprisingly little difficulty or opposition, it was soon agreed by the Ministry of Defence and Western Wessex TAVRA that "Le Marchant" could become the Battalion's new home – easily housing both Battalion HQ and Headquarter Company, who duly moved in during October 1972. Unfortunately, the sports field on the south side of the square had been sold off, and the old Officers Mess building had been demolished, but the huge main barrack block, the Keep, the Sergeants Mess and the garages were still there and in relatively good condition. The interior layout of the main block – with large rooms on every floor – was somewhat difficult to alter to provide a substantial number of offices and stores, but it was gradually adapted and changed to meet the various needs, and, as hoped, the place became the heart of the Battalion. The Keep housed the Quartermaster's stores for a good many years, and the Warrant Officers & Sergeants Mess was restored to its former use. Initially, there was no Officers Mess, and they therefore joined the senior NCOs for a drink after training on drill nights, and 'made do' in various places for dinners and parties. In due course, however, alterations were made to provide an ante-room on the ground floor and a dining room on the first floor.

There was no Battalion Camp that summer, and all the Companies went abroad individually – to Cyprus, Germany and Gibraltar. As the reports in Chapter 5 show, in their very different ways, those visits were extremely successful.

Exercise Wessex Marches in 1971 having been decreed (by Battalion HQ at least) a 'good thing', the Training Major decided to repeat the formula, and Wessex Marches II took place on Salisbury Plain in December 1972. It certainly maintained the Battalion's reputation for "active, rugged and sock-'em training"[26] – for the weather was even worse than for Wessex Marches I; although there was to have been a three-hour rest period on the Saturday afternoon, so gruelling were the tasks, and so awful were the wind and rain that it was cancelled and the whole Exercise finished early on the Sunday.

A major factor in the success of all those exercises (including even the mobilization one) was that at that time recruiting was buoyant, and the turnout at weekends was therefore extremely good. In March

1972, the Battalion was only a few short of its establishment of 736 all ranks, excluding the PSIs – a huge figure, because of the six-Company organisation – although by the end of the year, the actual strength was somewhat below that figure, and continued to drop until early in 1974.

Desmond Redding finished his tour as the Training Major in the autumn of 1972. With his warm smile and sense of humour, commanding presence and voice, a very positive approach, and outstanding professionalism, he had been a quite tremendous asset to the Battalion, and there was great and genuine regret in all the Companies at his leaving. The two big exercises, State Trust I and II, could not possibly have taken place without his organisational and planning skills. The inestimable benefit to him of having learned most things about the TA at the hands of 1 Wessex was not, however, to be wasted, for his next appointment but one was to command the 2nd Battalion – which he also did with great panache. His successor, Robert Jarman, was slim and pale; a brilliant staff officer, who had been the Adjutant of 5th Glosters in the early 1960s, he paid meticulous attention to detail, and had a well-known propensity for correcting anything that seemed to him to be inappropriate or out of place – some wag once said that "The only sound you can hear in a Rolls is the clock ticking, and in the Training Major's Mini all you can hear is the Training Major ticking". His work on the planning of the Colour Presentation Parade, due to take place at Camp the following year, was quite faultless. Some members of the Battalion found his wit rather too caustic, but, although not outwardly a 'soldier's soldier', he was nonetheless extremely sympathetic to the needs and problems of individual soldiers and junior NCOs.

Not content with planning and organising many major Battalion events in the south-west and mid-Wales during 1971 and 1972, as well as organising live firing of all the support weapons on Salisbury Plain and at Lulworth, and various training cadres, Battalion HQ (or, perhaps more correctly, the CO) continued to be smitten with ideas for training in unfamiliar places and unusual forms of transport. So in April 1973, in Exercise State Trust III – why the name was considered sufficiently enticing to be used three times is a complete mystery – the

Battalion were taken by British Rail to Norfolk, for a weekend on the Stanford PTA. The long and (it has to be said) tedious journey started at Exeter, and went via Sherborne, Andover, Westbury and Reading, picking up the Companies in turn on the way; then around the north of London on that mysterious route normally only used by freight traffic, and onto the Kings Cross-Norwich line. Dumped in the early hours of the Saturday morning at Brandon, a small station on the edge of the training area, the Battalion marched straight there – and, after a 24-hour battle, about which virtually no-one seems to remember anything except that it was B Company against the rest (and that, naturally, B Company claimed they had won!) – the whole process was repeated in reverse. C Company's return to Dorchester was memorable – for although the NCOs and soldiers got off the train at the right station, the officers remained fast asleep in their compartment, and the train continued on its way to Exeter with the TA Centre keys in someone's pocket. The careers of the Company's command team, and the risk of a mutiny by everyone else, were saved by the telephone and a fast driver!

C Company seemed to attract misfortune (albeit saved from disaster by good luck) more often than the others:

> The ammunition box was clearly marked "Blanks". But when the soldiers on a night exercise squeezed the trigger…… the sky was lit up by live tracer bullets.
>
> Yesterday the Army was holding an enquiry to find out just how real bullets had got into the wrong box. The shots were fired on Bovingdon training area at Clouds Hill, Dorset.
>
> Sixty Volunteers for Dorchester were advancing on their objective when Company Commander Martyn [sic] Evans ordered "Fire!". The men opened up with FN light automatic 7.62 rifles. The tracers flashed. And Major Evans ordered: "Cease fire!"
>
> An Army spokesman said last night "A check of 350 rounds of ammunition marked "Blank" revealed that one carton of thirty rounds was 'live'. No-one was hurt, and there was no damage to property."[27]

Initially, the Battalion was responsible for training all its own recruits, but in 1972 it became standard policy for that to be done at Regular Depots – and The Prince of Wales's Division Headquarters at Lichfield ran an extremely successful initial course in October that year, with another being held at Wyvern Barracks in Exeter in April 1973. The arrangement continued until 1975, when it was decided to revert to in-unit training, and successful recruits cadres were held several times each year.

One of the un-sung stalwarts of the Battalion was the REME Armourer Staff Sergeant, Peter Cracknell, and his contribution to its overall success was very properly recognised in the 1973 New Year's Honours List by his being awarded the British Empire Medal – the first of a good number of its members to rceive it over the next 22 years. See Appendix 5.

The major event of 1973 was the Presentation of Colours in June, on the middle weekend of Annual Camp at Knook Camp, near Warminster – and that is the subject of the next Chapter. By late on the Sunday evening after the Parade, however, the Battalion was fully back in training mode, already out on the Plain for a week of very different soldiering – which, as an extremely provocative challenge, incorporated the training part of the annual Fit for Role inspection – and that is covered in Chapter 5.

The last major training weekends in 1973 were the Battalion Skill-at-Arms Meeting in September, and Exercise Autumn Foray on the Plain. The former was held at yet another unusual place – Bisley ranges in Surrey, the 'mecca' of both service and civilian competition shooting – and it was certainly the first time that a major unit had done its 'classification' there for many years, possibly if ever. The quality of the shooting may not have been better than if the Meeting had been at home, but going there was all part of the business of widening the horizons of the Volunteers. The Exercise, organised by HQ South West District, involved many other TA units. Among some of the tasks set for the participants:

> the intricacies of laying a start-line near Imber village at 0300 hours in the morning did little to ruffle A Company's feathers, and the Company subsequently put in a night attack on Imber with verve, enthusiasm, white light and much shouting.[28]

B Company, with a very big turnout, was the enemy, but its successes

appear to have been limited to an attack on one of the friendly forces'
A Echelon (which rocked the soup and woke-up a helicopter pilot),
and the capture, by one of its patrols, of a Light Infantry Company
Commander – who, deprived of his boots, seemed disinclined to try
to escape.

---

[1]   *BB*, Winter 1967.
[2]   *D&DRJ*, October 1967.
[3]   *BB*, Winter 1969.
[4]   *Ibid*, Summer 1972.
[5]   Lieutenant Colonel John Roberts in conversation with the author.
[6]   *BB*, Winter 1967.
[7]   All the Camps up to 1980 are covered in Chapter 5.
[8]   Practicing the guarding of, and the withdrawal over a river or railway bridge that would
      be blown up to impede an advancing enemy.
[9]   *D&DRJ*, October 1967.
[10] *BB*, Winter 1968.
[11] *RHRJ*, Spring 1968.
[12] D&DRJ, June 1969.
[13] *The Duke of Edinburghs Royal Regiment Journal*, September1969. NB: In these footnotes,
      from here on *The Duke of Edinburghs Royal Regiment Journal* is referred to by the
      abbreviation *DERRJ*.
[14] Notwithstanding that the "CO" in "Stratco" stood for "Company" in "Strategic Reserve
      Company" they were always known as Stratco Companies.
[15] With a new rifle platoon in Barnstable, which, under the very positive initial leadership
      of Sergeant Beer, managed to raise half its establishment in the first four weeks of its
      existence.
[16] His old TA battalion was 4th/5th Royal Hampshires, which had retained much of the
      ethos of the Parachute Battalion it had been during World War 2.
[17] An old saying in The Gloucestershire Regiment.
[18] *BB*, Summer 1972.
[19] Anon.
[20] *BB*, Summer 1972.
[21] *BB*, Summer 1972.
[22] *1 Wessex – A 5-year Retrospect* (Produced by Bn HQ 1972).
[23] *DERRJ*, April 1971.
[24] *BB*, Summer 1974.
[25] Part I Orders 17 July 1972.
[26] *BB*, Summer 1974.
[27] A cutting from an unidentified Dorset paper in the scrapbook.
[28] *BB*, Summer 1975.

CHAPTER 4

THE PRESENTATION OF COLOURS

Saturday 16th June 1973 was a perfect English summer's day – blue sky, huge and puffy white clouds in the distance, and not too hot – and in a curious way the old, hutted, and in the winter often bleak, Knook Camp, near Warminster, was exactly the right setting for a ceremonial parade of a West County TA Regiment. The huge elm trees on the east side of the sports field-turned-parade ground were magnificently in leaf, the camp staff had mown the grass to perfection, and all around the rolling downs of Salisbury Plain created a theatre for a performance of that very special piece of Army ritual, a Presentation of Colours.

Major efforts were made by the Headquarters of The Prince of Wales's Division to get HM The Queen, the Duke of Edinburgh or the Prince of Wales to make the Presentation, but sadly that did not prove possible. As the Battalion covered such a huge geographical area, there were no other members of the Royal Family, or even senior members of the peerage, who 'related' to the whole of it – and it was felt that it would be invidious to ask the Colonel in Chief of one of the Wessex Brigade regiments to make the presentation. 1t was therefore decided to invite the Commander in Chief, United Kingdom Land Forces, General Sir Basil Eugster KCB, KCVO, CBE, DSO, MC, MA – a Guardsman, who had been extremely impressed when he came to see the Battalion in Camp at Lydd in 1971 – to do so on Her Majesty's behalf.

The question of what was actually going to be embroidered on the Colours might not only have turned into an almost insuperable problem, but also created a considerable amount of ill-feeling. Many in the four (originally six) Regular Regiments understandably wanted to see their badge or badges on the Regimental Colour, and some even thought it would be appropriate to have, say, three battle honours won by TA battalions from each. Wide consultation took place within the Battalion, however, and the very large majority felt quite unequivocally that, as the Battalion was both a new battalion and a new regiment, which had never earned a battle honour, there should be neither 'old' badges nor battle honours on either the Queen's Colour or the Regimental Colour. As the Regular Regiments were 'affiliated' to the Companies, and not 'parent regiments', they really had no grounds for disagreeing – and therefore the only symbol, apart from the centre badges with the Battalion's title on the Queen's Colour, and the Wyvern on the Regimental Colour, was the motto, "Their Land to Defend" on the Regimental Colour. No doubt to some people's surprise, the result, although unusual, looked extremely distinguished.

The great day was the middle Saturday of Camp, and the whole of the first week was given over to drill parades and rehearsals, the bulling of boots, the blancoing of belts, Band practices, and all the thousand and one jobs needed to be done to make the occasion as near perfect as possible – although a good proportion of the Battalion was able to relax with sport in the afternoons. Two quite excellent PSIs – the RSM, WO1 Mick Chappell, and WO2 Ted Kimberley (who was later to become the RSM of the Royal Hampshires) – had the responsibility of getting the Battalion's drill up to standard, and after the parade was over it was universally agreed that the Volunteers had achieved a pitch of performance of which most Regular battalions would have been extremely proud. It speaks volumes for the enthusiasm of those two, and their 'light touch' with the Volunteers, that no tempers were lost, no one was sent off parade branded a serious walking disaster (let alone a disgrace to humanity and his mother, or a congenital ***** idiot), and that, by and large, the practices and rehearsals were enjoyed by everyone. The Padres told a joke at the beginning of each full rehearsal. To avoid being ribbed by the rest of the Battalion, the officers, including the CO and the 2I/C, were put through their sword drill at 6.30 each morning. The sense of excitement palpably grew throughout the week, as all the threads of the planning were drawn together, and the weather was obviously set fair.

The planning for Operation Procol, as it was called, had begun in May 1972, as soon as it was known that the making of the Colours had been started, and that formal permission had been given for their presentation. Eastern and Western Wessex TAVRAs were persuaded to provide the colour belts for the Ensigns, and their swords were presented by Wilkinson Swords Limited; other swords, for those who did not have them already, were borrowed from the Regular Regiments and the old and bold; scarlet jackets, with all the accoutrements, were 'acquired' for the Corps of Drums from various sources, the Marines at Lympstone lent them white helmets, and the drums were emblazoned for the first time. Crockery, cutlery and glasses for the parties after the parade were hired, spectator stands were provided by the Royal Engineers at Longmoor, and the RCT Squadron at Old Sarum lent a VIP Land Rover; roadside verges were cut by the County Council, and the stalwarts of the Wessex Brigade Recruiting Team were brought in from Exeter to contain and entertain 300-400 regimental children while everyone else had tea.

Although there was some initial cynicism in the Companies, the 'chiefs' had hoped for some while, of course, that the parade would finally achieve a sense of real unity within the Battalion – and indeed it did. It had been thought from the early days that a modest 'aid' to that might be the wearing of items of dress that were unique to the Battalion. Consequently, in 1968, a stable-belt had been introduced that was quite unlike most others in the British Army, and, until one got used to it, somewhat startling – in the regimental blue, rather than the traditional two leather straps, it had a large square silver buckle carrying the regimental badge. Then, in the course of all the thinking that went on about the parade, it occurred to someone (possibly Robert Jarman) that a lanyard to be worn by all ranks with No 2 Dress would be another, albeit small, contribution to the same end. It was alternate strands of hodden grey and black. The former was the Scottish homespun cloth made by mixing black and white fleeces; it is thought to have been first used for military uniforms in 1859 by the London Scottish Rifle Volunteers, and subsequently became a traditional colour for the 19th century Volunteers generally.[1] The latter commemorated the 1st Rifle Volunteers of Devon, formed in 1881). Although some claimed that it looked more a piece of electric flex, it was in fact a very smart, understated, addition to the uniform, and everyone was proud to wear it.

When Colonel Sir Joseph Weld retired as the first Honorary Colonel of the Battalion in 1970, a well-known and much respected West Country

Territorial, Colonel W ('Bill') Q Roberts CBE, DSO* was appointed to succeed him. Originally commissioned into The Somerset Light Infantry in 1936, during the Second World War Colonel Bill had become one of 43rd (Wessex) Division's most distinguished commanding officers, and a legend as a strong leader; he won his first DSO commanding the 4th Dorsets and the second with the 5th Wiltshires. A genial, but by 1973 somewhat rotund, figure with a fine moustache, in 'civilian life' he was the Land Steward (or Land Agent) for the Duchy of Cornwall in Gloucestershire, Somerset and Wiltshire. He proved to be a marvellous choice – he only gave advice when it was asked for (and then of the wisest sort), he was popular with all ranks, and he endeared himself to the CO, if only by invariably saying, as he got into his car at the end of a visit, "Smells good, m'boy; smells good".

His usual command of almost any situation was, however, somewhat shaken when the author and the Training Major, Robert Jarman, asked his permission for three officers – the CO, John Roberts (the Second in Command) and Mike Tulloch (the Adjutant) – to be mounted on the Parade. He reddened, spluttered a little, and said it was an outrageous suggestion, but that if it were put to him in a letter, 'with reasons' he would think about it. His reply was characteristic:

> Duchy of Cornwall Office
> Edward Street
> Bath
>
> 3rd May 1973
>
> Thank you for your letter of yesterday. I still think that horses are an anachronism for an Infantry Battalion on such an occasion, much as I like them myself. However, far be it for me to stand in your way if you have MOD approval and also that of General Eugster. All I hope is that you do not fall off or are seen disappearing over Salisbury Plain in a cloud of dust!

The idea had originated, with much laughter, one evening over the Battalion HQ Officers' drink after a Drill Night, when conversation turned to the Parade, then only three or four months away. The suggestion was immediately and understandably pooh-poohed by the two Volunteers involved (whose only experiences of riding had been at a pretty tender age on someone else's pony), although not by the Adjutant, who was an adept horseman. It was raised again, however, somewhat more seriously the following week, and it was not long before officers and senior NCOs in the Companies were saying to all and sundry "Have you heard – the CO, the Second-in-Command and the Adjutant are going to be on gee-gees for the Parade!?" By then, there was no way out of it, so what had started as a genuine joke quietly became a fact – and in the event it was undoubtedly one of the many things which helped to make the occasion so special.

Using those 'It's whom you know' skills, in which they both excelled, the Training Major and the Adjutant had discovered that it would be possible to borrow three magnificent horses from the Royal Military Police in Aldershot, and for the 'wannabe' riders to have lessons from one of their riding instructors – although in the event he was generous enough not to put his pupils through quite the same rigours as he would had they been recruits in his own Corps. Nevertheless, in some magical way he managed to instill sufficient confidence in the CO and 2I/C – the Adjutant did not need to be given it – that at the end of the 'course' he was able to agree that there was relatively little likelihood of their coming to grief in front of General Eugster, the Battalion and all the guests. They therefore 'passed-out' of the awe-inspiring riding school – following which the QM and the wives of some of his staff made three extremely smart saddle cloths. The fact that there were indeed no mishaps on the day was without question entirely due to that riding instructor, and to the character and training of the horses. They were brought to Knook Camp, with their grooms, several days before the Parade, and by the time they had 'attended' three rehearsals they knew exactly when to move and where to go. That was something of a contrast with the arrangement reputedly set up by a long-serving CO of one of the Glosters' Territorial battalions before the Second World War. They were never a 'horsey' lot, but the officer in question fancied commanding parades from the saddle, and invariably used the same borrowed mount. No-one could understand, however, why an orderly always walked at the horse's head throughout the parade – and it was not until after a change of command that it transpired that each time the CO had to move anywhere, the orderly murmured in the horse's left ear "No milk today, thank you, milkman". It has to be recorded, however, that John Roberts did leave one rehearsal halfway through, in the feared "cloud of dust" and grimly hanging onto his reins – but he managed to pull his horse up a mile or two away on Codford Down. It was said that it was more this feat of bravery, rather than his charismatic leadership of B Company and his contribution as Second in Command to the general successes of the Battalion, that was deservedly recognised shortly after the end of Camp by his promotion to Brevet Lieutenant Colonel.

The preparation was hard work for everyone:

After our arrival at a rather desolate Knook Camp, it was not long before we had everything in good order, with the Company flag up and the men settling into their new quarters. Things got under way on the Sunday morning, with the whole Battalion on parade. We knew that we had under a week to prepare for the parade, and so we were ready for a lot of drill. Before long every man knew what part he would be playing on the day, and it was pleasing to know that E Company was represented in each of the four guards. During the first week a tremendous amount of work was done by all; stands and tents appeared around the grass parade ground, and the standard of kit and drill improved daily; and the 'trial' Colour Party were seen around the camp, carrying their dummy Colours, often with the Colonel, the Second-in-Command and the Adjutant in close attendance. It was not until Wednesday, after a dress rehearsal, that we knew 2/Lieutenant Evens of the Company was to carry the Regimental Colour.

As a break amongst all these preparations we had two afternoons of sport, and, with limbs aching from many rehearsals, were given a change of exercise on the football pitches. The Thursday afternoon was relatively free except for a rather dubious wet weather rehearsal, and it was hoped to have a Company party in the evening. This regrettably was not possible as we were the Duty Company, and so it - was decided to have one shortly after Camp was over. By Friday everything seemed to be dropping into place. The marquees were up and the chairs ready, and final adjustments were being made during the last rehearsal. The Camp's ground staff had worked wonders with grass-cutting and whitewashing – and all we could now pray for was fine weather.[2]

The day before the Parade, the customary message of loyal greetings was sent to Her Majesty The Queen, to which she replied:

16th June 1972
Buckingham Palace

Please convey to All Ranks of the 1st Battalion The Wessex Regiment (Rifle Volunteers) on the occasion of the Presentation of Colours today my thanks for their message of loyal greetings which I much appreciate.

Elizabeth R

The four Guards, each of 90 all ranks, were commanded by Company Seconds-in-Command – Captains Barry Staig, Fred Fifield, Larry Thornton-Grimes and David Ryan – and the Colour Party was Lieutenants Ian Taylor (Ensign for the Queen's Colour) and Peter Evens (Ensign for the Regimental Colour), CSM Bamber, and Sergeants Keith Reade and Bill Morris. The combined forces of The Devon Band of The Wessex Volunteers (as it was still officially called) and The Hampshire & Dorset Band, with their Bandmasters (WO1 E F ("Nobby") Knowles and WO1 J Parrott) and the Corps of Drums under the Drum Major (Colour Sergeant G W Kerswill) numbered over 90 – a magnificent sight, and one rarely seen on any regimental parade. They played 'all the best tunes', including *Young May Moon* as the officers fell in, the marvellously jaunty *Hey, Look me Over* during the Inspection, *On the Square* during the Presentation and *Great Little Army* for the March Past – as well, of course, as *The Farmer's Boy*.

It was decided to commission a large oil painting of the Parade. Various enquiries were made and artists' studios visited, and finally Miss Joan Wanklyn, a well-known painter of equestrian and military subjects, who had a particularly strong connection with The Royal Horse Artillery, agreed to do it. She quickly became enthusiastic, and spent much of the first week of camp making pencil sketches at rehearsals – and of the heads of the main participants in the Parade, which she subsequently gave them as gifts. The RSM was a skilled military artist himself, and when working on the picture after Camp was over, Joan Wanklyn would ring Battalion HQ and ask Mick Chappell to send her a pencil drawing of a bayonet scabbard, or a soldier's leg showing how his No 2 Dress trousers fell over his boot. Apart from the fact that the grass was perhaps too bright a straw colour, and not as green as it was in reality, the finished picture was a splendid record of a marvellous occasion, and it was suitably hung in Le Marchant Barracks.

The Parade followed the full form in the Manual of Ceremonial, and began with "the ancient and honourable custom" of the Consecration of the Colours by the Chaplain General to the Forces, The Venerable Archdeacon J R Youens CB, OBE, MC – in the course of which he prayed:

> that they may be an abiding symbol of our duty towards our Sovereign and our country, and a sign of our resolve to guard, preserve, and sustain the great traditions of bravery and self-sacrifice of which we are the proud inheritors.

General Eugster carried out his inspection from the VIP Land Rover, and, after presenting the Colours, he addressed the Battalion:

Colonel Lee-Browne and Gentlemen,

It is a great honour and privilege for me to present these colours to the Ist Battalion today on behalf of Her Majesty The Queen. This is the first occasion that your Battalion, newly created in 1967, has received Colours – though, of course, you are the heirs to the Territorial Battalions of six of our most distinguished Regiments of the Line, who all carried Colours emblazoned with the names of famous battles. Just as they won distinction and displayed those qualities which have made our Army famous over three centuries. so also will you. You have a high heritage to live up to, but no-one here today, watching you on this parade can have any doubt that you are worthy successors to the traditions you inherit.

Field Marshal Alexander once said that a ceremonial parade impeccably performed can never fail to be a source of inspiration to those who watch it or take part in it. A ceremonial parade, moreover, provides an occasion for men to express pride in their Regiment and pride in the profession of arms. Today I have been inspired, as I'm sure all your guests have been, by your bearing on parade, and I would like to congratulate each one of you on a fine performance. I would also like to congratulate your excellent Bands, and your PSIs who no doubt have worked hard to practise you for this parade.

England today has one Army whose Regular and Volunteer elements compliment each other as never before in our history, and it is an Army to which we can all be proud to belong. The Volunteer element is, to my mind, the best recruited, and the best trained and equipped which the country has ever had. I saw for myself, two years ago, the high standards of training and the general efficiency which your Battalion has achieved, and today you have demonstrated the same high standards in a more traditional sphere.

I know that I can entrust these Colours to you today in the knowledge that they will be the symbols of the splendid spirit of the Battalion, and symbols also of the distinctions achieved by your forefathers. This has been a memorable occasion for me, and I know it is one that all of you will be proud to say you took part in. I wish the Battalion all the success it deserves in the future.

What marvellous words, and how right he was! Without the totally different challenges which the Regular Army has to face – of which active service is obviously the greatest – occasions such as this become the highlights of a TA unit's history, and it is not fanciful to believe that, although General Eugster's words would not have been specifically remembered by many for all that long afterwards, what he said about the Battalion's standards and the Parade remained true for the remaining 22 years of its existence.

It was as well that the Training Major, whose great attention to detail was one of the main factors behind the success of the day, had directed that there should be in attendance at the edge of the parade ground a smart soldier with a wheelbarrow and shovel – and he actually had his moment of glory: as the CO finished asking the General's permission to March Past, his horse (having, like the other two, so far behaved itself impeccably) decided to relieve itself, then and there, of what appeared to be several days' worth of substantial meals. It stood at the equine equivalent of attention, but gently heaving, and then deposited a vast pile which the General, Colonel Bill and Major Chris Rimmer (acting as the General's ADC for the day) were left to contemplate as the CO returned to his place in front of the Battalion. To much laughter – actual from the spectators on the stands and scarcely concealed from those on parade – the gallant soldier arrived at the double with his equipment and 'did his thing'. Mistake-free though the whole Parade had been, the incident relaxed the tension at exactly the right moment, and heads were held even higher, arms swung even more positively, and the sense of élan could not have been greater as the Battalion marched off to tea.

For all ranks and the 1000 or so guests in marquees beside the parade ground, that was itself a magnificent affair, complete with strawberries and cream. The regimental cooks, with some help from the South West District Catering Adviser and his staff, excelled themselves, not only then but in the evening as well. After the guests had gone, the Battalion settled down with their wives and girlfriends to enjoy themselves – there was a Ball in the Officers' Mess, and parties in both the WOs' and Sergeants' Mess and the Junior Ranks Club.

All the effort put into the day had, without any question whatsoever, proved really worthwhile, and Colonel Bill (inadvertently imputing his own special expression of praise to General Eugster) wrote to the CO the following day:

> I enclose copy of a letter from the Commander-in-Chief, and no doubt you will have had one yourself. I thought that Saturday was absolutely first class, and I am proud and honoured to be the Honorary Colonel of 1 Wessex. I know that an immense amount of effort was put in by All Ranks into making the parade such a success, which reflects the utmost credit upon you and your Staff. There was a marked absence of flap throughout the whole proceedings, and the General told me that "the battlefield smelt well" when he drove into the camp – you can always tell! We met a number of old friends and thoroughly enjoyed ourselves, and once again I must thank you for all your hospitality. Will you please pass on my heartiest congratulations and thanks to All Ranks of the Battalion. Well done indeed!

In true Volunteer spirit, over half of the total cost of the occasion was contributed by the Battalion itself – every man at Camp gave up a day's pay – and the figures make interesting reading 27 years later:

Receipts	£	Expenditure	£
Regular Regiments' grants	100	Drummers' uniforms &	
TAVRA grants	312	emlazoning drums	737
Day's Pay scheme & draw	2,141	Ensigns' ceremonial	
CO's Fund	804	accoutrements	58
PRI	241	Colour belts & helmet fixtures	161
Drums Fund	196	Invitation cards	125
TA Centre lettings	77	Postages	19
Swill rebate	1	Programmes	465
		Teas	562
		Drink:	
		Officers (estimated)	400
		WOs & Sgts (amazingly)	156
		Junior ranks	538
		Tentage	138
		Cushion hire	5
		Mobile loo hire	36
		Battalion draw prizes	295
		Fittings for saluting base	2
		Junior ranks dance	45
		Sundries	75
	3,872		3,867

It takes the TA to make a profit on a ceremonial parade!

––––––––––

[1]   From a Note by Major I P B Taylor in *The Bulletin of the Military Historical Society*,
      November 1994, and other research.
[2]   *D&DRJ, November 1973*

––––––––––

1st Battalion The Wessex Regiment (Rifle Volunteers)

Parade State for the Presentation of Colours

Battalion Headquarters

Commanding Officer	Lt Col MS Lee-Browne TD MA
Second in Command	Maj JD Roberts TD
Adjutant	Capt MM Tulloch
Regimental Sergeant Major	WO1 MJW Chappell
Padres	Rev JF Parkinson CF
	Rev Fr MP Reid CF

Colour Party
Ensign for The Queen's Colour: Lt IPB Taylor
Ensign for The Regimental Colour: Lt PM Evens
Escort: WO2 JS Bamber, Sgts KM Reade & W Morris

A Company
Maj PJM Whiteman TD MA
Capt AM Grazebrook
Lt RJ Poole
Lt RD O'Neill, MA
Lt RN Hungerford
WO2 HW Marriott

B Company
Maj MAR Oakley TD
Capt FW Fifield
Lt ARC Peel
Lt RAH Nunneley
C/Sergeant M Heigho

C Company
Maj PJA Robson TD MA LLB
Capt LE Thornton-Grimes
Lt DK McIver
Lt R Gillam
2Lt HR Astin
WO2 K Gover

D Company
Maj AF Ravenhill TD
Capt BC Staig TD
Lt DM Fuller
2Lt BK Hudson
WO2 PA Reader

E Company
Maj CA Rimmer
Capt RHB Wood
WO2 GA Beer

Headquarter Company
Maj PL Jacques
Maj JJ Price (QM)
Maj PW Tucker TD MA MB (RMO)
Capt DC Ryan (IO)

Continued overleaf

Capt JJ Loftus (QM2)
Lt CRM Kewish (RSO)
WO2 FG Sheppard (RQMS)
WO2 GV Crawley (CSM)

Bandmasters
WO1 EF Knowles & WO1 J Parrott
Drum Major
C/Sgt GW Kerswill

CHAPTER 5

ANNUAL CAMPS: 1967 – 1973

1967	Stanford Primary Training Area
1968	B Company: BAOR (Lüneberg Heath); Signal Platoon: BAOR (Osnabrook); remainder: Sennybridge PTA
1969	A Company: Berlin; C & part of HQ Companies: BAOR (Soltau); remainder: Otterburn PTA
1970	D Company: BAOR (Soltau); remainder: Stanford PTA
1971	A Company: Wyvern Barracks, Exeter & Salisbury Plain PTA; B Company & part of HQ Company: BAOR (Soltau); E Company: Crowborough Camp (Sussex); C, D & remainder of HQ Companies: Lydd/Hythe PTA
1972	A Company: Cyprus; B & C Companies: BAOR (Lüneburg Heath & Soltau); D Company: Schleswig-Holstein; E & part of HQ Companies: Gibraltar
1973	Knook Camp, Heytesbury; Salisbury Plain PTA; Composite Company: Gibraltar

———

"Camp" has always been the highlight of the TA training year. Before 1967, it had almost invariably taken place in the UK, and one of the many exciting aspects of being a member of one of the new TAVR NATO-committed battalions was the fact that a high proportion of Camps were abroad.

Training for TA battalions with a NATO role was initially intended to be on a three-year cycle, from basic training in the first, to platoon company tactics in the second, and a full battalion Camp abroad every third year. Not surprisingly, however, life turned out to be rather less simple and straightforward than that – and between 1968 and 1976, the pattern was never consistent. During that period, at least one company in the Battalion went abroad on its own every year, and was either attached to, or 'sponsored' by, a battalion of (almost always) the Regular Regiments or occasionally an armoured regiment. In 1972, the Battalion and three other NATO battalions each contributed a company to a composite battalion that went to Cyprus for a fortnight (each company itself being a composite one, with its members being drawn from across its own battalion). Another year, a composite company formed from within the Battalion spent the fortnight in Gibraltar on its own. From 1977 onwards, however, the whole Battalion went to Camp together (albeit very occasionally less one or two 'detachments' training elsewhere), and, like all TA NATO battalions, it was normally alternately at home on one of the major UK training areas (Lydd & Hythe, Otterburn, Salisbury Plain, Sennybridge or Stanford), and in BAOR with 4 Division and later in Schleswig Holstein and Denmark with the United Kingdom Mobile Force (Land).

The 'abroad' Camps were particularly looked-forward to, thoroughly enjoyed, and extremely worthwhile in training terms. They gave the Volunteers excellent experience of 'real Army life' – and (as well as on courses that were attended by both Regulars and Volunteers) there was considerable amusement and personal satisfaction to be gained from seeing how long it took the Regulars to discover that one was actually in the TA! It must be remembered that what was routine for the Regular soldier was an adventure for the Volunteer. Driving from Devizes to Germany and back in a military convoy could well have been drudgery to the hardened BAOR professional – but to the eager amateur soldier, however, it was an event to remember, particularly for one who had never been abroad before.

Camp has always been a compromise between training and fun. It is probably true to say that, in the 'old (i.e. pre-1967) days', although the training was treated perfectly seriously when it was actually happening, that was almost always only between breakfast and tea, often with a good break at lunchtime, and it was fairly rare to spend more than one night out in the field. For many 'hardened Territorials', pre-Camp visions of "What is happening this year?" included thoughts of getting-away-from-the-wife; spending virtually every evening and the middle week-end (which normally lasted from mid-day on the Saturday until first parade on the following Monday morning) enjoying possibly a lot of serious drinking; 'a little bit of fun' starting in, say, the pubs of Thetford or the café nestling in the corner of the beach at Holywell Bay, near Newquay; and social activities in the Officers' or Sergeants' Messes.

From 1967 onwards, however, whether at home or abroad, things were very much the reverse – and by the mid-1970s what had become known by both the Regular Army and the TA as "R & R" [Rest & Recuperation] was usually limited to only one day of the middle week-end, with "Company Smokers" [parties] on one evening, and (depending on the location of the Camp and the training programme) possibly one other 'evening off'. A lot of hair was let down then, but the 'brutal and licentious soldiery' only misbehaved themselves seriously on very rare occasions, and (as in the 'old days') happily little or no harm resulted to 'persons or property'. Any physical damage caused was normally made good the following day, and there does not seem to be any evidence at all that the birth rate in the districts around the various camps increased above the norm each Spring. For all, or virtually all, the junior ranks, tough training, little sleep and dreadful weather notwithstanding, Camp was a really good holiday; that was obviously not quite so for the officers and SNCOs responsible for making everything work; but for all ranks, however, it was a fortnight in an utterly different world from that in which the other 50 weeks of the year were spent – and the fact that a substantial number of Volunteers completed anything between 10 and 15 (and sometimes even 20) Camps speaks for itself.

As in the Regular Army, courses are an essential element of TA life, and they were nearly always mandatory for a Volunteer who wanted promotion. They varied from the 'cushy' Unit Water Duties and Signals to the very taxing Section Commanders', Platoon Sergeants' and Platoon Commanders' Courses, and somewhat more cerebral Company Commanders' Course, run by The School of Infantry in either the Welsh mountains near Brecon or at Warminster. A fortnight at Brecon was both mentally and physically tough, and almost all of those who went on the latter undoubtedly 'walked taller', had greatly enhanced their military skills, and were well equipped to cope with the responsibilities that promotion would bring them. Every year, some Volunteers did their courses in lieu of Camp, but the really keen ones would do both.

No doubt because of a combination of the planning and organisational skills of the Regular Permanent Staff, good leadership in all the companies, and the demanding nature of the Battalion's various roles, it is true to say that (possibly with the exception of Sennybridge in 1985) there was never in fact a 'bad' Camp, either for individual companies or the whole Battalion. They were always demanding, and by and large thoroughly enjoyable. Had they not been, of course, most of the Volunteers would have 'voted with their feet', and the younger ones would never have got TA soldiering 'into their bones' – that state of mind which compelled them to come back to drill nights, weekends and Camps, weeks, months and years on end because they felt it stimulating and worthwhile. Each year hundreds of Volunteers returned home "tired, dirty and smelly, but with that contented feeling that we had completed our task and had not been found wanting".[1]

Many of the quotations in this and the following other two Chapters about Annual Camps could not better illustrate the enormous difference in attitude between the old TA and the TAVR. In many of the pre-1967 regimental journals, reports of Camp merited but a few lines written in a deadpan style which seemed to reflect no great enthusiasm for the training side of the event:

> Camp at Stanford P.T.A. was a great success. All members enjoyed the training, wich was very interesting. [We had] time off for seeing the Norfolk countryside.[2]

Following a period of intense training, the Signal Platoon left for Annual Camp in Okehampton, probably better qualified as a whole than for some time past. We were now to put this training to the test, and Captain Long had prepared a particularly complicated exercise for this purpose. Due to the many social functions arranged, the exercise had to be held in the first few days of Camp. The object of the exercise was to test the individual initiative of those taking part, and to practice voice procedure and the operation of the 62 set over distances of more than 15 miles in places. Changing frequency onto one of the three different nets, driving experience over the difficult country lanes, map-reading and griddle etc, were all incorporated.[3]

1967

The whole Battalion – East Wretham Camp, Stanford Practical Training Area (1–15 July)

"......our wives have very little idea of how much hot air has been expended as we try to be as different from each other as possible."[4]

"They went to Camp, as one of their officers expressed it, as five private armies, but they settled down into a happy, well co-ordinated entity, and long-serving volunteer officers were rejoicing at having an infantry battalion that was something near full strength. There were nearly 500 men in camp."[5]

The main object of the Battalion's first camp was, of course, that everyone should get to know everyone else – and that did not initially prove to be an easy task. Someone said that the Officers' Mess needed to be five-sided, so that each Company could have its own corner, and the officers, in particular, found it quite difficult to convert what had been casual acquaintanceships formed at say pre-1967 South West District TEWTs [Tactical Exercises without Troops] into a willingness (whenever training was on other than a company basis) to rely on the military efficiency and skills of relative 'strangers' on a night exercise or on the range. Nevertheless, it began to happen, and at the end of the fortnight the majority went home feeling that the Battalion was made up of extremely nice and very competent Volunteers, and that "it was going to work":

On 'day one', however, there were purely practical problems to be addressed:

> At once we found that the administrators – having been used to accommodating [an 'old'] TA battalion comfortably, with enough beds for about one-third of the paper strength[6] – had been left behind the times. The Companies overflowed into haphazard and hastily erected tents littered about the camp area.[7] Luckily, however, the weather was on our side, and everyone accepted the makeshift conditions with tolerable good grace, although a good number of extra square feet were needed in the dining hall.
>
> Camp training was built around two 48-hour schemes, one in each week, and the first of these was designed to practise the Battalion in the occupation of a defensive position and the establishment and attacking of demolition guards. Much time was spent digging, repairing and discussion of slit-trenches and gun-pits, but in between we found time for some patrolling and an attack on the enemy's guarded bridge. We were pleased to be told that the patrolling was generally rather competent, but the attack, founded on a very subtle pincer movement, was frustrated somewhat by the amputation of one of the arms before it reached the objective. The other stormed the bridge with magnificent panache amidst a holocaust of pyrotechnics, and saved the prize from destruction; unfortunately the umpires ruled that only two or three would have made it alive, so a certain amount of weight had to be given to the enemy's fanciful boast that he had succeeded in withstanding the onslaught.[8]

Much of the second week was taken up with Internal Security training – seen in a somewhat romantic light by a Devonshire newspaper reporter:

> A rabble of refugees – clamorous, ragged and ill-shaven – advanced in the river bridge brandishing sticks. The soldiers, calm and unflinching, met them at the barrier. There were scuffles and a few desperate characters were chased as they made a dash for freedom. Warning shots were fired and soon the suspects were being searched in a barbed wire compound. The soldiers were men of The Wessex Volunteers. So were the refugees, enjoying this masquerade enacted to give realism to the first annual training camp of a new unit of the Territorial and Army Volunteer Reserve.[9]

and a little light-heartedly by one of the participants:

> After giving a widely-acclaimed road-block demonstration, the Company was pitched into the rebellious kingdom of Tottinvar on Exercise Mush Tamaam. We were allotted the role of reserve Company, which led to a frustrating time dashing to the scene of unrest to find that either someone else on our side had got there first, or that the enemy (provided by our own ferocious Support Platoon, aided by mercenaries from [1 Glosters'] Recce Platoon) had given up waiting for us and gone somewhere else. The whole thing was much enlivened, however, by the loan of a couple of RAF helicopters, which flew hither and thither dropping packets of troops to quell the unruly Arabs. Unfortunately, WO II Keitley was dropped to such effect that he had to retire with a damaged ankle, and another casualty was Sergeant Morris of the Mortar Section, who became so ferocious in an ill–controlled riot that his arm went home in plaster.[10]

Showing early signs of what was to become its traditional laid-back style – which implied that war was a dirty and nasty business not to be involved in if at all possible – C Company's report in the October 1967 issue of the *Devonshire & Dorset Regimental Journal* covered Camp in one paragraph:

> It was no surprise that the Company went to Camp at Stanford PTA 101 strong – the strongest Company in the Battalion....... CSM Gover did splendid work, and behind the scenes CQMS Rigler made the very best of difficult Q facilities. The Support Platoon teams under Lt C Fookes swept the board in the Battalion Support Competitions, being placed first and second. Sgt Vater and CSM Knight (PSI) take credit for the know-how they taught in the Dorset TA, and since formation. Cpl Dyas and Cpl Stainer commanded two very good rifle sections. Many Lance Corporals in old TA units had to revert in order to join TAVR II. Such men as Ptes Chant, M. Jones, C T Murphy, Theobald, Welch, Lord, Desmond and Bewley showed their skill in the field and are to be thanked for their actions. Both Captain Speakman and Captain Jeanes had the opportunity of commanding the Company on exercise.

While B Company's report was laconic in the extremein pre-1967 style. All it said was:

> Camp was the usual highlight of the training year, and was held in Norfolk. The first week was taken up with firing platoon weapons, followed by a three-day Demolition Guard Exercise. All platoons excelled themselves at digging.[11]

1968

B Company – Lüneberg Heath Training Area, BAOR (22 April– 6 May)

> "......the CO on a flying visit being unable to find the Support Platoon from the air by helicopter because they were supposedly so well hidden.......and Lieutenant Lowden desperately trying to find carriers for all his gin on the return journey."

This was almost the first time that virtually any Volunteer, whether he had served in one of the predecessor TA battalions or joined the Company since its formation, had ever done any training outside the United Kingdom.[12] The Company was sponsored by 1 D & D, who gave them tremendous support – planning and providing the enemy for two three-day exercises, (the first involving a Squadron of 17th/ 21st Lancers in Centurion tanks), and lending an APC for the use of Company HQ:

> It was undoubtedly an outstanding Camp, everyone without exception learning something new about unfamiliar equipment, unfamiliar tactics, or simply independent company administration in the field for a sustained period[13]

and, indeed, some learnt about possibly unfamiliar pleasures on the middle Saturday, when:

on arrival in Hamburg, 99% of the Company made straight for the

Rieperbahn, whilst the Company Commander insisted on taking the Second-in-Command and Lt Lowden to see the Botanical Gardens.[14]

All the Companies had by now learned to 'cultivate' their local newspapers, to keep themselves 'in the public eye' and encourage recruiting – but it has to be said (without in any way decrying the valuable job which the papers and their editors undoubtedly did) that most of the reporters had their own very idiosyncratic way of describing military activities and organisation, mentioning the huge variety of jobs the Volunteers did, and bringing in little 'human touches'. *The Southern Evening Echo* for 8 May 1968 reported the fortnight in a good example of the style of those papers:

PART-TIMERS BACK IN DEAR OLD BLIGHTY

With a gruelling fortnight behind them – it ranged from roughing it in slit trenches to a 2 am tour of Hamburg's nightlife – Hampshire men of The Wessex Volunteers have just returned home from Germany.

The troop [sic], who make up B (Hampshire) Company have done their annual training on heath and forest land near Soltau, about 30 miles from Hamburg. Keeping a distant eye on them were the 1st Battalion The Devon & Dorset Regiment, camped out 15 miles away.

Their camp nestled among thick fir trees, but no-one was in when I called. To find these "new Territorials" who will serve as an instant extra arm for the Regulars in an emergency, we bumped over the training area's tortuous terrain. We came across pockets of them dug in after a two-day exercise in the field. Weary but cheerful, they told of the test exercise, which had involved preparing a bridge for demolition and a night withdrawal to defensive positions.

Flew out in April

They were men from areas ranging from Basingstoke to the Isle of Wight, and had flown from Gatwick to Hanover on April 22 after an advance party had travelled by sea on the Dover-Ostend route with the equipment. The flight back was last Friday – and the return meant sleeping rough on the Thursday night as equipment and tents had been loaded for transport.

In command of the Company was Major John Roberts of Winchester, and a visitor during the camp was the Volunteers' Commanding Officer Lieut. Col J Sellars.

Reorganisation of the Army's reserve forces into volunteer divisions has meant that thosenow serving are of the keenest calibre. The "part-time Army" is a key part of their lives – an and nothing will stop them attending parades or camps.

Bank test in Camp

A bank examination did nothing to stop Winchester bank clerk Lieut. Ian Taylor (24) of Leigh Road, Eastleigh, going to Germany. He went to camp, but took his two-day examination under canvas, with an officer of the Devonshire-Dorsets standing by as invigilator. Marriage has been uppermost in the minds of two Isle of Wight "buddies", but they too have managed to keep to their training programme. Lance Corporal Colin Upton (22) of 2 Middleton Terrace, Cowes, who works at the Thornycroft shipbuilding yard at Southampton as a draughtsman, gets married on May 25. With him at camp was a friend who will be his best man – Pte. Michael Blow (23) of Oakfield, Station Road, Wootton[15], who was married five weeks ago. L/Cpl. Upton was his best man.

His second love

Pte. Blow, a sheet-metal worker with the British Hovercraft Corporation, had a honeymoon at Torquay, and then prepared to meet his second love – the Volunteers.

Taking time off from driving Southern Vectis buses at Shanklin and Ryde were Pte. Albert Dennis (40) of 51 Carter Avenue, Shanklin, and Pte David Hallett of 6 Lower Highland Road, Ryde. Pte Dennis has changed Services. He was a stoker in the Royal Navy until 1968, and joined the Territorials six years ago. Two Volunteers hailing from Winchester are Pte. Johnny Ramalingachetty (25) of 67 Wales Street, who came to England from Mauritius six years ago and now works as a supervisor in the doughroom of the Brazil pie factory in the city; and Pte. David Berry (21) of 43 Fox lane, Stanmore, a heating engineer with Dicks of Winchester Ltd.

Second trip overseas

Winchester butcher Pte. Tom Gardner of 2 Warren Road, Winnall, has been abroad twice with the Territorials. After National Service with the Greenjackets, he went to Munster with the 4th/5th Bn The Royal Hampshire Regiment TA, linking-up with the 1st Royal Hampshires.

Longest serving man in the Company is Company Sergeant Major Ronald Witt (37) of 16 Hinton Crescent, Thornhill, Southampton, who has a record of 17 years as a Territorial after having done his National Service with the Dorset Regiment in Vienna. He was a Sergeant Major at the age of 23, and is a foreman at the Pirelli General Cable Works at Southampton.

[There then followed details of another six members of the Company, whose occupations included working for HM Stationary Office and the Ministry of Labour, and one whose address was curiously given as '407, North Tidworth'.]

Left to own initiative

During the fortnight's camp, the Devonshire-Dorsets played "enemy" to the Volunteers – and left them almost completely on their own. The idea behind the training programme was to give the Volunteers the chance to run their own affairs without assistance. They set up their own field kitchens, did their own administration, and operated exactly as if they were on active service. Training in troop-lifting by helicopter, exercises with Centurion tanks, platoon training and lessons in driving armoured personnel carriers were additional to the two-day exercise in the field.

Training nights for the Company (when recruits will be welcome)

Winchester: Newburgh House, Tuesdays; Newport IoW: Drill Hall, Drill Hall Road, Wednesdays; Basingstoke: Drill Hall, Penrith Road, Thursdays. Time in all instances is 8 pm.

———————

Signal Platoon – Osnabrook, BAOR (28 June–11 July)

In June, Captain George Simey and Colour Sergeant Vodden took the Signal Platoon to 1 D & D, and it proved to be a very worthwhile and enjoyable fortnight. The majority of the training was, naturally, signals-oriented – and the Volunteers were very pleased to discover not only that they had exactly the same equipment as the Regular battalion, but that there were even more items with which they would be issued in due course. There were, however, a number of other attractions – including first-time-ever rides in APCs and the new amphibian personnel carrier, the Stalwart – and the Platoon beat their much fitter and more experienced Regular colleagues at football 5–2.

As one of the local papers said when they got home "Without wanting to make it sound too obvious……it was a signal success".

———————

Remainder – Sennybridge Primary Training Area (Early May)

Weather-wise, it was an extremely unpleasant fortnight, with driving rain or mist nearly every day. The Camp and training areas were shared with several other units, and both were full to bursting point – but nevertheless it proved to be really worthwhile:

> Breconshire is doubtless a charming spot when a watery spring sun is peering inquisitively through the morning mist, and only the busy chattering of the starlings interrupts the placid permanence of the moor. No doubt even the gaunt Beacons melt into benevolence when they reach into a clear blue sunny sky. Early in May 1968, however, Breconshire was, for the most part, windy and wet. When it is windy and wet, Breconshire is foul.
>
> Only three rifle companies came to Sennybridge. The first week-and-a-bit of the camp was given over to cadre instruction, and a duplicated exercise was attempted by companies on successive days at the end of it. Of the cadres there is little to say; Camp is the most important part of the training year, and plenty of basic training got done. Sennybridge is a camp with a wide range of local training facilities and, as a result, it is nearly always full. This meant that while on some days our shooting was due to start at six a.m., on other occasions it could not start until the afternoon and was due to continue until nine at night. These hours were not as bad as they sound, however, and training was enlivened by a trip to Castlemartin to see and learn about tanks (for many people, for the first time), and a visit from Captain Grist, 1 Glosters, attached to the Army Air Corps, accompanied by his helicopter.
>
> The exercise at the end of the fortnight was a complicated and lifelike advance to contact affair, although, as all such exercises must, it took place in a bit of a vacuum. The weather got worse and worse, and worse again, so that as dusk was closing in, the last few hours were abandoned to avoid prejudicing the success of the following day's field firing. The exercise had been fairly successful, though conditions were appalling, for it helped to convey the air of chaos and devastation which is probably characteristic of any 'real' battlefield.

(Your correspondent is sure he left half his belongings in the mud at Smelly Jam, or was it Ribald Aunt?[16])

Camp had to end on a Friday night, instead of the usual Saturday morning. The lack of accommodation appears to be such, nowadays, that not only is every camp over-full, but there is a queue of incoming units waiting at the gate for outgoing ones to leave. It was a good fortnight, based on the principle that you must walk before you can hope to run, and everyone must have learned something.[17]

This Camp was the best ever undertaken by any member of C Company. Despite the wet – and Wales is wet! – the fortnight's field firing was a tremendous success........[which] was in no small measure due to the Training Major, Major Dick Jury, D & D, who planned a very complicated programme using all the ranges.

Your correspondent is glad to say that the Company found time, energy and money to have an evening party which will long be remembered. CSM Gover discovered a pub in a place he was pleased to call "Yer to Glynis", and the whole Company arrived at this very with-it establishment in two coaches. The young ladies of South Wales were not backward in coming forward, and the evening passed quickly. The Company Commander felt that it would be tactful to leave before the end.......

It is no coincidence that C Company have won the Battalion Champion Company Cup for the first time.[18]

Camp this year was an unqualified success for everyone except the Band and Drums. After practising for a solid week, the Beating of Retreat was cancelled at the last moment on account of bad weather.[19]

1969

A Company – Berlin with 1 Glosters (Dates not known)

"Berlin, here we come!"[20]

———————

The Company were flown by the RAF to Berlin, setting out "with the intention of showing the Regulars what we are made of", and they managed to fit in an amazing amount of field training. There were a night navigation exercise; an orienteering competition held in the Spandau training area, adjoining the barricade forming the boundary between the Russian and British Sectors – in the course of which it was realised that in Berlin, magnetic North is on the "wrong" side of grid North; the grenade range; a section battle-drill competition; a morning of PT and the assault course; initiation into the mysteries of tanks (from 9th/12th Lancers) and 432 personnel carriers (from the Glosters and 1 Staffords); and a morning practicing (or more probably messing about in) assault boats on the River Havel. Some members of the Company went on border patrols with the 1 Glosters Reconnaissance Platoon – certainly as close to active service as almost anyone in the Company has ever been – and there was a church parade on the Sunday morning, following which the Company marched past Lieutenant Colonel Tony Streather, the CO of 1 Glosters. The fortnight ended with the quite inappropriately named Exercise Wessex Dragon, involving patrolling, company in defence, three river crossings in 36 hours, and finally the 'statutory' company attack. On the R & R side, one night there was a Company party in the barracks to which a number of members of 1 Glosters were invited – but, owing to a rather rash statement from a member of the Company 'in his cups', the entire Regular Corporals' Mess turned up. Subsequently, to the Company's great credit, they accepted a decision that, to avoid any untoward incidents, they would not inspect the bright (or very dim) lights of one of the world's most celebrated 'nite-life' cities until the last night of Camp. That was an astute move on the part of Peter Whiteman and the Company Sergeant Major, Dick Keitley, who must have realised that everyone would be utterly tired, and so would be virtually incapable of enjoying the delights on offer.

......how tired is perhaps shown by the soldier who was sitting with his friends in the front row of a 'strip' club one evening and who fell asleep. The performing fräulein obviously took this as a deep insult, for, having finished her act and removed all her clothing, she went over to this soldier and shook him and shook him and shook him. But he didn't wake!

Among many places visited during 'working hours' were East Berlin, including the Russian War Memorial in Treptow Park where lie the remains of some 25,000 Russian soldiers who died in the capture of the city at the end of the war, and the newly-erected Wall, some 10 feet high, positioned on the Russian side of the old and rusting dannert wire which marked the actual boundary between the Russian and British Sectors. Near the point from which the orienteering sections set out was the grave of a refugee who had not made it, and we noticed the tremendous difference between the people of East and West Berlin. The former looked care-worn, unhappy and despondent; the latter, affluent, contented and confident. Of course, one was looking out for this contrast, as a result of what one had been told, but nevertheless, it was extremely obvious. The Volunteers had had a wonderful experience, particularly in terms of seeing quite a lot of the 'Russian presence', and they came home, by Britannia to Luton, in extremely good spirits. Not only that, but (as true members of A Company) they also came home in some style too, for (more like the end of wars in the 19th century than exercises in the late 1960s) there were duty-free champagne bottles sticking out of many small packs. [21]

This Camp was another example of a Company getting a very good idea of Regular Army life. They trained on their own, but with help from their hosts in the running of three cadres, and in the provision of umpires and enemy. In fact, the Glosters bore the brunt of the Company's administration, leaving them free to carry on with training, and, indeed, 'bent over backwards' to help them in every way they could. There were always many advantages, and few disadvantages, for a Volunteer Company spending its Camp in BAOR.

C Company – BAOR (Soltau) (28 June–12 July)

.....it is important that some record of C Company's activities should be set down so that wives and girlfriends can, in some cases at least, corroborate their men's military stories with the facts.....

[They] will be glad to know that we DID spend Camp at Soltau in West Germany. The dates were June 28 to July 12. Members of the Company DID fly to Hanover in a Boeing Jumbo Jet; they DID fly in helicopters and drive 432 Armoured Personnel Carriers; they DID get blisters on one or two company exercises, and became acquainted with pastel-green chemical warfare suits and respirators; they even had the energy – some of them – to play volleyball and run round an orienteering course. They also paid Hamburg a Saturday visit – but the exact facts relating to that are a little difficult to tabulate and readers will understand the writer's reticence.

There is little doubt that this year's camp was a great success – many have said that it was the best they have attended. There can also be little doubt that a pure Company camp has much in its favour. The numbers involved are such that everyone feels he knows the next man and that a minimum of time is spent "hanging around". Under its own management, a Company very quickly becomes a unit with an identity and a spirit all its own.

The Volunteers of Dorset were very lucky to have 17 soldiers from HQ Company at Trowbridge with them; these Wiltshiremen became a happy part of C Company in just next to no time. Our thanks go to Captain Speakman and CSM Crawley for all their help.

The Company lived in a splendid tented camp sited in a pinewood. Support Company 1st Bn The Devonshire and Dorset Regiment acted as hosts, and no praise can be high enough for all they did to make the camp a success. We owe much to Major Bullocke, CSM Thacker and all their Company, for they planned the training, built the camp, administered our supplies and food, and acted as umpires and enemy. Sgt. Gigg was a pillar of strength on the Q side, Sergeant Oxland, who spent two years as a PSI with Dorset TA in Wareham, gave wonderful help to Capt. Speakman in providing canteen facilities. CSM Thacker, a very good friend from the old Dorset Regiment, was a ball of fire, night and day, while CQMS Cook and Sergeant Burlock ran first-class section and platoon demonstrations.[22]

HQ Company

The new HQ Company at Trowbridge began to form-up in the Summer of 1969, in readiness for the move of Battalion Headquarters from Exeter in November, and was sufficiently established to be able to go to Annual Camp. It nevertheless split into two: CSM Crawley led a party that went with C Company to Soltau (see above), and the rest joined B, D and the 'old' HQ Companies at Otterburn.

Remainder – Otterburn Training Area (Date not known)

> "…..one of our outstanding 'funnies' was the shaken expression on the faces of the OC and the 2IC, having blown over 30 'blinds' on the 36 and 94 grenade ranges in one afternoon – fuses got increasingly short towards the end…"[23]

According to a Berkshire local paper, 350 all ranks of the Battalion attended, and because "Obviously with all that live ammunition flying about there had to be stringent safety measures", the Royal Berkshires' TAVR III cadre came too and provided some of the range staff. Most of the Volunteers were from B and D Companies, with their support platoons, and they trained very hard:

> We went north to Otterburn Training Area, most of us for the first time. A local pressman who accompanied us described the area as "snuggling among the cloud-capped Cheviot Hills high in Northumberland". The Company favoured less poetic descriptions, but, during the middle weekend, most found something to snuggle, and the rest at least managed to get high!.....The first week, which some thought would never end, was devoted to field firing. All platoon weapons were fired by day and night, and section and platoon tactics practised *ad nauseam* on the many and varied field firing ranges. By the end of the week, however, the efficient and aggressive manner in which the platoons worked gladdened even the Company Commander's heart, in spite of the superior and professional manner he has adopted since his successful course at Brecon. (Offers for 120

unused rifle slings to the 2IC, please).

The 2IC, Captain Ravenhill, was heard to mutter "Serve you right" when the Colonel announced that Major Heavens was to command the Battalion on Exercise Chevy Chase during the second week, but his amusement dissolved when the CO continued with the news that would command the Company. Rumour has it that the two of them then vanished for the complete weekend to prepare orders, etc. for the exercise, but CSM Reader, who knows them better than that, was able to assure the Company that they were only up to their old tricks.[24]

Two days in the middle of the second week were devoted to Exercise Chevy Chase. The training area had become (as training areas do) an imaginary Commonwealth country, "Mogul", rich with oil and under threat from a nearby Communist country – and the Battalion had been flown in to act as an internal security force. The Training Major had 'acquired' three RAF helicopters – one of the pilots of which achieved a modest amount of fame by remarking during the initial loading and unloading practice: "You'll know if we are going to crash because I shall go very pale!" – and a good number of Volunteers managed to get airborne, if only for ten minutes. The Communist enemy was provided by 1 DERR from Catterick, and they were beaten by the end of the first day – but at one point, forming up for an attack on them, D Company were themselves attacked by a real enemy in the form of hundreds of tiny black and white insects "that descended in their hordes, anxious to get their teeth into any exposed flesh that they could find". The Duke of Edinburghs having returned to their barracks, 60 Volunteers from the 4th Bn The Parachute Regiment 'dropped in' after dark to replace them. Needless to say, they were soundly routed by both Companies not long before the end of the exercise – after which D Company prepared for, and carried out, a night shoot, and then marched for an hour back to Camp.

The B Company Notes were again brief and laconic in the extreme – all they said was:

We went to Camp in July at Otterburn, and spent an outstandingly useful fortnight on the excellent field firing ranges where we fired every company weapon live. The Bn exercise involved us in the IS [Internal Security – e.g. as in Northern Ireland].......helicopters, etc., and we completed a very satisfactory test exercise with the Company in the advance to contact using live ammo.[25]

1970

D Company – Soltau with The Blues & Royals (Dates not known)

"The thought of a company of soldiers lined up in a well-known department store on a Saturday afternoon, waiting to use the Polyphoto machine, caused a photographer to be dragged from his bed at a very early hour on the Sunday morning."[26]

The original intention was that the Company should go to Germany with the 1st Bn The Royal Irish Regiment, but (for reasons now unknown) they "flatly refused to leave Catterick" – and, not surprisingly, the Volunteers were somewhat reluctant to go to bleak Yorkshire instead. Their next proposed sponsors were the 1st Bn The Kings Own Scottish Borderers – who, not a little alarmed at the idea of entertaining 120 or so part-time soldiers from Reading and around, promptly made a successful application for a posting to Northern Ireland. As a result, The Blues & Royals drew the short straw, but, whilst extremely efficient and helpful, the general consensus of opinion among the senior members of the Company was that a fortnight was not long enough for them to get to understand the TA ethos!

Training was hectic, comprehensive and exhausting……and [we] prepared a fair proportion of the Soltau Training Area for later cultivation by digging in at every conceivable opportunity…….All work and no play? We descended upon Hamburg on the middle Saturday and, like moths round the light, congregated in the Zillertall, where the Commanding Officer, Lieutenant Colonel Paul Freeland, was acclaimed Conductor of the Night, but failed to teach the German band to play *The Farmer's Boy*. Those who had not visited the city before rapidly completed their education, and despite all the stories, everybody seemed to make it back to camp.[27]

<u>Remainder – Stanford PTA (Dates not known)</u>

"We even went on a route march on Saturday morning between a guest night and church parade – but such was the spirit that it degenerated into a gallop, in an effort to cure Patrick Lambert's hangover. It did! ….."[28]

The weather was simply amazing for the whole fortnight – "probably the most enjoyable [Camp] that A Company has enjoyed since The Wessex Volunteers were raised in 1967"[29] In the first week the training was entirely Company- and cadre-based. Most of the second was taken up with Exercise Wessex Jacket – an 'all-singing, all-dancing' affair, with bridge demolition guards, daylight and night withdrawals, the occupation of a defensive position, a dawn search-and-destroy operation; a battalion attack, tank hunting and wood clearing – and an internal security exercise. Added to that heady and exhausting brew were "the firing by the Training Major, who is no longer with us, of a 'tactical nuclear device'", and much air activity – helicopter lifts to and around the training area, repeated air strikes by a Hawker Harrier making the new fighter's first-ever operational sortie with troops, and regular visits from Canberra photo-reconnaisance planes and Phantom fighters. A rifle company from the 4th Bn The Royal Green Jackets (based in Buckinghamshire and Oxfordshire) provided a resident 'rent-a-crowd', and seemed to enjoy themselves.

E Company (which had converted from being HQ Company at the beginning of the year) certainly did so:

When the last notes were written, we were preparing for our first appearance in public as a rifle company, so we went to annual camp at Stanford filled with mixed feelings. Everyone's concern was "Were we going to be up to the right standard?" The Support Platoon were more modest than the rest of us, and went to Netheravon for a week's crash course before they felt ready to come out into the open. By all accounts, Netheravon had as much of a shock as we did at Stanford. Does any normal person do an hour's battle PT before breakfast every day while on a course, and enjoy it? When they joined the rest of us, it was obvious that they were changed men. Not only did they seem to know what they were doing, they even doubled! During our battalion exercise, Corporal Philbin was so pleased to be in charge of a Mobat that he went four days without sleep.

The Support Platoon's visit to Netheravon had a curious sequel. At the end of camp, when everything was packed up and the whole Battalion was preparing to leave, a solitary policemen arrived. Someone had stolen a portable bar from the Sergeants' Mess at Netheravon, and he wanted to search all the vehicles in case our Support Platoon was responsible. As the thing was bigger than a trailer anyway, and our platoon only had Landrovers, the whole business was ridiculous. The policeman wandered around for a bit on the MT Square and admired the Battalion's transport, but he eventually went away. Then the Military Police arrived, and although they said that we were uncooperative, we eventually persuaded them that the whole incident was somewhat comical. It was however a pity, and spoilt a very successful visit to Netheravon.

Patrick Lambert set a very tough pace and a good deal of very hard training was done. Some of us were out on night exercises three nights running, in addition to the normal daytime training. The curious thing was that the more we worked the more it became enjoyable – in a twisted sort of way. Not even our night shooting could be played clean. This took place half an hour before dawn, after patrolling since dusk, carrying all the ammunition. During most of camp the troops lived in a constant state of readiness for an ambush, and they used anxiously to count the heads of the officers and other instructors. One of our difficulties was fitting in any time off, and we became known as the Company without civvies. We tried to be first out of camp in the mornings and seemed always to be last in at night.....

During the second week of camp, there was a four-day exercise, and despite a certain lack of sleep, the Company found it a welcome rest after Company training. Many valuable lessons were learnt, not least of all by the CO; during a night withdrawal, he arranged for E Company to be ambushed by 4RGJ. Having neglected to occupy the ambush position alongside the enemy, Colonel Freeland was amazed to be clouted on the jaw by one of our enthusiasts when the ambush was sprung. From the first shot being fired, it took us but four minutes to vanquish the enemy, and go on our way rejoicing! When the exercise ended, the Battalion marched back to camp in prewar style,

with the Drums beating and all the trimmings. E Company brought
up the rear. Halfway home, A Company, in front, turned off the road
to avoid a cattle grid and found that they had marched up a cul-
de-sac. They were followed by B Company, who were followed by C
Company, who were followed by Uncle Tom Cobley-and-All – all, that
is, except E Company who halted in their tracks and cheered the other
Companies to the echo as they wheeled and countermarched. When
we got back to camp, we had a proper Company party, for the first time
since the Regiment was formed, and went home feeling very pleased
with ourselves, if a bit weary.[30]

A Company was asked to provide a demonstration for a USAF Open
Day at Lakenheath on the middle Saturday – a tactical airborne
landing from a USAF transport plane, and an assault up a hill held by
a resolute enemy, supported by F-100 Super Sabre jet fighters – before
a crowd of 15,000 spectators:

As only a Platoon of "Good Guys" and a section of mortars was
required, volunteers from the Company were called for. The enemy
was provided by the Anti-tanks and Company HQ. Preparations
proceeded without hindrance; BFAs for SLRs and GMPGs (at that
time, unheard of in a Volunteer unit) miraculously appeared, as did
three years' allocation of blank, thunderflashes and smoke grenades,
plus 58 Pattern equipment that the soldiers purchased themselves.
The great day arrived and the enemy departed for Lakenheath and
their hill, while the "Good Guys" went to Mildenhall, home of the
61st Tactical Air Squadron, USAF, so that they could be flown into
Lakenheath. The C130B covered the six miles between the two
airbases in about half an hour. (Not a mis-print – we flew around
in circles becoming sicker and sicker.) The assault force landed on
the main east-west runway, the aircraft (for some curious and un-
military reason) actually reversing up to our disgorging point; we
rapidly disembarked and, led by Lieutenant RJ Poole, set off for our
forming-up point, with the mortar section under Sergeant Marriott.
The C130B took off and we were on our own.

We advanced and almost at once came under fire from the enemy
(a determined cohort, commanded by the Captain Ryan, WO2 Keitley
and Sergeant Mears consortium). Thereupon three years' worth of
blank and pyrotechnics were expended in a 'Brocks' Benefit, ably

The Honorary Colonels:
Colonel Sir Joseph Weld   Colonel W Q Roberts
Major General G C A Gilbert   Major General M J H Walsh

The Commanding Officers (1)
Lieutenant Colonel J A Sellars   Lieutenant Colonel P R B Freeland
The Author   Lieutenant Colonel L C Tremellen

The Commanding Officers (2)
Lieutenant Colonel J G T Southwood & Lieutenant Colonel C W E Coppen-Gardner
Lieutenant Colonel P A Goddard & Lieutenant Colonel R J Pook

The Commanding Officers (3)
Lieutenant Colonel T B Dutton   Lieutenant Colonel G E Brady
Lieutenant Colonel P J Cable   Lieutenant Colonel A P B Lake

The Officers at Stanford, 1967

Back row:

Lt PEQ Long Lt PD Pomeroy Lt LE Thornton-Grimes Lt BC Staig Lt DC Ryan Lt TP Lowden Lt CHR Fooks Lt   MAR Oakley Lt BACarte Lt IPB Taylor

Middle row

? ? Capt AF Ravenhill Lt FW Fifield Maj TMC Anstey Capt EG Churcher Capt GRS Simey Capt TKE Jeanes Capt PJM Whiteman Lt AM Grazebrook Lt PA Lintott

Front row

Rev Fr MP Reid Capt PG Marriott The Author Maj JD Roberts Maj GE Fulford Lt Col JA Sellars Maj R Jury Maj MW Evans Lt LKJ Courtenay Maj PE Allen

A Company at Stanford, 1967

The 5 Glosters at Camp in 1910

Le Marchant Barracks, Devizes c. 1910

Le Marchant Barracks c. 1910

The plaque on the Keep

Le Marchant Barracks c. 1995

The Presentation of Colours – 16 June 1973
(oil painting by Joan Waklyn)

The Presentation by General Eugster

The March Past

The Bands and the Corps of Drums

The Commanding Officer, the Second-in-Command & the Adjutant

Some of the Officers on the Parade

Lt I P B Taylor   2Lt H R Astin 2Lt B K Hudson Lt A R C Peel   LT R J Poole
Lt P A Lintott   Lt D K McIver   Lt R Gillam   Lt P R R Evens

Rev F J Parkinson   Lt C R M Kewish   Capt B C Staig   Major P L Jacques
Capt F W Fifield   Maj C A Rimmer   Capt A M Grazebrook   Capt J J Loftus
Capt D C Ryan   Rev Fr M P Reid

Maj P W Tucker   Maj M A R Oakley   Maj P J M Whiteman   Capt M M Tulloch
Maj R A F Jarman   Lt Col M S Lee-Browne   Capt J J Price   Maj J D Roberts
Maj P-J A Robson   Maj J N Speakman   Maj A F Ravenhill

Plus ça change? – B Coy? 7 Royal Hamps in the Ardennes, January 1945

Lance Corporal Robin Fraser
(Front cover of TAVR Magazine, Vol 47/7 – 1977)

Excercise Tango Test, 1979

assisted by the flight of four F-lOOs making low-level passes at the hill. The signal that the attack was successful was a 1-ton Wombat Carrier disappearing in a cloud of white smoke over the horizon and the CSM lying on his back with his legs in the air. The hill was assaulted and taken, and we re-formed in dead ground out of sight of the public.[31]

After it was all over, the Company learned that the commentator, introducing the demonstration over the tannoy, had referred to the Company as "The Platoon of the Royal Army", and subsequently USAF journals reporting the day said that the event had been provided by the "Brigade of Royal Wessex TA". The rest of the Battalion was not allowed to forget that for some while.

1971

"Plans do not always work out"

B Company – Soltau (5–19 June)

"No luxuries such as tents or hot shaving water this time."

……..we trod the now familiar path through RAF Lyneham – this time bound for Hanover and finally the Soltau training area on the southern edge of Lüneburg Heath. Arriving at about midday on Monday 7th June, B Company had settled into its tented camp by the evening. Early next morning, however, the camp was empty again, as the troops moved out on an exercise lasting till late on Friday. This was to be a tough exercise, with each soldier carrying his normal battle load and nothing else. In any case, there was no time to prepare them for it, and the opportunities for sleep were to be few and far between. During the next four days the Company was exercised in a wide variety of different tasks, advance, attack by night and day, defence and patrolling, to list a few. The weather again took a hand, and the rain, which started on the Tuesday, was to stay with us for the whole of the rest of the exercise, making the tough training even tougher. On

Friday "Half Time" was called, and the Company withdrew to its tents for the two days of the weekend. This was spent in visiting the bright lights of Hamburg on Saturday and in a more leisurely tour around North Germany on Sunday. Come Monday, it was back to soldiering and the mixture very much as before until the flight back to UK on the Friday.[32]

C & D Companies and the remainder of HQ Company – Lydd & Hythe Training Area (Dates not known)

"…..as part of a 3-day,16-stand range circuit…with one hour allotted to each activity, which varied from filling 1500 sandbags….."[33]

––––––––––

This was principally a 'shooting Camp', making full use of the best range facilities in the United Kingdom, and with tremendous help from members of the Small Arms School Corps:

We were blessed with fine weather and, although we cursed the shingle of the huge complex of ranges, we were much better shots at the end of the fortnight than we were at the beginning. There was a somewhat excessive number of distinguished visitors 'from above' (including the GOCs of Southern Command and South West District, General Sir Basil Eugster and Major General John Douglas-Withers; four TA Colonels; our two TAVRA Secretaries, and the famous Brigadier 'Bala' Bredin, the Colonel of the Devon and Dorsets – most of them, no doubt, keen to check whether the Volunteer CO was doing everything that his staff told him). All in all, we had a very worthwhile and enjoyable time.

At that point, the Commanding Officer, Training Major, Adjutant and Quartermaster all relaxed, fondly thinking that in due course E Company would go off to Malta into the capable hands of 41 Commando, Royal Marines. Only a few days later, however, at just five weeks notice, the visit was cancelled for political reasons, and a substitute camp had to be arranged. Luckily, we were able to get Crowborough in Sussex, and training took place on the Lydd/Hythe ranges, with much the same programme as the main part of the Battalion had some six weeks earlier.[34]

––––––––––

E Company – Crowborough Training Camp (August)

"[When we went to the ranges,] it was interesting to see the variety of targets which were engaged from one fire order."[35]

The Company must have been extremely disappointed at not having a 'holiday-Camp' after all, but to judge by the cheerful tone of the reports in the D & D Regimental Journal, everybody was determined to make the re-arrangement work well:

During June and July, we began to sweat about Malta, as the news gradually got worse. The pace of preparation hotted up, and jabs and KD uniforms became quite a topic of conversation. The news broke in the middle of July that Malta was off. Major Anstey and Captain Simey were both at Bisley at the time, and had several hectic days trying to shoot, arrange (with the help of the Training Major) a new venue for Camp, butt mark, book new training areas (with the same help), do a bit more shooting, fix Camp recces, go back into the butts, and generally enjoy themselves.

There must be something beneficial about being hectic, as on Tuesday July 13 both Major Anstey and Captain Simey were decorated. In peacetime, it must be a very rare event indeed for this to happen to two officers in the same Company on the same day. Major Anstey won The Queen's Medal for the Best Shot in the TAVR, and Captain Simey was awarded the Territorial Decoration......

On arrival at Crowborough Camp, and before our baggage had had a chance to touch the ground, we found ourselves in the OC's office for a training conference, and with yet more amendments to the amended programme......there were not many training areas or ranges available. There was, however, a small dry training area at Pippingford Park, complete with lake, which was generally under-used, and here each platoon in turn spent a half-day learning about assault boats and watermanship. This training was in the capable hands of our PSI, Sergeant Foster, and at the end of each session he was kind enough to go 'overboard' so that we could practice getting him back in the boat. One platoon thought that if he was silly enough to go jumping in the lake then he ought to be left where he was! The area was really too small for the rifle platoon to deploy tactically, but in the second week it proved ideal country in which to set an ambush.

When we were not occupied at Pippingford Park, we found ourselves firing on either the Hythe or the Lydd ranges. Unfortunately, Crowborough Camp is about one and a half hours drive away, so a lot of time was wasted in travelling. It also created problems with transport, which were only solved by hiring civilian coaches – so that sometimes the MT square looked more like the start of a Bank Holiday outing, with hayboxes, cooking equipment, etc., all disappearing into the boots of the coaches.

There is no doubt that in the TAVR we do not have enough live firing, and so having those excellent ranges was of great benefit to all in the Company. On the battle shooting ranges, the soldiers were able to put into practice much that they only knew in theory, and the NCOs were also trained in giving fire orders. Practice does indeed help to make perfect, and by the end of our two weeks sections were all engaging the same target. The night firing also proved interesting, and there were, as is usual on these occasions, a number of the younger soldiers with itchy trigger fingers firing at shadows and stones thrown over their heads by the DS [Directing Staff].

The Support Platoon did not have many facilities for specialist training, and for the most part did all the training that the Rifle Platoons did. There was a day of live firing on the middle Saturday, but the ammunition was somewhat limited. The Anti-tank Section had ten practice rounds, but as the range faces out to sea, and they had not allowed for fishermen straying into the danger area, they had difficulty in firing even those. The Mortar Section had 72 rounds, but here too the restrictions on the range are such that it is difficult to provide an interesting shoot. During the second week we had a visit from the GOC, General Sir Basil Eugster, who came to Hythe to see us and watch us at our various tasks. We were very fortunate in being allowed to use the Range Officer's hut to entertain Sir Basil to lunch. It was at this lunch that we discovered that the Company 2IC makes an excellent cup of coffee! We were also surprised to see one of the Company quarter-ton vehicles with four silver stars on it, and there was speculation as to whether or not some long awaited promotion had come through at last. Despite the setback of not going to Malta and the problems of a camp some distance from the training areas, there is no doubt that generally the Company had a successful fortnight.[36]

A Company – Wessex Brigade Depot, Exeter and Salisbury Plain (14 – 28 August)

> After the E Company saga, Battalion HQ breathed a collective sigh of relief, had a good lunch in a pub, and opted for a little Egyptian PT [an afternoon nap], again fondly congratulating themselves on how well things had worked out. That was, however, wishful thinking! Five days before A Company should have gone on a fortnight's attachment to the 1st Battalion The Royal Regiment of Fusiliers [1 RRF], its 'parent' Regular battalion in 5 Brigade of 3 Division, at Kirton-in-Lindsey in Lincolnshire, they were sent to Northern Ireland – and, for an unprecedented second time that summer, the 'Instant Camp Switch' had to be flicked to 'On' and some quick readjustments made.[37]

As always in that sort of situation, it is who, not what, you know that matters – and within about 48 hours of learning that the Company would not be going to the Fusiliers, the Training Major, Desmond Redding, had made arrangements for them to spend the first week at the Wessex Brigade Depot in Exeter and on Dartmoor, and the second on Salisbury Plain. The entire staff of the Depot were marvellously supportive, providing accommodation, instructors and training areas – so that almost the only amendment to the orders for the fortnight was to delete "Lincolnshire" and substitute "Devon and Wiltshire".

Initially, the Company very understandably thought that the first week would be a considerable let-down, and a poor alternative to a week in a Regular battalion's barracks, but in the event it proved to be highly enjoyable – for, although much of it was spent in cadre training, the teaching, largely by Regular instructors from the Depot and 41 Commando's base at Lympstone, was of a very high standard. There was also a 36-hour exercise on Dartmoor, a 'work-up' for the second week:

> It was a success, in that it removed the cobwebs, even though we did nearly lose one Mortar Sergeant and his Land Rover. Sergeant Marriott never realised how fit he was until he bogged his vehicle, and had to run a very long way after a slowly disappearing Company

fighting a battle across Dartmoor to get assistance.[38]

The second week, on the Plain, was quite astonishing because, although the exercise planned for 1 RRF was 'cut down' to company size, all the supporting elements were retained:

> And it was certainly an ambitious exercise! The *personae dramatis* read as follows: "A Company in the leading role, a troop of Centurion tanks from the Royal Hussars, a Scout helicopter provided by the Army Air Corps, a flight of RAF Wessex helicopters, RAF photo-reconnaissance Canberras, and finally RAF Phantoms and USAF aircraft making air-to-ground attacks".
>
> [It] started with a bang and continued so for four days. Gradually, however, the *personae dramatis* deserted the Company and joined the enemy. In the beginning, when everybody was on our side, we captured bridges, cleared woods and buildings, and decimated the enemy wherever we found them. As the days passed, however, more and more of that 'support' went over to the enemy – a platoon from 1 D & D, who were initially, of course, soundly routed several times a day. Our allies having turned their coats, we found that we were having to dig in on hill-tops, being photographed and strafed by ground attack fighters and being attacked both by day and night by tanks and infantry. It all ultimately led to a reverse slope by the side of a wood where we dug shell scrapes in the dark. Dawn not only brought warmth from the sun, but also heat from the exhausts of a brace of screaming Phantom fighters who roared over our defences at zero feet until the arrival of the enemy infantry and armour which swept through our position. That ended the exercise and it was just a short march back to Westdown Camp, for a hot meal, a bath and sleep.
>
> It was an excellent exercise, ambitious, realistic and tough. Many lessons were learnt and techniques improved. It is encouraging for us Volunteers to realise that someone must think that it is worthwhile to lay on such a professional exercise for us. We appreciate that our training must be limited, because of the little time that we give to soldiering, but we try, and try very hard, to be as good as regular infantry soldiers in our training. We train to be a down-to-earth infantry company, and the way in which the Company conducted itself during Exercise Swansong shows that it can deal with the different phases of war in a fast–moving exercise.[39]

Lieutenant Roger Poole, however, had his own, very different, first week of Camp – he spent it as a guest of the Regular Army, being member of a District Court Martial, and stoutly claimed afterwards that it was the first occasion in peacetime that a TA officer had ever done so.

1972

There was no Battalion Camp as such this year, and all the Companies went their separate ways.

A Company and part of HQ Company – Cyprus (Ex Amber Light: 19 August–2 September)

"…..the perils of the midday sun and what it could do to you….."[39]

Annual training was this year spent in Cyprus. Preparations for this event started early in the year with vaccinations and inoculations, and the issue of olive green tropical uniform. and warnings of how displeased the Army would be if you suffered from heat exhaustion, Recruit training was concentrated in Gloucester, and the PSIs worked very hard to ensure the success of the move out. The net result was 150-odd soldiers at Brize Norton airfield climbing into a Britannia aeroplane in the early hours of August 19. Six hours later, and on only three working engines, the Company landed at RAF Akrotiri and embussed for Alexander Barracks, Dhekelia Sovereign Base Area. Here we were to become "X" Company of the "Amber Light Infantry", being joined by Stratco Companies from the Light Infantry Volunteers, the Yorkshire Volunteers and the 2nd Lancastrian Volunteers. The ad hoc battalion formed from these four Companies was commanded by Lieutenant Colonel B M Lees, (The Light Infantry); the 2IC, QM and MTO were respectively our own Training Major, Major Desmond Redding, our QM, Major Jack Price and our MTO, Captain Jim Loftus.

The programme was divided into two distinct parts; the first week was individual training, and in the second there was company training, a Battalion exercise and an Inter Platoon Competition. For week 1 the Battalion was split into various Cadres. Working in groups with soldiers of other companies and training with them was at first a strange experience for most of the Wessex soldiers; however, within a very short time it was realised that we were all in the same army – even if you couldn't understand the dialect of the soldier next to you. During this first week the cadres visited the local training areas, Troulli, Athena Forest, Pylla and the infamous Goshi or Moonbase as it came to be known, with its bare rocky hills, no wind, no vegetation, lizards, snakes, and the heat of the August sun. The middle weekend found the majority of the soldiers around the island in hired cars, taxis and coaches. Most of the well-known spots were visited – Nicosia, Kyrenia, Famagusta, Salamis, Larnaca and Limasol. It would be impossible here to mention some of the adventures of A Company's soldiers, but all had a good time – A Company soldiers are full of initiative!

The second week started with a move to the Evdimou Training Area near Episkopi, some three and a half hours driving from Alexander Barracks. The first night involved a company patrol exercise, and as soon as this finished we started a battalion cordon and search exercise. The enemy were provided by the 3rd Royal Anglians. They were lodged atop what appeared to be Mount Everest and, as befell our luck, we were the cordon company for the cordon and search operation. Marching through vineyards laden with ripe grapes has its advantages, but when it came to the hill climbing, we were grateful for our general good health and morale, helped by the early morning physical exercise conducted by Private Devlin (ex 1 Glosters) during the first week. After this phase, the Battalion, without a rest, moved north. Now came a drawn-out night march again up hills, so that by dawn we were in position to do a sweep through a wooded area containing a company's worth of enemy. This task completed, we set about organising our teams for the Inter-Platoon Competition. Five stands were set up, and at each stand was a specialist who asked members of each platoon questions according to his rank. The subjects covered were first aid, signals, map reading, weapon handling and general knowledge. On completing this phase, the platoons were able to get a little rest before preparing for a patrol competition and, immediately on completing that, they had a night forced march of some seven miles. The four Platoons from A Company came 1st, 3rd, 4th and 5th out of the 16 teams in the battalion. The competition was the end of the military training; Friday was declared a shopping day, and the Company arrived back in Gloucester on the Sunday afternoon.[41]

B & C Companies – Lüneberg Heath & Soltau Training Areas, BAOR (30 September–13 October)

"We were under canvas and near the river – and so, with the density of the foliage, were cold during the day, and bitterly cold at night....."[42]

By this time, both B and C Companies had new Company Commanders. Martin Evans had, partly on grounds of ill-health, handed C Company over to Major Peter-John Robson; another solicitor (who so-generously never charged his clients who were members of the Company for any work he did for them), he was one of the most un-warlike officers the Battalion ever had on its books, but without any doubt he headed its happiest-ever Company. The new Company Commander in Reading was Major Andrew Ravenhill, who worked for the Atomic Energy Authority, and he too ran a cheerful and effective Company. The two Companies combined for this Camp, and (except, of course, for the road party) flew from RAF Brize Norton to Hanover, and then drove to:

> a tented camp on the training area. For all except the recruits, it was a one-night stay in camp, and then straight out on Monday for a five-day exercise with much practice in the patrol and surveillance role. Tough exercises of this type have become the standard pattern in B Company, and the resulting improvement in personal and sub-unit administration has been remarkable. The Company marched back into camp on the Friday in time for a few hours of well-earned sleep before the weekend.....During the second week, the Company joined together with C Company in an advance to contact exercise. With 150 soldiers on the ground, this was more of a commander's battle, but, lasting four days, extended everyone in both Companies. In all, a very satisfactory and worthwhile Annual Camp.[43]

The training for the first week culminated in a company attack on [B Company's] position. This was a complete success because the whole of the "enemy", except for their Command Post, was away at the time attacking our own position. Likewise their attack was also a complete success! ......On Saturday we had our first day off after what had been a rather gruelling week and we went to the Reinsehlen Camp for showers, which were very welcome after a week's crawling around in the field. Feeling more human after this we boarded coaches for Hamburg for Exercise *Reap Creep* and, from the ensuing stories, magnified, no doubt, by the German beer, it would appear that a good time was had by all. After a bit of sight-seeing and football on the Sunday, we then started off again with Phase II of our exercise. On this, [the two Companies] became a joint Company with command being alternated between the two Company Commanders, our "enemy" being the Support Company of 1 Glosters in their APCs, who proved to be a most realistic and entertaining enemy. Training was very varied, and varied from section, platoon and then company attacks with night infiltration, to a series of platoon tasks in conjunction with helicopters. This went on for 24 hours a day for three days, by which time our stay was coming to an end, and on the Thursday we started packing up Camp, handing out the pay, having a Company photograph taken, followed by last minute shopping, and in the evening both Companies had their parties. By midday on the Friday, we were back in UK after a hard, gruelling and, in retrospect, enjoyable Camp.[44]

D Company – Schleswig-Holstein with 1 DERR (21 October– 5 November)

> "......the Company Commander and the 2IC rushing over to BAOR in April to do a recce and see if everything is fit for the soldiers...."[45]

.....our aim is to be trained so as to take our place with confidence alongside our Regular counterparts. The crunch will come when we stand patiently in line at Luton waiting to board the charter flight to Schleswig-Holstein and 1 DERR. Those members of our affiliated Regular Battalion who trained in that area last year may well be surprised, even amazed, to hear that we are currently launching a recruiting campaign, the theory behind which is the inherent attraction of just such a prospect.[46]

We have continued our activities in Berkshire and Wiltshire, many of which lead directly to our forthcoming visit to Holstein as a fourth rifle company for 1 DERR.......our D-Day is 21 October, when we assemble in Reading *en route* for the northern part of Germany. Having read the 1 DERR reports in the previous volume of the Journal, some members of the Company view the prospect with some trepidation, but no doubt all will be well. The delights of service in the TAVR, and a visit to BAOR in particular, have been sold hard with great success. We have attracted 35 recruits in under six months before we called a halt in time to ensure a standard of training commensurate with our commitments. As first step in that direction we held three intensive cadres to ensure a good basic state of training for them.[47]

HQ Company (the remainder) – Gibraltar with 2 RRF (May)

Off we flew in May to the sunny Med! Needless to say, the first week's weather was worse than that at home, but the second week provided the sun we were all looking for. The MT Platoon 'ran up' a vast mileage total in two weeks on an area of less than three square miles, and received much praise from their Regular opposite numbers. The RMO [Regimental Medical Officer] was kept busy helping run the clinic and tramping up Med steps with the Signal Platoon. Someone dreamt up the idea of battle PT and the Company Commander and RSO [Regimental Signals Officer] bravely led the early morning folly up the various steep hills surrounding South Barracks! All good things, however, come to an end, and soon we were gone in an RAF Brittania, leaving many new friends behind. A further 30 members of the Company are now off to Cyprus with A Company.[48]

1973

The whole Battalion - Knook Camp, Salisbury Plain (9–23 June)

"It was a day to remember all our lives….."[49]

───────────────

This was the first complete Battalion Camp since 1967. The Colour Presentation Parade – covered in the next Chapter – occupied the whole of the first week, and the second week was spent on a Battalion exercise on the Plain.

The contrast could not have been greater, and only a staff officer with a very curious sense of humour, or a very special point to make, could possibly have decreed that the training part of the year's Fit For Role inspection would take place in the week immediately following a major ceremonial parade – but that is indeed what happened:

> If a unit ever tried to prove that the V in TAVR stands for versatile, we were certainly that in this extraordinary period of two weeks, from the glitter of ceremonial to the reality of digging-in yet again on the Plain[50]

The first three days were spent in a bivouac area, practicing section and platoon drills, as well as the business of routine in the field – all under the close scrutiny of Major General Hugh Cunningham, and some of his staff from HQ South West District at Bulford. A large, relaxed, man, with a heart-warming smile and marvellous at talking to people, the General was one of those people who always left one feeling better for having been with, and he was extremely well disposed towards the Battalion. Indeed, so much confidence did he seem to have in the ability of the Training Major, the Adjutant and the QM to keep the Battalion going in the right direction that, during the first year after his arrival at the District Headquarters, the CO only ever seemed to met him at cocktail parties! Thanks mainly to efforts of the Permanent Staff, the administrative part of the inspection had already gone extremely satisfactorily earlier in the summer – and with everyone determined to do well, the training side of the Report made

1 WESSEX

CORRIGENDA

Page number

56   List of names: Captain E G Churcher was R Hamps;

113   Central heading: "Practical" should be "Primary";

221   "[General Lane]" should be in commas, not brackets;

239   First paragraph: "outside the Light Infantry" should have been deleted;

289   Last five lines: these should refer only to 1 Wessex;

407   Left hand column: Majors Roberts and Fifield should have been shown as Lieutenant Colonels;

409   Left hand column: Lieutenant Colonel Durant also commanded B Company in Swindon;

420   Left hand column: "(previously A Coy and later OC HQ Coy)" should be added to WO2 Heatley's entry;

447   Under "TA Battalions (post 1967) – 4th Bn The Devonshire & Dorset Regiment":
            Line two should read "(Originally referred to as 3rd Bn)";
            The page reference immediately after "Chap 8 *passim*" should be "275-276".

very flattering reading. The weather also tested us – for, in contrast to the glorious warm sunshine of the previous week, it poured with a vengeance, virtually non-stop – but, after the Battalion's six years' practice at working in the wet, it mattered not a scrap. After the inspection was over, the Wednesday afternoon was spent watching a spectacular fire-power demonstration at the School of Infantry, and for the last two days:

> ......the Battalion was divided into North and South forces and, operating from different positions, began a 36-hour exercise. E Company was the South Force under the control of Major Chris Rimmer, and soon we were dug in ready and waiting in our defensive position. Both Forces had a fragile 'booty' to look after, in the shape of three WRAC officers. Patrolling was active throughout the night, during which the enemy position was located, and the exercise culminated in a Force attack on [North Force's] position. It was not until breakfast time on the Friday morning that the last of South Force returned to Knook Camp, ready for a well-deserved shower and some hot food. This exercise brought Annual Camp to a close – a special one which will long be remembered by those who took part.[51]

F Company – Gibraltar – Exercise Jangle

In August, 120 Volunteers, drawn from across the whole Battalion to make up an *ad hoc* "F" Company under the command of the Training Major, Robert Jarman, were lucky enough to go on a second Camp in Gibraltar – where 1 RRF (no longer the 'parent battalion' for A Company in its Stratco role) were efficient and genial hosts. The Company departed from the new Air Mounting Centre at South Cerney, being one of the first major units to use it.

B Company in fact provided the largest number (30) of soldiers, and three of the four platoons were commanded by A Company officers. If the truth be told, because the training facilities on The Rock are, to say the least, basic, it was more of a holiday than the usual strenuous fortnight. The most taxing activity appears to have been being chased to the top – well, nearly there – by a PTI and a couple of recently-out-of-Brecon corporals from 1 RRF to visit the apes. There was a good deal of drill, spit-and-polish for the privilege of providing ceremonial guards at Government House (which also involved being gawped-at by hordes of tourists), and there was a little shooting. With the help of the Royal Navy, the whole Company was seaborne at one time or another, in craft ranging from assault boats to frigates and submarines, and many took the opportunity of visiting Tangier at the middle weekend.

---

[1]   *RHRJ*, November 1984.
[2]   *BB*, Winter 1965.
[3]   *DERRJ*, October 1966.
[4]   *D&DRJ*, October 1967.
[5]   *Exeter Express & Echo*, 15 July 1967. There were in fact 505 all-ranks.
[6]   Because in the middle 1960s that was all that went to Camp.
[7]   "The Officers' Mess staff are still recovering from the shock of sleeping on the ground." *D&DRJ*, October 1967.
[8]   *BB*, Winter 1967.
[9]   *Exeter Express & Echo*, ibid.
[10] *BB*, Winter 1967.
[11] *RHRJ*, November 1967.
[12] Although 4/5 Royal Hampshires' Camp in 1966 had been with their Regular Battalion in Germany.
[13] *Ibid.*, November 1968.
[14] *Ibid.*
[15] In due course to become the Company Sergeant Major.
[16] Codewords such as these are used to mask the identity of a feature on a map.
[17] *BB*, Winter 1868.
[18] *D&DRJ*, October 1968.
[19] HQ Company Notes: *Ibid.*
[20] *BB*, Winter 1969.
[21] *Ibid.*
[22] *D&DRJ*, October 1969.
[23] *RHRJ*, November 1969.
[24] *DERRJ*, October 1969.
[25] *RHRJ, November* 1969.
[26] *DERRJ*, April 1970.
[27] *Ibid.*
[28] *D&DJ*, October 1970.
[29] *BB*, Summer 1970.
[30] *D&DRJ*, October 1970.

31   *The Back Badge*, Winter 1970.
32   *RHRJ*, November 1971.
33   *D&DRJ*, October 1971.
34   Source unknown.
35   *D&DRJ*, February 1972.
36   *D&DRJ*, February 1972.
37   Found in the Battalion scrapbook – source unknown.
38   *BB*, Winter 1971.
39   *Ibid.*
40   *Ibid.*, Winter 1972.
41   *Ibid.*
42   *D&DRJ*, May 1973.
43   *RHRJ*, May 1973.
44   *D&DRJ*, May 1973.
45   *DERRJ*, April 1970.
46   *Ibid.*, April 1972.
47   *Ibid.*, October 1972.
48   *Ibid.*
49   *Ibid.*, Autumn 1973.
50   *Ibid.*, October 1973.
51   *D&DRJ, November 1973.*

CHAPTER 6

A VARIED LIFE: 1974–1980

"Hacking holes in chalk is a necessary, but time-consuming,
part of TA soldiering"[1]

The B Company Notes in *The Royal Hampshire Regiment Journal* of
November 1974 commented:

> At last, having been formed for seven years, the Battalion has achieved
> a corporate identity, and all the Companies wear the same uniform and
> badges ......however, we must never lose our links with the County
> Regiment.

By and large, that hope was well fulfilled over the whole of
the Battalion's existence, bearing in mind that the battalions of
the Regular Regiments were rarely stationed in the UK. Without
exception, the early Camps, when individual Companies (sometimes
made up to strength with members of others) went to one or other
of those battalions in BAOR, were a huge success, because a real
effort was made to give the Volunteers a thoroughly worthwhile
fortnight. The various Regimental Headquarters, however, rarely seem
to have displayed much interest in either the Battalion as a whole,
or the Companies to which they were "affiliated". In that respect
the decision to "affiliate" rather than to "parent" was unfortunate
– although, as mentioned elsewhere, it did enable those Companies,
and thus the Battalion, to acquire their own identities sooner than
they might otherwise have done. There were, of course, some good
links – the Colonel of the Glosters took the salute at A Company's
annual Back Badge parades yearly from 1968 until 1972 – but, on the
other hand, when D Company transferred to 2 Wessex, the DERR
Journal made no mention of the end of the direct succession of the
TA battalions of The Royal Berkshire Regiment. The PSIs in fact
provided the strongest links, even though in 1986 they would give up

wearing their own regimental badges in favour of the Wyvern. There were, of course, a number of occasions when the Companies either paraded with, or 'stood-in' for, their Regular colleagues on ceremonial occasions – and there was a reasonably constant two-way trickle of personnel between the Regular Army and the TA. Some Regulars, on finishing their 'time', came into the Battalion, and, likewise, there were always a number of Volunteers who had acquired a real taste for soldiering and transferred to the Regular Army; for example, in 1979 11 members of A Company did so, and in 1977 two young officers, Lieutenants James Falkner and Richard Howman both of D Company left to take up Short Service Commissions with, respectively, DERR and D & D.

A most important morale booster at the beginning of this period was the issue, in February 1974, of the latest DPM [Disruptive Pattern Material] combat kit to all ranks – for months afterwards, everyone seemed to be walking taller!   Other new clothing – particularly waterproofs – took longer to arrive, but the Volunteers nevertheless managed to survive:

> The autumn day opens with sunshine, blue sky and not too much cloud – at least overhead. A long march, then perhaps practicing a bridge demolition guard and lots of patrolling, and little sleep lie ahead. Nevertheless, it could be a good weekend. Clamber out of the 4-tonner, check one's kit, 'get fell in'. Half an hour after setting off, the weather has changed completely. Black clouds in the west, and the rain begins, not much more than drizzle to start with, then it takes on a persistent feel, and it is obvious that it has set in for the day.
>
> Gradually the rain begins to penetrate one's combat trousers – first at the knees, then down the legs. Socks are the next to get wet – but some wise souls wear a plastic bag between them and the boot. Hitch the large pack up on the shoulders a bit, and change shoulders for the rifle. Hands go pink. Some of the breakfast-time anticipation of a good weekend starts to falter. Gradually, everyone realises that they are wet through to the skin, and aren't going to get dry until tomorrow. There's no warmth in a basha. Puddles, mud, sodden grass up to the knees. Nevertheless, one or two jokes, a break with perhaps a square of chocolate, some cajoling from the Platoon Sergeant – and imperceptibly spirits rise.[2]

Lieutenant Colonel Colin Tremellen of the Duke of Edinburgh's took over command in December 1973. In the mysterious ways of the British Army, he had had no previous experience of the TA, and it was unclear how his previous job – a member of the Directing Staff at the Sudanese Staff College – had prepared him for this particular posting. During the weeks of his take-over, he became more and more bemused by the differences between the way the Regular and the Territorial Armies worked – for example, the fact that any Volunteer could (but in practice rarely did) say "I'll turn up if and when I want to – not when I'm ordered to!"; or that, although in the Regular Army the management of the financial accounts of the Companies and Messes had to be passed around the officers every six months, if (as was the case from time to time) in a TA Company there were only two officers, other than the Company Commander, there was no alternative to their handing the account backwards and forwards to each other every six months – and, indeed, whether or not they had any knowledge of military accounting. He soon, however, got into his stride, and led the Battalion with considerable flair and a light touch.

He quickly realised that keeping the Battalion up to strength was the key to worthwhile training and high morale, and so he made recruiting, and the retention of trained soldiers, absolute priorities. Until the early 1970s, across the whole country, recruiting had been relatively easy; as time went on, however, wastage – i.e. the outflow, of almost exclusively junior NCOs and soldiers – from virtually all TA units became an increasingly serious problem, and it's corollary, recruiting, therefore became increasingly important. By the beginning of 1974, the TA as a whole was only 75% fully recruited (compared with over 100% in 1967), and the Battalion's total volunteer strength had dropped from nearly 750 to just under 550 over the previous three years or so. After tremendous efforts, however, by the end of 1975 it was 28 officers and 635 other ranks – a marvellous achievement by all concerned – and the highest ever strength after that was 35 officers and 639 other ranks (on a total establishment of 730) in October 1977.[3]

Colin Tremellen had two Seconds-in-Command – the first was Major Peter Whiteman (previously the second Company Commander of A Company), and he was followed by Major Andrew Ravenhill (who had likewise been the second Company Commander of D Company). Although often regarded as a 'non-job', the role of the 2IC was in fact particularly important in a TA battalion with a Regular Commanding Officer. As the senior Volunteer, he was the CO's adviser on the peculiarities, strengths and vagaries of TA soldiering – and on the rare occasions when a 'Regular v. TA difficulty' arose, he could help to resolve it, or 'protect' the Volunteers against a somewhat over-enthusiastic new CO or Training Major who (as he would in all likelihood readily admit) was only part-way to the top of the 'learning curve'. The 2ICs were a valued link between the Regular officers at Battalion HQ and the Companies; they worked closely with the Training Major in planning Battalion-organised training; and from time to time, of course, COs gave them the extremely useful experience of commanding the Battalion on an exercise. Peter Whiteman retired from the TA when he gave up the job, sadly with no formal recognition of the tremendous amount he had done for the Battalion, and A Company in particular, since 1967. Andrew Ravenhill, however, went on to a staff job at Headquarters, South East District; then, to the great pleasure of the Battalion, his enthusiastic and devoted service was recognised by his becoming the second 2IC to be promoted to Brevet Lieutenant Colonel (John Roberts having been the first), and he transferred to South West District as the G1 Training (TAVR) [the senior officer in charge of TA training].

In July 1974, WO1 James Parrott, the Bandmaster of the Hampshire and Dorset Band, retired after an astonishing military career spanning a period of very nearly 50 years – in the course of which he was awarded the Military Service Medal, the Long Service & Good Conduct Medal, and the Territorial Efficiency Medal with a Bar. He enlisted as a Boy in Cairo in October 1924 in the Band of the 1st Bn The Royal Hampshire Regiment, in which his father was then serving. In January 1925 the battalion moved to India, and with them he took part in many operations on the North West Frontier. In March 1937 he returned to England to go on a course at the Royal Military School of Music, Kneller Hall. During the Second World War, he was first in the 1st/4th Royal Hampshires, and he then rejoined the 1st Battalion in Sicily, and took part in the invasion of Italy as a platoon sergeant. He was taken prisoner, and not released until the end of hostilities in May 1945; he then served as CQMS at the Regimental Depot until the termination of his 21-year engagement. Soon after the end of the War, he entered the Civil Service, and became a clerical officer in the Orderly Room of the Green Jackets' Depot at Winchester – where he was still working at the time of his discharge from the TA. Having played with a number of civilian bands, in late 1954 he was at last been able to renew his involvement with military music – he joined the 4th Royal Hampshires as the Band Sergeant, and a year later he was promoted to WO1 and appointed as its Bandmaster. The Band acquired a very good reputation, and (like the Devon Band) they never played better than on the Colour Parade the year before his retirement.

Over the four years since its formation in 1971, the 2nd Battalion had found its geographical layout particularly difficult. It covered the area between Bletchley in Buckinghamshire and Weymouth, via Slough, Maidenhead, Reading, Basingstoke, Portsmouth and Poole – although that was simple compared with the spread of the 1st Battalion over 13 TA Centres from Reading to Barnstaple, and from Cheltenham to Newport on the Isle of Wight, with Swindon, Gloucester, Bristol, Basingstoke, Winchester, Dorchester, Poole, Exeter and Plymouth in the middle. In 1974 it was therefore agreed between the two Battalions that some reorganisation was needed. The Headquarters, United Kingdom Land Forces at Wilton and Eastern Wessex TAVRA were persuaded that the proposals were sensible – and accordingly, as the first stage, on All Fools' Day 1975 the 2nd Battalion took over the TA Centre at Penrith Road in Basingstoke from the 1st Battalion. Then, some two years later, in July 1977, under the somewhat oddly named Exercise Overlap, D Company in Reading (but not its detached Platoon in Swindon) was 'exchanged' for the 2nd Battalion's D Company in Poole. Although no one probably realised it at the time, those were the first of many steps in the gradual 'dismemberment' of the Battalion which went on for the next 18 years. The Poole Company had been raised from The Dorset Territorials, who (like the 1st Battalion's C Company) also stemmed from the 4th Dorsets and 294 (Dorset Yeomanry) Field Regiment, Royal Artillery.

At the time, the Battalion understandably felt that, in D Company, it was losing a strong limb, and getting a replacement of totally unknown quality. In the event, however – perhaps partly because of a sense of 're-connection' with its previous history – the new Company relatively quickly became well integrated into the Battalion, and imbued with its spirit. The Battalion accordingly now had two Companies in Dorset, but none in Berkshire, and its spread was reduced from seven counties to six.

One small event took place in September 1974 that epitomises the basic generosity of soldiers, be they Regulars or Volunteers. C Company had traditionally had an annual exercise on Alderney (by courtesy of HMS *Hardy* of the Royal Naval Reserve) – and this time they "took the opportunity of repaying the Island for past hospitality, and presented a garden seat to the Old Peoples' Home. The seat had very largely been made by volunteer members of the Company, and was erected by Corporal L Webb and helpers".[4] The following year, they managed to amass a positive flotilla for what can only be referred to as a jaunt, for, in addition to HMS *Exmouth*, they had a large launch from the Royal Engineers at Marchwood, on Southampton Water, and a Fleet Auxiliary Tender from the Portland naval base.

On the retirement of Colonel Bill Roberts as the Honorary Colonel in 1975, Major General Glyn Gilbert CB, MC was appointed to succeed him. General Glyn had had a very distinguished career; he originally joined The Lincolnshire Regiment, and won his MC with them in Belgium in 1944; he transferred to The Parachute Regiment, and in due course commanded their 10th (TA) Battalion; he was then successively the Commander of the 44th Parachute Brigade, the Commandant of the School of Infantry, Commander of the 3rd Division in BAOR, and finally the Commandant of the Joint Warfare Establishment at Old Sarum. Very much a 'soldiers' soldier' of the best 'old-fashioned school', his experience and helpful advice were of tremendous value to three Commanding Officers of the Battalion, and, probably attracted by the twinkle in his eyes, the Volunteers always enjoyed talking to him.

Not often did the activities of Government departments, other than the MOD, have an impact on TA soldiering, but a highly unpopular change in the Inland Revenue's policy over pay occurred in 1975:

[At Camp] some recruits were the first to suffer the juggernaut of the
Inland Revenue. TAVR pay has always been subject to Income Tax, but
it has now been decreed that Tax be deducted before the soldier receives
his pay, and tax is deducted at the standard rate regardless of personal
circumstances. This led to the iniquitous situation of the recruit who
was not liable to Income Tax at all receiving only two-thirds of his pay,
and facing a long delay in fighting the Inland Revenue for a refund.
Although the recruits coped extremely well with the military aspects of
the cadre, they were unable to come to terms with a considerable loss
in income, and we have unfortunately lost some good soldiers through
their unequal struggle with bureaucracy.[5]

That year the whole Battalion was meant to go to Camp in Cyprus.
However, after some 30-40 years of antagonism between the Greek
Cypriots and the Turkish Cypriots, in July and August 1974 Turkey had
invaded Cyprus, with the intention of ethnically cleansing the Greek
Cypriot population and annexing as much of the island as it could, to
create a purely Turkish state. The Turks finished up controlling about
a third of the island, and it was obviously inappropriate for the British
Government to increase its troop levels by 500-600 soldiers, even if
they were only there for a very energetic holiday! As a result, the 1975
Camp took place at Haltern near Munster – and, with 1 Irish Guards
as the sponsor unit, it was very successful. A full report is in Chapter
7, as there are of all the other Camps between 1974 and 1980.

The moves of Headquarter Company from Exeter and Trowbridge
to Devizes had left the Corps of Drums [often referred to as the Drums
Platoon[6]] 'stranded' in Plymouth, and it became increasingly difficult
to encourage and look after them. For eight years they had been an
integral and much respected part of the Battalion, and it was with
considerable regret, therefore, that it was decided to disband them
there, and raise a new Platoon at Devizes under the CSM, WO2
Morris, and Drum Major Veale. Although recruiting was initially slow,
happily a number of former Duke of Edinburgh's' drummers 'came out
of the woodwork', and, with the great expertise and encouragement
of those two senior NCOs, it was not long before the Platoon were
performing with the skill and élan of their predecessors.

Major out-of-Camp activities in 1975 included a CPX [Command

Post Exercise] in bitterly cold weather in April; in September, Exercise High Flyer on Salisbury Plain, set by South West District and involving NBC drills and much use of helicopters; and, two months later, on 8 November, the granting to C Company of the Liberty of Bridport – a very unusual honour indeed for a sub-unit. Two guards of 50 each and the Colours, plus the Devon Band and the Corps of Drums, together also 50 strong, were on parade, and the occasion was a particularly happy one – for which great credit is due to the efforts of the Company Commander, Major Nick Speakman. Another very successful achievement was the participation of HQ Company in the Devizes to Westminster Canoe Race, spurred on by their new Company Commander, Major Michael Oakley – who had previously commanded B Company, and was anxious to rid HQ Company of its image as the Cinderella of competitive activities. The weather was freezing and generally dreadful, and the course gruelling (particularly as the canoes had to be carried at the run to get round locks and other obstacles), but two of the three teams entered duly finished up outside the Houses of Parliament. Last, but certainly not least, there were a number of social activities – the WOs & Sergeants' Mess very successful Christmas Draw Party at Devizes, and Officers' Dinner Nights at Warminster and Devizes, a Ladies Night at Trowbridge and a Summer Ball at Tidworth. In this connection, mention must be made of the first Officers' Mess Colour Sergeant, Dirk Bate-Jones. He had been that for 4 Devons, and his easy efficiency and warm personality without question guaranteed him a place in the Battalion on formation day. Apart from the fact that he was an extremely fine small-bore shot, and represented the Battalion on numerous occasions, under him the Mess was organised to perfection. He was, like so many of his colleagues throughout the Army, a combination of minder, mentor and god-father to the young officers: "Come on, sir – don't talk so much – you're on parade in three minutes, and I hope you haven't left your Sam Brown in your room…." or "If I were you sir, I'd stick to beer or you'll have a very thick head in the morning….". He had a broad Devon accent, a marvellous smile and a lovely sense of humour – it was a sad day for the Battalion when he retired.

The Battalion's report in the TAVRA *Newsletter* (*No 10*) for 1975 concluded:

> All in all, it has been a fascinating year – full of achievement, enjoyment, surprises and the inevitable occasional failure. The variety of training, visits, ceremonies and social activities has shown that life with the TA is never dull, should as often as possible be fun, and is always rewarding.

Life in the TA was, indeed, never dull – for example:

> Since the last notes appeared, we have been kept extremely busy. It all started in March [1976] with what appeared to be a simple Battalion Exercise named "Wessex Puddle" – or was it "Muddle"? – down on the Bovington Training Area. Infantry-tank co-operation was what it was all about. It was the first time that some of our younger soldiers had seen Chieftans and Scorpions 'in action', churning up the sand only a few yards from their dug-in positions. Swanning around the training area were, in addition to the tanks, reece vehicles, Rovers, Bedford 4-tonners – and fire engines. Fire engines? Yes, fire engines. Some nameless soldier decided it was time he had a cup of tea so he 'brewed up' with his hexamine [individual, solid fuel] cooker, and then in view of the tactical situation he decided to 'cam up' [camouflage himself] using some of the very dry heather that covers the area. Hence the sudden appearance of the Dorset Fire Brigade – and, believe you me, there is nothing in any Military Manual that covers fire engines taking part in a military exercise. No wonder the CO, Lieutenant Colonel Tremellen, gave up command, and departed for the peace and tranquility of the Prince of Wales Divisional Headquarters.[7]

A major success in 1976 was that of an A Company team under Lieutenant Philip James which came seventh out of some 45 in the Reserve Forces Association's International Patrol Competition near Stuttgart in West Germany – a series of varied and challenging tests at intervals along a twenty kilometre course. The event was very well organised by the Bundeswehr, and the team were generously hosted by German Reserve officers. A Company achieved another feather in its cap by becoming able to put up a "No vacancies" sign on the front door of the Eastern Avenue TA Centre, as it was fully recruited up to its establishment.

Also in 1976, after 11 year's devoted service to the Devon Band, WO1 (Bandmaster) EF ("Nobby") Knowles MSM handed over the baton to WO1 (Bandmaster) Roy Hibbs. The Devon Band had been a good one, both in musicianship and drill, for many years, but under Nobby it became one of the finest in the TA; as mentioned below, with the Hampshire & Dorset Band, it played a major part in the Queen's Jubilee Royal Review, and it was a great pity that he was not able to direct it then – he would have just loved it! The two Bands were well matched, and the Battalion was so lucky to have them. Their excellent reputation in the South West meant that ex--Regular bandsmen who had retired to the Plymouth, Devizes or the Andover areas often joined, and both Bands accordingly included former Regular Band Sergeant Majors, Staff Sergeants and Sergeants who had been perfectly happy to drop several ranks simply for the pleasure of being able to continue playing. The entry in the Battalion's Part I Orders for that change of Bandmasters showed that 'snakes and ladders' play a part in Army life – "WO1 Knowles voluntarily reverts to Lance Corporal", and "Bandsman Hibbs is promoted to substantive WO1 (as Bandmaster of the Devon Band)" in one jump. Both Bands worked extremely hard – for example, in 1977, in adition to its commitments within the Battalion, the Devon Band had a public engagement every month, including a Christmas concert for Exeter schools, a Plymouth Reserve Forces parade, a parade for the 100th Anniversary of St John's Ambulance, several Old Comrades Reunion dinners and the British Pony Association's Show at Exeter.

1976 was the last year that the Battalion was split up for Annual Camp – A Company went to BAOR, and the rest to Cultybraggan in Scotland – and from then on (apart from those doing courses, and sometimes detachments of Support Platoons going to specialist ranges) everyone spent the fortnight together. That undoubtedly had a strong stabilising effect on the Battalion as a whole later on, particularly (as related in Chapter 8) between 1986 and 1992, when it lost five Rifle Companies to either the 2nd Battalion or 4 D & D. The major activity after Camp was Exercise Winter I, for which the 2nd Battalion provided the basic enemy, and there was a positive army of supporting (and sometimes additional enemy) troops – detachments from the Royal Marine Reserve; 266 Battery; 100 Field Squadron, Royal Monmouthshire Engineers (Volunteers); 219 General Hospital, Royal Army Medical Corps (Volunteers) and the part-Regular, part TA-manned Army Air Corps [AAC] 666 Squadron from Netheravon. From the Regular Army came detachments of 14th/20th King's Hussars, 22 Engineer Regiment RE, and the 2nd Light Infantry; the RAF provided fighter-ground-attack simulation, and the Bristol and Oxford University OTCs, and Marlborough College CCF, all took part.

Colin Tremellen had had a very successful two-and-a-half-year tour, and before Camp in May 1976 he handed over command to Lieutenant Colonel Bill Coppen-Gardner MC – an extremely positive Royal Hampshireman, who was the "very model of a modern" Regular Lieutenant Colonel. He began his military career as a National Serviceman in the Glosters in 1953, but transferred to the Royal Hampshires in 1955 when he was granted a Short Service Commission; subsequently he took a Regular Commission, and he won his MC in operations against the Mau-Mau in Kenya. Although he often seemed somewhat aloof, he had an engaging personality and a good sense of humour; the Battalion appreciated his belief in hard training, and under him it became increasingly effective in the field.

Many years' observation of infantry officers has shown that, in a very broad sense, they fall into three distinct types. The first thinks that if you can't organise yourself to get out of your barracks into the field quickly and efficiently, there's no point in being fit to march to wherever you are going, and that small arms training is therefore a waste of valuable time; the next believes that unless you are really fit, being good at administration or having a battalion of marksmen won't help you win the war, because you simply won't get there; while the third takes the view that if you can't shoot straight when you do, there's no point in having started out in the first place. It is not therefore surprising that over, say, any ten year period, each of the Commanding Officers tends to be a different 'type' from his predecessor – with the result that the units with good COs finish up being well-trained in every aspect of infantry soldiering. That was certainly so for the Battalion over the whole of its existence – and (excluding the author from the judgement) every one of the COs made very different but quite tremendous contributions to its success. Bill Coppen-Gardner was, however, an exception to that 'pigeon-holing', for he was not only a brilliant organiser and a great encourager of fitness throughout the Battalion, but he was also very keen on shooting.

It almost goes without saying that virtually all the officers and NCOs wanted to improve their military skills and, the part-time nature of TA service notwithstanding, to become as professional as their Regular Army counterparts. Except for the specialists such as cooks and signallers, mortarmen and anti–tank gunners), the place to achieve that was The School of Infantry, which (as already mentioned in the previous Chapter – and for most of the period covered by this book) had its Officers' Divisions at Warminster, its NCOs' Training Wing at Brecon, and a Support Weapons Wing at Netheravon. Although the courses were extremely testing, both mentally and (particularly in the case of the NCOs' Courses) physically, they were also immensely stimulating, and almost invariably the many Volunteers who went on them came back full of enthusiasm and ideas for improving the training of 'their' part of the Battalion, and very appreciative of the efficiency of the School and the quality of its staff. It is not therefore surprising that, within only a few years of the Battalion's formation, the School's ethos had very much become the Battalion's too, and Warminster/Brecon the Battalion's 'spiritual home' – so much so that, following the amalgamation of the Battalion in 1995, it was decided that Warminster was the most appropriate place in which the Colours should be laid up. They are in cases fixed to the main staircase wall in the Hythe Officers' Mess there. (See footnote to Appendix 4)

In addition to the two moves of Battalion HQ and HQ Company in 1969 and 1972, and the periodic losses of companies to other TA battalions, there was almost perpetual internal reorganisation of one sort or other. For example, B Company's Support Platoon was originally in Basingstoke, but in 1971 the TA Centre there was, at somewhat short notice, handed over to 2 Wessex, so they moved into Winchester; then, in 1979 they moved again, this time to a new (although not purpose-built) TA Centre on the former RAF Andover airfield, most of which was occupied by the huge and curiously-named

Regular organisation, Logex (Army). The biggest change of this period, though, affected all the Support Platoons in the Battalion. Ever since 1967, each rifle company had had one, consisting of detachments of both mortars and anti-tank guns. In 1978 the Battalion adopted the '650' establishment (i.e. the total number of all ranks) – and that was seen as a good opportunity to rationalize the wide spread of support weapons across the it's area. Bill Coppen-Gardner accordingly decided to concentrate the detachments with just two of the Companies – A Company's Support Platoon becoming the Battalion's Anti–tank Platoon, and B Company's Support Platoon becoming the Battalion's Mortar Platoon. From both the training and operational points of view, that made sense, because it concentrated the expertise in two places instead of having it spread over five – but there were two disadvantages. The first (albeit only relatively short-term one) was that a number of members of A and B Companies had to be trained as anti-tank gunners or mortarmen from scratch – although some of the A Company Mortar detachment did not think that the conversion was going to be all that difficult: "It's exactly the same – you just put the round in the other end" – while a corresponding number in C, D and E Companies had no alternative but to revert, understandably not very happily, to being ordinary riflemen. The long-term disadvantage was that the new structure took away from those three Companies some important 'rungs on the promotion ladder', from which a fully trained rifleman, or a young NCO, could move sideways into a support detachment, and thus have a change of scene and experience, before going back to a rifle platoon again, probably on promotion. For a Volunteer in Dorset, Berkshire and Devon who was keen to work his way up the ladder, there was therefore definitely less to look forward to – but few, if any, actually resigned as a result.

The Battalion was involved in two of the major events celebrating HM The Queen's Silver Jubilee in 1977 – the Review of the Reserve & Cadet Forces at Wembley Stadium on 30th June (which was actually part of a three-day Services Musical Pageant), and then a Review of the Reserve & Volunteer Forces of Avon in Bristol on 8th August. Both were unique occasions. The Wembly Review was believed to be the first time that Volunteers from the reserves of all three armed services (as well as the Cadet Forces and the Royal Observer Corps) had ever paraded together before the Sovereign; a major review of the Army had almost certainly not been held since the first Queen Elizabeth inspected her forces at Tilbury on 8 August 1588, when the Spanish Armada was threatening these islands. "Her rough-hewn soldiers can hardly have failed to take inspiration from the bejewelled figure in their midst. 'Let tyrants fear,' she said, in terms calculated to woo her audience, 'I have always so behaved myself that under God I have placed my chiefest strength and safeguard in the loyal hearts and goodwill of my subjects'....." In what a later generation would think of as a Churchillian mode, she was resolved to die rather than surrender. But unlike Churchill, she could play the card of gender, and it is this declaration that has come ringing down the ages: "I have the body of a weak, feeble woman, but I have the heart and stomach of a king – and a king of England too....".[8]

Nearly 400 years later, the Review was 'dreamed up' by the Ministry of Defence at fairly short notice, and, because every one of the major TA units provided participants, the logistics of getting those involved to Wembley from all parts of the UK proved to be extremely complicated. Although there was only one rehearsal, 'on the morning', everything nevertheless seemed to go off very well. The 1 Wessex contingent was perhaps luckier than most, in that the Battalion was at Camp; 30 strong and representing all five Companies, it was commanded by the irrepressible third OC of A Company, Major David Ryan – "whose heroic efforts to speak to Her Majesty from the middle of the Stadium resulted in his losing his voice for the rest of Camp"[9] – and both the Devon and the Hampshire & Dorset Bands were privileged to be included in the six which made up the massed bands for the parade. Some former members of the Battalion may still have a copy of the long-playing record of the event.[10]

A major element of the Silver Jubilee celebrations was the Queen and Duke of Edinburgh's 'progress' (as it would have been called in Elizabeth I's time) around the whole of the British Isles in the Royal Yacht *Britannia*, calling at many ports and islands on the way. Due to visit Bristol in any event, they were invited by one of the strongest supporters of the volunteer services in the south-west, the Lord

Lieutenant of Avon, Colonel Sir John Wills Bt TD, to review the
Reserve & Volunteer Forces based in the County. The event, held
in Bristol on 8 August 1977, was a major undertaking, organised by
Headquarters South West District, and:

....with the greatest co-operation from the City authorities and the
Police, the whole of the City Centre was closed for the morning;
spectator stands had been constructed, and unit displays erected on
the open spaces and gardens around which traffic normally flows. The
City Surveyor deserved a medal for the way he agreed to have his
precious flowerbeds turfed or boarded over without so much as raising
an eyebrow, and he produced a forest of flagpoles on which all the unit
flags made a marvellously colourful show. It is, of course, eventually on
the details that any occasion of this sort succeeds or fails:

"What is the maximum load for these paving stones – will they take
    a 10 tonner?"
"It has definitely been decided that the Royal Princes aren't coming,
    so you can plan accordingly";
"How do you get the first – or is it the 21st – gun to coincide *exactly*
    with the opening of the Royal car door?"
"And who *actually* opens the door of the Lord Lieutenant's car?"
"The Royal Princes are, after all, coming";
"Yes, there are electric plugs in the flowerbeds";
"No, the Band can't possibly play that….. ";
"Tell the City Engineer that we need 12, not 11, flagpoles there, so
    the spacing will have to be altered";
"Unfortunately, we have now heard the Royal Princes will definitely
    not be coming after all…...";
"Can we dredge the basin to get HMS *Upton* right up to the
    Neptune Statue?"
"Does a High Sheriff take precedence over a Brigadier?"
"Does the Guard of Honour march off leaving HM on the saluting
    dais, or does she leave first?"
"Royal Naval Auxiliary *what?*"
"Can a Police car radio net-in with 37 Signal Regiment's Pye radios?"
"We have now, finally, heard that only Prin….."   ;
"Will the Mounted Police Escort stop here, or….. ?
"When should …?", "How can the ….?", "Where may ….?", "Which

....?"11

A positive army of VIP spectators – the Lord Lieutenant and the Vice-Lord Lieutenant, Deputy Lieutenants, distinguished "Elder Statesmen of the TAVR" (as they were described in the immensely detailed, 22-page, Operation Order), as well as representatives of both TAVRAs, senior officers of all three Regular Forces and the participating units, ecclesiastical and educational dignitaries, mayors and councillors, and Avon MPs – was ensconced in the best stand. On their arrival at the northern end of the Centre in one of the royal Rollses driven down to Bristol specially for the visit, Her Majesty and the Duke of Edinburgh were greeted with that 21 gun salute fired by 266 Battery, and they then inspected a Guard of Honour provided by 6 LI, parading the Queen's Colour of the old 4th/5th Battalion of the Somerset Light Infantry. That over, the Queen and The Duke were introduced to a number of the VIPs, and they then spent over half an hour touring a comprehensive and elaborate series of static displays by the participating units, stretching down the Centre from the War Memorial almost to the Neptune Statue at the head of the water in Broad Quay. Her Majesty, accompanied by the Lord Lieutenant, the Lord Mayor, and the author (who, as the TA Colonel (East) in South West District, was responsible for all the military aspects of the day), visited the stands of A Company's Speedwell Platoon, 37 Signal Regiment, 3 Troop RMonRE, 219 General Hospital and the Bristol University OTC. Her Majesty was particularly interested in the oil painting of the Battalion's Colour Presentation Parade displayed on A Company's stand, as the artist Joan Wanklyn had recently painted some of the Royal horses; David Ryan (to whom the CO seemed to have granted the exclusive right to be the Battalion's senior representative at Silver Jubilee events, and who had presumably recovered his voice) showed her around the display – which included support weapons and some of the Battalion's ceremonial accoutrements – and she spoke very relaxedly to several of his Volunteers. The Duke of Edinburgh, escorted by Lieutenant Colonel Keith Brown (a tremendously staunch member of the TA for many years, at that time the Commanding Officer of 37 Signal Regiment, and who later followed the author as the Chairman of the TAVRA), went to 266 Battery, 6 LI, 245 Squadron and 395 Air Dispatch Troop

RCT, and the Royal Observer Corps. Both The Queen and The Duke visited the joint stand for the Sea Cadets, the Army Cadets, the Air Training Corps and the Combined Cadet Force The two escorting officers had the task of ensuring that their charges arrived at Broad Quay simultaneously – a difficult one, because The Queen's party went down the west side of the Centre, and The Duke's party down the east side, 100 yards or so away, and were largely invisible to each other – but all went well, and the royal couple genuinely seemed to enjoy themselves.

The proceedings, particularly at the start of the day, were lightened in several ways. The Queen and Prince Philip had arrived on the previous afternoon in the Royal Yacht *Britannia* at the Royal Portbury Dock at Avonmouth, which The Queen then opened. One of the Royal Princes came too, and a special programme had been arranged for him during the Review; received wisdom has it, however, that he was persuaded to spend the evening in *Britannia's* Petty Officers' Mess, apparently with disastrous effects, for his programme was cancelled first thing in the morning. Then, before arriving in the Centre, their Royal Highnesses had visited a school in Filton, and enjoyed themselves so much that they over-ran the allotted time; getting on to the M42, the royal driver, with a Rolls Royce Merlin engine under the bonnet, therefore put his foot down, with the result that they arrived in the Centre only a few minutes after the planned time – with the police escort quite some way behind. The very 'on-side' senior policeman in charge of the non-military side of the visit, Chief Inspector Mike Challis, was found by the author some ten minutes later, walking about with a face like thunder – which seemed a little curious, given that everything was now going exactly according to plan; when asked what his problem was, he replied "The bloody royal car – it was going so fast, we couldn't keep up with it". Then, having inspected the Guard, and found it well polished and expert at its drill, the Queen asked the Guard Commander whether she and the Duke should return to the very smart all-perspex saluting dais – one of the many on which they had already stood in the course so far of their 'pilgrimage' around the country. When invited to do so, an unmistakeable voice from behind her said, quite audibly, "Oh, God – not again!"

A most pleasing aspect of the Queen's Jubilee was that two members of the Battalion were named in the Birthday Honours list for services to the TA. Another of its irrepressible characters, Captain (as he then was) Jim Loftus, the TA Quartermaster, was appointed an MBE. A Gloster, he had been captured by the Germans just before Dunkirk, rose after the War to become an RSM, and then reverted to the rank of private twice – first when, after retiring, he joined the 5th Glosters, and then again in order to get into A Company.   Secondly, Sergeant Norman Tout of E Company was awarded the British Empire Medal – in particular for acting as the Platoon Commander of No 17 Platoon in Plymouth for nearly three years. They were both really well-merited rewards for many years unstinting service, and the senior ranks in the Battalion were pleased for them – and furthermore Major Andrew Ravenhill, WO2 Harry Mower and Corporal (as he was then) Ken Chivers of C Company were awarded the Queen's Jubilee Medal.

After all that parading and polish, and a 'warm-up' on Dartmoor, the whole Battalion went to Camp on the Stanford PTA, with most of both weeks being taken-up with exercises designed to test both infantry skills (including everybody's favourite occupation, digging-in) and personal stamina. 1 DERR lent instructors for support weapons cadres, excitement was provided by helicopters from 665 Squadron AAC and the German Bundeswehr, while on the final exercise fighter-ground attacks by the RAF and the USAF accompanied the live firing of mortars and GPMGs [General Purpose Machine Gun]. In addition to all that, a number of Volunteers went soldiering abroad in addition to their UK Camp: two teams each spent two weeks in Cyprus with 1 Glosters, who were carrying out troop trials of the Army's new Clansman radio in a non-temperate climate; with the help of a very generous grant from Western Wessex, David Ryan, yet again in the limelight, took a party to stay with a Bundeswehr unit – spending, from all accounts, appreciably more time visiting various sights and innumerable bierkellers than in soldiering; and an indubitably more rugged time was spent by a composite platoon from both 1 and 2 Wessex with 5 Queens during their Camp in Norway. Finally, a group of five officers and five other ranks gained a great deal of experience by going to BAOR to take part in 2 Division's CPX Exercise Queen's

Crown – presumably so-named in view of the Silver Jubilee celebrations – intended to test unit and sub-unit headquarters' procedures at every level. The very sophisticated radio equipment, with its inbuilt security system, was a considerable eye-opener to the Volunteers, making a mockery of the traditional 'voice procedure' in which the use of codewords provided the only safeguard against a listening-in enemy, and which at that stage the TA still used. The last significant training event in an exceptionally busy 12 months was Exercise Octoberfest on Salisbury Plain, attended by over 400 Volunteers:

> …in which 1 Wessex acted as enemy to the whole of 44 Independent Para Brigade, supported by German and French paras. It was billed as the highlight of the year – and it would most certainly have been so if bad weather had not prevented the Paras from dropping in. Even so, the Exercise was extremely enlightening and worthwhile, as it offered, for the first time for most people, an opportunity of operating with APCs and of working with Regular Bundeswehr soldiers. The two [Bundeswehr] platoons attached not only showed their efficiency and expertise, but also demonstrated how a front-line Government's awareness of the 'threat' is reflected in good equipment, clothing and training. As a finale to the Exercise, all participants were treated to a firepower demonstration which amply convinced everyone of the lethality of modern weapons and ammunition.[12]

while the year ended with an astonishing series of 'leaps up the ladder' by Private Gigg. As WO2 D B Gigg, he had been the senior PSI in E Company, and, happy to relate, on his retirement from the Regular Army he became a Volunteer. His enlistment date was 15 November, and he was promoted to Substantive Corporal on 16 November, to Substantive Sergeant on 17 November, to Substantive Colour Sergeant a day later, and finally on 19 November to WO2, as the CSM of E Company.[13]

1978 began with the cutting of the first sod of the site of a huge new TA Centre at Derriford, on the Tavistock Road out of Plymouth, by the Lord Lieutenant of Devon, Lord Roborough. It would bring together 17 Platoon of E Company, 232 (Petrol) Squadron RCT and its REME Workshop, and 211 (Wessex) Field Hospital RAMC – who were all scattered over the city in extremely unsatisfactory accommodation

– and also provide accommodation for a Company of the Devon ACF. The cost was estimated at £700,000.

The following months saw two successors to the 1971/72 Wessex Marches:

Why Offa ever had cause to build his Dyke to keep the English out of Wales will never be understood by those members of B Company who took part in Exercise Wessex Walker I at Sennybridge in February. The weather could have been worse, and it was a good thing that it wasn't, as the Exercise involved movement from the south-west corner to the north-east corner of the training area, travelling on foot across the grain of the country. The pity of it was that the very poor visibility prevented live mortar and GPMG (SF) [GPMG delivering 'sustained fire'] in support of the advance. The Company can feel justifiably pleased with its ability to endure the adverse weather conditions and testing nature of the exercise.........Welsh Nationalist propagandists may argue, of reservoirs supplying water to our northern cities, "Welsh water for Wales"; B Company's sentiments are that they can keep it![14]

Exercise Wessex Walker II took place on Dartmoor in March – luckily after the very heavy snow-storms, although vestiges still remained, and at one point the range road was still blocked by a drift. Useful training at section and platoon level was carried out, against an active enemy for a change. A large and successful fighting patrol interrupted the enemy's slumbers on what was a rather cold, damp and cheerless night. For once, our friends from the RAF turned up trumps by flying in rather adverse conditions, though not always to the exact destination, startling an enemy group by landing right on top of them. Some soldiers from the Island will be eternally grateful to the RAF for flying them home to Newport in record time.[15]

Shortly after that, three light anti-tank gun teams joined the RWxY at their Camp in Gibraltar. Despite its limitations, both for training and R & R activities, the Volunteers enjoyed going there, for – with the exception of Cyprus, which had been visited by several elements of the Battalion – the place could not have been more different from anywhere else known to almost everyone. It was good experience to work with a different TA unit – and to be able to swank a little in front of the Yeomen about their specialist skills!

There was another big and significant ceremonial parade on 29 April 1978. For some while, the Mayor and Councillors of Devizes had wanted to commemorate the Battalion's association with the town. The Freedom of the Borough – with the traditional right for units of the Armed Services to march through it "with Colours flying, bands playing, drums beating and bayonets fixed" – had been granted to The Wiltshire Regiment in 1950, and transferred to the DERR in 1973. One of the odder effects of the Government's reorganisation of the local authorities in 1977, however, was that (in common with a good number of similar-sized places) Devizes had ceased to be a borough, and became a town instead – as a result of which it was legally unable to confer any further Freedoms. The Battalion was therefore 'adopted' by the town – the only civic honour it ever received[16] – with the somewhat unusual "Liberty of the Town, the right to use the arms of the town in any way it thinks fit". The traditional right to a "Ceremonial March" could no longer be granted formally – but the request to have one after the Adoption ceremony was (not surprisingly) readily agreed. For the first time in 28 years, therefore, the military again marched through Devizes. Three month's of drill practice, mainly on an individual company basis, ensured that it was an excellent parade.

The Lord Lieutenant, Lord Margadale, was there, and The Mayor, Councillor Major A C Clark, arrived with a positive train of two Mace Bearers, two High Constables, the Town Clerk, the Custodian and the Mayor's Officer. Accompanied by the Honorary Colonel, General Glyn Gilbert, the Mayor inspected and addressed the Battalion, and then presented the Letters of Adoption – in exchange for which, on behalf of the Battalion, General Glyn presented the Town with an inscribed silver salver. After the Mayor had taken the salute on the March Past to the exhilarating strains of *The Farmer's Boy*, the Battalion exercised its Liberty in exactly the same way as it would have had it been granted the Freedom (except without fixed bayonets) – with colours flying and drums beating, the Bands playing all the right tunes, and stripped-down Land Rovers bringing up the rear. An excellent tea provided by the Town soon turned into a rather more alcoholic celebration, and the day was deemed to have been a great success:

The Parade to mark the Adoption of the Battalion by the Borough of Devizes was the first time that the Battalion had been involved in a formal parade since the Presentation of Colours five years before, so it's not very often that the Company is called upon to undertake such things. Together with D Company, we shared the honour of providing two half-guards as Escort for the Colours. Having formed up in drizzling rain in one of the more discreet parts of Devizes, the Parade, of three guards in all, marched on with the Colours and the combined Bands for which the Battalion is responsible. The Padre had done his work well, for as we drew up in the Market Square the rain stopped and the sun shone. Being Market Day in Devizes. a fair proportion of the local populace turned up to see what had so rudely disturbed their Saturday routine.[17]

The Parade appointments were:

Honorary Colonel: Maj Gen GCA Gilbert, CB MC
Commanding Officer: Lt Col CWE Coppen-Gardner, MC
Second-in-Command: Major AF Ravenhill TD
Training Major: Major PM Baxter
Adjutant: Capt SWJ Saunders
Regimental Sergeant Major: WO2 MSO'F Cook

	No 1 Guard	No 2 Guard	No 3 Guard
	Gloucestershire	Dorset &	Devonshire
	& Wiltshire	Hampshire	& Dorset
Guard Commander:			
	Major RD O'Neill	Major IPB Taylor TD	Major PV George
Second-in-Command:			
	Capt ASP Cook	Capt MJ Baggs	Capt LE Thornton-Grimes
Subaltern:	2Lt RG Lee	2Lt NS Pope	Lt DP Heath
Guides:	WO2 Reade	WO2 Worthy	WO2 Gigg
	WO2 Heatley	WO2 Cundy	WO2 Needs
	CSgt Mower	CSgt Blow	CSgt Denty
	CSgt Clapham	CSgt McManus	CSgt O'Connor

Colour Party

Ensign for The Queen's Colour: Lt PM Evens
Ensign for The Regimental Colour: 2Lt JD Temple
Warrant Officer: WO2 Gould, Sgt Diggle & Sgt Blake

The Devon Band of The Wessex Volunteers
The Hampshire & Dorset Band (TAVR)

———————

'Proper soldiering' was, however, what the Battalion rightly felt was thier real *raison d'etre*:

> Although ceremonial duties are an accepted and important part of soldiering, and all those who took part in the parade felt very proud to be there, there was a definite desire in the Company, and in the Battalion as a whole, to get back to some serious training in the run-up to Camp.[18]

but nevertheless 'in-house' social activities were certainly never forgotten. It was, however, always quite difficult to arrange Officers' and WOs & Sergeants' Mess cocktail parties, dinners, and occasionally balls, because they obviously had to be held at weekends – on almost every one of which during the entire year several of the companies, or the whole Battalion, were out on training in different places, more often than not a long way from Devizes. For all the senior ranks to depart at 5 o'clock on the Saturday evening, to climb into their 'glad rags' and collect their wives or girlfriends, was neither the sort of disruption in training that fitted the ethos of the Battalion, nor commended itself to the soldiers! Possible future functions therefore had to be 'pencilled into' training diaries many months in advance, and to a certain extent that affected their spontaneity. A rather less enjoyable, but very necessary, sort of partying was the giving or returning of hospitality to 'local dignitaries' and business people to introduce them to (or remind them of the existence of) the TA in general and the Battalion in particular – and they were often held in conjunction with training evenings at TA Centres.

Lieutenant Colonel John Southwood of The Royal Hampshire Regiment took over as the sixth Commanding Officer of the Battalion in November 1978 and served until 1981. Quietly very effective and a most capable planner, his tour, like Bill Coppen-Gardner's, was marked by a great deal of active and demanding training – including a strong continuation of support for shooting generally and for the Battalion team in particular.

Although time on the ranges had played a significant part in training during 1978, in terms of results sadly things did not go well. Indeed, somewhat embarrassingly, the Inspecting Officer for the Battalion's Fit for Role inspection in the autumn commented that individual shooting skills left a certain amount to be desired. While two young soldiers (Lance Corporals Dade of E Company and Ferguson of C Company) distinguished themselves, for the first time in many years C Company failed to win the South West District SAAM [Skill At Arms Meeting] at Bulford. Success was hard to come by at the TA Skill At Arms Meeting [TASAAM] at Bisley too, and the Battalion team's best efforts could only get them second place in its 'own' competition, The Wessex Volunteers' Cup, and ninth place (out of 73 teams) in The Dragon Trophy, the major unit championship – although that was certainly nothing to be ashamed of. In 1979, however, the Battalion shooting team covered itself in glory at Bisley. Not only did they win the most coveted trophy in TA shooting, the China Cup for the Section Match (so big that at least six people are needed to carry it), but Corporal Robin Price of C Company (the son of its original CSM, WO2 Tom Price) won HM The Queen's Medal – following in the footsteps of Michael Anstey, who had done so in 1971.

In January 1979, at John Southwood's instigation, 1 Wessex became the first TA battalion to 'fight a battle' with the Army's newest training aid, the Battle Group Tactical Trainer (BGTT) at the Royal Armoured Corps Training Centre at Bovington in Dorset:

> The Trainer enables the Commanding Officer to exercise commanders in fighting a defensive battle under realistic conditions – by the use of computers – without deploying the Battalion. The Company Commanders, having received their orders, went out on the ground to recce their positions. They then returned to a giant map covered with symbols representing their positions. "Red Symbols" appeared and

the battle developed. Computers were used to check engagements, and give accurate and final results. The Company Commanders relayed their messages to the Battalion Command Post as the battle progressed. In another room camouflaged vehicles and 9 x 9s[19] were arranged to simulate a Battalion Command Post in the field, complete with gunner, intelligence and control cells, all equipped with a radio link to the Battle Room. Thus the CP was well tested. At the end of the exercise, the computerised Casualty Analysis showed that we had knocked out ninety enemy APCs and thirty of their tanks. Enemy mortar and anti-tank fire had neutralised fifteen of our sections, which just enabled us to emerge on the credit side in this computer battle.[20]

There were two section competitions in 1979, the first of which was the South West District March and Shoot, over a weekend before Easter, This took place on and around the Bulford ranges, and consisted of a ten mile march in full fighting order, followed by a timed shoot. Every company and the support platoons entered teams – and the results were very satisfying, with the Anti-tank Platoon coming a close second, and five of the Battalion's other teams in the next nine places. The second competition was the Battalion Inter-Section Competition, Exercise Wonderful Wessex, at Sennybridge on 7 and 8 July. Each section was tested on a live firing exercise, a dry[21] section attack, and an overnight patrol base exercise, with 22 SAS [Special Air Service] acting as enemy. D Company from Poole were the winners, scoring 4,285 out of a possible 4,500 points, and the Anti-tank Platoon repeated their earlier success by coming second. During the competition, the Battalion was visited by Major General Sir John Acland, CBE, the GOC South West District, who was entertained to lunch in a Range Warden's target shed – served in true 1 Wessex 'field-style' from a five gallon dixie on to a tin plate, eaten standing-up, and without the white tablecloth and silver candelabra that a very large number of TA units still seemed to think *de rigeur* when senior officers visited them on field training.

Following the usual August 'shut down' – during which time there was no training and the Permnent Staff took 'block leave' – there was the usual weekend practicing mobilisation drills (carried out as part of the UK Home Defence Exercise, Scrum Half) in preparation for what would undoubtedly be an important Camp. For that, the Battalion went in October to the area of the Hartz Mountains in BAOR, where it took part in 4 Armoured Division's major exercise of the year, Full House. The fortnight began with a 'proper' complete mobilisation exercise; having gone through all the procedures in their TA Centres, 440 members of the Battalion travelled, mostly through dense fog, to Devizes, and then flew to Munster or Hanover, and from there they deployed straight onto the training area for two days of company training before the Exercise began. The biggest undertaking of the year, this is covered in the next Chapter – a substantial part of an extremely thoughtful article by Major Adrian Grazebrook, then commanding Headquarter Company, which was published in the *British Army Review*,[22] and which is proof, if it were needed, that some TA officers think very seriously about what they are doing; then the CO's semi-formal report, and finally comments from two Companies in *The Royal Hampshire Regiment Journal* and the *Western Wessex Newsletter*.

In 1979 there was a repeat of the 1968 national fuel crisis that severely constrained the ability to travel in military vehicles between TA Centres, and from TA Centres to training areas:

> The Battalion's allocation of fuel for the 1979/80 Training Year is 83,400 litres. In the first three months, we have already used 43,600 litres. Coy Comds and SPSIs must only permit essential journeys to take place, and are to make the maximum use of hired transport.[23]

A major part of that usage had been the getting of all the Battalion's vehicles up to Cultybraggan in Scotland for Camp in May. On the other hand, literally just a few litres sufficed for the Hampshire & Dorset Band, as they spent their single week's Camp in Portsmouth, playing for the presentation of Colours to the Second Battalion. Needless to say, of course (certainly to those who are familiar with the military 'system'), nine months later, in February and March 1980, so little fuel had been used, there was so much available that it proved quite difficult to use it all up. In 1968, the situation had been similar:

> ......the Battalion ran out of petrol (at one stage the permanent staff

were talking in terms of pints rather than gallons), but then on the 29th March some incredibly clever person in the M—y of D—e, or somewhere like that, told us that we could have 300 gallons so long as we used it between the 27th [sic] and the 31st March....[24]

– and for once the standard rule that "If you don't use your allocation this year, you can't carry the unused amount forward to next" was quite meaningless.

When the name "Territorial Army" was abandoned in favour of "Territorial & Auxiliary Volunteer Reserve" on 1st April 1967, a large proportion of the public thought that the Territorial Army had been completely abolished, and that the volunteer spirit embodied in the initials "TA" had accordingly died. Despite considerable publicity, the initials "TAVR" never became remotely as familiar to the general public as "TA" had been. Indeed, from the outset there was confusion as to what they actually stood for, and even many serving members thought that they meant "Territorial Army Volunteer Reserve". On 7th August 1979, therefore, with a view to recapturing the recognition and support of the country at large, and to the delight of almost everyone who had served in the old TA, the Ministry of Defence officially reinstated the name "Territorial Army". Moreover, appreciable efforts were made to ensure that people realised that, with its modern organisation, equipment and commitment, the country had a much better Reserve Army than before, and that the concept of a single army of Regulars and Reserves was now well established. The B Company 'scribe' for *The Royal Hampshire Regiment Journal* commented:

The TAVR is dead – long live the TA! The reorganizations of 1967 swept away many of the less satisfactory aspects of what was then considered a Reserve Army. A new purpose manifested itself amongst those units which sprang from the reorganization, and although during our short existence our role has changed several times, we now have one which is unique amongst the TA infantry battalions. We think, and we hope justifiably, that this selection reflects the regard that others have for 1 Wessex. It follows that necessarily our standards must be high, and in a way it is a pity that the decision to change from TAVR back to TA has been taken. The old TA had a reputation, deservedly or otherwise, of Saturday night amateurs, and in this battalion we have worked extremely hard to demonstrate that that image is false……..If Armageddon arrives, 1 Wessex will immediately take its operational place alongside regular units as part of the UK contribution to the NATO defence of North West Europe. Possibly our fears about the change in title are unfounded, but the main purpose was to reawaken public interest in an organization that many people outside the Services believed had ceased to exist.[25]

No doubt largely because of the lack of general public awareness of the TAVR and indeed the 'old' TA over the years since 1967, (which, it is unquestionably true to say, resulted from a serious disinclination on the part of the MOD to fund publicity properly) recruiting was gradually getting more and more difficult:

> Like the rest of the TAVR, we suffer from the general malaise of the Great British Public's disinterest in the Reserve and Regular Forces, and we are having to recruit hard just to stand still. For example, 40% of our strength are classed as Recruits, and much time and effort is being spent in basic training skills, rather than in perfecting formation training, the stage which our training cycle has reached.[26]

During 1979, a total of 147 recruits were in fact enlisted,[27] and roughly the same number terminated their TA service and left the Battalion. In many cases, soldiers did that – without the inconvenience of having to complete a lot of forms, or even the embarrassment of telling one's platoon sergeant that you had just "had soldiering" – by simply ceasing to turn up for training.[28] Over the years, usually for no obvious reasons, the Battalion's actual strength went up and down, but thankfully the 'downs' were never serious enough to affect the operational requirements. The "establishment" of every Army unit is its official strength assuming that it is fully manned, although for various reasons it was quite frequently changed – and in 1967, in the euphoria of the reorganisation and re-tasking, almost every unit of the TA (including 1 Wessex) was recruited to over 100% of its establishment. In due course the numbers dropped, but the strength of the Battalion does not seem ever to have been less than 75%. The 'lean years' were the 1970s – and, for example, over the eighteen-month period from

December 1977 to July 1979, the strength of the Battalion slipped from being approximately 100 short of its then establishment of 37 officers and 695 other ranks (87%) to around 150 below it (80%). In the same context, after the initial 10 years or so of the Battalion's existence, for the first time the turnover (or 'coming and going') of officers began to increase quite substantially, and – although the number 'on strength' remained virtually constant – by 1980 only four of those who went to the first Camp at Stanford were still serving in it.

Several Battalion exercises took place in 1979, and the most important of these was undoubtedly Exercise Tango Test, an FTX on Salisbury Plain at the end of October, the purpose of which was to practice working with tanks. The Queen's Royal Irish Hussars at Tidworth kindly provided a squadron of them, and the first phase was an advance to contact, with Imber Village as the final objective. This was taken and held overnight. The second phase was to withdraw to a new defensive position, involving two Bridge Demolition Guards. The move was completed in six Sikorsky helicopters from the German Army, specially flown over for the exercise. Once in its new positions, the Battalion assisted the withdrawal of the tanks, before blowing the bridges – simulated with some devastating explosions provided by RMonRE.

The annual Fit for Role inspection went off very well – during the visits to the TA Centres by the GOC's minions, no 'brew-up' kit was found concealed in a piano, and no broom cupboard was opened to reveal a dead-drunk cook stuffed in by the PSI in a last-minute panic, as once actually happened in one of the pre-1967 Wessex TA battalions[29] – and the comments of General Acland in the Report were:

1. I am pleased to see that the Battalion is fit for its role, and congratulate those concerned on the successes achieved in a number of fields during the year.
2. I emphasize that:
    (a) There is a continuing need for closer attention to the rules on pay and accounting;
    (b) Every effort should be made to improve Personal Weapon Test results.
3. These two matters apart, the inspection discloses a very satisfactory

state of affairs, and I am particularly pleased by the energy and enthusiasm with which training is planned, and by the willing assistance given to CCF and ACF units.

The last important events of 1979 – which had been an amazingly busy year – were the formal opening of the two TA Centres mentioned above. In November, The Lord Lieutenant of Hampshire, Colonel The Earl of Malmesbury, performed the ceremony at a refurbished building for the much-moved Mortar Platoon (which had originally been B Company's Mortar Detachment) on the former RAF airfield at Andover, and in December the new Lord Lieutenant of Devon, Field Marshal Sir Richard Hull, did the same for the big, brand-new one in Plymouth. There, all three units involved provided demonstrations of some of their skills:

> One of the participants on 211 Field Hospital's stand was a very new recruit, who had not yet been issued with his kit – so he was put to bed as a casualty, with only his head visible outside the sheets. Luckily the Field Marshal did not ask to see his wounds......[30]

This is an appropriate point at which to pay a warm tribute to the Lords Lieutenant of all the counties in which, from time to time, the Battalion had Companies. In rotation, they each acted for a year as the President of whichever of Western Wessex or Eastern Wessex TAVRA 'their' counties came under, and, although in that role they were naturally more involved than the other Lords Lieutenant, without exception, and year after year, every one of them maintained a real interest in the doings of all the TA units in their respective counties. With their military backgrounds (universal in those days), they were able to offer wise advice to the CO and Company Commanders, and with their warm personalities and genuine feelings for people, they would talk, without the slightest difficulty, to anyone – be they a brand-new recruit, the TA Centre caretaker, or a Company Commander. Knowledgeably interested in what was happening in the Battalion, they were always welcome visitors. Particularly memorable were the brothers Colonel 'Tim' Gibbs in Gloucestershire and Field Marshal Sir 'Rowley' Gibbs in Wiltshire, The Earl of Morley in Devon, Colonel Walter Luttrell in Somerset, and somewhat later Lieutenant

General Sir Maurice Johnston in Wiltshire and Henry Elwes, Esq., in Gloucestershire.

Lord Lieutenant's Certificates were the honours given at County level to members of the Reserve Forces and Cadets (in the case of the TA normally NCOs and other ranks, but very occasionally officers) for long and exceptional service:

> Our sincere congratulations are extended to Corporal John Gorman of 1 Platoon on his well deserved award of the Lord Lieutenant's Certificate.......it recognises the quiet distinction with which he has served us since 1976. He personifies all that is best in the Volunteer soldier with a devotion to duty second to none. He is a splendid NCO who thoroughly deserved this fine award. We were also delighted that his wife, Margaret, was able to be with him when the presentation was made at the Cirencester home of Her Majesty's Lord Lieutenant for the County of Gloucester. Well done indeed.[31]

1980 was the year of Exercise Crusader 80 – the biggest post-war exercise for the entire Army and much of the Royal Air Force, both Regular and Volunteer, intended "to demonstrate our national ability to reinforce NATO's Central Region, and to fight in conjunction with our Allies on the ground and in the air to defeat any aggression towards the Alliance."[32] Taking place in the UK and Germany, it entailed a quite astonishing amount of detailed organisation and hard training. Indeed, it appears to have taken up so much that the Company Notes in the various regimental Journals said virtually nothing about any other activities between January and September! For the NATO units, "Crusader" was made up of three separate Exercises – Square Leg (mobilization), Jog Trot (the road journey to Germany) and Spearpoint (the 1 British Corps field training exercise).

Exercise Spearpoint was the largest exercise carried out by the Corps for many years – and the Corps Commander, Lieutenant General Sir Peter Leng KCB, MBE, MC had under him 94,000 troops, with 880 main battle tanks and over 350 helicopters. The cast included three full British Armoured Divisions with supporting troops, reinforced by 7 Field Force (of which the Battalion at that time formed part) and 30 Engineer Group (Volunteers); the American Texas-based

2nd ("Hell on Wheels") Armoured Division, and the 3rd German Panzer Brigade. Finally, there were four companies of German reserve soldiers, while in the air the Belgian, British, German, Netherlands and United States air forces all took part. The enemy at its greatest strength was two full armoured divisions, another German Panzer Brigade, a "disruption Brigade", consisting of the Headquarters 2nd (United States) Airborne Brigade with, under command, a British and an American Parachute Battalion, and two British and one American air-mobile infantry battalions, and finally a "diversionary Brigade" consisting of British and American Special Forces and "locally raised partisans".

Looking forward to the fortnight, the A Company notes in *The Back Badge* for the summer of 1980 provided a thoughtful over-view:

> Every BAOR Camp is a showcase for the part-time army – the effectiveness of Territorial Army battalions on the ground is being assessed. They are working with Regular units, and are bound to be compared with them. The build-up to a German Camp tends to dictate the progress of TA training and organisation. Technically, training in the TA should follow a three-year cycle. The first year is devoted to individual training, the second year to section and platoon tactics and the third year to combat team and battle group tactics. A German Camp, however, demands a different set of priorities. Participants in a divisional exercise cannot retire for an afternoon because a combat team attack is not in this year's training cycle.
>
> Training in the UK is the bread and butter of the Battalion's life, but the visit to Germany provides a landmark in that existence – the sole reason for recruiting, training and motivating the Volunteers. It is a veiled glimpse of 'the real thing' – the awful prospect for the Territorial Army exists. Since 1945, there have been various limited overseas conflicts, and political and industrial unrest at home, but the TA has not – since 1956 – been employed in any of these. It will be employed in grave national emergency, or not at all. It may be assumed for a NATO committed battalion that, if ever required in operations, they are likely to take the form of a large-scale war in Europe. Thus the exercises in Germany are a dress rehearsal for operations in earnest in a way which internal security training in Imber[33] (for example) could never be. For these reasons, the build-up – the gathering of

momentum for the fortnight's visit to Germany – extends over a year or so. Germany provides the focal point for training and recruiting efforts. During the intervening years it is convenient to send people on courses and attachments, and to have a taste of adventure training and sport – but only a taste, as the Volunteer's training time is very limited. There is particularly little time for any of that in 1 Wessex in 1980. Recruiting must take place to fill the gaps in the order of battle; the new recruits must be enlisted in time to be adequately trained before the exercise. The training emphasis is placed upon the Battalion's BAOR role, and the types of task likely to be encountered in a BAOR operation.

Members of the TA are in it because they enjoy it. They like the training, they like the companionship, and they feel they are doing something worthwhile. A divisional exercise in BAOR cannot be guaranteed to provide the genuine daily training pleasure which a TA private soldier seeks, but each individual will make any effort he can to be there, for it is widely recognised that if UK training can be fun, the German Camp is what the commitment is all about.

In 1980 the preparation and planning has been going well. The paper strength of A Company and the Anti-tank Platoon is now only a dozen or so short of establishment. Already, however, it can be seen that about 15 individuals are, for perfectly valid reasons – job moves, family commitments, increasing years – no longer active members, and recruitment has to go on all the time to keep the strength and effectiveness up. Just as in the Regular Army, a lot of the recruits are under 20 and we have a young Company. It is a far cry from the old Territorial Army days when more of the training took place in the bar than in the field. What we do welcome is a leavening of experienced people with a background of regular or volunteer service elsewhere to balance and guide the enthusiasm of the young soldiers. Weekend training over the last six months has been very much directed towards the BAOR role. No single event has been remarkable, but all the training has been progressive and worthwhile. The writer cannot recall seeing the contents of water bottles frozen solid in the UK before, as they were on one Saturday night in January, but no doubt that is a regular event elsewhere.[34]

The B Company notes[35] reported the practical preparations:
Spring sprang hopeful in the Company's collective heart, and Company

Headquarters took to the field in April for a Battalion CPX. This was followed in May by a defence exercise on Salisbury Plain which also incorporated heliborne assaults from Wessex helicopters......The final part of the exercise consisted of a night move to Crossing A,[36] where a reserve demolition was established. At dawn, A Company attacked out of the sun and finished the exercise. This was the first of many demolition guards carried out by the Company during the summer. Along with the rest of the world (or so it seems) we are destined for Exercise Crusader 80 and, it is thought, a bridge somewhere in Germany. With this in mind the Company has exercised – to be more accurate, dug holes – over most of Salisbury Plain, and at Longmoor where the ground is far softer. At least once a month the same ritual has been practised; that is almost every training weekend. The only major exception was a very damp and soggy weekend field firing at Sennybridge. Crossing C, rather like Christmas, normally comes but once a year, but in 1980 it seems to have been every other week. [In July] the Company was given this favourite crossing over the Avon to defend against all comers. Tanks from the Queens Royal Irish Hussars helped the Company fend off attacks from 2 Wessex, descending from the skies by helicopter; sappers from the Royal Monmouthshire Royal Engineers disturbed the peace with loud bangs when they blew trenches – usually long after they were needed; OPs [observation posts] lurked on every hill, often in out-of-bounds areas; and enemy frogmen floated down the Avon, alarming moorhens, trout and our sentries. At one stage the tanks were not too sure whose side they were on when they rolled unconcernedly across our 'minefield'; and why is it that 2 Wessex can get helicopters that actually land and take off rather than ring up and say the weather is too bad? By September, guarding bridges will have become second nature. The Company is full of confidence that it can deal with all manner of Orange forces appearing from whatever direction in whatever national garb. Everyone is looking forward to Crusader (with the exception of an anonymous junior NCO from the Island who has an aversion to compo [tinned food]), and it is satisfying that a TA battalion like 1 Wessex has been given such particular tasks within the plan. Never before has the TA been in the field in the same place in such numbers, so the Company will be very much on its mettle. And even if it rains, the digging will not be through solid chalk.

———————

Full reports of Exercise Crusader '80 are in Chapter 7.

Despite the huge amount of time and energy taken up by the preparations for Crusader, many other excellent things happened during the year. Recruiting improved and wastage was reduced; in the tough and challenging District Inter-Section Competition in May, three of the Battalion's teams came 2nd, 3rd and 4th, only just being beaten by a strong one from Bristol University OTC. Then there was a second visit to the BGTT at Bovington – with "model troops and tanks", and tape-recorded explosions and noises of tanks, guns and aircraft helping to create realism – that proved testing and instructive for the Battalion and Company Command Posts.[37] Finally, shooting went from strength to strength. First, C Company re-found its previous form and virtually swept the board at the South West District Small Arms Meeting, and then the Battalion team surpassed itself in the TASAAM at Bisley – winning the supreme accolade of the Dragon Trophy for the Major Unit Championship, as well as the Volongdis Cup (Light Machine Gun), the Daily Telegraph Cup and the Mullens Trophy (both for rifle sections), and, for the second time, the Wessex Volunteers Cup (Fire-and-movement Section competition), presented to the TA Rifle Association by the Battalion in 1968. That meant that in just over a year, the Battalion had won all the major TA shooting competitions at Bisley.

Over the next few years, however, more and more cups and prizes, both at District Meetings and at Bisley, went to units whose training obligations and war roles enabled them to spend considerably more time practising than front line units could. From 1982 onwards, 1 Wessex's war role required appreciably more training time to be devoted to major exercises with the Regular Army than was the case even for many other NATO battalions – and after its successes in those years, the additional work-load imposed by the reorganisations that are the subject of Chapters 8 and 10 gradually reduced its ability to produce really good Bisley teams, and it was sadly unable to take any further part in TASAAM after 1990. Nevertheless, for the moment, the successes of 1979 and 1980 were followed by more in 1982, 1984 and 1985 – the five *anni mirabili* of competition shooting for the Battalion – and full details can be found in Appendix 5.

Early in December 1980 the Battalion RC Padre, Father Eddie

Peach, hit the national headlines in a totally un-military context:

The Frightened Priest….and the strange things that went bump in the night

Sound in the night so terrified Catholic priest Father Edward Peach that he thought the Devil himself was outside his door. He was woken by monstrous deep breathing, scuffling and thumping, he told a Court yesterday.

It was 3 am when the strange noise disturbed the young priest in his presbytery room. "I thought it was a monster of some kind. It was a devilish sound" he said. "I do not have a very vivid imagination, but at that time of the morning, awaking from a deep sleep, I thought it was something to do with the devil. I picked up a walking stick to defend myself and I went to the door".

On the landing he saw the cause of the commotion. It was Miss Maria Cavarra, housekeeper at the Presbytery in Bridgewater, Somerset, a County Court Judge was told. The well-built woman was rushing along the corridor and throwing herself against the bedroom door of parish priest Father John McReynolds. Father Peach, who is a curate, told Bridgewater County Court: "She was kicking Father McReynolds's door and she was saying that he had a woman in his room. She said that if he didn't open the door, she would go in and drag the woman out. It was just like something you might see on television. She was behaving like a jealous wife".

Miss Cavarra was sacked because of the rumpus, said Father Peach.

Yesterday she sued Father McReynolds for £250 damages for clothes, books and other possessions which she claimed had become unusable or lost while stored at the presbytery when she left. Father McReynolds said "Miss Cavarra was dismissed for making the rumpus outside my room. The door still hangs in splinters for anyone to see. She had become convinced that there was a lady in my room". Cross-examined by Mr Nigel Long for Miss Caverra, Father McReynolds denied that there had been a woman in his room several nights that week.

Dismissing Miss Cavarra's claim, and awarding costs against her, the Judge said she had been unwise to cause the disturbance which led to her dismissal.[38]

Finally, to round off the year there was a 'first ever' for the Battalion,

the CSM of A Company, WO2 Robin Heatley, was commissioned
into the Regiment. Having previously been a member of the 5th
Glosters, he joined the Battalion on its 'Day One' as a Corporal in
the Mortar Platoon; he became the Battalion's Master Shooting
Coach, and after his commissioning he continued to serve in it until
1991 – by which time he had become Major Heatley commanding
Headquarter Company.

---

1   *RHRJ*, November 1980.
2   Anon.
3   From then on, numbers continued to drop across the entire TA. In May 1977, the
     Battalion's strength was 33+610 (730 all ranks); by March 1978 32+593 and by June
     1979 31+545. There are no extant records after that.
4   *D&DRJ*, December 1974.
5   *RHRJ*, November 1975.
6   Because on mobilization it provided a battalion with its stretcher bearers.
7   *DERRJ*, Autumn 1977.
8   Clive Aslet: *Landmarks of Britain* (Hodder & Stoughton, 2005 pp.290–291).
9   *BB*, Winter 1977.
10   Produced by Pye Records (PKDN 2002).
11   Article by the author in *BB*, Winter 1977.
12   *BB*, Summer 1978.
13   Part I Orders 12 December 1977.
14   *RHRJ*, May 1978.
15   *Ibid.*
16   Although, as mentioned above, C Company was awarded the Liberty of Bridport in
     1976.
17   *RHRJ*, November 1978.
18   *BB*, Winter 1978.
19   Framed tents.
20   Western Wessex TAVRA *Newsletter No 11*, 1979.
21   I.e. with unloaded weapons.
22   No. 62, in August 1979.
23   Part I Orders, 19 July 1979.
24   *BB*, Summer 1968.
25   *RHRJ*, May 1980.
26   *Ibid.*, November 1978.
27   When the TAVR was first established in 1967, it was possible to enlist for 2, 3 or 4
     years, but as from 1 October1979 that could only be done for 3 years.
28   The subsequent task of recovering uniforms and equipment from those who simply
     walked-out, or writing off the cost of irrecoverable items, was one the worst aspects of

being a Company Colour Sergeant (CQMS).

29 Not surprisingly, the incident was not reported in the Regiment's Journal, but the author heard of it at first hand.

30 *The TAVR Magazine*, December 1979.

31 *BB*, Winter 1985.

32 1 British Corps information card sent on 15 September, possibly to all participants.

33 A village on Salisbury Plain, originally taken over by the Army at the start of World War II, and used for a wide variety of training.

34 *BB*, Summer 1980.

35 *RHRJ*, November 1980.

36 Crossings A, B & C were, in 'military-speak' three Bailey bridges across River Avon near Netheravon.

37 Western Wessex TAVRA Newsletter No 12, 1980 – where "models" was, it is presumed inadvertently and with no intention of referring to the participants, printed as "nodels".

38 *The Daily Mail, 9 December 1980.*

———————

CHAPTER 7

ANNUAL CAMPS: 1974–1980

*"The week-end manoeuvres were many and varied, but
space and decorum forbid their publication here."*[1]

1974	Stanford PTA
1975	BAOR – Haltern All Arms Training Area
1976	A Company: BAOR – Reinsahlen; remainder: Cultybraggan, Perthshire
1977	Stanford PTA
1978	BAOR – Osnabruck, Münster and Hartz Mountains
1979	Cultybraggan
1980	BAOR – Exercise Crusader 80

1974

The whole Battalion – East Wretham Camp, Stanford Training Area (6–21 July)

Luckily, the weather remained fairly favourable throughout the fortnight. Cadre training occupied the first ten days, and although that meant that all the Companies were split up, it was generally agreed to have been extremely well run.

Our last Notes should have left the reader waiting with bated breath for news of the Company's 1974 Annual Camp. It was not intended, however, that the breath should be held bated for quite so long, and apologies are due and given for the non-appearance of these notes in the previous issue of *The Back Badge*. The area provides excellent infantry training ground, not least because it is virtually flat. Frog Hill, the only feature of any height, is thus an ideal reference point and, indeed, the majority of exercises used this wooded knoll at one time or another for starting, finishing, resting, replenishing, recce-ing, order--grouping, marching to, marching from or returning to if lost. Although a Battalion Camp, the work in the initial ten days was performed in cadres and thus the Company was split up. With the exception of the Wombat, all the Company weapons were fired on the various ranges, and there was no shortage of ordnance. The ranges are a major feature of Stanford PTA, and their wide variety enabled most people to improve their marksmanship under realistic conditions, and to improve their knowledge of, and gain experience on, the less usually used of our weapons.[2]

The last three days were taken up by an arduous and exciting three-day inter-Company competition, Exercise Final Furlong:

A Company entered four teams. The event was a competitive one and the various serials were, with the exception of the shooting, run on a timed basis. The first day started with a short assault course, and teams moved quickly on to an orienteering course which had to be covered with accuracy and alacrity to stay in the running. A move to the ever-present Frog Hill provided a rest and food before the start of a night march. Those teams which started sufficiently late, or which started early and suffered 'navigational errors', earned the bonus of being able to pick early morning mushrooms of varied toxic content for breakfast.

After the night march and another rest, there was a forced march to a river crossing. Unfortunately, some of the A Company teams suffered from the fact that the effects of inflation had not reached their assault boat and crossing times suffered as a result. Other teams devised ingenious and sometimes successful methods of completing the course. Following the river crossing, there was a short shoot on a range, after which the weary brethren returned to Camp. The next morning another forced march took place, ending at the 'Final Furlong'. This was a 220-yard assault course with a variety of obstacles, and which thoroughly tested the strength and determination of all who took part.

In the final analysis, although 'A' Company did not win any of the prizes, they did extremely well in the marching and shooting events, and were the only Company to end with four complete teams, a result which spoke well for the enthusiasm and 'togetherness' of those who took part.[3]

To the surprise of everyone, including themselves, the winners were HQ Company. Another report, somewhat aggressive in its third sentence, came from B Company:

> ....Not so well managed was the first day of Annual Camp, when the Battalion had to report to East Wretham Camp at Thetford half-way through the second half of the World Cup Final. Those of the Company who hadn't disappeared on courses or were at Bisley went to Sunny Stanford, where the emphasis was on cadre training. Once again it amply demonstrated that B Company is way ahead. Placed alongside soldiers from other Companies, individuals always stood out in appearance, bearing, individual skills and youth. Cadres were dispersed to Companies during the second week of Camp for Exercise Final Furlong, "planned by our old master and past-master of fiendish feats of physical discomfort".[4] This was an inter--section competition designed to test navigational skills and endurance over two days. Despite the competition being supposedly inter-sectional, few teams were commanded by junior NCOs, and the majority were officer-led – with one, even though it may be churlish to say so, being blatantly gladiatorial. All credit must therefore go to Corporal Knight and his merry band from the oft-discredited and mocked wheeled cavalry unit from Basingstoke[5]. Unable to emulate our previous successes on Wessex Marches, they saved the Company's honour by coming third, We are able to show our readers another historic photograph of 'Private-Major' Fifield at the top of the 12-foot wall, with the nether face of another most senior individual, two members of a team full of high-ranking 'privates' that nearly carried off the Training Major's Prize.[6]

1975

The whole Battalion – BAOR: Haltern All Arms Training Area (31 May–14 June)

> "......the camp site where we spent the fortnight did not appear in the AA Continental Touring Guide....."[7]

—————

"The announcement at Annual Camp at Stanford last year that the Battalion was to go to Cyprus in 1975 was the signal for the Turkish Invasion of the Island. Needless to say, we are no longer bound for cheap sun-tans there this year!"[8]

"Few, perhaps, will have had the experience of the Company Commander, who approached the German/Dutch border post from the German side at the head, as he thought, of a convoy of some 30 vehicles – only to find the back half of his convoy approaching the same border post from the Dutch side at the same moment"[9]

—————

For the first time, the Battalion travelled as a complete unit to an overseas Camp – at Haltern All Arms Training Centre, south of Münster. The move out was accomplished in four parties, air advance, air main, vehicle advance and vehicle main. The air advance party, consisting of the command element, flew from Luton, while the main body moved through movement control at South Cerney and flew from Brize Norton to Düsseldorf. At one stage air main was routed to Hanover, and the switch to Düsseldorf happily shortened the flight by that well-known aircraft, the 4-tonner. Both vehicle parties took the same route, on different days. After company packets married up at Dover, Townsend Thoresen delivered the convoys safely to Zeebrugge. All credit is due to the drivers who made both trips without a single accident.

We owe a debt of gratitude to the 2nd Royal Tank Regiment, who provided the muscle to erect the majority of the tentage required to house the Battalion on a small camp site at Lavesum. The site is intended for use by company groups, so our presence tended to stretch the local resources somewhat. It was a welcome change after the backwoods of Soltau on previous trips to find running water and, to a limited extent, electricity. The field firing ranges did not offer much, but by dint of hard work and enterprise the Permanent Staff created some interesting and enjoyable practices. The Company spent the first two days on the ranges, a disadvantage of which was the time that it took to post and recover sentries and hoist innumerable flags. During this time the weather was not on our side, and some of the training value was lost. Fortunately, however, it changed very much for the better for the Company's excursion into the woods on a two-day map reading and navigation exercise from a bivouac site. In fact, the weather held good for the remainder of our stay, and it was very different returning to the field firing range after the exercise – and so dry that we set it alight.

The Friday was taken up by a visit to Münster, where 4 Guards Armoured Brigade laid on a most impressive display of all their hardware, and that rounded off the first week; on Saturday morning the Battalion dispersed to all parts of the earth – Münster, Dortmund, Düsseldorf and Amsterdam. Surprising though it may seem, no one was found absent on the following Monday, when the Company went out on a 24-hour exercise in the Advance to Contact phase against a defending force from A Company. Having cleared the axis, the Company took up a defensive position and managed to put out as many defence stores as the opposing force did in two days. The inevitable dawn attack went in, supported by a troop of real tanks from 2 RTR, and in the end honours were about even.

The helicopter exercise was cut short, and we had to be content with a morning's familiarisation with them instead of being able to use them tactically. The UEO [Unit Emplaning Officer] is still protesting his innocence in arranging for part of the Company to be the last chalk back to the LZ [Landing Zone], to rope down in the presence of the Commander of 4 Guards Armoured Brigade – the chalk leader being 29 (years old)! A sports afternoon was arranged, and the Company trooped out to the local swimming baths, which afforded excellent facilities. The insistence that everyone wore a bathing hat caused some interesting combinations of dress, as those at the end of the line ended up with the pretty flowered ones. The afternoon gave everyone a chance to be among the local population, and very pleasing on the eye they were too. 1 Irish Guards, our sponsor unit, who looked after us exceedingly well, sent down a platoon of 432s [armoured troop-carrying vehicles], and the Company took its turn with familiarization with the vehicles and had an opportunity to use them for a short mechanized attack. The vehicles may save the laborious business of getting from A to B, but on a scorching hot day they are really a mixed blessing. All too soon for some, it was time to see the vehicle parties away to the UK, and the last Friday was taken up with administrative chores to unwind the camp site and prepare for the Quartermaster's nightmare, handing it back; and so, clutching duty-free booty, the Battalion deplaned in Brize Norton and dispersed from there.

It is interesting for some members of the Company, for whom this was the fourth excursion to BAOR since formation, to compare what was achieved on previous visits, and it is certainly true to say that the higher the formation the more Parkinson's Law applies. Nevertheless Camp was interesting and enjoyable and those that went will remember it with pleasure.[10]

The Battalion arrived at 0130 hrs on a very cold and wet Sunday morning, and each man was passed a sleeping bag and a torch, and sent packing to his tent......During the weekend....the local brews were sampled and found fit for human consumption.[11]

A NATO battalion doing its Camp in BAOR always attracted a good number of senior visitors, anxious to see whether their protection in the event of war was in good hands – and this year they included Lieutenant General Sir Jack Harman, the Commander of 1 (BR) Corps; Brigadier Dick Randall, the Deputy Commander of South West District; and Brigadier Michael Hicks, the Deputy Commander of 4 Guards Brigade, as well as the Director of Volunteers, Territorials & Cadets, Major General Peter Shapland and others. The Press Relations Officer at South West District, Peter Clare, and a reporter from *The Wiltshire Times* also came for a few days, and their reports were of good recruiting value.

1976

A Coy – BAOR: Reinsahlen (near Bremerhaven) (4–18 September)

For the first time since 1970, when it became the Battalion's Stratco Company, in September A Company went – 118 all ranks strong (including a few from other Companies, but less a number of A Company recruits who went with the rest of the Battalion to Cultybraggan) – to be the fourth rifle company of its new 'parent battalion', the 1st Bn The Worcestershire and Foresters Regiment [WFR], for 19 Airportable Brigade's Exercise Clam Fury. The first week was spent exercising with the "Woofers", as a work up to the second week's very impressive Exercise:

After a brief stay in Reinsahlen, the Company moved to a wood north of Bremerhaven for the first week. Various aspects of training were carried out, including vehicle anti-ambush drill, an extremely active patrolling exercise, minefield laying, an attack on a demolition guard, and a demolition guard itself. The main lesson learned, however, was "how to live in the field" for a much longer period than the average weekend. Administration for the week, three hours drive from the base camp, brought many problems, and usually the way to solve them! Inclement weather and ill-timed downpours were at times disheartening, but the presence of a local gasthof enabled the Company to get wet inside as well as out.

Return to Reinsahlen allowed time for helicopter and tank familiarisation, and the usual administration, to take place before the second week. Time was also found for a trip to Hamburg for the many soldiers who wished to visit the famous Art Galleries and Museums – at least that is what they said!

The second week began with a night move taking more than three hours, to an area south west of Hanover. The Company was to be the Battalion Reserve for 1 WFR, who were the Route Activation Party for the Brigade. A night spent in a hide saw one quick counter attack and then a move into the Company position. Digging of fire and shelter trenches was achieved with varying degrees of ease, depending on whether the platoon area was near the railway, the graveyard or in a turnip field.

The week-long Brigade exercise was the largest in scale that most members of the Company will have experienced, and the sight of an American Airborne battalion being lifted by helicopters, the manoeuvring of a regiment of tanks, and a complete APC battalion provided a valuable view of our likely role. It also provided excellent opportunities to practice, on a grand scale, all the aspects of the training which we practice during the year in the confines of our Drill

Halls and (usually) on Salisbury Plain.   [It was] a hard and successful Camp, and all who took part can derive a great deal of satisfaction from their performance.[12]

———————

Remainder – Cultybraggan & Barrybudden Ranges (between Dundee & Carnoustie) (5–19 June)

"The camp was originally purpose-built to contain prisoners of war; present-day occupants enjoy the place no more than the previous residents did."[13]

"A fortnight in Scotland taught us that the water shortage problem is entirely regional."

"Constantly wet underfoot, this Exercise sorted out the chain smokers! However, the mountain scenery was breathtaking (a pun!)."

———————

Cultybraggan was new to the whole of the rest of the Battalion, and particularly good for adventurous training, with climbing, abseiling and canoeing on Loch Earn. There was much of that, to avoid the risk of tedium in what was otherwise very much a 'the-mixture-as-before' Camp, with the rest of the fortnight devoted to individual training, and low-level platoon and company tactics. The two Support Platoons did, however, escape to Otterburn for a week's live firing with, by curious chance, 3 WFR – the TA battalion of 1 WFR for which A Company provided its additional Stratco company. Members of 27 Army Youth Team from Devizes provided excellent instructors for the adventurous training, and 7 Regiment, Army Air Corps lent a Gazelle helicopter (with, sadly for a few 'wanna-be' pilots, someone to drive it) for virtually the entire fortnight – all most welcome. 85 soldiers who had all joined within the previous 12 months successfully completed a Recruits Cadre; that was around 13% of the Battalion's strength, and indicates the extent of the perpetual 'turnover problem'.

From now on, the entire Battalion went to Camp together every year, and individual Companies no longer did so on their own.

—————

1977

The whole Battalion – Stanford PTA (25 June–9 July)

"......a delightful training area......"[14]

—————

A major Battalion exercise made very good use of four German helicopters, as well as Scouts and Alouettes from 665 Squadron AAC, and FGA [Fighter Ground Attack] support was provided by several Phantoms – and a Canberra which, it was said, had to finish its sorties photographing us from above by ten o'clock in the mornings, as the military museum where it 'lived' opened at half past ten. A Company's GPMGs in the sustained fire role, covered a night flanking move by the rest of the Battalion, using live ammunition; for most of the platoon, it was their first experience of live firing other than on a range, and it is a tribute to the high standard of training that the Battalion was not decimated.[15]

—————

The popular cry after it was all over was "Brill". It is never easy for the Volunteer Army to make the change from civilian to soldier, and so leaving the comfort of a hutted camp to set off into the woods on the first morning, without a day to shake down, came as rather a rude shock, especially as it was forbidden to return to Camp to collect anything that had been left behind. The first three days were spent on a Company exercise run at that level, practising all phases of war, and including "character-building" elements such as lack of sleep, hunger and the inevitable sore feet. The return to the amenities of the camp was therefore most welcome. The following three days were spent on range work, enjoying what are now excellent facilities for live firing, and much valuable benefit was derived from the modern ranges and the most helpful attitude of the range staff. After a morning of sporting activity on the Saturday, the Camp emptied, as everyone headed for the fleshpots of East Anglia – the Officers' and Sergeants' Messes to dry out after a combined Dinner Night. The Monday morning of the second week dawned bright and early with the Commanding Officer's O Group at 0730, starting a four-day Battalion exercise during which all phases of war were practised. In essence it involved moving anti-clockwise round the whole of the outer parts of the training area. During the course of the exercise considerable quantities of Norfolk soil were moved, helicopter support was provided by 101 Kondor Battalion of the German Army, and fighter-ground attack by the RAF, although in the final Battalion attack they gave the impression that they were taking part in another exercise. 1 Staffords [1st Bn The Staffordshire Regiment] provided the bangs and the Guards Depot some enemy. A feature that not many of the Company will see again was live firing by GPMG (SF) and mortars by day and night during the course of the exercise, as part of a fire plan. Even so, some members of the Company remained singularly unimpressed, commenting that all it did was prevent them from sleeping!

Having steadfastly refused to take recruits, our decision was entirely vindicated by the sight of recruits with other Companies falling by the wayside during what was a tiring and strenuous, though highly rewarding and worthwhile exercise. Needless to say, sufficient reserves of energy were found to celebrate at a Company Party, wash away the scars of war, and swap lies over the triumphs of the previous few days. A very happy and high-spirited Company returned to Camp in very high order.

Although the phrase was sometimes used in jest, in all seriousness it does sum up the Camp – "Good 'ere – in'nit?!"[16]

1978

The Hartz Mountains, Münster and Osnabrück, BAOR – 4 Armoured Division's Exercise Full House (13–29 October)

"......and for eleven days occupied either draughty barns or holes in the ground...."

The unusually large number of articles and reports about this late October visit to BAOR – the first time that the whole Battalion had taken part in a major exercise there – confirms that it performed very creditably, and that (no doubt at least partly on that account) by and large it was regarded by all ranks as one of the best ever.

4 Armoured Division's, and a Danish Armoured Regiment's, Exercise Full House was a series of exercises on the foothills of the Hartz Mountains, barely 30 miles from the East German border, designed to test various aspects of the Division's training. It was in fact becoming evident that HQ UKLF and the Divisional planners did not really appreciate the practicalities of getting the NATO battalions to the battlefield in BAOR (or wherever else they might be needed) with all their equipment, and ready to fight – on which subject, in his acutely perceptive article in the *British Army Review*[17] Adrian Grazebrook wrote:

> The 1st Battalion The Wessex Regiment (Rifle Volunteers) is a non-mechanised infantry battalion. It forms part of Fourth Armoured Division, and is as much an integral part of the Divisional battle plan as are the regular units based in BAOR. It cannot be regarded as a reserve battalion which might turn up, or might not; for the number of regular battalions allotted to the BAOR divisions is not sufficient to free TAVR battalions like 1 Wessex from a specific role in the Divisional deployment.
>
> If these battalions are to perform the tasks allotted to them by their divisions then:
> (a)   They must be able to reach the battlefield before those tasks have gone by default;
> (b)   Equipment and training must be of a standard which will enable them to be effective in the performance of their role.
>
> They go to BAOR for their annual fortnight's camp one year in three (soon to be one year in two). This year, 1 Wessex took part in the 4 Armoured Division exercise, named Full House, which ran through the second half of October.
>
> Full House did not take the form of a single Field Training Exercise but rather of a series of exercises and training phases, each designed to train or test one part or another of the Division. Thus, during its

fortnight's training, 1 Wessex began with a mobilisation exercise; then, for a day, provided the men to enable other units to practice their procedures for receiving war reinforcements; then spent five days of Combat Team and Battle Group training within the Battalion (with the aid of D Squadron The Queen's Own Hussars and supporting arms), and finally took part in Exercise Rock Steady as part of Task Force Hotel (H) in a two-sided exercise, controlled by Divisional Headquarters. This lasted some four days, though part of that time was spent by the soldiers in a concentration area, as the battle unfolded.

None of the phases of training was of particularly long duration, but the purpose of the Battalion's visit to Germany must principally have been to consider what it could put into the field in a time of emergency, and to assess how it would perform as part of a Task Force. We took four hundred and forty officers and soldiers, including attached personnel; we have our own doctor, padre and paymaster. The Battalion was reorganized into three rifle companies of three platoons each, a 120mm anti-tank platoon and an 81mm mortar platoon.

Mobilisation notices were sent to all Volunteers some days before camp began (Friday 13 October – not an auspicious day on which to start a war); the main party, travelling by air, assembled at their widely dispersed local drill halls (fourteen in all) after work on that Friday afternoon. Chartered buses brought everyone to a central mobilization point, so that by the Saturday morning the battalion was assembled. It is impossible for any Volunteer unit to predict with absolute certainty exactly which Volunteers will arrive on the ground on the day, so the rest of the night was spent updating the previously prepared air-loading manifests and passing the medical, pay and documentation teams. By dawn the administration was complete, and the first party was on its way to the departure airfield.

The result of this rather dryly catalogued chain of events was that the main body arrived, in the case of the early flights, at German airfields in well under 24 hours after the individual soldiers had reported at the drill halls, despite the adverse weather. In terms of real emergency, however, there would be a vastly increased demand for flying time. In addition to the Volunteer battalions, there would be home-based Regular battalions and stores to fly out, and, presumably, families to be brought home.

In any event, it may well be unrealistic to expect a battalion of Volunteer soldiers to arrive on the ground within a day or so following the actual mobilisation. How soon they will get there, following the need for mobilisation, will depend as much as anything upon the timing of the political decision to call out the TAVR. If a battalion such as 1 Wessex is to arrive in reasonable strength and order, this decision is likely to be necessary at least a couple of days before the actual mobilization begins, to ensure that every Volunteer receives notice of it, and has sufficient chance to organize his affairs at home and work to enable him to go to war with confidence.

1 Wessex's move was not confined, however, to an air party. The whole of the Battalion transport – over 60 vehicles – came by road and sea, with drivers and co-drivers accounting for about one-third of the Battalion strength. This party had to move two full days before the main body left the ground, in order to arrive at Hanover at much the same time. As is customary, civilian car ferries were used to get them across the channel.

The tactical capability of the Battalion would naturally be severely limited by the absence of its vehicles, and it is presumed that in a 'real scenario' not only the troops but also all the vehicles, stores and equipment will have to be transported by air to enable the Battalion to be effective at or shortly after the time of arrival of the main body. There are, however, probably few TAVR Infantry units which have worthwhile experience of preparing and loading vehicles for air travel[18], and it can be foreseen that in the event of an emergency mobilization the assembly and preparation of the vehicles and equipment for the journey will take at least as long as the gathering of the soldiers. Unless stores and vehicles have been largely pre-packed (thus rendering them useless for training), much of the work could not be carried out until after the soldiers have arrived to do it, and the time taken to get the Battalion to Germany would be correspondingly increased.

The third choice, a road party via the channel ferries, hardly seems practical in time of emergency, with so many other demands likely to be made upon channel crossing facilities and with the need to mobilise one third of a battalion, in effect, at least two days sooner than they could be expected to arrive in the battle area with their vehicles. Even allowing for inescapable delays and hiccoughs, it can be foreseen with some confidence that a unit such as 1 Wessex could appear on the battlefield, with its equipment, some four or five days after the announcement of mobilisation and perhaps some two days after the soldiers began to assemble. On arrival, each battalion would move straight into the role which has already been allotted to it, a role which might well involve its deployment as part of a mixed task force of the type seen in Germany in October.

In Exercise Rock Steady, Task Force H consisted of 1 Wessex, 1 Cheshire [1st Bn The Cheshire Regiment] (a mechanised infantry battalion) and 1/FAFR, a Danish Battalion consisting of two mechanised companies and one tank company, The Queen's Own Hussars complete, with a Squadron of the 16th/5th Queen's Own Lancers, Artillery and Engineer support. The scenario was typical of a BAOR exercise, the friendly Task Force being ordered to deploy from a concentration area to a defensive position, to hold an advancing mechanized enemy. The exercise involved the move into and preparation of a position, with the appropriate battle procedure, a withdrawal and the occupation of fresh positions to the rear. The threats of chemical and heliborne attack were present and exercised.

The Volunteer infantryman is not used to manoeuvring over large tracts of virgin farmland, in unknown terrain and surrounded by a civilian population. He is diffident at first about trespassing in the fields and buildings of the local people, following years of learning to respect private property and Schedule 1 land in the UK. However, once that initial shyness has worn off, the relative freedom from training restrictions provides him with a welcome feeling of freshness and realism, after a usual diet of Salisbury Plain, Otterburn or even the more hospitable Stanford PTA. He has always had a certain independence of approach in a tactical setting, and this will often enable him to overcome his comparative lack of practice in basic infantry techniques and procedures. Thus, in defence, he will respond to the challenge of digging a well proportioned hole, and will still have an inquisitive interest in what is taking place after hours of cold and dark, when his regular counterpart, who has seen it all so many times before, is finding routine defence a bit of a chore. The Volunteers, who may know their battle procedures a bit better in theory than in practice, will nonetheless be trying to the last to 'get it right' and think themselves through to a solution to their problems.

Thus were 1 Wessex able to occupy and defend their front on level terms with the units digging in beside them. With the addition of Swingfire to the battle group armoury, they were able to mount an equivalent anti-tank defence to that of their neighbours, and their logistic elements seemed, at least for the short duration of the exercise, able to function quite adequately.

A Volunteer in a NATO battalion may do only forty or fifty days training during the year, but he is training only for war in BAOR (and, of course, to perfect his basic skills towards that end). He does not have to concern himself with internal security, with the mechanics of APCs, or with a great deal of barrack administration or ceremonial. He should, therefore, be regarded in BAOR terms as being able to speak the same language as his regular counterpart, even though he may speak more slowly and often has to think before opening his mouth.

So the defensive position was dug, occupied and held in the approved manner, and there was a chance in the CP for a relative newcomer to the BAOR battle scene to reflect upon one or two apparent difficulties which may well affect not only the TAVR, but any battalion engaged in this sort of contest.

One wonders how long hand-digging will continue to be an acceptable method of getting underground against an enemy with substantial capacity for air recce and an abundance of long range artillery. In difficult ground, it will always take some hours to furnish a position with its full complement fire and shelter trenches, tiring the soldiers and placing them at risk of discovery and destruction before their protection is complete. Even with the aid of a mechanical digger, preparation of a position is bound to be an extended business, Perhaps only the use of explosives can get a battalion underground in an acceptable time.

1 Wessex generally expect their communications to work (rather than merely hope that they will) and in this respect we had no difficulty in falling in with the regular elements attached to us and talking to other units in the line. We become more and more dependant upon radio communications these days, as weapon control systems become more sophisticated and logistic requirements increase. Electronic warfare was not practiced on Rock Steady, but interference with radio communications must be one of the most effective ways of eliminating a unit's indirect weapons and restricting the flexibility of its troops and direct fire power. Perhaps the superior capabilities of Clansman [then the Army's latest radio system] will inhibit an enemy's ability to disrupt communications, but it seems likely that units such as ours will probably remain equipped with Larkspur [the previous system] for some years to come, and could find it difficult to keep talking against

an enemy determined to prevent them from doing so.

When the withdrawal phase of the exercise came round, it was relatively unhurried and unharried by enemy pressure, but such problems as there were arose when a number of composite units were trying to move a lot of vehicles to different destinations at the same time. It must be difficult to control an effective mixture of mechanized and airportable infantry where extensive or rapid movements are concerned. One can imagine the non-mechanized element being severely limited in movement when confined either to its feet or soft-skinned vehicles on roads which may frequently have become cratered and impassable, or choked with refugees.

Exercise Rock Steady was a success, however, and the Battalion generally contrived to be in the right place at the right time, looking the right way. The soldiers enjoyed their camp; they felt it was something akin to the real thing, and they gained greatly in experience and morale by working with and being treated as a regular battalion.

It is equally important that regular units and staffs should gain confidence in the ability of the Volunteers to perform their battle tasks. We hope and believe that this exercise will enable the regular soldiers and commanders who took part in it to view the appearance on the battle map of volunteer battalions without alarm and that they will now assume that such units will get to the battlefield and are quite capable of fighting a conventional European war when they do so.

––––––––––

For those 'on the ground':

The outward journey was enlivened by the VC10 carrying B Company, which overshot the runway in dense fog on the first approach, and converted 120 agnostics into ardent Christians in a very few seconds. We thought that was bad, but worse was to come. German autobahns with twenty metres' visibility reduced most passengers to bloodshot-eyed zombies after 120 kilometres.[19]

In the first week, Phase 1 was company training as part of the Division's Reinforcement Exercise, which for B Company did not go quite as planned or expected:

Early start for the Company phase of the Exercise. Short march to a defensive position. It was only after checking his map that the Company Commander, Major Taylor, noticed that a most unfortunate mistake has been made: the map he was issued with was of the geological structure of the area, and the pretty colour that was chosen for the defensive position in fact denoted an outcrop of granite. 24 hours later we were down to three feet, six inches. Naturally, the next order was "Fill in and move off".

When we arrived at the Company's base location we found our four-star accommodation behind a huge, steaming manure heap – what a great reception we received from our Permanent Staff, WO2 Jesty and C/Sgt Copping! The straw in the pigsty had been changed, and the cows moved over to make room for us. "Home from Home" – how quaint![20]

For Phase 2, the Battalion exercised with a squadron of tanks from The Queen's Own Hussars as enemy, a troop of Swingfire anti-tank missiles and eight RAF Wessex helicopters. The Division's two-sided Exercise Rock Steady took up most of the second week. 1 Wessex was part of Task Force H, with 1 Cheshire, the QOH, and 1/FAFR – "Well, we were told that it was a Danish tank battalion, for they all sounded like the man in the Smurf song"), and the general feeling afterwards was:

> We were able to prove that a TAVR unit can fit into a Regular formation, play its part and fulfil its role. It was a demanding exercise, calling for stamina and the ability to react quickly to the tactical developments as they occurred. It was a rewarding experience for the Battalion.[21]

The final two days were spent in Münster and Osnabrück, for a really enjoyable time with three of the Regular Regiments, 1 D & D, 1 Royal Hamps and 1 DERR. The regimental journals give the impression (either true or false) that there was little done apart from socialising – the high point of which was a magnificent Beating Retreat by the Bands and Drums of all three battalions, followed by parties in all the Messes for not only them but also 1 Glosters, who had recently arrived in Münster after a year and a half in Northern Ireland.

A semi-formal report of the fortnight was given by the Commanding

Officer to the Honorary Colonel, General Glyn Gilbert:

I am happy to report that our fortnight's training in BAOR went extremely well. As you know, we mobilised here on Friday 13 October, having sent our road party of 63 vehicles on ahead. We flew out to Germany on the following day, and the Battalion went through the reinforcement procedures in 4 Division before settling into a battalion concentration area on the Sunday.

The first two days, during which we were visited by D[eputy] Com[mander] South West District, were devoted to company work-up training. I had previously specified that positional defence, night withdrawal and demolition guards should be practiced – all under NBC conditions.

There followed a Battalion Exercise on the R[iver] Liene, during which I endeavoured to stretch the companies and test the CPs in particular. We moved on to three bridges over the river at night, and held them the following day. D Squadron Queen's Own Hussars were under command at this stage, and I used them as a controlled enemy pretending to be the forward element of an M[otorised] R[ifle] Regt. We withdrew at night into a closely wooded area well back from the river, after blowing the bridges.

Having dug in again I persuaded the armour to advance up the rides towards the company positions, and there followed a series of infantry/tank engagements which we won! The squadron then withdrew.

The following morning we mounted a two company heli-borne attack over the river and destroyed the supposed MR Regt HQ. This in fact went well, except for the fact that the RAF decided to fly away and refuel between insertion and recovery, and the subsequent withdrawal of B and E companies was therefore less than realistic. I had deliberately kept my orders simple, so that the S[upport] H[elicopters] could not make any error. *C'est la guerre.*

After a short rest, we moved north east to within a few miles of the E[ast] G[erman] B[order] and went into the Divisional Concentration Area. Brigadier Gordon-Lennox, the Task Force Commander, gave orders at 1300 on Sunday 15 October and we moved, once again at night, into positional defence to the east of Braunschweig. Our Battle Group now consisted of the following:

1 Wessex (org into 3 Rifle Coys, and A1 and A2 Echelons, with 6 Mobats and the Mortar platoon)
1 ATGW [Anti-tank Guided Weapon] Battery (Swingfire)
2 Sects Air Defence (Blowpipe)
1 Field Battery (Abbott)

There followed a screen battle, after which the minefield lane, left for the withdrawal of QOH and 16/5 Lancers, was blown by 1 Wessex – a few nerve wrecking hours for me, not wishing to leave the armour the wrong side of the minefield!

The enemy T[ask]F[orce] (Brig Barry Lane), then attempted to breach the minefield but failed. At this time we were pleased that we had sited our Atk weapons carefully, and subsequently received the Comd's praise for this, as well as our slick battle procedure and good digging.

The enemy then got round the obstacle to the north and the whole TF withdrew at night; 1 Wessex moved back to hold two bridges over which the TF would subsequently withdraw if the tanks lost the second battle. They didn't, and after the bridges had been attacked abortively by a helicopter *coup-de-main* force (Duke of Wellingtons [1st Bn The Duke of Wellington's Regiment] as enemy) the exercise came to an end.

At the subsequent debrief, the Brigadier was kind enough to say that we had done well and gave the impression that we had held our end up successfully in very august company. After a day to clean up, we split up and went to 1 D & D, 1 R HAMPS and 1 DERR. A highly successful and enjoyable last two days ensued. Because of the pressure of the previous twelve days, I had asked the COs to make them fun, and they did. The finale was a Retreat carried out by all three Bands at Münster – a most moving and memorable experience. Parties in the various messes followed, and we returned to UK the following morning. The Regular Battalions really put a tremendous effort into making us feel part of the family and undoubtedly succeeded. They were marvellous.

I have no doubt that, as a result of the rigorous nature of the first twelve days, we shall lose some soldiers, but I am equally sure that we shall gain even more once the war stories start to circulate round the West Country. Our strength was 31 officers and 407 soldiers, and by keeping the echelon to a minimum we had three good rifle companies in the field, and I feel sure that we would have given a good account of ourselves in the event. Lastly, command at all levels was thoroughly tested. The Battalion CP was under pressure throughout and came through it all well. That is not to say that there are not a number of things to put right![22]

Although a good proportion of the Battalion had been to Camp in Germany several times before, it was always very different from training in the UK:

> Little incenses a volunteer soldier more than going on an exercise which is overflowing with tanks, APCs, helicopters, and even real foreigners, only to find that the battle is invariably half a mile away and that his magazine is as full on day three as it was when he first loaded it! But if there were some private soldiers and junior leaders for whom the tactical work might have seemed unrewarding, there can be no doubt that the training was extremely valuable and the experience gained, albeit unconsciously, by all ranks will stand them in good stead if mobilisation is ever required. Although there were mixed views (as there always are) about the exercise, there was nothing but praise from all ranks for the hospitality offered during our final two days in Germany by 1 DERR in Osnabrück. It is impossible to imagine a regular battalion giving a greater welcome and taking more trouble to entertain its volunteer counterparts and memories of this highly successful visit will certainly outweigh recollections of drab hours of darkness in the Hanoverian trenches. By all accounts 1 D & D and 1 R HAMPS meted out similar treatment to the other Companies of 1 Wessex who visited them……… Nothing can do more to enhance the respect and understanding of the volunteer for the regular and (we hope) vice versa than contact both on the training ground and in the bar.[23]

1979

Cultybraggan & Barry Budden Ranges (between Dundee & Carnoustie): (2–16 June); Support Platoons: Otterburn (1 week)

Almost by definition, a home-based Camp in the year following a successful one on a major exercise abroad was something of an anticlimax – but this was the third year in the training cycle, which once again was mainly devoted to individual training. A very large number of people accordingly volunteered, or 'were' volunteered, for courses in lieu of Camp – young officers, platoon sergeants, section commanders, drivers, cooks and signallers. For those who did go to Scotland, contrary to what those members of Battalion with previous knowledge of it were expecting, the weather was particularly kind. There were nine specialist cadres – for Recruits, Junior NCOs, Tank Killing, GPMG, Signals, HGV driving, Adventure Training, as well as live firing for the Anti-tank and Mortar Platoons on the Otterburn Ranges in Northumberland, and non-specialist cadres run by the Companies – the aim of which was to raise standards generally, and most of the second week was taken up with Exercise Wessex Wedge, particularly designed to stretch and test junior commanders, which was:

> .....an arduous three-day infiltration and patrolling exercise moving over the Highlands to the Cultybraggan Training Area, where each of the Companies patrolled against the Drums Platoon, and resisted with surprising ease patrols from the Stirling Company of the 1st/51st Highlanders [another TA NATO battalion]. As an example of what the TA sometimes gets up to, the Highlanders were actually only supposed to have been involved for one evening – in fact a two-hour Drill Night – but they did not arrive on the training area until about 2200 hours, and finally left it at 0400, after a Battalion dawn attack in time to go home, get shaved and go off to work.[24]

1980

BAOR – Exercise Crusader 80 (14–27 September)

The Battalion, now part of 1 Armoured Division, went to Germany and took part in Exercise Crusader 80 – one of the most extensive exercises undertaken by the British Army in the post-war years. Company attendances were very high – including the Anti-tank

Platoon, A Coy went 125 strong, and E Company took 80 – and in all 540 Volunteers turned out. The crossing to the continent involved 53 vehicles and trailers on ferries and other specially chartered ships, and flights from 7 civilian airports, as well as RAF Brize Norton and Lyneham. The Battalion's main task was the provision of demolition bridge guards – and so, throughout the summer, every Company had spent weekend after weekend "practising the drills" – another expression for digging yet more trenches on Salisbury Plain, and then filling them in again. Hardened Volunteers who had already been to BAOR a couple of times or more feared that there would be all the usual waiting about for hours and hours, and the 'order, counter-order, disorder' scenarios that are the main features of almost every big exercise – and they were not proved wrong. Nevertheless, although it turned out to be a really exhausting Camp, which in some ways just seemed to go on and on, the general verdict after the event was that it had been a worthwhile fortnight:

The outward journey involved coaches to Devizes and then [one of the barracks in] Windsor; Jumbo jet to Gütersloh; train, coach and the 4-ton trucks to Sennelager, and finally, having married up with the road parties, a long drive to the training area near Verden. That move out (and the subsequent return to the UK) went reasonably smoothly, and we arrived within the 48 hours allotted to the BAOR reinforcements. Exercise Spearpoint was the main training for the company, and we prepared to perform a relief on a bridge which was to be attacked with an American parachute drop. According to *Spearpoint News*, we defended the bridge valiantly and there were photographs to prove it. However, we did not actually arrive on that particular bridge until the day after the attack. The fog and confusion of battle revealed itself very rapidly and, after many orders and counter orders, we eventually launched a company attack on another bridge, supported by an unexpected helicopter force which appeared in the middle of the operation. After dispelling the American invaders, we spent a night on the bridge and moved the next morning to perform a relief on the original bridge. That the operation took place smoothly is a great tribute to the company, as on arrival at the bridge it was found that chaos reigned supreme: the roads to it were completely blocked by armour and soft skinned vehicles, and the area must have contained elements of almost all the friendly and enemy forces taking part in Spearpoint. However, the bridge was occupied and duly blown the following morning. The next phase for us was a long withdrawal, and a period of some days guarding key points in an area far to the west of our original position, where we were subjected (whether intentionally or unintentionally) to many false alarms and excursions. During an earlier wood clearing operation, the following conversation took place:

> "Hello 2, this is 1 – send Sitrep – over".
> "2, We have a contact but this really is a gargantuan task, more for a company than a platoon – over".
> "1, How many enemy are there? – over"
> "2, One dead and at least two more – over".
> "1, (deleted) – out".

Clearly a case of two's company, three's a divisional task.

An extremely hazardous second wood-clearing operation at last light marked the end of the Exercise for us, and we began the long return journey via Falingbostel – and, after the post-exercise admin, the Company enjoyed itself in the bright red lights of Hamburg, That the recovery was long and tedious goes without saying; the Company arrived back at its home locations in the early hours of Sunday morning, and the vehicle party later the same day. Although extremely tired, the drivers managed to pilot their vehicles without accident and this is a great tribute to their fortitude.[25]

while two other Companies' views of the Camp were:

B Company was just one very small cog in the enormous machinery of the Exercise, as the move to Germany quickly made all those taking part aware. The road party drove to Harwich overnight from Winchester, via Devizes, arriving in time for breakfast, after having been overtaken by a rogue wheel from a trailer. That morning the vehicles were loaded on to a very smart Danish ferry – whose crew, we hope, would be just as keen to provide their services for 'the real thing' – and all personnel started gorging themselves on the Scandinavian food provided free by a generous commissariat. Evening found the road party in Zeebrugge, marshalled into a huge convoy of some 200 vehicles. Driving on motorways through Belgium and Holland is not very exciting at the best of times; at night at 25 mph it is at best mind-blowingly dull, and at worst downright dangerous. Fortunately the drivers managed to stay awake for enough of the time to avoid any accidents, although errant vehicles could be seen meandering into the fast lane and back every so often.

Meanwhile the Air Party had moved from Devizes to Heathrow, via [a barracks in] Windsor and caught a 747 to Germany, the flight being enlivened by a stewardess advising against smoking whilst wearing an oxygen mask. Having survived the rigours of a Belgian train and the efforts of the movements staff to convert order into chaos, road and air parties were reunited at Sennelager. The Battalion then motored to its destined workup area north of Soltau. With a farmyard and barn as its firm base, the Company carried out two days' training around a nearby bridge. Unfortunately the water table lay only a foot down, so trenches soon became ponds, and (not to be outdone) the Command Post a swimming pool. The weather was typically North German autumnal – wet.

The day the Battalion moved to its exercise task was hot and clear. A sixty-mile drive along autobahns and main roads led to the release point, and at last the Company moved forward to the bridge it had been detailed to guard. As our relief of a company of the Irish Guards was carried out, heavy transport aircraft could be seen dropping huge numbers of paratroops some five miles to the south. Furthermore, helicopters were seen landing behind woods two miles to the east. The Company took up its positions as soon as possible, and everyone tried to find their bearings and generally what was what, as the Irish Guards rapidly withdrew to the west. It was soon apparent that all the aerial activity was enemy, and that Orange forces were deploying to threaten the bridge. Two Orange Land Rovers tried to 'bounce' the bridge, but were deemed destroyed by the umpires. Suddenly the fields to the east were full of American paratroopers advancing behind smoke. At the same time the heliborne force converged, and the eastern end of the bridge disappeared in a welter of smoke grenades and thunderflashes. A brisk counter-attack led by "Conroy, VC" ensured that possession remained with B Company. The fast rattle of Armalite rifle fire heralded the approach of the Americans on the other bank, and despite heavy fire from SF in the section trenches, they were soon on the bridge, busy firing at their own forces on the opposite bank - an understandable mistake in the confusion.

The next day found the Company still at the bridge. Armoured vehicles had continued to stream over the bridge during the night. Reports of enemy reconnaissance a few miles to the east came faster and thicker; real, live, Liaison Officers arrived; umpires began to take interest again; and spectators and the media arrived in droves. Enemy pressure began to build up on the eastern bank, but eventually the code-word was given, and a large bang indicated that the Company had successfully accomplished its task.

Then began our withdrawal on foot, clad in NBC [Nuclear Biological & Chemical] suits and carrying everything but the kitchen sink, in temperatures nearing the eighties, on what proved to be the hottest day of the Exercise. The Battalion regrouped some 20 miles behind the front line, passing numerous mechanical casualties of the retreating Division on the way. While most people were taking advantage of the cover of a large barn to wring out sodden clothing and reduce offensive body odours, the powers-that-be ordained a gas attack. Once everyone had realized that it was not a cruel joke being played by the umpires (who like sensible men were walking around in shirt-sleeve order and crisp, pressed denims), the attack was dealt with in earnest. The relief of taking off a respirator at the end of that phase was exquisite.

For the remainder of the Exercise the Company was deployed with the role of Rear Area Security, and life was really quite pleasant and relaxed. Rumours of marauding SAS abounded, but none were ever seen. Perhaps the comprehensive patrol programme scared them away into someone else's patch. The area was rather more prosperous than where we had been for the work-up training, and consequently it was quite difficult to find a suitable farm. The search [for the SAS] was, however, all the more worthwhile when our host farmer was found to have a most athletic-looking daughter who, unlike most, was not locked away out of sight as soon as the Company drove through the farmyard gates. Our farmer was not reluctant to share his cellar either – as a surprised sentry discovered one night, and was not slow in accepting the hospitality.

A pleasant time was had by all, patrolling rural countryside on foot and in vehicles. The ideal OP [Observation Post] was at the top of an old Wachtturm, which happened to have a thriving Gast-stube at its foot. The final operation was to clear a pocket of infiltrators holed up in dense forest. Naturally our friends the helicopters who delivered us to the scene put us where they thought we ought to be, rather than where we thought we ought to be, and it was not until dusk that the enemy were located and assaulted.

The journey back was uneventful. For the road party, the nightmare of trying to stay awake behind endless lines of vehicle lights stretching ahead up the autobahn; for the air party, a pleasant 36 hours in Sennelager before flying into Heathrow by 747 in the early hours of a Sunday morning. The road party landed at Marchwood, and were only a very few hours behind the air party in reaching Winchester.[26]

Once the shooting season was over, training for Crusader took top priority and it seemed no time before we were mustering at Dorchester. Many readers will be only too familiar with the journey out, so suffice it to say that we formed the largest single chalk [group of passengers] of the 400 pax [individuals] and we were unloaded from our Boeing 747 Jumbo Jet at Gütersloh in 19½ minutes. The subsequent task of reuniting 400 men with their 800 pieces of baggage had to be seen to be believed!

After 24 hours work-up training in the area of Verden, we joined Exercise Spearpoint – where our initial task was to take over a demolition guard on a bridge over the Hildesheim Canal. Recce completed, the Company Commander awaited the arrival of the Battalion main body as if direct from UK. As they arrived, so did the American Airborne drop and at the same time four Harriers 'destroyed' our bridge. B Company were more fortunate and were able to take over their bridge, but only to be attacked by the Americans and dislodged from the near side of it. C Company then put in a spirited and successful counter attack, although it was not long before the Americans were back in greater strength and recaptured the bridge. Next morning we were able, with B Company, to re-occupy our positions, and over the next 24 hours we carried out a successful joint demolition guard, withdrawing hastily at the last but with all Blue forces safely over and the bridge blown. We were then moved to the Rear Area, halting briefly in the 1 D & D area en route. We became responsible for security in a part of the rear area and for the next three days mounted an intensive patrolling campaign which was more reminiscent of Northern Ireland operations except that 'Noddy suits' [NBC protection] were in evidence. Finally, we moved back to Falingbostel to prepare to move back to UK, and to spend one day on R & R. It was here that, under the guidance of Capt. Nick Gray, the PR Officer of 1 D & D, Donald Mildenhall from the *Western Gazette* caught up with us – with the result that shortly after our return home we had the kind of Press coverage in our local papers that only Donald seems to be able to produce.[27]

The very fact that Camp was almost always the highlight of the training year meant that the return to life in the TA Centre, and familiar training areas did not have much attraction:

> ....after Exercise Crusader 80, the remainder of the year was something of an anti-climax. Week-end training has been taken up with upgrading boards, range work, Remembrance Day parades, house clearing at section level (to shake off the excesses of the Christmas Party the evening before), a Company Inter-Section Competition, and, latterly, a Battalion exercise on a rather cold and snowy week-end attacking and defending Imber village.
>
> By virtue of the pattern of training at week-ends, the Company tends to become rather fragmented, but during the two weeks at an Annual Camp procedures become slicker, teamwork improves remarkably, and tremendous comradeship is engendered. Some of this disappears at the end of the fortnight, but by having training based on the sections it was hoped to preserve these important aspects, while at the same time improving the standard of shooting by more frequent visits to ranges. What upset the apple-cart was the large, and indeed welcome, influx of recruits. There is no doubt that the present economic climate has a lot to do with the buoyant state of the recruiting market, but it still does not alter the fact that, despite careful briefing, many recruits do not fully realise what will be asked of them, and several fall by the wayside.[28]

---

[1] *BB*, Winter 1975.
[2] *BB*, Summer 1975.
[3] *Ibid.*
[4] Major Fred Fifield.
[5] The Battalion's Mortar Platoon.

6   *RHRJ*, November 1974.
7   *DERRJ*, Autumn 1975.
8   *RHRJ*, May 1975.
9   *DERRJ*, Autumn 1975.
10 *RHRJ*, Winter 1975.
11 *D&DRJ* Winter 1975.
12 *BB*, Winter 1976.
13 For those who would like to refresh their memories of the Camp, pictures of it can be found at www.geo.ed.ac.uk/scotgaz/features/moregpix7987.
14 *D&DRJ* (E Company Notes), December 1977.
15 *BB*, Winter 1977.
16 *RHRJ*, November 1977.
17 No.69, August 1979.
18 1Wessex did in fact have some, as the result of the 1972 Exercise State Trust air-move to Yorkshire.
19 *RHRJ*, May 1979.
20 Capt HR Astin in *ibid*.
21 *Western Wessex TAVRA Newsletter* No 10, 1978.
22 Letter in the Battalion scrapbook.
23 *BB*, Summer 1979.
24 *RHRJ*, May 1980.
25 *BB*, Winter 1980.
26 *RHRJ*, May 1981.
27 *D&DRJ*, January1981.
28 *Ibid*.

CHAPTER 8

THE FIRST REORGANISATION: 1982–1986[1]

It is now necessary to interrupt the general year-by-year narrative to consider the major reorganisation of the TA that was planned and agreed (or at least accepted) between 1982 and 1986, as it affected South West District, and its highly significant effect on the Battalion. Ever since the root-and-branch changes of 1967, of course, there had been internal change of some sort within individual battalions and regiments, particularly of the locations of platoons and similar sub-units. Given, however, that in almost every walk of life re-organisation was becoming more and more common, it is perhaps surprising that the TA as a whole had survived without a major one for 15 years.

From 1974 onwards, the Ministry of Defence had initiated a number of studies into the TA, and in that year the Majury Committee[2] considered many of the anomalies that had existed in the infantry order of battle since 1967, and as a result many of the minor ones were corrected. The most significant study, however, titled *Wastage in the TA*, was carried out in 1978 by the then Director of Volunteers, Territorials & Cadets, Major General Peter Shapland – an enthusiastic supporter of the TA, whose son, Tim Shapland, was commissioned into the Battalion, became the 2IC of B Company in the mid-1980s, and then commanded the short-lived C Company in Newbury. Despite its title, the study addressed many aspects of TA soldiering, and two of its main conclusions – universally accepted as being true – were that "Too many TA units recruit from too wide an area" and that "In too many parts of the country, identity with the old TA units has been lost."

Although no immediate action was taken to address those problems, in due course General Shapland's recommendations were adopted as part of the Conservative Government's 1981 Defence Review[3], which announced a substantial expansion of the TA, for use both at home and abroad. The established strength would be increased from about 59,000 to 86,000, with a considerable number of new units being formed, mainly in the 'teeth arms'. There would be a "Key Plan for the TA Enhancements", to be implemented in two phases – Phase I (which was announced in March 1982) over the years 1982–1986, and Phase II between 1986 and 1990.

Under Phase I, so far as the TA Infantry was concerned, in order both to improve the protection of the vital rear area of 1 (BR) Corps in BAOR and to standardise the number of rifle companies in the NATO battalions at four, additional ones were to be raised by the 5th Bn The Royal Irish Regiment, the 3rd Bn The Royal Regiment of Wales and the 51st Highland Volunteers. Secondly, all the NATO battalions, including 1 Wessex, were authorised to form reconnaissance platoons; and, thirdly, anti-tank platoons were to be formed by those NATO battalions that, unlike 1 Wessex, did not already have them. There would also be increased establishments and better equipment for certain Home Defence battalions, to improve the defence of key points in the UK. All those enhancements would happen in 1984 and 1985.

In the event, it was A Company that was tasked to form not only the Battalion's new Reconnaissance Platoon from the Rifle Platoon in Cheltenham, complete with eight Fox Armoured Recce Vehicles and several PSIs, but also an Assault Pioneer Platoon. Even given the attraction of becoming wheeled, it says much for the general enthusiasm in the Company that almost three-quarters of the members of the Recce Platoon quickly volunteered for the five-week familiarisation course. The Assault Pioneer Platoon started life in Gloucester; it was commanded by Sergeant Peter Blake, a devoted and long-serving member of A Company; he revelled in being allowed to sport the traditional beard of the Pioneer Sergeant, and to appear on ceremonial parades with a white apron and a silver-headed axe, and in due course he became a WO2. Over the next few years, however, the Platoon became something of a football, moving to Cheltenham, back to Gloucester, and then to Cinderford.

Because the pre-1967 TA had no specific task, there was little incentive to make training really appealing and challenging. In terms of individual skills, the 'peak' was perhaps to survive an 'escape and evasion' exercise and to get one's "classification" on the range [attain a minimum standard of shooting], while (if memory serves right) there was little tactical field training other than crudely executed platoon, company and battalion attacks; for example, defence (including digging-in), OP work and serious patrolling were only very rarely, if ever, on the programme – and it must almost go without saying, therefore, that an immense amount of hard work was necessary to ensure, in quite a short space of time, that the Battalion could do all that was expected of it. There had to be completely different types of training, and a new attitude to it – but (by courtesy of the Permanent Staff) the first happened and the second was achieved very quickly – and that effort paid off handsomely, for in 1982 there was a dramatic and exciting change in the Battalion's role.

The United Kingdom Mobile Force (Land) [UKMF(L)] – the UK's contribution to NATO's Ace Mobile Force (Land) [about which see page 287] – had been formed at Aldershot on 1st April 1978 as 6 Field Force, and its infantry element consisted of 3 regular battalions and two TA battalions, the 10th Bn The Parachute Regiment and the 5th Bn The Queen's Regiment. In January 1982, 6 Field Force became 1 Infantry Brigade in 3 (UK) Division and moved to Tidworth – and the marvellous news was received that, as part of those changes, 1 Wessex would be 'promoted' to become the sole TA battalion in the Brigade, replacing 10 Para and 5 Queen's. It was, of course, an excellent reflection of the efforts and achievements of virtually every single member of the Battalion, but particularly the vision of the COs of that period – Bill Coppen-Gardner, John Southwood and Terry Dutton – and their Training Majors.

The planning of Phase II of the Key Plan, led by Lieutenant Colonel Henry Joynson of HQ United Kingdom Land Forces, started in the autumn of 1982 – and it quickly became known as "the Joynson Plan", or just "Joynson". The Ministry of Defence, however, then sensibly realised that this was an excellent opportunity to build on the conclusions of not only the Majury and Shapland Reports, but others as well, and Joynson therefore became a review of the entire structure of the TA. In operational terms, Phase II had two main, interlocking, objects – to concentrate a number of very spread-out TA major units into more realistic geographical areas (one of the objects of which, it was said, was to make it easier for TA officers to command them), and the provision of more infantry for the defence of the United Kingdom.

As time would show, however, whilst it was relatively easy to expand and "restructure" the TA on paper, with the planners full of ideas for reorganising virtually everything, on the ground things were often seen very differently. In many cases, and in various parts of the country, not only in 1967 but now again, insufficient account was taken of the strengths of old regimental identities, loyalties and geographical interests – the bedrock on which the characters and strengths of the regiments of the British Army had been built up over several hundred years. Furthermore, many of the proposals (certainly as they affected the Infantry) failed to recognise the extent to which not only the original 13 NATO battalions, but also the new units (such as the Royal Wessex Yeomanry) formed in 1971, were already fast acquiring those qualities in their own right. The planning for the reorganisation necessitated not only very wide consultation, but also the 'floating' of many alternative scenarios – which naturally led to a very large number of rumours circulating everywhere; there was 'in-fighting' between Regular regiments having axes to grind in terms of their own TA interests; and regrettably many TA battalions were virtually treated as mere pawns in a game of chess, with new proposals and counter-proposals appearing, so it seemed, almost monthly. It was all very unsettling.

In December 1982, Colonel Joynson, having visited the Headquarters of both South East and South West Districts, proposed that 1 Wessex should:

> 1. 'Provide' an additional Home Defence Company in South East District, by transferring the very well recruited B Company in Hampshire to 2 Wessex (which had, of course, already acquired D Company in Reading in 1975); and

> 2. Exchange the equally well-recruited E Company in Devon for the under-strength, Bath-based, A Company of the 6th Bn The Light Infantry – which would also move its Battalion HQ and HQ Company from Bath to Bodmin, so that they were more in the centre of its rifle companies.

Whilst that would, of course, achieve both the objects of Phase II, it would also result in 1 Wessex losing its unique five rifle company establishment – so that it would be left with A in Gloucestershire, a new B Company (ex-6 LI) in Bath, C in Dorchester and D in Poole. That idea was firmly opposed for two very valid reasons.

Both 1 Brigade and the UKMF(L) were commanded by Brigadier Edwin Beckett, and he argued strongly against the proposed transfer of B and E Companies. His reasoning was that it was the nature of his Brigade's role was to deploy rapidly, and that it therefore depended heavily on its infantry organisation; its concept of operations relied on anti-tank weapons and the ability to hold ground, and the key factor in that 'defensive posture' was therefore the availability of the maximum number of infantry companies. The 'exchange' of 10 Para and 5 Queen's for 1 Wessex had already reduced the number of companies in the Brigade from 20 to 17, and the matter was further complicated by an MOD proposal that Regular 'A' infantry battalions would reduce from four rifle companies to three. The Brigadier consequently claimed, with considerable justification, that to lose yet another company would seriously jeopardise the Brigade's operational effectiveness, quite apart from the fact that the proposal would require negotiation with the other NATO countries involved about the frontage that the Brigade would no longer be able properly to control. Not surprisingly, from the safety of its offices at Wilton, the Headquarters of the United Kingdom Land Forces [HQ UKLF] strongly disagreed. Brigadier Beckett then pointed out that 1 Wessex were a well-recruited and well-motivated unit, and that:

> [They] have recently completed one exercise season, including a demanding FTX in one contingency area. They are now familiar with he concept of operations with their 5 company organisation. Considering the problems of a TA unit training with a formation, particularly in such a complex role, it would be undesirable to introduce a major change at this stage.
>
> They have contributed a great deal to the cohesion of UKMF(L), and it would not make sense to reorganise them at this critical stage in their development. Certainly the redeployment of one company from the UKMF(L) role to Home Defence would be seen as a detrimental step.[4]

Bearing in mind that the Battalion had only been in the Brigade for eleven months when he wrote that, it was praise indeed, and a heart-warming endorsement of the Battalion's capabilities – and, although those two Companies would leave the Battalion in 1986 and 1987, the 1 Brigade role was not affected.

Then, in very cogent letters to Lieutenant General Sir Edward ("Ted") Burgess (the Commander of the UK Field Army and Inspector General of the TA)[5], the GOC South West District, Major General Michael Gray and the TAVRA both argued against the proposals on the grounds that, firstly, they were likely to create serious recruiting difficulties for 1 Wessex, and, secondly, that the cost of altering the Bodmin TA Centre (part of the old Depot of The Duke of Cornwall's Light Infantry) to accommodate 6LI's Battalion HQ and Headquarter Company would involve the taxpayer in a substantial, and in the TAVRA's view unnecessary, expenditure of around £1 million. That reorganisation would also, of course, create the need to re-role and enhance the training skills of A Company 6 LI.

A good number of factors must have been taken into account in making the decision to give the Battalion what was in all probability the best Infantry role in the entire TA. After 15 years in 4 Division, it had acquired a good deal of experience of the 'BAOR scenario', and was clearly regarded as capable of fulfilling its new role. Its location around Salisbury Plain was a major advantage – it would obviously have been difficult for, say, the extremely good 1st Bn The Yorkshire Volunteers to exercise with the Brigade, and very possibly to get to wherever it was needed speedily enough in the event of mobilisation. Quite apart from the boost it gave to everyone's morale, the change was definitely a 'Good Thing' from the Battalion's point of view, in that it would be a bigger cog in a smaller machine, and there would be a much closer liaison than had been possible with the Division and more opportunities of training with Regular battalions. Needless to say, though, the Battalion knew exactly why it had been chosen!

When the transfer of B and E Companies was first proposed, within the Battalion it was hoped that, following the loss of the Reading Company in 1975, that would be the 'final disaster', and that there would then be no further 'raids' on the Battalion. What is not known, though, is whether in the Ministry of Defence or HQ UKLF there was at that stage an underlying, but unrevealed and certainly not yet 'thought out', long-term intention that 1 Wessex – being a 'one-off' TA regiment without a Regular parent regiment to protect its interests (as, for example, 6 LI had) – would eventually be completely broken up in order to allow the re-creation of former TA battalions for the Regular Regiments. It is probably true to say that when the Reading Company was lost in 1975, with the Battalion by then well established as one of the leading ones with a NATO commitment, it never seriously occurred to anyone within it, or closely connected with it, that worse might be to come. Nevertheless, although the Battalion had by now acquired its own special identity, and had never enjoyed particularly strong ties to the Regular Regiments, the author believes that if at that stage the wheel had gone full circle and it was decided that all the Companies should be returned to their original 'parent' regiments, or their successors, for all practical purposes at the same time, the Battalion would probably (although somewhat reluctantly) have accepted that.

On 18th February 1983 a meeting to discuss Phase II (the formal title of which was *The Long-Term Organization and Deployment of The Territorial Army*) was held in Historic Room 27 at the Ministry of Defence in Whitehall – perhaps an appropriate setting, given the 'breaks-with-history' nature of the business! It was chaired by the Under-Secretary of State for the Armed Forces with responsibility for the TA, Mr Jerry Wiggin MP (who had in fact served as a TA officer in The Royal Yeomanry between 1975 and 1978), and around the vast table were gathered the Vice Chief of the Defence Staff; General Burgess; the Director of the Territorial Army & Cadets (the jolly and hugely pro-TA Major General Dick Gerrard-Wright), and several other generals; Lieutenant General Sir Peter Hudson, the Chairman of the Council of TAVRAs, who had been the previous Inspector General and was one of the keenest supporters of the TA ever produced by the Regular Army; and the Chairmen of all the 13 TAVRAs. After the draft Plan had been outlined, each Chairman was asked to comment on it, so far as it affected 'his' area. As was to be expected, some of them positively welcomed the proposals, and some accepted them resignedly, but the author (then in fact only the Chairman designate of Western Wessex) spoke very strongly against the B & E Companies/ 2 Wessex/6 LI idea – and the Under-Secretary "noted his concern, and undertook to re-examine the proposals".[6]

HQ UKLF then realised, somewhat late in the day, that there was a requirement to protect Plymouth – the largest town south of Bristol – and in particular its Royal Navy dockyard, but, although Cornwall itself was adequately 'covered' by the two companies of 6 LI in Camborne and Truro, there was not the recruiting potential in east Cornwall to enable it to raise a third company for that task. Furthermore, there were no Home Defence infantry companies in either Devon or Dorset, and accordingly strong arguments in favour of at least one, if not two, being formed there. They could not, however, operate independently of a TA battalion, and the nearest existing one was 2 Wessex, but as its 'territory' closest to Devon and Dorset was Hampshire, it was too far east. It soon became obvious, therefore, that a possible solution was to create a new, three-rifle company, battalion in Devon and Dorset – and who better to base it on than E Company of 1 Wessex? How to achieve that, however, with minimal disruption of existing units, and without upsetting strong, some long-established, and some not-so-long established, regimental interests, was a daunting task – and so the scene was set for months and months of wrangling between the interested parties.

Although RWxY, a light reconnaissance regiment, covered several Districts in the UK (and thus did not meet the 'concentration' objective of the Key Plan), it was never a potential major victim of the Joynson Plan. Nonetheless, the fact that the round journey from its D (Royal Devon Yeomanry) Squadron in Barnstaple to the RHQ in Cirencester was some 260 miles had always been a major logistical problem. That, the idea of a new battalion, and the fact that there were 1 Wessex Companies in Devon and Dorset, led the Colonel of D & D, Colonel Michael Bullock, to take up the 'new Home Defence battalion idea', and propose to the Prince of Wales's Division[7] in a letter of 21 March 1983 that it should be the 3rd (TA) Battalion of his Regiment. It would have its Battalion HQ and Headquarter Company in Wyvern Barracks, Exeter, and be formed by taking over and re-badging 1

Wessex's C Company in Dorset and E Company (both of which would therefore have to re-role, as it were, 'downwards' for Home Defence, and with E Company reverting to being a Headquarter Company again); the Plymouth Platoon would be expanded into a company; and either D Squadron, which had detachments at Barnstaple, Tiverton and Totnes, would be taken over or 1 Wessex's Barnstaple Platoon would be expanded into a company.[8]

Whilst the idea of 'rejoining' their county regiment naturally appealed to many, or even most, of the original members of C and E Companies who had served in the 4th Dorsets or the 4th Devons, it is probably fair to say that most of their present members felt that their real loyalty was now to 1 Wessex – and by then, of course, some 16 years after the Battalion was formed, there were not in fact many of the first ones left. In Battalion HQ, and all the other Companies, it was felt that the loss of C and E Companies would cause tremendous disruption and ill-feeling within the Battalion, and in those two Companies possibly a considerable loss of morale, because their disappointment at the change to a less demanding role might not be more then balanced by the return to their affiliated Regiment. Furthermore, it was undoubtedly a blatant promotion of purely regimental interests, at a time when the re-creation of TA battalions for Regular regiments was definitely not on the MOD's already extremely complicated agenda. Objections to it were made not only by the CO, Lieutenant Colonel Terry Dutton, but by everyone else involved, in the strongest possible terms. In the event, the proposal did not become part of the official agenda at that stage, but it would rear its head again two years later, albeit in a slightly different form, with very serious consequences for 1 Wessex.

Only a week later, however, on 29 March 1983, after further discussions with the TAVRA, General Gray (who, as a Gunner having no 'regimental axe' to grind, was genuinely trying to arrive at a solution that, if not welcomed, would at least be generally acceptable to all concerned) proposed to General Burgess, as an alternative to the exchange of 1 Wessex's E Company for A Company 6 LI, that:

1.   E Company should re-role (still 'downwards') to form part of the new Battalion in the South West, which would have its Battalion HQ and HQ Companies in Plymouth, and take in the existing B and C Companies of 6 LI in Camborne and Truro;

2.   1 Wessex would replace E Company with a new Company in Swindon based on the existing detachment of HQ Company there; and

3.   To replace its B and C Companies, 6 LI should recruit new rifle ones in Bristol and Weston-super-Mare (and keep its Battalion HQ in Bath).

Two months after that, on 27 May, Colonel Bullock – who had obviously been hawking his plan around the corridors of power, and apparently imagined that it stood a good chance of being adopted – wrote to Major General Barry Lane, the Colonel of The Light Infantry (then the Vice Quartermaster General, but soon to become the GOC South West District) hoping that he [General Lane] would "*support [me] in opposing any fancy or contrived titles such as 3rd Bn The Wessex Regiment*".[9] He went on to say that "*The term "Wessex" has never had much significance in Devon, even though it may mean quite a lot further east.*"[10] A senior staff officer at South West District commented in a letter to HQ UKLF "Those who say [this] are surely looking with their blind eye".[11] That request and statement completely ignored several facts. The first was the admittedly obscure one that four TA battalions of the Devons had been part of 134 and 136 Brigades in 45 (Wessex) Infantry Division (a 'duplicate' of 43 (Wessex) Infantry Division) between 1941 and 1944[12]; the 4th and 5th Bns of The Dorsets, one of the antecedent regiments of The Devonshire & Dorset Regiment, had fought with considerable distinction as part the 43rd (Wessex) Division in the 1944/45 campaign in North West Europe – and, although the 5th Bn was disbanded, the 4th remained in it until the 1967 reorganisation (as did, incidentally, 5 DCLI); there is a memorial to the Division at Rough Tor on Bodmin Moor; most importantly, however, before their amalgamation in 1958, both The Devonshire Regiment and The Dorset Regiment, and after it The Devonshire

& Dorset Regiment had been part of the post-War Wessex Brigade, whose Headquarters were in Exeter. Colonel Bullock then wrote to The Prince of Wales's Division at the beginning of July, starting his letter with some wishful thinking: "While I know that I am preaching to the converted….", and then emphasising his view that forming 3 D & D was the only realistic way of producing the new Home Defence battalion. He then went on, however, to give the impression that he and General Lane had agreed that, if that proved impossible, it could be formed from 6LI's two rifle companies in Cornwall, badged Light Infantry, and two "in Devon" wearing D & D badges; its title would be the very clumsy "The Light Infantry & Devon & Dorset Regiment Volunteers (LIDDV)" – which even he admitted would be "something of a mouthful"! It is difficult to see how that idea would have been much to the advantage of the D & D, and it would have resulted in the creation of the first-ever battalion in British post-Haldane military history to have a mix of heavy and light infantry companies – hitherto a completely unthinkable concept.[13]

In the event, General Gray's proposals were adopted without amendment in HQ UKLF's first Plan for the Phase 2 Enhancement, which was issued as a paper on 25 August 1983, and then as a formal document – *The Territorial Army Expansion 1986-1990*[14] – in 1984:

6. The second phase of the TA expansion programme is more ambitious. It will begin in 1986 and run until the end of the decade. We have now decided what measures should be implemented during this phase in order to achieve our goals, although final details of some measures remain to be determined and the names for some of the new units which we propose to raise have not yet been decided. (The names used to designate new infantry battalions in this paper are for convenience only at this stage). While many measures involve the raising of new units, some are concerned with adding equipment and manpower to existing units. In devising our plans, operational requirements have determined our choice of which new units to raise and where to raise them. However, we have also taken into account recruiting potential and regimental traditions. In particular, we have taken the opportunity to restructure the Territorial Infantry to meet the criticism contained in the Shapland Report (1978) that "too

many TA units recruit from too wide an area. In too many parts of the country identity with the old TA units has been lost." It has been our aim, therefore, to reduce wherever possible the geographical spread of units, although there are some cases in which other considerations have prevented us from doing this.

7. An important factor in achieving our goal of raising the strength of the TA to 86,000 will be the ability to recruit officers and men of the right calibre. A sustained effort will be necessary.

8. In Phase II we plan to raise six infantry battalions, three for service in Germany and three for Home Defence. We also plan to raise a Yeomanry squadron and a new Air Defence regiment, and to add further batteries to the three existing Air Defence regiments. As to logistic and support arms, we intend to raise a new Transport squadron, a further Field Ambulance unit and a new Ordnance unit. Two more ADR squadrons will be formed and considerable enhancements will be made to other logistic units. One notable measure is the planned formation of a TA Army Air Corps squadron equipped with Scout helicopters, the first such unit. We also plan to increase the number of guns in Field Artillery regiments; to improve infantry equipment, including the introduction of LAW [Light Anti-tank Weapon] 80; and to increase the number of mortars which are allocated to the TA Infantry battalions in 2nd Infantry Division........

18. In South West District, we have given much thought to ways of preserving the historical and cultural identity of Cornwall in the TA of the future. To meet the operational requirement in the area we propose to raise a new three-company battalion of The Prince of Wales's Division in Devon and Cornwall. It will have its Headquarters at Plymouth and will take over the Camborne and Truro companies of the 6th Battalion The Light Infantry (Volunteers) and the Exeter company of 1st Battalion The Wessex Regiment (Rifle Volunteers). In determining the name and structure of this new battalion full account will be taken of its traditional antecedents. 6th Battalion The Light Infantry (Volunteers) will replace its Camborne and Truro companies with new companies in Bristol and Weston-super-Mare, while 1st Battalion The Wessex Regiment (Rifle Volunteers) will relinquish its Winchester and Exeter companies and form a new company at Swindon. Its Headquarter company will move from Swindon to Devizes [sic].

Disregarding the D & D's views, however, and albeit "only for identification purposes", the proposed new battalion was given the title "3 Wessex". The possibility that it might be adopted – particularly as E Company would, initially at least, be its best-recruited and best-trained component – had, of course, very considerable attraction for both Wessex battalions, and the 1st Battalion's newly appointed Honorary Colonel, Major General Mike Walsh, wrote strongly in favour of the idea to the Colonel Commandant of the Prince of Wales's Division, Major General Lennox Napier.[15]

That there was a need for a new major Home Defence unit in the District had in fact been accepted without question – even 1 Wessex could not argue otherwise. The District Headquarters, the TAVRA and the three regiments concerned had, however, been set the extremely difficult, if not impossible, task of finding a solution that would meet that need without seriously upsetting anyone. Both the MOD and HQ UKLF were determined that Regular regimental interests would neither 'drive' nor obstruct changes that needed to be made for good *operational* reasons, but neither the D & D nor The Light Infantry were willing to accept that. The whole business therefore rapidly became, and continued to be for the next year, near to chaotic, with letters flying in every direction, meetings at all levels (although rarely involving the COs of the TA units concerned), red-hot telephone lines and conversations in the gents lavatories of many headquarters and officers' messes. Happily, however, both General Gray and Brigadier Starling, the fairly recently appointed Secretary of the TAVRA, kept calm, trying to come up with a more realistic scenario, and generally see fair play all round.

Spread over Avon, Somerset and Cornwall, 6 LI was without doubt vulnerable to some sort of re-organisation. Understandably, however, General Lane did not want to absorb any part of 1 Wessex and thus 'contaminate' any part of his green-uniformed 6 LI with 'heavy, redcoat' infantry of the line – and, indeed, he never seems to have said (at least on paper) that he was receptive to Colonel Bullock's proposal. He was totally opposed to the whole 3 Wessex idea – and he wrote angrily and at great length to General Gray, protesting that he (General Lane) had not been properly consulted about proposals which directly affected one of his Regiment's TA battalions, and that by supporting the 3 Wessex suggestion General Gray had been improperly interfering in the affairs of another regiment (i.e. The Light Infantry); he further claimed that, if implemented, the plan would not only be extremely unpopular in Cornwall, but also have a seriously adverse effect on The Light Infantry as a whole.[16] He then said that he was content that D & D should form the new TA battalion (be it 3 D & D or 3 Wessex), leaving 6LI as it was, but with the addition of a new company in Weston-super-Mare. General Gray's reponse was courteous and clear:

> Very early in the Joynson Studies I appreciated that the regimental implications were far wider than just South West District. I therefore recommended that they must be co-ordinated by HQ UKLF. General Ted [Burgess] agreed to do this through the Director of Infantry...... Throughout all this we have worked within the guidelines given to us by HQ UKLF. I believe that, contrary to your surmise, we have consulted within the District far more widely than would normally be the case......... I can understand your regimental dilemma and anger, but a finger should not be pointed at this Headquarters, who have worked extremely hard on the plans and have been sensitive to local regimental feelings, doing all that was asked of them.....I believe that this all looks a little different when viewed from a District Headquarters.[17]

It was abundantly clear that the proposals for implementing the Phase 2 Plan pleased neither 1 Wessex or The Light Infantry, nor virtually any of the senior officers with interests in the District. The GOC, General Grey, stood between a rock and a hard place – and sadly he did not get the great credit he deserved for his efforts to achieve the fairest solution for all concerned. Needless to say, snippets of information about the situation quickly found their way to the Battalion and 6LI, and rumours started to spread – so HQ UKLF were told, mildly but firmly:

> These proposals have been developing since the end of last year. It is inevitable that consultation should be extensive. In fact it would have been wrong if this had not been the case. Needless to say, units have got the drift of what is being discussed, and it is beginning to have an unsettling effect. It would be a mistake to allow this uncertainty to drag

on into 1986 [the original implementation date for Phase 2]. Hopefully
the deployment decision, whatever it is, will be made soon.[18]

The uncertainty did indeed drag on, with yet more conferences,
meetings and papers – largely on the questions, firstly of whether,
in terms of the size of their population and hence their recruiting
potential, the towns in which it was proposed there should be new
companies could actually 'support' them (in addition, of course, to any
existing units); and, secondly, of the cost to the TAVRAs of providing
the extra TA Centres that would be needed.

The Ministry of Defence and HQ UKLF were obviously well aware
of the general feeling of unease and uncertainty that the Defence
Review had generated within the TA, and they had also known for
some years that an increasing number of Volunteers found themselves
at some stage in their TA careers (whether they were long or short) in
conflict with their civilian employers – specifically because they were
members of the TA. Notwithstanding the fact that TA service almost
certainly made almost all of those who experienced it better fitted to
do their 'real' jobs, many Volunteers were being actively discouraged
from joining in the first place, or from spending too much of their 'off-
duty' time soldiering, so it was said, to the detriment of those 'real'
jobs. Increasingly often, they were not – as they had almost invariably
been 10–15 years earlier – allowed an additional 15 days off, over and
above their normal entitlement, so that they could go to Camp and
have a family holiday as well. In the hope that it might be able to
prevent an appreciable number of members of the TA deciding to
leave on account of both uncertainty about their military futures and
employer hostility, the Government sensibly decided to try to persuade
employers of members of the TA to 'do their bit for defence'. Although
an appreciable number of Volunteer (usually private) soldiers preferred
not to let their employers know that they were in, or intended to
join, the TA[19] – at the beginning of April 1984 the Secretary of State
for Defence, Michael Hesletine, wrote to all those employers whose
identity was known to the various units:

Dear Employer

I am writing to you about members of our volunteer reserve forces, in particular in the Territorial Army (TA), who work for you or under your supervision.

The TA plays a vital part in our defence strategy. It is also highly cost-effective; it provides over 25 per cent of the mobilised strength of the British Army for about 4.5 per cent. of the Army's budget. Since coming to office, the Government has given a high priority to increasing the size of the TA and improving its operational capability. To this end we have embarked on a programme to expand it to a strength of 86,000 by 1990. We are also expanding the Royal Auxiliary Air Force, and we have plans to increase the size of the Royal Marines Reserve.

But the Government can only do so much to foster recruiting and enhance the training and effectiveness of our reserve forces. Inevitably, we rely on the dedication of the volunteers themselves, and I readily acknowledge the debt we owe to them and their families for their commitment to the security of our country, and the preservation of our way of life.

To equip him (or her) for his military role the volunteer must be properly trained. This involves him in a number of weekend and evening training programmes throughout the year; but of critical importance is attendance at the annual 15-day period of full-time training. Meeting this commitment invariably involves considerable personal sacrifices on the volunteer's part. I realise that it can also cause considerable problems for employers, particularly small employers. However, the qualities of leadership, self-discipline and initiative inherent in TA training are as important to the community and as beneficial to the employer as they are to the Armed Forces.

I am now appealing to all employers to adopt a policy of encouraging their employees to join the volunteer reserve forces, and of allowing those who are members of these reserves time off to attend training. I recognise that many of you already do this, for which I am very grateful.

This will be especially important this year when, in the autumn, a large number of TA soldiers will be participating in Exercise Lionheart, a major military exercise designed to test our plans for reinforcing the British Army of the Rhine.

I appreciate that what I am asking of you will not be easy, but by responding in this way not only will you be making your own important contribution to our national defence but also helping yourself by developing, through service in the reserves, the personal qualities and potential of those volunteers in your employ.[20]

The reorganisation business rumbled on across the whole of the county during the 1983/1984 winter, and there seemed to be little prospect of agreement being reached on the titles of several of the new battalions – or even, in the case of the one in South West District, as to how it was going to be formed. A not insignificant diversion – which did not affect the Battalion in administrative or operational terms, as it was under the command of 1 Infantry Brigade – was the formation on 2 April of a new Headquarters based in Exeter, 43 Brigade, to relieve the pressures on HQ South West District at Bulford, and to correct the imbalanced military presence in the south west. The bulk of the District's 18,700 Regulars were at the eastern end, while most of the TA were in the west – so it was ill-placed to "supervise TA training, oversee Home Defence and to liaise closely with the Civil Authorities in the largest areas of population in the South West."[21]

Then, on 4 April 1984, some nine months after "3 Wessex" had been first suggested, HQ UKLF sent a signal saying that the title of the new battalion in South West District would be "3 Wessex (Devon & Cornwall)", badged as Wessex but wearing green berets! The previous day, the Director of Infantry, Major General Colin Shortis, CBE – who had been appointed the Colonel Commandant of The Prince of Wales's Division in 1983, and succeeded Colonel Bullock as the Colonel of The Devonshire & Dorset Regiment early in 1984 – had written in the first of those capacities, to all the Divisions of Infantry, the Districts, the TAVRAs and the Ministry of Defence as follows:

1. In reference A [A letter from MOD (ASD 2 TA), 21st March 1984], I have been instructed by DASD [the Director of Army Staff Duties] to give him my recommendations, as Director of Infantry, for the names for the four battalions which are to be raised in Cleveland and North Yorkshire; London; Devon and Cornwall; and Greater Manchester and Cheshire. In doing this I am to take account of regimental and local opinion, and to consult in particular with DTA

& C (and through him with the TA Council and TAVR Associations), and with HQ UKLF.

2. The purpose of this letter is to ask the Colonels Commandant of the Divisions concerned to send me their recommendations for the proposed title of the new battalion or battalions in their Division. *In the case of the new battalion in Devon and Cornwall, the Colonel Commandant Prince of Wales's Division* [i.e.General Shortis himself], *in which the new battalion will be, is to consult with Colonel Commandant The Light Division before recommending an appropriate title and/or other measures to recognise the historical antecedents of the new unit.*[22]

3. In formulating their advice Colonels Commandant are to take account of the statement published in reference B, and in particular paragraph 6 which is reproduced at Annex A for ease of reference. However, any proposal must meet the following criteria:

a. Any particular historical, regimental or county affiliation can appear in the title, but the cap badge worn must be that of an existing regiment in the Regular or Territorial Army order of battle. We are not in the business of setting up new small regiments.

b. Any title proposed must have the overall support of the large majority of those actually concerned i.e. the volunteer officers and soldiers as well as the civil population and local authorities. Although Colonels Commandant will wish to consult TAVRAs on this, DTA & C is asked to forward a definitive statement to me reflecting the views of the TA Council and TAVR Associations on the names proposed.

c. The adoption of a particular regimental title gives no special right to manning by regulars from a particular Regiment, and all regular appointments will continue to be filled from the best men available on a Divisional basis.

d. The recruiting areas of territorial and regular battalions of the same Regiment should coincide, and the adoption by a territorial battalion of a particular regular title and badge must not be mandatorily imposed on those with a different affiliation.

4. I believe that the choice of the right titles and the reinforcement of the regimental and county links will play a major part in our

ability to recruit both our new and existing battalions. History shows that imposed solutions seldom last, and I therefore welcome this opportunity to obtain your and, through you, the views and wishes of the people on whom we will rely to man these units. For this reason, it is important that the proposals I forward are the ones that will gain the maximum local support to reinforce the volunteer spirit and local pride which is so much part of the TA Infantry, and if in doing this we can also enhance the links and mutual support between regular and territorial battalions, then so much the better.[23]

It seemed at the time, and still seems, that the right hand had little idea what the left hand was saying, for it was not easy to reconcile HQ UKLF's proposal of 4 April with General Shortis's letter, and it is far from clear what the second half of paragraph 3d meant. It was, however, quite obvious to all that his instructions, as they applied to him in paragraph 2, were specifically intended to result, sooner or later, in the creation of a TA battalion of the D & D.

On 6 April, General Barry Lane wrote to the author (who had become the Chairman of the TAVRA a few days earlier):

We are bedevilled, unnecessarily in my view, by the structure of this new battalion. I wish I had been involved in it from the beginning. I really must seek your help in resolving it if we really have to go down this path. We cannot alienate Cornwall – or my Regiment – in the search for two more companies in the South West. We have to find a solution which is acceptable, and which does not leave Cornwall without a Light Infantry presence at a time when [that presence] is being strengthened throughout the rest of the Regimental area.[24]

but did he think about alienating 1 Wessex, and to whom should the solution also be acceptable? By virtue of being the GOC South West District, he was also the Major General UKMF (L), and, some three weeks after that, he wrote to HQ UKLF about the implementation of Phase 2 in the District, including these paragraphs in his letter:

UKMF(L).......I am reviewing the role of 1 Wessex within UKMF(L), since *I believe that it may be being employed beyond its capability*,[25] certainly when compared with the tasks given to other TA battalions in 1(BR) Corps; there is probably no justification for a fifth company in the long term, although the timing of any redeployment should be related to any change of role.

Peacetime Structure of TA Infantry – 1 Wessex. There is at first sight and on current plans no operational reason to delay any change the role of the Company [sic – but presumably he meant E Company], but its standard of training will be better sustained by leaving it under the command of 1 Wessex until alternative command arrangements are properly established.[26]

Those two paragraphs appear to be somewhat inconsistent with each other, but it is difficult to see the first one as other than an attempt to belittle the Battalion – and there is no evidence whatsoever that either 1 Brigade, HQ UKLF or, indeed, anyone else in the UKMF(L) were in any way dissatisfied with its performance. Indeed, as mentioned in Chapter 12, at Camp that year in Schleswig Holstein, taking part in 1 Brigade's Exercise Bold Gannet, it had many important visitors, and that would surely not have been the case if it was not well capable of holding its own with the Regular Army. The fact that it retained its challenging and important role for another eleven years (albeit with a two-year break in 1992–1994 to allow it to recover after its final reorganisation) speaks for itself.

Four other names were put forward as alternatives to HQ UKLF's proposed "3rd Bn. The Wessex Regiment (Devon & Cornwall)". D & D and the Light Infantry wanted "3rd Bn. The Devon & Cornwall Rifle Volunteers", the TAVRA suggested "3rd Bn. The Wessex Regiment (Duke of Cornwall's Rifle Volunteers)", and the Colonel Commandant of The Prince of Wales's Division, the very level-headed Major General Laurence Napier, proposed "3rd Bn The Wessex Regiment (Devon & Cornwall Volunters)".[27] The TAVRA consulted widely – with the COs of 1 Wessex (Philip Goddard, who was, ironically, a Light Infanteer) and 6 LI, the Company Commanders of the Companies that would be involved, the six Lords Lieutenant, and the senior TAVRA members in all six counties – and the most acceptable (or least objectionable) suggestion was held to be the third; nevertheless for a few months, "DCRV" became the standard reference for the new battalion. General Shortis, however, felt that there was "compelling advantage" in the adoption of "3rd Bn. The Devon & Cornwall Volunteers" *as a battalion of The Wessex Regiment, but not so named.*[28] because:

> .....to impose The Wessex Regiment title would be ill-judged on the grounds that: (a) The title "Wessex" is regarded as foreign in Cornwall, as Cornwall had never formed part of Wessex. As such it would tend to be misunderstood and to repel rather than attract local support in Cornwall, and (b) The existing Wessex Company in Devonshire is thinly recruited, and a more positive link with the county title, and with the existing regular County Regiment offers the prospect of more effective local support in the future.[29]

and, most curiously, he also said:

> The Wessex Regiment badge was imposed by Colonel Commandant The Prince of Wales's Division [i.e himself] against the wishes of the Colonels of both Regiments [i.e. D & D and The Light Infantry] concerned who would have preferred a new and unique capbadge. By definition, the battalion will be part of The Wessex Regiment although not so named.[30]

but how he did not know that the 5th Bn The Duke of Cornwall's Light Infantry had formed part of 43 Division throughout the Normandy campaign in 1944–1945, or why he decided that the new battalion should be part of a regiment for which he had scant regard – and what "by definition" meant – is anyone's guess.

That idea could not possibly have appealed to The Wessex Regiment, and in any event it was, of course, verging on the ridiculous, not only as a military concept, but because the DCRV would be unlikely in the extreme ever to have a first or a second battalion in the future. Nevertheless, in August, quite astonishingly and for reasons that are likely to remain totally obscure, that title was formally approved by HM The Queen.[31]

The possibility of The Wessex Regiment acquiring a third battalion did, however, lead General Mike Walsh and the Regimental Council to put forward the idea – already successfully adopted, with MOD approval, by the three battalions of The Yorkshire Volunteers – of establishing a Regimental Headquarters, with a Regimental Colonel and a Regimental Adjutant. Both would be TA officers already employed at District Headquarters, and would thus become 'double-hatted', and their task would be "to co-ordinate the recruiting, the career-planning for TA officers and other ranks, certain administrative matters and aspects of training" of the battalions. The proposal was strongly endorsed by Brigadier Joe Starling, but because, in the event, the "3 Wessex" proposal never came to fruition, and a third battalion of The Wessex Regiment was never formed, the idea was dropped.

Everything then went strangely silent for almost two years – the waiting period before the implementation of Phase 2 began – during which time E Company remained steadfastly part of the Battalion, and no further discussions about reorganisation were held or proposals put forward.

On 1st April 1986, however, as part of Phase II – and, indeed, implementing the original proposal made by Colonel Joynson back in December 1982 – B Company ceased to be part of 1 Wessex, and became B Company of 2 Wessex. The original intention had been that the Company would leave the Battalion in 1984, but Philip Goddard had strongly objected to the idea, on the very sensible ground that it had never been intended that the replacement B Company in Swindon (initially known, to avoid confusion, as F Company) would be operational before 1 April 1986[32]– and his point was taken[33]. One significant result of the change in the timing of the move, however, was that by the time it took place they had recruited so well that they were 20 over their establishment. Just before the transfer eventually took place, the writer of the Company Notes in the *Royal Hampshire Regiment Journal*[34] said:

> Yes, it is with curiosity, rather than any other feeling, that we prepare to make a slightly more intimate acquaintance with that other lot. I use the word "intimate" advisedly; it has come to our notice the 2nd Battalion has among its ranks a WRAC [Women's Royal Army Corps] platoon.

The formation, and the subsequent loss, of the new B Company is covered in the next Chapter.

In the previous month, an infinitely worse scenario from 1 Wessex's point of view began to be discussed, undoubtedly at the instigation of General Shortis, who had just handed-over as Director of Infantry and become the GOC of North West District – the formation of a new, entirely Devon & Dorset TA battalion along the lines he had previously suggested back in May 1983. It would 'acquire' not only E Company but C Company in Dorchester as well, and, rather than taking in 6 LI's Cornish Company, raise one in either Newton Abbott or the Torbay area; Battalion HQ and HQ Company would be in Plymouth. The loss of C Company could, it was said, be offset by A Company concentrating in the Gloucester area, and the formation of a new Company at Speedwell in Bristol from the existing A Company Platoon there.

A senior staff officer in the Director of Infantry's office wrote to The Prince of Wales's Division at Lichfield:

> We know that the new battalion's disposition and title have created controversy and correspondence between HQ Prince of Wales's Division, HQ The Light Division, HQ SW District and Western Wessex TAVRA. The current situation is unknown to us......but we need to have some idea of the direction and likely outcome of the discussions we suspect are in progress.[35]

and in a letter to Brigadier Joe Starling, the very straight-forward Divisional Brigadier, Brigadier 'Bill' Turner of the DERR, said:

> We have nothing to offer, and have informed Warminster accordingly. I join the ranks of the confused. My reading is that General Colin Shortis and General Barry Lane have played it very close to the chest."[36]

The formal proposal for the formation of 4 D & D (as the new battalion eventually became) was set out in a paper by General Lane, still the GOC, on 9 April 1986. The only change from General Shortis' plan was that Battalion HQ and a newly raised Headquarter Company would be in Exeter, rather than Plymouth. The requirement that 1 Wessex should recruit a new company in Bristol to compensate for the loss of C Company remained unchanged.

The Wessex Regimental Council met on 26 April 1986, and immediately after it, General Mike Walsh wrote to Lieutenant General

Sir John Akehurst, the new Inspector General of the TA (who, after his retirement, was to become an able, much appreciated and greatly respected Chairman of the Council of TAVRAs):

> The present Phase 2 Plan has resulted in restructuring of both 1 and 2 Wessex. These changes have been accepted by all ranks, and everyone has worked hard to ensure that our operational role has not been affected. We now understand that yet more restructuring is under consideration which overall could result in 1 Wessex, over a period of 2/3 years, losing three rifle companies, restructuring a further rifle company and having to raise two new companies. In view of 1 Wessex's training and operational commitment, these proposals are, we believe, unacceptable. As Chairman of The Wessex Regiment Council I would advise you that the Council will strongly oppose any further major changes to the 1 Wessex deployment. Furthermore, we would appreciate being briefed and consulted in order to prepare our case.[37]

On 1 May, General Shortis sent a letter to General Akehurst, Major General Edward Jones (the ebullient Director General TA & Cadets, who after he left the Army became Black Rod in The House of Lords, and was yet another extremely popular Chairman of the Council of TAVRAs), Major General Sir David Thorne (who had recently taken over as the Director of Infantry from General Shortis), Brigadier Starling and others – but, seemingly as a direct snub, not to General Mike – giving his "fullest support" to General Lane's plan. He somehow knew of that TAVRA's proposed "Torbay alternative" but:

> While I understand [the TAVRA's] concern for stability in 1 Wessex I have to say, on balance, and irrespective of any Regimental feelings, that this is not a good solution since it could only defer the issue not resolve it.

clearly demonstrating that in the end, one way and another, he intended, to get C Company for 4 D & D. The Honorary Colonel reacted immediately with a letter of some force:

> I am both saddened and surprised that, as Colonel Commandant of the Prince of Wales's Division, you are recommending that the GOC

> SW District's revised plan for the deployment of the Territorial Army
> in the SW "be agreed and promulgated as soon as possible". You have
> a specific command responsibility to The Wessex Regiment. At no
> stage have you consulted or given consideration to their operational
> and training commitments. Not only is this a clear breach of military
> courtesy, but also, in the view of the Wessex Regiment Council, a
> failure to carry out your duty to a regiment of your Division.[38]

but, as another snub, he never received a reply. Brigadier Starling
pointed out that it would be manifestly unfair for the Devon &
Dorsets to get their TA battalion back when the chances of any of the
other Regular Regiments doing so as well were at that time remote in
the extreme, and Eastern Wessex also wrote to South West District
condemning the turbulence that the proposed changes would inflict
on the Battalion.[39] Brigadier Starling and the author then came up
with that "Torbay alternative" plan as it became known, to avoid 1
Wessex losing C Company to 4 D & D – which was that 4 D & D
should instead recruit a new rifle company in Newton Abbott (as had
in fact originally been suggested by General Shortis), and an additional
platoon at Exmouth. The author again consulted the Lords Lieutenant
and the senior members of the TAVRA, and, with only two predictable
exceptions, they all approved the new proposal.

It is easy to understand the deeply-held wish of every regiment in
the British Army at the time to re-acquire the TA battalion it had lost
in 1967, to strengthen the links within the regiment between Regulars
and Volunteers, and to maintain an 'uncontaminated' presence in
its county or counties (particularly in those areas where its Regular
battalion was unlikely to be seen regularly). On the other hand, because
there was no 'commonality' of names between the Regular regiments
and 1 Wessex, and the Regular Regiments were only "affiliated", and
not "parent", regiments, they consequently had less contact with,
and perhaps less interest in, the respective TA companies than would
probably otherwise have been the case. The Regular Regiments did
not therefore all seem to appreciate the extent to which, by that time,
1 Wessex had acquired its own identity, fierce pride, local links, and
the respect of so many members of the Regular Army. It wanted to
retain its unity and those strengths just as strongly as The Devonshire

& Dorset Regiment, and initially The Light Infantry, wanted to dismember it for their own purposes. Regular regiments with 'power bases' were able to protect and enhance their interests, while those TA ones without 'clout' were seriously at risk. It is a fact of military life that senior officers are sometimes appointed to jobs that inevitably put them into the position of having a major conflict of interest, and they are able to use their power as servants of the whole or part of the Army for the benefit of their own 'private armies'. That was happening now, and 10 years later it disastrously led to the total demise of the Battalion. The author must, however, admit that, as his remit as the Chairman of the TAVRA was unquestionably to help everyone within its area of responsibility arrive at the most acceptable and practical solution to any dispute or problem, and that he therefore had to give up his primary loyalty to 1 Wessex, whenever possible he did his best to achieve for it at least some 'damage limitation' – provided only that that did not adversely affect any other existing units.

To that end, he spent four hours at home one Sunday afternoon at the beginning of June 1986 in a marathon discussion with General Shortis about the formation of 4 D & D. A forceful and persuasive officer, the General, although no longer the Director of Infantry, was still both the Colonel Commandant of The Prince of Wales's Division and the Colonel of The Devonshire & Dorset Regiment – and thus in a position of virtually unassailable power in relation to the future of 1 Wessex. It regrettably has to be said that, despite his protestations of impartiality, it was perfectly clear that he was wearing his own regimental hat and determined to take at least E Company, and if possible C Company as well. By the time of that meeting, as the result of many earlier discussions, it had in fact already been agreed (albeit extremely reluctantly) by both 1 Wessex and the TAVRA that there were good operational reasons for E Company being transferred to the new battalion, although it was not at that stage clear what its regimental affiliation would be. The sticking point, however, was C Company in Dorchester.

The argument went on, 'tooth and nail', for almost four hours – while the author's wife plied the General's driver with endless cups of tea – but by the end of it the author did not feel that he had conceded anything. One reason for that was perhaps the unique tradition in the TA in those days (which may still exist today) that when a TAVRA Chairman and a General met for the first time the Chairman addressed the General as "General" – but thereafter (except when it would have been inappropriate in the circumstances) by his Christian name. The principle behind that was that, as the senior representative of all the TA soldiers in his TAVRA area, but not being 'under command', the Chairman stood on the same rung of the ladder as the GOC, and hence virtually all other generals – and it provided the inestimable benefit of enabling the former to talk to the latter 'man-to-man' without inhibition.

General Shortis based much of his argument on the "disappointment" which would be felt in Dorset if the new Battalion did not include C Company, and he seemed quite unable (or unwilling) to accept that for 1 Wessex, which had just begun the task of raising a completely new B Company in Swindon to replace the Hampshire one, to lose another Company would be a monumental blow. The author wrote to him a few days later:

> You talked much of compromise, as if it had to begin at this stage, but I think you fail to appreciate that 1 Wessex has already had to accept giving up B and E Companies. If 4 D & D were to include C Company, I cannot see that there would be any compromise on your part, because its transfer would only be a question of timing and mechanics, not principle. As Colonel of the Regiment, I believe that you should be thankful in accepting a Devon-based 4th Bn – particularly as, notwithstanding what you told me was the Divisional policy about TA battalions, the chance of any of the other Wessex Regiments getting theirs back seems a remote prospect at the present time.[40]

and to General Lane on 20 June:

> …..you will appreciate that having no Regular "parent" regiment to press their case in fact places [1 Wesex] at a considerable disadvantage – were it otherwise, I am sure that they would have many 'big guns' supporting them. In the circumstances, as I have already said to Colin on several occasions, I believe that, as Colonel Commandant of The Prince of Wales's Division, he should be concerned almost more for 1

Wessex than for his own Regiment.

Almost the only person to support General Shortis outside the Light Infantry seemed to be General Lane – who, in all the to-ing and fro-ing, had managed to remove the threat to 6 LI's Cornish Companies. Everyone else, however, from the Inspector General of the TA, the Lords Lieutenant of all the counties in which 1 Wessex had a presence, 1 Infantry Brigade, to Brigadier Joe Starling of the TAVRA, was unanimously supportive of 1 Wessex. Brigadier Joe also pointed out that, as well as reducing turbulence in the Battalion, the "Torbay alternative" would avoid the risk, anticipated by the TAVRA on demographic grounds, of a failure not only to enlarge A Company's Platoon in Bristol into a complete Company, but also to form a replacement Platoon in Gloucestershire – and, furthermore, it would save around £150,000 in building works.

A month or so later, General Lane proposed another solution to General Shortis: as had already been agreed, 4 D & D would have its Battalion HQ and Headquarter Company (formerly E Company 1 Wessex) in Exeter, with Rifle Companies in Plymouth and the Torbay area (almost certainly in Paignton) – and it would also form a Recce Platoon in Weymouth, which would give it a presence in Dorset. C Company, however, would remain in 1 Wessex, and even the idea of a new company in Bristol could be forgotten about – although as things were to turn out some years later, it was in fact only shelved. To almost everyone's amazement and relief, that was accepted by General Shortis, who wrote to the author:

> The position of myself and my Regiment on this matter has not altered in any way whatsoever, but I reflected very carefully both on our conversations and on all the issues involved and felt that it could only lead to serious damage to relationships and the well-being of The Prince of Wales's Division if I were to continue to press our case at the present time.

A further satisfactory aspect of the compromise was that E Company would not transfer to 4 D & D until the new rifle company in Swindon was at least 'up and running', if not yet completely fit for its role, and that did not in fact happen until 1987. In the event, however, as explained in Chapter 12, the "Weymouth solution" was in fact never implemented in that form – but there was still to be one more, and immensely disappointing, loss to the Battalion: The Devon Band would be transferred to 4 D & D – although, happily, the Hampshire & Dorset Band would continue to be administered by the Battalion, and in effect still 'theirs'.

It has, however, always been one of the great strengths of the Army – both the Regular Army and the TA – that when there has been any amalgamation or reorganisation of Infantry regiments, after all the proposals and wrangling, the discussions held and positions taken, the successor units have nearly always turned out to be extremely successful. So far as the Volunteers were concerned, that is undoubtedly because, in the last resort, the large majority of them were much more interested in whether or not they could continue to serve at all, than in which cap-badge they wore[41], and broad minded enough to make real efforts to ensure that almost any new arrangements worked really well.

———————

[1]   Most of the material for this and the subsequent Chapters which deal with the re-organisation of the Battalion is taken from the author's files of original and copy correspondence, and papers, passing between many of those involved in the discussions. Permission to use those documents in which Crown Copyright exists has been given by the Ministry of Defence.

[2]   Chaired by Major General James Majury (late Royal Irish).

[3]   Command Paper 8288.

[4]   Letter to HQ South West District 9 December 1982.

[5]   Dated 13 December 1982 and 18 March 1983.

[6]   Minutes of that meeting.

[7]   Letter of 21 March 1983.

[8]   Annexe to *ibid*.

[9]   Author's italics – from a letter 27 May 1983.

[10] Ditto.

[11] Letter 12 July 1983.

[12] http://en.wikipedia.org – 45th Wessex Infantry Division.

[13] Some 20 years later, of course, in 2006/2007, The Devonshire & Dorset Regiment, The Royal Gloucestershire, Berkshire & Wiltshire Regiment (formed in 1994 by the amalgamation of The Gloucestershire Regiment and The Duke of Edinburgh's Royal Regiment) and The Light Infantry joined together to form the 1st Battalion The Rifles,

part of a newly-created "large large regiment" in The Light Division. The Glosters had in fact narrowly avoided amalgamation with the Royal Hampshires in 1970 (as the result of a change of Government) – shortly before which some wag had suggested that, contrary to appearances, the Sphinx might not be female after all, and the following appeared in the RHRJ: "To marry the Sphinx and the Tiger/We early decided was out/Our decision is even more right as we hear/That the sex of the Sphinx is in doubt".

[14] Defence Open Government Document 84/02 – exact date of publication not known.

[15] Letter 1 July 1983.

[16] Letter to General Gray, 12 September 1983.

[17] Letter 18 October 1983.

[18] Letter from South West District, 12 July 1983.

[19] In due course, however, they became obliged to do so.

[20] *Hansard* 9 April 1984.

[21] HQ South West District Directive of 26 March 1984.

[22] Author's italics.

[23] Letter 3 April 1984.

[24] Letter 6 April 1984.

[25] Author's italics.

[26] Letter 25 April 1984.

[27] Letter to General Walsh, 6 July 1983.

[28] Author's italics.

[29] Annexe to letter from General Shortis to the Deputy Director of Infantry 8 May 1984.

[30] *Ibid.*

[31] Director of Army Staff Duties' letter 6 August 1984.

[32] Letter from 1 Wessex to HQ UKLF and others, 4 Jan 1984.

[33] A copy of the extremely clever draft MOD "network" [flowchart] for the forming of, inter alia, the Company is on Plate 22. The boxes on the top line are the earliest start date ($\emptyset$ = April 1986), the serial number and the earliest finish date; the middle line is the project; the bottom line shows the latest start date, the duration and the latest finish date.

[34] May 1986.

[35] Letter 17 March 1986.

[36] Letter 25 March 1986.

[37] Letter to General Shortis, 30 April 1986.

[38] Letter 8 May 1986.

[39] Letter to HQ South West District, 12 May 1986.

[40] Letter 5 June 1986

[41] One of the finest examples of that was Colonel J D Bryant, TD**DL. After National Service in the 13th/18th Hussars, he joined the Royal Gloucestershire Hussars; he then transferred to the North Somerset Yeomanry/44th Royal Tank Regiment, which became the North Somerset & Bristol Yeomanry; in 1967, he remained with the NS & BY when it merged with the Somerset Light Infantry (TA) to form the Somerset Yeomanry and Light Infantry. He commanded Bristol University OTC, after which he joined the All Arms Pool of Watchkeepers in the British Army of the Rhine, then transferred to 6th Bn The Light Infantry – and he finally finished his TA service as Honorary Colonel

of 57th Signal Squadron, Royal Signals. 7 different cap-badges – and (his claim to
fame in this book) while he was with the RGH in the late 1960s he acted as the 'Honorary
Armoured Adviser' to 1 Wessex, helping John Sellars with the planning of several major
exercises!

_____

CHAPTER 9

THE VARIED LIFE CONTINUES: 1981–1987

Two letters received in the Battalion during January and February 1981[1] (faithfully reproduced here) showed that not everyone who joined the TA found the life to their liking:

> Dear Sir,
> with reference to your letter dated 17th October 1980 – Riminder of Non-Payment of debit Voucher. I have only just returned (17th January 1981) from France after serving 3 months in the French Foreign Legion and 2 months in Prison for desertion and I would appreciate it if an arrangement could be made for small weekly payments could be made off the debit until I am able to find work.
> Yours sincerely,
> XXXXX

> Dear Sir,
> I am writing to you to tell you that I have stopped coming to the meetings and that I would like to hand in all my kit.
> the reason why is because after the recruit cadre I know that I could not die or kill some body for some thing I do not believe in. Apart from that I could not kill some body as it says in my bible in the Ten Commandments Thou Shalt Not Kill. And I believe in the word and I will not go against the word of God.
> Now I spend my Tuesday nights at prayer meetings and my Sundays in the Pentecostal church in Tiverton.
> Yours faithfully,
> XXXXX
> Ephesians 6.17

John Southwood finished his tour of command on 31 March 1981 – and his next job was in the office of the Director of Army Public Relations, where, among other things, he thought up the famous, and very effective, national recruiting poster: "If you were the enemy, would you know the difference?" – a picture of two totally indistinguishable camouflaged soldiers, Lance Corporal Bond of 1 Royal Hamps and Corporal Bachelor of HQ Company (no less!) 1 Wessex, advancing with fixed bayonets.

His successor was a Gloster, Lieutenant Colonel Terry Dutton, MBE – whose father had been in The Wiltshire Regiment. He was a graduate of the Royal Military College of Science – and as captain of the RMA Sandhurst Rugger XV he had followed tradition by later playing for the Army. He was a good leader, measured and firm in his approach, with a great ability to get on with anyone, be they a general or a private soldier's girlfriend, and a good sense of humour; he really identified himself with the Battalion, and greatly enjoyed his tour of command. The middle and last years of his tour, 1982 and1983, were made particularly dificult by the reorganisation proposals which were the subject of the previous Chapter – but he stoutly defended the Battalion's position in the face of powerful onslaughts from both D & D and The Light Infantry, and happily, for various reasons, the Battalion underwent no actual changes for another three years.

Following Exercise Crusader 80 and the immense effort put into it, 1981 was a year of unremarkable but very serious and demanding training – internal cadres, external courses, exercises on Salisbury Plain and elsewhere, company weekends and drill nights, an October Camp at Reinsehlen in BAOR (see Chapter 11) and, of course, there was a modest amount of social activity as well. Just how serious and demanding training had in fact become – or perhaps always had been – is well illustrated by the following list of activities that was carried out by B Company in the four summer months of 1982 – in addition, of course, to two drill nights a week for the majority of its members:

8/9 May: The Company fired its Annual Personal Weapons Test and a major Company FTX was held, with the Company reunion on the Saturday night.

22/23 May: A Company Attack week-end on Salisbury Plain; the Company practised all aspects of attack and fighting through, from section to company level, plus patrolling, recce and ambush.

5/6 June: A Company Defence week-end, again on the SPTA (with the usual rock-hard ground).

19/20 June: The Battalion Field Firing week-end on Salisbury Plain. Training consisted of platoon anti-tank ambush, 84-mm and 66-mm field firing, NBC, 84-mm sub-calibre stalk, bayonet fighting, and field defence TEWT, all in 36 hours.

3/4 July: A withdrawal week-end, based on the Longmoor Training Area.

10/11 July: I Infantry Brigade's Medium Anti-tank Weapons Concentration on the Lydd Ranges. The Company provided 12 teams for this shoot; notwithstanding that all the other teams were from Regular battalions, 1 Wessex won overall, and B Company now leads in the 66-mm/84-mm Brigade shoots. The week-end consisted of an assault course with outdoor sub-calibre shoots, AFV recognition (all teams were said to be sitting an Open University degree course in this subject next year), and shooting at moving targets.

24/25 July: A week-end on the Isle of Wight – a pleasant change from Salisbury Plain – with a march and shoot competition, NBC training (including shooting), a GPMG concentration, and a lot of camouflage and counter-surveillance work.

7 August: The next of the Company's shooting days.

14/15 August: A Battalion FTX[2] with Chinooks, the digging of a battalion defence position, fighting off heliborne attacks, etc.

21/22 August: Briefing week-end for Camp. "The usual talks – security, pay, etc" – plus a lot of NBC[3]

The same sort of pace was consistently maintained throughout the Battalion month after month, year after year – for example, in 1984:

Immediately after the Easter break, in April there is to be a weekend Inter Fire Team Competition, a FIBUA [Fighting in built-up areas] training weekend at Longmoor and participation in the Gloucestershire County Show with a large Recruiting Stand. In May the Annual Personal Weapons Tests and Bounty Tests, in June off to Annual Camp in Norfolk, but before that the Battalion Skill at Arms Meeting.[4]

Two training weekends a month – one for the Companies on their own, and the other for the whole Battalion – was the norm for everyone, and very occasionally there were three. For a few individuals, however

– such as the 'chiefs' in the Companies who had to plan future training, members of Battalion teams (particularly the shooting team), and officers who had to audit the various Company and Battalion accounts every six months – there was almost certainly bound to be yet another weekend at least once a quarter. It should not be forgotten, too, that not only were the CO and the Training Major, and sometimes other members of Battalion HQ, 'by definition' out on all Battalion weekends, but also for at least one day of almost certainly four or five other weekends out of six or seven they were visiting the Companies or the specialist platoons on their own training weekends, and other activities of one sort or another.

Working at that pressure, of course, often put a huge strain on the family lives of the married Volunteers and Permanent Staff, and on the relationships of probably most of the rest with their girlfriends. It was, however, very rare indeed for an officer or NCO to leave the Battalion for 'domestic pressure' reasons – for which the greatest possible credit was due to their ladies.

For all that effort and hard work, members of the TA were paid at the lowest rates for their equivalent rank in the Regular Army without any increments for length of service. In 1982 they were:

Recruit	£10.38 a day
Trained soldier	£11.08
Lance Corporal	£12.68
Corporal	£16.84
Sergeant	£19.45
Colour Sergeant	£20.59
WO 2	£23.52

and in addition Volunteers could claim travelling expenses at the rate of 9.3p a mile, with a (very generously, tax-free) 'allowance' for attending drill nights at the derisory rates of 75p for soldiers, 87p for NCOs and £1.09 for officers. There was also, however, the Bounty:

As we approach the end of the financial year our thoughts and efforts are concentrated on the final 'dash' towards qualifying for the Annual Bounty......The Bounty is a non-taxable lump sum paid to all members of the TA annually, subject to qualification, on the following scale:

[in 1982/83] – first year of service £150; second year of service £275; third and subsequent years £400. To 'qualify' for his Bounty, a member of the TA (Infantry) must have:

> Completed 27 day's training, of which 15 days were at Annual Camp, or attended an approved course of not less than 10 working days in lieu of Annual Camp;
> Attended the appropriate number of training days specified by Bn HQ as being of particular importance (known as Red Days);
> Been available for Army Service for the complete 'Bounty year';
> Fired his Annual Personal Weapons Test (APWT);
> Been of the correct medical category and sufficiently fit to take his place in the unit for its war role;
> Passed the Fitness Tests, at the minimum standard; and carried out the Nuclear, Biological and Chemical [Defence] and First Aid Tests.

It can be seen that these lump sums are not purely a "handout", but proper rewards for loyal and efficient service.....[5]

In April 1981, a rare and particularly pleasing event took place: WO2 Tony Cundy of B Company – who, as a Colour Sergeant, had been awarded the BEM in 1973 for his tremendous success in commanding the Isle of Wight detachment – was commissioned after 16 years in the ranks. He immediately took over the Mortar Platoon in Andover, and his achievement was publically recognised in a full-page spread about him and the Platoon in the *Andover Evening Advertiser*[6] In due course he rose to become a popular Company Commander of B Company. Another, but rather different, achievement was that of WO2 Bernard Wray RAMC, of the Battalion's Medical Section, who won the 26-mile, 375 yard Devizes Marathon in 2 hours, 47.34 minutes.

A sadness in the same year was the death of Captain Geoffrey Foreman, a retired Gloucester Bank Manager, who had been the Paymaster of 5th Glosters for a good many years. He was too old to transfer to the TAVR in 1967, but he volunteered to become the Treasurer of A Company's Wessex Club at the Eastern Avenue TA Centre, and he looked after its accounts with the greatest possible efficiency and dedication. One of life's gentlemen, totally non-military in his appearance apart from his moustache, both before and after 1967 he endeared himself to countless officers (including the author) who were Account Holders responsible for the funds of the individual Companies, the Officers' and WOs & Sergeants' Messes, etc. for his ability to explain the mysteries of (as was the system in those days) double-entry book-keeping so simply that they never forgot it.

Major Peter Tucker began his TA service in 1955 as the Regimental Medical Officer of the Royal Devon Yeomanry, but he transferred to the Battalion in 1967. A GP in Midsomer Norton, near Bath, he was one of those people who did a magnificent job almost completely unnoticed. Much of his work was extremely routine – mainly "doing medicals" (as it was known) on almost every potential recruit in all five Companies, to check that they were healthy enough to stand the rigours of life in a NATO battalion. Doing that entailed driving very long distances to the various TA Centres – in the winter months through fog, rain and sometimes snow – going through the same procedures (which, by the early 1980s, he must have done well over a thousand times), and then driving home again, almost always late at night. At Camps, he occasionally had major problems to deal with, but by and large the Battalion was extremely healthy, and serious accidents were few and far between. He was a gentle, almost shy, person, but with a happy and positive grin, and a manner that exuded a quiet confidence; as he went around the Battalion he would run an eye over the officers, the senior ranks and the longer-serving soldiers – whom he obviously got to know pretty well – and if he felt uneasy about someone, perhaps looking heavily overworked, limping or not very fit, there was always a word of sensible advice. He was very properly made an MBE in 1981, and his retirement the following year was a sad day for the Battalion.

At the end of 1981, after six years as an exemplary Honorary Colonel, General Glyn Gilbert retired, and his place was taken by another "Para" – Major General MJH Walsh, CB, CBE, DSO, DL – an event that was reported in 8 local newspapers! General Mike was commissioned into the King's Royal Rifle Corps in 1946; he served at the Small Arms School at Hythe, and in Malaya; he then went to the Australian Staff College, became a Company Commander at Sandhurst, took command of 1 Para in 1966, and won the DSO with them in Aden; after commanding a Commonwealth Brigade in Singapore in 1976, he became the GOC of the 3rd Division, and his last job was as the Director of Army Training. On retirement he was appointed a CB, and soon afterwards he became the Chief Scout. Both an "officers' officer" and a "soldiers' officer", he had a wonderfully broad smile, was always brimming over with enthusiasm, and when asked for advice invariably gave wise answers. No one could have fought harder for 1 Wessex's interests in the very difficult times that lay ahead.

One of General Mike's first duties was to present WO2 Norman Minty of the DERR, the senior PSI with D Company in Bournemouth, with the Long Service & Good Conduct Medal for 15 years' service. In due course, he was commissioned as a Quartermaster and served with the Royal Regiment of Wales. His family had an amazing connection with the Wiltshire Regiment, for not only were his father and grandfather, but also his great grandfather, long-serving members of it – the last was a canteen sergeant during the Indian Mutiny.

No doubt urged on by him, D Company dreamed-up a probably unique publicity stunt:

> There was a Conductor on a Bournemouth Transport bus today who was not collecting fares — instead he was directing music on the top deck of an open one. Bandmaster John Quaye exchanged a conductor's rostrum for the stairwell on the bus. From there, he led 23 members of the Devon Band of Wessex Volunteers through numbers from My Fair Lady, Mary Poppins and Serenata. This unusual venture was all part of a recruiting campaign for D Company of the 1st Wessex Regiment (Rifle Volunteers) who are based in Bournemouth. WOII Alan Hobbs, the permanent staff instructor at the TA Centre in Holdenhurst Road, explained they were after about 100 volunteers aged between 171/2 and 25 who would be required to spend two weekends a month with the regiment, in addition to two hours each Tuesday. The one- hour tour around Bournemouth was a face-showing exercise which caused more than a few surprises for people around the town. It was also a new experience for bus driver John Jones – he was given a free ticket to drive anywhere in the town. He said that it was the first time he had simply been told to "Drive where you please". After the tour the bus went back to its normal route along the coast.[7]

Lieutenant Colonel Malcolm Carr OBE, DL, who had succeeded Lieutenant Colonel EGB Moss as the Secretary of Western Wessex in 1971, retired in 1982. A Light Infantryman, he was approachable, hardworking, thorough and efficient, with a good sense of humour, a strong, deep voice and a characteristic laugh; he had been an outstanding Secretary, and all the TA units in the six counties were very sorry indeed to see him go. Although he retired early and voluntarily, he maintained that it was not because he didn't enjoy the job!

His successor, who could not have been more different, was Brigadier JG ("Joe") Starling, CBE, MC, ADC – one of the post-war Army's great characters, and who was quickly to become almost certainly the most remarkable figure in the world of the Reserve & Cadet Forces. Originally enlisting in The Suffolk Regiment, he won his MC as a young officer in the Malayan jungle. In due course, he transferred to The Parachute Regiment, and, after exciting service with them in the Middle East, he took over command of its much-feared, Glasgow-based, 15th (Volunteer) Battalion. He then became the Regimental Colonel of The Parachute Regiment, and his last appointment before retirement was as the Deputy Commander of South West District. Fair- and single-minded, well-organised, and a lateral thinker, his only object in life – to the almost total exclusion of anything and everything else, except keeping his long-suffering and laconic, but happily robust, wife Iris happy – was, as far as he possibly could, to ensure that all TA and Cadet units in Western Wessex were properly accommodated, fully recruited and generally happy. He talked almost as fast as a machine gun fired bullets, and his boundless energy, quick brain, his negotiating abilities, and a burning desire to 'get things right' were an inspiration, and endeared him, to everyone. His ability to see early on in any particular situation what might be possible and what was likely to prove impossible – and hence to decide whether to press on with an idea or abandon it – was a great asset. He firmly believed that a Volunteer with the right credentials, and able to give the necessary time to the job, should be preferred to a Regular officer for the command of a TA unit – and to those who got it he invariably gave his fullest support.

Joe Starling's scurrilous stories about soldiering, and some of those with whom he had formerly served[8], may have surprised a good many people outside the 'military system' with whom he came into contact – and he did have a propensity to tell not very polite (but almost always very funny) ones to audiences which included ladies. However, that was a small price to pay for his tremendous energy and capability. An almost uniquely 'gung-ho' soldier, he unusually combined all three of the 'officer philosophies' mentioned in Chapter 5, and in TA Centres and Cadet huts he achieved legendary status with his lecture, performed over the years to hundreds of incredulous Volunteers and Cadets, on How to Survive in Any Conditions Almost Anywhere in the World – during the course of which he produced from various parts of his uniform and body a mind-boggling collection of rabbit snares, candles, knives, mini-saws, energy-giving tablets, razor blades and countless other items which might be useful to a cut-off or escaped soldier. Another of his many idiosyncrasies was his habit of writing minutes of meetings – usually of some of the TAVRA's County Committees, which, more often than not, he regarded as a waste of time and effort – either while they were going on, or even (some said) before they began. Western Wessex's *Newsletter*, and various other publications were almost invariably enlivened by military cartoons – typical ones of which are reproduced on Plate 21.

Most of the work of the TAVRAs related to the TA and the Army Cadet Force – and although they had an involvement with the Royal Naval Reserve [RNR], the Royal Marine Reserve [RMR] and the Royal Auxiliary Air Force [RAuxAF] as well, it was quite limited. They were, however, genuinely representative of all the Reserve Forces, and for that reason, they were pretty cumbersome. Western Wessex had approximately 150 members – the majority of whom had TA interests. Its President was one of the Lords Lieutenant of the (originally six) counties in its area on an annual rotation; until the 1990s the Chairman had always been a retired TA Colonel, but since then retired senior members of the RNR and the RMR held the appointment – and there was a Vice-Chairman for each county, as well as for each of the RNR, the RMR and the RAuxAF. There were Selected Members, mainly senior serving or retired officers of the TA, with a few from the other three Reserve Forces; Ex-Officio Members –

the Brigadier commanding 43 (Wessex) Brigade in Exeter, the current TA Colonel for the western end of South West District (who was also the Deputy Brigade Commander), the COs of all the major TA units and the two OTCs, the OCs of all the minor units, the County Commandants of the Army Cadet Forces, and their equivalents in the Air Cadets and the Sea Cadets; then there were Representative Members from employers' and employees' organizations, and the county councils; and finally Co-opted members, people who did not fit into any of the many slots in the organisation, but who it was thought could make a useful contribution to it. That 'cast list' was much the same in all the other TAVRAs.

The Associations normally only met in full once a year, for their Annual General Meeting – how un-military! – which included 'progress reports' from all the units (latterly, and often thankfully, distributed beforehand), and a talk on military matters by the GOC or the Brigade Commander, or occasionally on a related subject by some other distinguished person. The proceedings concluded with a lunch that was always regarded as the most important element of the day, and usually finished at about teatime.

Although the Secretaries were responsible for the day-to-day running of the Associations, and for all dealings with the Ministry of Defence and HQ UKLF, the basic decision-making at local level was in the hands of an Executive Committee, and subsidiary Finance, Works (i.e. Buildings) and Recruiting Committees – and from the late 1980s onwards the TAVRAs all had an Employers Liaison Committee. The Secretary naturally attended all their meetings, and most of the Committees would meet five or six times a year, but sometimes more often. The Executive Committee was approximately 20-strong, and the Secretary would be supported as necessary by the Association's full-time Finance and Works Officers – so that there could be proper discussion and quite often 'then-and-there' decisions on, for example, requests from COs for help with an expensive recruiting campaign, or perhaps a visit by a number of Volunteers to some foreign part (which on close examination might sometimes be found to have actually little to do with TA training!), or even for the consideration of an upgrade of a TA Centre.

The TAVRAs were, as mentioned above, like other aspects of the TA, curiously unmilitary, even semi-democratic. Unless there were strong financial or other non-operational reasons for doing or nor doing something, decisions relating to the TA in general (as distinct from issues only affecting one or a few units) – for example, the allocation as between units of funds received from MOD for recruiting – were arrived at by agreement; the author does not remember any question ever having to be put to a vote.

The final 'tier' in the TAVRA structure were the County Committees – each county having its own – which in effect replicated the TAVRA General Purposes and Recruiting Committees, 'one level lower', with the addition of one or two interested members of the local community, usually significant businessmen, and sometimes local headmasters and the local police. Those Committees met usually twice a year (one for their AGM – without lunch!) at one of the larger TA Centres in rotation, normally under the chairmanship of the Lord Lieutenant of the County. Attendances varied, it has to be said, from 'reasonable' to 'sparse'. Their purpose was to pick up 'groundswells' of opinion among the Volunteers for the benefit of the TAVRA, to report the 'current state of play' in the various units in the county, and, perhaps most importantly, to 'sell' the Reserve Forces to a few hopefully interested civilian members:

The Gloucestershire Meeting was held in our TA Centre at Carne Place on 22 October 1986, with both ourselves and our friends of A (RGH) Squadron, The Royal Wessex Yeomanry involved in the administration. The Yeomanry with their usual style and panache produced the small eats and Dry White, whilst, after a talk by the Company Commander, Major Peter Stanley, the "PBI" laid on a display of weapons and equipment. The Meeting was voted a success and many complimentary letters were later received.

That event provided us with a dress rehearsal for the much bigger Avon County Meeting seven days later, held in the Speedwell TA Centre in the Fishponds area of Bristol, where we are represented by 2 and 3 Platoons. Our co-producers on this occasion were 245 Ambulance Squadron, RCT. Representing 1 Wessex were members of 2 and 3 Platoons, the Anti-tank Platoon, the Assault Pioneer Platoon, the Recce Platoon, the Mortar Platoon and those two

stalwarts Corporals Jock Nelson and Maurice Vizor of the backroom
staff. Major Peter Stanley repeated his address, the VIPs (including
various 'Captains of Industry' in the Avon area) listened intently, and
then heard the views of one of our young volunteers, Philip Lines.
In the subsequent question period he ably and cheerfully fielded
more fast balls than Ian Botham at Lords. He was totally undaunted
by the seniority and position of his audience and created the best
possible impression of a first rate TA Volunteer. Our thanks and
congratulations to him on his fine performance.[9]

but generally speaking the Volunteers did not think that – other than
in briefing the civilian members – the County Meetings really achieved
anything worthwhile. For the military members, it was to a large extent
a question of telling people either what they knew already, or things
about other units in which they frankly had little interest – because
all the serious discussions about buildings, PR and recruiting, financial
needs and so on took place as needed direct with the Association staff
or at the Executive Committee meetings. Nevertheless, the obligation
to hold them was accepted with good grace.

The provision of buildings for the TA and the Cadet Forces (as
well as, although to a much lesser extent, for the RMR and the
RAuxAF) was the biggest responsibility of the TAVRAs, and not
surprisingly it produced the biggest headaches too. Particularly
after the end of the Cold War, ever-tightening financial restrictions
imposed by every Government in its efforts to contain or reduce
defence expenditure meant that the buying of a site and building a
new Centre on it, the enlarging of or substantially altering an existing
Centre, or sometimes the conversion of a non-military building into
one, required the strongest possible justification. If any major unit
wanted to form a new platoon, or change the location of an existing
one – usually for recruiting reasons – it was the TAVRA's job to satisfy
both the GOC and HQ UKLF that the population of the potential
catchment area was sufficiently high to provide an adequate 'pool'
of recruits on a continuing basis, and thus justify the cost involved.
The Shapland Formula (for calculating the local recruiting potential)
was still invariably the 'touchstone' for measuring that pool. It was,
however, extremely rare for there to be a new build or conversion

in a town where there had not been a TA presence since 1967. In the case of a proposed new platoon location, the Battalion and the Company concerned also had to be sure that a sufficient number of already serving, experienced, Volunteers would be willing to transfer to the new platoon in order to give it a 'flying start', without seriously affecting the efficiency of the 'parent' Centre; that might well entail their travelling appreciably further than they already were from their homes for drill nights and weekends – even up to another 15-20 miles. 'Out-station' Centres were both a blessing and a bore – the former because they increased a Company's potential manning position, and provided more opportunities for giving greater responsibilities to young officers and NCOs, and the latter because they needed supervising by the senior management team (both the Volunteers and the PSIs) who had quite enough to do at Company HQ anyway. Overall, however, they definitely proved their worth – for example, it is unlikely that E Company would have remained viable for so many years without the Barnstaple Platoon.

A Regular soldier's view of the TA at this time was provided by WO2 RB Wright of the Glosters, the senior PSI with A Company between 1981 and 1983. At the end of his tour, he wrote:

> The Senior Permanent Staff Instructor's job is to advise and assist the Company Commander on all training matters as detailed in the Commanding Officer's Training Directive and his forecast of events. To make the job really interesting, he also assists in the running of the training ammunition account, a fleet of vehicles, the TA Centre itself through the Western Wessex TA Association, general security, health and safety at work, etc., etc. Because of the very nature of the TA, all training is done either at weekends or weekday evenings. As you would expect, this promotes a fairly active and involved life style.
>
> The TA soldier receives any and all instructions through the post, so once a month we would post 180 letters to the far corners of the counties of Avon and Gloucestershire – and even further afield, Colchester! Our team consisted of the Clerical Officer, myself and, if I was very lucky and they were not forewarned, the Anti-tank PSI and the QPS1. These latter two had a canny knack of knowing when the mail-out day would happen, and avoided it like bubonic plague. At any rate, after four hours of addressing, stamping and filling envelopes

with programmes and weekend instructions, the mail would eventually reach the post box.

The training done is obviously influenced by the time available. Everyone's favourite for the move to either ranges or training areas for the weekend – "Don't forget to book the transport!" – is to go late on a Friday evening, the alternative being to start very early on a Saturday morning. The first thing I noticed working with TA soldiers was the enthusiasm they put into their training and the general standard they achieve. Range days are, of course, enjoyed by all, and produce a mixed bag of results from very good to the not-so-very-good.

My first year's Camp took us to that Caribbean look-alike area, Soltau. The weather was booked twelve months in advance and didn't let us down, for it rained solidly for two weeks – no, I tell a lie, the sun appeared as we prepared to depart from the airfield at the end of Camp – but with grim determination the soldiers stuck with it, and had a worthwhile time. The second year took us to Putlos and Exercise Bold Guard. My, what a friendly lot the Germans are up there, I must have put on two stones – all that coffee and apple strudle! In many German villages; we were offered bicycles, showers and heated accommodation by friendly locals, all readily and eagerly accepted by cold, tired TA Tommies.

On each TA camp, everyone has a twenty-four or thirty-six hour period of R & R. This can be taken locally, or on pre-booked coaches to Hamburg, Kiel, Hanover or whatever main metropolis you find yourself near. The soldiers rush off to visit the museums, cathedrals and parks, or whatever else takes the fancy of TA and Regulars when they visit such distinguished German cities and towns.

The moves to and from Camp are a PSI's nightmare. Many boxes of pace-maker batteries are exhausted, both prior to and during the moves to and from Camp. Returns, returns, more returns, next of kin (NOK) cards, employers' certificates and medical documents. "SPSI will complete Company Nominal Rolls of all those attending camp" – but I was never really sure who <u>was</u> with us until the Hercules touched down on the other side. Still, many attempts and many insertions and deletions later, we somehow managed to do it. Collecting NOK cards was a nightmare: reminders by letter containing a stamped addressed envelope for reply – no reply; therefore phone holder of card or near relative to pass on a message – telephone invariably answered by a dear old soul complete with NHS hearing aid, etc: "Please ma'm, could you tell Pte. Bloggs to return his NOK form." Pause: "It's half past four, sonny." Oh well, back to the drawing boards!

I can, however, look back on a very enjoyable time with the TA. I can reminisce on some hard times, good times, but always plenty of laughter. Despite the sometimes difficult administration problems posed by the dispersal of platoons scattered over a large area, the TA soldiers always managed to turn up in the right kit and nearly always at the right time. The type of training done is very similar to that of regular soldiers, albeit a little more 'condensed' due to the time available. It was a very hard two and a half years with many weekends and evenings, but also very enjoyable.

Finally, I would like to take this opportunity to thank all members of 'A' Company 1 Wessex for the many kindnesses shown to me and my family over the whole period. I now have many good friends scattered about Avon and Gloucestershire who, I am sure, I will meet again soon. Stay loose.[10]

Reciprocally, as it were, almost without exception the PSIs were greatly appreciated by the Volunteers:

Both have been first class assets to the Company during their tours, and will be sorely missed. Without exception, all ranks have gained enormously from the experience of soldiering alongside these fine representatives of the Regular Army. Both were 'sent off' in the now traditional way – the so-called 'formal' Company 'do', and the more relaxed and light-hearted lunch (with drinks) in the Club, attended by all the TA Centre staff. To both stalwarts and their families go our very best wishes for their futures.[11]

––––––––

Although Colour Sergeant Paul Lewis's heart always lay with his own battalion, he nonetheless did an excellent job as Permanent Staff Instructor in the stores and in the field. [His successor] has shown an amazingly swift grasp of the frustrations and delights of the TA, and looks set to follow in his predecessor's very successful footsteps. His tour cannot have been all bad – he collected his Colour Sergeant's crown and a wife.[12]

One of the minor consequences of the Battalion's important role was that a large number of very senior officers were always wanting to 'see how things were going'. These visits produced two quite separate reactions – almost invariably one of irritation before the event, because of the interruption it would cause to training, but pleasure afterwards if (as happily was almost invariably the case) everything had gone well. For example, in 1981, the Inspector General of the TA, Lieutenant General Sir Frank Kitson, well known for his lack of conversation, brought NATO's CINCENT [Commander in Chief, Central Europe], the magnificently named General Dr F von Senger und Etterlin to watch the Section Competition. According to a local newspaper, however, they seemed to have visited a different unit, and the reporter also clearly thought the outgoing CO had made such a good job of running a pretty dilapidated training camp that he had received instantaneous promotion through as many ranks as Private Grigg had a few years earlier:[13]

> Individual skills and section competitions were held in the annual 1 Royal Wessex Territorial Army exercise on Salisbury Plain at this weekend. The events were highlighted by a visit from Gen Dr F von Senger und Etterlin, Commander-in-Chief central area [sic], NATO with the deputy Commander-in-Chief UKLF, Lieut Gen Sir Frank Kitson, in his capacity as Inspector General of the Terrritorial Army. Their visit on Saturday coincided with the handing-over of Westdown Camp by Lieut Gen Sir John Southwood to Lieut Col Terry Dutton. The exercise demanded high standards of skill in a variety of tasks.[14]

General Kitson's successor as Commander of the UK Field Army and Inspector General, General Burgess – who, after his retirement, was to become another popular Chairman of the Council of TAVRAs – also came to the 1981 Camp, as did the GOC South West District, General Michael Gray. There was in fact a steady stream of visitors of one sort or another – it was, of course, very convenient for the MOD to have a NATO battalion within 90 minutes drive of Whitehall, and HQ ULKF one less than 30 miles away. Presumably, however, the 'top brass' liked what they saw, or 1 Wessex would not otherwise have remained in a major Regular Army formation.

It is interesting that, because of the huge geographical dispersion of the Companies, and the fact that most officers and NCOs were solidly based wherever they lived and had their civilian jobs, few Volunteers transferred from one Company to another; indeed, it was once suggested that there were probably more changes and transfers of Companies and their titles. Consequently, there was little or no sense of competition between Volunteers of the same rank, whether officers or NCOs (as there understandably might be in a Regular battalion) – so that, except in fairly unusual circumstances, Captain A or Sergeant B of 'Y' Company, and Captain C or Sergeant D in 'Z' Company would not be vying with each other for appointment as the next company commander or colour sergeant of their own or another company. It is also of note that it was extremely rare for a Volunteer to be 'excluded', and resign, because he was unpopular with his colleagues.

Two thoroughly well-liked Volunteers were the A Company cooks, Corporals "Jock" Nelson and "Nobby" Hall, whose skills were such that they won the 1982 South West District Cooking Competition with an "exquisite chicken supreme" – although why it took two Corporals to produce only one dish between them was not revealed. When Corporal Hall finally 'hung up his hat', the A Company Notes in the Summer 1984 issue of *The Back Badge* paid him a handsome tribute – such a good illustration of the tremendous loyalty and versatility of so many long-serving TA soldiers that it is worth quoting in full:

Mr. R A Hall, known universally and with affection as "Nobby", first donned khaki as a young National Serviceman at Plymouth in August 1951, and found himself a member of the Royal Hampshire Regiment. He spent the whole of his National Service in BAOR, apart from a short spell "tin bashing" in the old underground training centre at Goodge Street, near Tottenham Court Road, in London.........On leaving the Royal Hampshires, Mr. Hall decided to keep up his soldiering as a Territorial, and so joined 5 Glosters HQ Company, then in the old Drill Hall in Painswick Road. He remained with 5 Glosters until the battalion disappeared in the re-organisation, and joined A Company on its formation in the new Drill Hall in Eastern Avenue. His initial occupation was that of railwayman, but when the opportunity arose he joined the civilian staff of A Company as a driver.

He is a Driver during the day, but a Corporal on Drill Nights and at weekends. In his long service with the TA he has attended Camps in Cyprus, Gibraltar, BAOR, and the UK. In fact, he has travelled abroad far more as a Territorial than ever he did as a National Serviceman. A loyal and faithful servant, Mr. Hall has been a tower of strength in A Company, and although he had to change his cap badge to the Army Catering Corps – age finally beat him as far as the Infantry is concerned – he remains first and foremost a " Gloster". Long may he remain so.

Chicken supreme probably never appeared on training in the field, and the normal food was "compo", or the Composite Ration Pack; for those readers who have never sampled its delights, a brief description should make their mouths water. The compo ration was a small crate containing food for 14 men for one day. To give variety, there were seven types of crates, labelled A to G, one for every day of the week and each containing a different 'menu' – and the precooked meals could be heated on either the collective petrolgas stoves or personal hexamine cookers. As the compo rations were chiefly made of preserved food, their use had to be kept to a minimum. In addition to the A to G crates, therefore, there was another set of crates of the same size, cleverly numbered 1 to 3, which were to be accompanied by fresh bread, rather than biscuits. Some of the basic meals contained in the various crates were stewed lamb, pork and vegetables, oxtail and beans, beef and kidney gravy, steak and vegetables and salmon. The other contents of, for example, a crate D were (the brackets giving the number of cans or containers) bacon (3), sardines (8), concentrated soup (2), cigarettes (a box of 50), margarine (1), vitamin enriched chocolate (14 bars), sweets (2) and matches (1 packet), salt (2 bags), tea, sugar, and powdered milk (3), preserved vegetables (3), biscuits (1), pudding (3), soap (1 packet) and lavatory paper (84 sheets).

During the period covered by this Chapter, by far and away the most important events were, of course, the transfer of the Battalion from 4 Division to 1 Infantry Brigade, the loss of B and E Companies (see Chapter 8) and the formation of the new B Company, but there were a number of significant changes affecting individual platoons – two moving, the raising of a new one, and the demise of a fourth.

When B Company's Support Platoon was moved to Andover in 1979, a new 7 Platoon was raised at Basingstoke, but unfortunately it failed to get properly off the ground and was disbanded; by 1980, however, the Company's numbers were increasing elsewhere, and in January 1982 it acquired another TA Centre, the fifteenth in the Battalion – Blighmont, in Millbrook on the outskirts of Southampton. For a refurbished 'old' drill hall, it had excellent facilities, and Lieutenant Bill Conroy did a marvellous job in re-establishing the Platoon and getting it up to full strength. In Dorset, by 1981 C Company had found that (although the Platoon Sergeant, Ken Chivers, had been a tower of strength to a succession of regularly changing Platoon Commanders) its 9 Platoon at Wallisdown in Poole was geographically too remote for it to remain a successful element of the Company; so at the end of that year it moved to the Bincleaves TA Centre in Weymouth, formerly the home of B Company the 4th Dorsets. There, it was hoped, "the old Dorset association will be revived and a strong presence re-established there" [15], and that indeed proved to be the case. In both instances, Eastern Wessex TAVRA could not have been more helpful – as it was to be in 1988 and 1989 in carrying out substantial improvements to the Company Headquarters TA Centre at Dorchester, in part of the 19th century Poundbury Barracks.

In 1984, a new Platoon for A Company was established in the former Herefordshire Light Infantry drill hall at Cinderford in the Forest of Dean – the first Glosters' or Wessex presence in the Forest for 66 years. Within 10 months, it had 20 'on the books', with four in the recruiting 'pipeline' and two about to transfer from another unit. In the same year, however, and with great regret, E Company's 19 Platoon in Barnstaple had to be disbanded. It had originally been formed in 1969, and ran extremely successfully under Lieutenant Patrick Lambert and a great 'son of Devon', Sergeant Fred Smale (who in due course became the CSM of the Company); Patrick Lambert was succeeded in 1972 by Peter Evens, then only an Officer Cadet, who was commissioned immediately before the Colour Presentation Parade, and stayed with the Platoon for an exhilarating six years, until 1978. Following his promotion to Captain and his appointment as the Company 2IC, they had a number of Platoon Commanders, none of whom, unfortunately, stayed more than a year or so, and eventually it proved impossible to find one at all, as a result of which there was such a dramatic drop in numbers that the Platoon was no longer viable. Peter Evens must have been slightly sad at his promotion to and appointment as the Company 2IC, for he had been the Ensign for the Regimental Colour on the Colour Parade, and carried one or other of the Colours on almost every subsequent Battalion parade until his promotion – after which, of course, he was no longer eligible to do so.[16]

A new Establishment for the TA published in April 1983 introduced Permanent Staff Administration Officers [PSAOs] – and in the NATO battalions there was one in each company. They were all ex-Regulars who had been commissioned from the ranks, and their varied former service was rightly considered to be most appropriate for the appointment. Their role was to relieve the company commanders of many of their administrative chores, and ensure that, so far as possible, they were provided with all they needed to train an effective and efficient company. Without exception, every one of those in the Battalion were 'stars' – a very experienced and special group of soldiers who made a marvellous contribution to the smooth running of the Battalion for the remaining 15 years of its existence. They were all very individual characters, each with a tremendous sense of humour, completely unflappable, and simply such nice people. For some unknown reason, a full job description for them was never published, but the rank was that of captain (with no promotion), so those who had been majors in their Regular service therefore had to revert. The first PSAOs with the Battalion were (with their Regular ranks) Major Reg Wallace MBE (late The Royal Tank Regiment)[17]with A Company and Major George Thomas (Glosters) with B Company in Winchester; Major Dougie McMeeken MBE (9th/12th Lancers) was in Dorchester with C Company – and he later joined the TA, and commanded both C and HQ Companies – while Major Gordon Burt MC (The Parachute Regiment) went to D Company in Poole and Major Jack Barrow MBE (DERR) to E Company. Captain Jim Foreman (RAPC – not to be confused with the Captain Geoff Foreman mentioned above) had already been appointed as the Battalion Administration

Officer at Devizes. As they retired, and the structure and layout of the Battalion ebbed and flowed over the years, they were followed or joined by Captain Jim Mitchell (9th/12th Lancers – B Company in Swindon) and Captain Richard ("Mad Nick") Nicholson MBE (RCT – C Company at Newbury), Major Roy Mawdesley BEM (REME – A Company), Major Michael Cornwell MBE (DERR – HQ Company, who later became the Battalion Administrative Officer), Major Tony Morgan (D&D – who had been the twelfth RSM of the Battalion – D Company in Poole), Captain Eddie Fry (Glosters – A Company and later C Company in Cheltenham) and Major Pat O'Brien (RCT – B Company in Bristol). They were a remarkable group of men!

To leap forward momentarily some 12 years, it seemed almost inevitable that, after the Battalion was amalgamated in 1995, the PSAOs would continue to meet – and they did indeed form a Dining Group, which still gathers regularly. The idea for it derived from the 'rolling audit' meetings, which were held at the Company locations in turn; in addition to auditing the accounts, they formed policy, exchanged ideas, put the wealth of their vast combined service experience to good use, and then dined together. The purpose was, of course, to maintain the bonds that were made, and to remember those that 'have gone before'. The ethos of the Group was that it should remain in existence until, echoing the ancient TA cry of "Last man out, close the door please", the last officer dines and dies. The Group had the use of an unusual piece of furniture: some years after the move of Battalion Headquarters and Headquarter Company to Devizes, the Officers' Mess acquired on loan from "Mad Nick" an enormous U-shaped courts martial table, once the property of the German Army, that he had 'liberated' from some very secret place when serving in BAOR. After the amalgamation, as a former member of the Royal Corps of Transport and at heart a died-in-the-wool 'truckie', he presented it to the Officers' Mess of the RCT's Duke of Gloucester Barracks at South Cerney, near Cirencester, the home of the Army's Air Mounting Centre – through which, over the years, a large number of the members of the Battalion had passed – and which became the regular 'home' of the Group's meetings. The only non-PSAO ever to be invited to become a member was Major Roger Coleman MBE

(R Hamps) the Battalion's last-but-one Quartermaster.

Some years later, in 2000, the former PSAOs commissioned a commemorative picture, which is reproduced in Plate 25. Of the symbols in it, CH is "Crazy Horse" (the nickname of Major Coleman); 108 refers to the A[rmy] B[ook] 108, the Regular soldier's Record of Service, and 397 was AB 397, the Army's main accounting ledger; and the six-pointed star represents the six original PSAOs. The names of those who are "involuntarily posted to the Great TA Centre in the sky are added as Higher Command dictates".[18]

It was fairly unusual for more than about twenty members of the entire TA to receive honours in the Queen's Birthday or New Year Honours each year, but the Battalion seems to have done rather better than many major units. During this period, two NCOs who were each an epitome of the best loyal and long serving Volunteer, were awarded the BEM. Colour Sergeant T Hoare of B Company, for his "outstanding" work with the Mortar Platoon in Andover since it formed, received it in the 1982 New Year's Honours – and WO2 (at the time Colour Sergeant) Budge in 1983. Arthur Budge had joined the Army Cadet Force in the late 1940s, became a Regular in The Duke of Cornwall's Light Infantry in 1959, went to Suez, and then served in 4 Devons from 1960 until 1967. He enlisted into E Company in 1969, was awarded the TEM in 1979, a bar to it in 1985, when, as the CSM of the Company, he finally retired. Then in the 1984 New Year's Honours, Colour Sergeant Martin Wright LS&GCM, a member of the Non-Regular Permanent Staff[19] with HQ Company, received the BEM; he had spent 22 years with the Royal Military Police, and on his retirement in 1978 he promptly joined the Battalion.

There was a double celebration on 18 June 1983, of the 75th Anniversary of the original formation of the Territorial Army, and the 10th Anniversary of the presentation of Colours to the Battalion. In the morning there was a "splendid parade" before a large crowd in Devizes. The Honorary Colonel, General Mike Walsh, presented Colour Sergeant Budge with his BEM; the Mayor inspected and addressed the Battalion, and then took the salute, following which the Battalion exercised its Liberty of the Town, with colours flying and drums beating. After lunch in the Town Hall, there was an Open

Day in Le Marchant Barracks, attracting over four thousand people, naturally including a substantial number of the wives, children and girlfriends of members of the Battalion. Not everyone, however, was happy with the occasion:

> The four-hour sealing-off of Devizes Market Place on Saturday morning for a big 75th Anniversary Parade has upset some of the traders. Spearheading their protest is Mr Frank Giles, proprietor of The Pie Shop, who said that several had suffered a substantial drop in takings as a result. "Why did the parade have to take place at a peak shopping period?" he asked. Why couldn't it have been on a Saturday evening, or on a Sunday?......The Town Clerk said that the time was fixed by the Army as suitable for their purposes. The Council said it was very honoured the 1st Wessex was holding a parade in the Market Place.....[20]

Although his tour of command was the normal length, Terry Dutton hardly seemed to have settled in before, in the autumn of 1983, his successor arrived. He was Lieutenant Colonel Philip Goddard of The Light Infantry. A 'cross-Divisional' appointment was almost unheard of in those days, and it caused a few eyebrows to be raised. Perhaps equally unusual was the fact that he was a qualified helicopter pilot, and had been attached to the Army Air Corps at Middle Wallop – but that definitely went down well within the Battalion, as he was adept at persuading more of his former colleagues to take a greater part in exercises than had previously been the case. In many ways he was lucky to command during the two-year 'lull' in the reorganisation of the Battalion which is the subject of the previous Chapter, in that, as a Light Infanteer, he very naturally had little or no experience or understanding of the ethos of, and the relationships between, the Regular Regiments, and probably knew very few of their 'principal players'. His tour therefore proved to be straightforward and without any major problems – and there was no doubt that he left the Battalion in every bit as good shape as he found it.

At Camp in 1983 (on the Stanford PTA), General Mike presented a magnificent cup for an Inter-Company competition, which was promptly and naturally named the Walsh Trophy – and the first winners were A Company. There was in fact already an Inter-Section Cup, which had been presented by John Southwood in 1980 and fought for a couple of times, but (for the "Life being what it is" and "Too much to do" reasons) it then stood on a shelf in the Officers' Mess silver room for a number of years. Similarly, there was no competition for the Walsh Trophy in either 1984 or 1985. In 1986, however, Philip Goddard decided that the Companies should battle it out for both trophies simultaneously, and Exercise Griffon's Jaunt – whoever invented the name badly needed a lesson in the mythological beasts of the south-west of England! – took place on Salisbury Plain in March. Every Company's Notes in its affiliated regiment's journal show that they were all in no doubt whatsoever as to their ability to prove to the rest of the Battalion that they were the best Company. It was a "gruelling" weekend on and around Sidbury Hill, near Tidworth. Despite a Friday night start – which, for obvious reasons, was not (pace Sergeant Major Wright above) popular with everyone, but nevertheless accepted on an occasional basis – the high turnout on this occasion was clear proof of everyone's determination to win. The conditions for both competitions were the same and taxing – on the Saturday going through a number of 'stands' on such diverse subjects as bayonet fighting, clay pigeon shooting, first aid and Kim's Game, followed by a night march – and then on the Sunday morning a 14km forced march and a falling plate shooting competition; the arctic weather conditions were another hazard, for drenching rain alternated with driving snow over the whole week-end. After a really hard-fought contest – "often strenuous, often hilarious" – A Company not only won back the Walsh Trophy, but took the Southwood Cup as well. Through the efforts of the newly-arrived Adjutant, Captain Guy Woodcock, the local press attended in some force, and much valuable publicity was achieved. The following year, 1987, despite much better weather, it was too much to expect that A Company would win the Trophy for a third time, and indeed it went to D Company in Poole; the conditions for the competition being in the discretion of the CO, this time it was based on patrolling, and involved night navigation, section attacks, first aid, NBC, close quarter battle shooting, and finally an assault course race.

It was to the credit of the 'chiefs' throughout the Battalion that training was always very varied, and – to return to the proper chronology of this Chapter – these are samples of what the Companies did on week-ends during 1984:

> The fertile brain of our Senior PSI, WO2 John Davies of the Glosters, produced one of those 'funnies' in the shape of an escape and evasion exercise, aptly named Pipeline. This took place in the Forest of Dean on 26 and 27 November, and involved small groups negotiating in the dark a particularly tricky area of the Forest, including going through the disused Welsh Bicknor Tunnel, abseiling, an aerial runway and a boat crossing. The overall distance covered was 22 miles. No injuries were sustained and perhaps more important, no one lost his way. A rumour that breakfast would be taken 'on the hoof' proved very unpopular, but fortunately our Q staff and their Haute Cuisine British Breakfast were just around the next corner! It can hardly be said that "a good time was had by all', but it was a worthwhile challenge for everyone.[21]

They say that the best working relationship comes when operating in a group of no more than ten people. The key element in an infantry company is the rifle section, and for B Company 1984 is "The Year of the Rifle Section". The majority of our nine elite section commanders gained their spurs on the Thetford NCOs' Cadre in July 1983, and since then we have given them every support to weld their sections into individual closely-knit teams. Lance Corporals Curtis, Figg and McColm have been promoted to Corporal, and others should follow soon....... Since October, therefore, we have concentrated on building up the sections. We have become experts in patrols, ambushes and OPs. The Company is grateful for the expertise of WO2 MA Horder (1 R Hamps) who, with his experience in Northern Ireland, has injected hard-nosed professionalism into our low-level tactics. We have tended to patronize Barton Stacey, not far out of Winchester, and Newtown, Isle of Wight, over the winter months, making use of local knowledge and contacts. 2nd Lt Peter Pay (who commands 6 Platoon) and WO2 BA Fitzpatrick have been excellent hosts whenever the Company have visited the Island.

By February we were ready to study "The Platoon" again. In the best traditions of the School of Infantry and Brecon, we formed a composite platoon from 'the management' and crossed Salisbury Plain in some style. The role of Platoon Commander was shared between Colour Sergeant RJ Hoare, who has recently been promoted to command 7 Platoon, and 2nd Lt Nick Goulding, formerly of Bristol University OTC, who is giving us eight months of his time before he departs to further his civilian career. Working nearly seven days a week, he commands 5 Platoon, captains our shooting team, is chief coach for the Section Competition, and acts as an able assistant to Lt-Colonel Rivers at the TAVRA Headquarters in Southampton......

Although we are currently short of platoon commanders and sergeants, there are five potential officers [in training] at Winchester, and in due course our section commanders will be aspiring to their third stripe. In the meantime, we would welcome members of the Royal Hampshire Regiment who, having left the Regular Army, would like to soldier on as volunteers. There are some good appointments to be filled, and they are vacant now.[22]

———

Early in the morning of 7th July the whole Company took itself off for what was to be its most popular training event of the season. A whole weekend of Adventure Training at Vauxhall Camp, Monmouth, had been arranged. It included abseiling 85 feet, climbing 15 feet and 80 feet, pot holing and canoeing and watermanship. In the immortal words of WO2 John Davies:

If you're frightened of heights, we'll drag you up;
If you're frightened of pot-holing, we'll drag you under;
If you're frightened of water, we'll drag you through it;
If you're frightened of abseiling, we'll drag you down.

2 and 3 Platoons made the headlines again by their participation in the Bristol City Docks Festival on 14th July. It was their task to battle against a team from the Royal Naval Reserve to carry cannons from one side of the docks to the other on pontoons. The assembled pundits were confounded as the land lubbers won hands down (or is it a pontoon!). The weather was fair to middling and all were wet one way or another.[23]

and sometimes the senior NCOs had to take on responsibilities at a higher level, when their training was seriously put to the test:

> During the year, because of the shortage of subalterns, senior ranks have commanded Platoons and Corporals have become Acting Platoon Sergeants. This was the situation on Exercise Bold Gannet in Denmark, in which some 85 members of [E] Company participated........The Platoon Commanders, WO2 O'Connor and Sergeants Tony Helm and Terry Carman, and Sergeant Christopher Stokes, Corporal Brian Harrison and Corporal Murray as Platoon Sergeants, coped extremely well (with, in some cases, very inexperienced soldiers), made their defensive positions most skillfully and ran successful Platoons.[24]

The following year, 1985, the more demanding 'out-of-Camp' training included A Company acting as enemy on the 1 Glosters' Exercise Pilgrim's Progress, held in deepest Wales, an "outing" that "provided the warriors with enough excitement to last the whole training year" and was "voted a huge success"; Exercise Wessex Whiplash, a Battalion FTX on Salisbury involving the usual mix of infantry tasks – the night occupation of a concentration area, helicopter moves by day and night, company attacks, the occupation of defensive positions, and patrol and ambush operations; and the Recce Platoon (which had only been formed some two years previously) had the first of their annual field firing tests at the Royal Armoured Corps ranges at Bovingdon, using their 3mm Raden cannons, for which they achieved a B grading. C Company had their own tough Operation Nutcracker on Salisbury Plain in December, and this report of it in one of the local papers gives a perhaps surprisingly authentic picture of Volunteer training:

> Mud is the only soft thing about Salisbury Plain, a winter wilderness for nearly 60 Dorset Territorial Army soldiers involved in Operation Nutcracker. Loaded down with kit and weapons, C Company of 1st Battalion The Wessex Regiment left Dorchester to drive to Wiltshire where they linked up with Fox armoured cars from Gloucester and other TA units from Wiltshire and Hampshire. I went with them, and was greeted by torrential rain and atrocious conditions as we waited near a massive open-cast cement works for the order to march out

into open countryside at midnight. Mist was our constant companion, often cutting visibility to a few yards, but we reached a hay barn from which we would attack the "enemy" armoured cars at nearby Grants Farm. Silently we moved forward to the tree-cloaked target, suddenly making contact in a blaze of gunfire and parachute flares which saw a few of the enemy escape.

What followed was a crippling march across the Plain to the rubble of Ladywell Farm. Stumbling and tripping on the uneven ground, breath rasping in my throat, I tried to keep up with C Company's commanding officer, Major Mick Cook, and his radio operator Lance Corporal Colin Valentine in knee-deep grass, tank track ruts and that strength-sapping mud. Major Cook, seemingly with personal radar, navigated us to where the cars [sic], now friendly, were waiting for C Company groups to come in.

A few minutes rest beneath a thorn tree, and we were off again to attack woods and a blockhouse, the long-suffering enemy being drawn from C Company recruits. Explosives experts laid charges as part of the attack, and when these went off there was another night-into-day series of flashes as mortars, parachute flares and automatic weapons stitched the night. The attack over, we tried to grab some sleep. My rumbling stomach later got to grips with egg and sausage sandwiches for breakfast in the wood before I went off with Corporal John Longley from Beaminster to join the "enemy", led by Captain Steuart Davidson-Houston.

They were in the deserted village of Imber, taken over by the Army in World War II, and their job was to fight the main body of C Company to give them training in FIBUA [Fighting In Built Up Areas]. Imber looked grim, with its hollow-shelled functional buildings, inside one of which was Private Gavin Robinson from Broadmayne, who had an unusual job. He volunteered to be a casualty, and spent a happy few minutes in front of me mixing blood, draping himself to cow entrails and going off to wait for the order to start screaming! Territorial Army enthusiasm was personified by Private Simon Luckett, from Weymouth. He spent the first wet, sleepless night of the exercise playing enemy in a mist-shrouded wood. It was his 19th birthday and he said: "I didn't get a birthday cake – just my rations."

When C Company attacked Imber, they did so in a mass of explosions and firing covered by smoke grenades. Inside our building it was bedlam, with spent rifle rounds ricocheting, off the walls to clatter on the galvanised iron floor, and all the time the shouts and screams of battle. After the village was cleared, Major Cook criticised the attackers for bunching, something which could lead to heavy casualties.

Off went the enemy again, and this time we went down a misty track to a blockhouse and trees which had to be defended against an afternoon attack. The explosive clash over, we wolfed down a meal and took part several hours later in a track ambush as rain pelted down and a strong wind blew. Flares lit the enemy convoy up like the fourth of July. Most of the C Company force then slogged across country in thick mud to meet the transport, and everyone was glad to pile into waiting lorries, for the weary trip back to Dorchester. Back at Poundbury Barracks, Major Cook said "I was pleased that everything went so well."[25]

In April 1985, there was universal approval of an increase in the Bounty to £175 in the first year of service, £315 in the second, and in the third year and thereafter £455 – all tax-free. No one ever joined the TA for the money, but it did help to keep the wives happy!

That year also saw the introduction of modern 'weapons' for administration, as distinct from use on the battlefield:

> The age of the computer is about to dawn in the Battalion, with each Company becoming an "outstation". Lt. Nick Goulding is busy working on "Big Brother" at Battalion Headquarters, producing programmes which are expected to give us instant information of an exotic nature in a wide range of subjects. There is no truth in the rumour that the Company Offices of the future will consist of nothing more than a clacking computer, reams of print-outs, a solitary Senior Permanent Staff Instructor and huge clouds of steam.[26]

Luckily, each Company HQ and Battalion HQ enjoyed the help of a lady Clerical Officer. Most of them were extremely competent; they mastered the computer systems much more quickly than the PSIs and those Volunteers who needed to use them, and without doubt added 'a little something' to life in the various offices. Although for the first six months or so after their arrival, their 'learning curve' in relation to the mysteries of staff duties and other military matters was very steep, they got there in the end:

> [She] is now firmly in the chair and having considerable success in her daily battle with the peculiarities of military life and the use of abbreviations. Who can blame the puzzled looks on receipt of messages like "This is the RSM, please tell the SPSI that he is to RV at GR 723419 on SPTA. He will require the Company's FFR and 2 x 9x9s "!! Never mind, Julie, it takes time, but you are very welcome to stay with us forever.[27]

Lieutenant Colonel Robin Pook of The Devonshire and Dorset Regiment became the ninth Commanding Officer of the Battalion on 1 February 1986. His two immediately preceding jobs had been 2IC of 1 DERR, and then a teaching post at the Royal Naval Staff College at Greenwich. Being an Army Orienteer, his arrival engendered a certain amount of apprehension on the part of some of the more physically challenged members of Headquarter Company and the various Company Headquarters – but, happily, during his tour there were no reported cases of Volunteers expiring beside rough tracks through the woodlands in any of the (by then) five counties.

He had only been in 'the chair' for two months when, on 1 April, the second of the major changes in the Battalion's layout and 'orbat' [order of battle, i.e. the composition of a battalion or larger formation in terms of its sub-units] took place – and B Company in Hampshire became part of 2 Wessex. That this was going to happen had, of course, been known since 1982 – but that did not lessen the great sense of loss. It was in fact, and perhaps surprisingly, felt more strongly in the rest of the Battalion than in the Company itself, who seemed to be somewhat relieved at having a rather less demanding war role, and hence not having to undertake such tough training as they had been used to for the previous 19 years:

> Yes, it is with curiosity, rather than any other feeling, that we prepare to make slightly more intimate acquaintance with that other lot. The word "intimate" is used advisedly – for it has recently come to our attention that the 2nd Battalion has among its ranks a WRAC platoon.[28]

[The change] will have little or no effect on the organization or kit within the Company. We are indeed looking forward to drawing some benefits from the new role, which is Home Defence. After many years of rigorous and sometimes very time-consuming training in a NATO role we are hopeful that the future will enable us to adopt a good solid life of training without having to travel great distances to Camp each year, and perhaps on occasions miss out on some of the "fun soldiering" that is important to all of us.[29]

B Company had been the epitome of the '1 Wessex ethos'. With the single-minded, tough approach of, in particular, their first three Company Commanders, they had shown what could be achieved in a TA unit with a really demanding war role. They proved that, with the right leadership, a major result of tough training is the creation of a marvellous *esprit de corps* – but the social side of the TA was never neglected, and the Company had just as much fun as all the others at discos, dinners and Christmas parties.

It was replaced by one formed 'from scratch' at the post-War TA Centre in Church Place, Swindon on the same date – known, until the 'old' B Company transferred to 2 Wessex, as F Company. Because Robin Pook was initially unable to find a Company Commander, for the first 18 months or two years Jim Mitchell, the PSAO, did a tremendous job in getting things going – and in due course Major Peter Booth took over, with Captain Neil Barrett as the 2IC. Swindon was, of course, a good recruiting area – but the Centre was shared with the Royal Wiltshire Yeomanry Squadron of the Royal Yeomanry (the senior Yeomanry regiment in the TA, which in 1995 would become the first NBC Defence Regiment in the Army), and there was no practical way of manning the front door, in effect for 12 hours a day, in order to be able to persuade potential recruits on their first visit to turn left inside the front door and become 'foot-slogging infantry', whereas by turning right they could in due course enjoy the thrills of driving armoured reconnaissance vehicles. Nevertheless, numbers increased well, and by 1987 the Company was almost 80 strong – including several Volunteers who had previously served with other Companies in the Battalion. It was able to attract young officers, and for a period it seemed as though there were almost enough to make up an 'Officers' Platoon': two who stayed in the Battalion for a good many years were Lieutenant David Gillingham, the son of the Battalion's RQMS, and Lieutenant Ed Borup. Lieutenant Jonathan Moss moved from A Company, and when he was joined by his brother 2/Lieutenant Justin Moss from Bristol University OTC, the Company acquired its very own "Moss Bros". Then came 2/Lieutenant Phillip Hall and Lieutenant Benjamin Lai (formerly with 5 RRF) – and at one time there were six potential officers on strength as well. The Company originally had two Rifle Platoons and an SF [Sustained Fire (Machine Gun)] Platoon, but after only three years, in 1989 the latter (although remaining at Church Place) would be transferred to the new Support Company, and a third Rifle Platoon raised in its place. Things had gone so well for the Company that it was a considerable shock that only six years after its formation, in 1992 the Company was unceremoniously transferred in its entirety to 2 Wessex. Apart from the very depressing loss of yet another Company, it was particularly unfortunate, given the immense amount of time and effort that had been put in to making the Company a viable part of the Battalion. Furthermore, because he stayed with the Company, in Jim Mitchell the Battalion also lost someone who, without question, was one of its inimitable characters; a law unto himself, he had very firm ideas as to what should and what should not happen, and he never showed any hesitation in telling anyone that – but even if people disagreed with him, they were never in any doubt as to his fierce loyalty, firstly to B Company and secondly to the Battalion. The latter was to be poorer without him.

Hitherto, the PSIs had worn their own regimental badges, rather than the Wyvern, but in 1986 it was agreed by the Regular Regiments that for the duration of their tours with the Battalion they should re-badge. That was a generous gesture, well set out in a letter from the Regimental Secretary of the Glosters to the Prince of Wales's Division:

> The Colonel of the Regiment [then Major General John Waters] considers that the obvious attractions to the Regiment of having its badges on display in its counties are outweighed by the adverse effect on identity and unity of multi-badging in a Wessex Battalion. He

believes that the latter overrides all other considerations when Wessex COs are required to train for an operational role, and inculcate a sense of unit identity and high morale.

Therefore, although a difficult decision to arrive at, he believes that, on balance, the PSIs should wear the Wyvern badge.[30]

and there is no evidence that they ever objected to doing so. It was support of that kind that brought Regular regiments and TA battalions a little closer together, and helped to foster the "One Army" concept – i.e. that the Regular Army and the TA were one, each dependant on the other – that had been 'invented' by the Ministry of Defence during the 1970s

Not to its own surprise, the Signal Platoon won the 1986 1 Brigade Line Laying Competition for its TA units for the fourth year in succession – undoubtedly due to the fact that

by June the Volunteers have usually completed two brigade CPXs, usually at Stanford, and Battalion CPX and an FTX – although it is difficult for them to keep up with the [skills they need] when the time available for that is two hours on a Tuesday evening and an average of one Headquarter Company weekend a month."[31]

In the 1986 New Year Honours, Major Mick Cook, the Company Commander of C Company in Dorchester, was appointed an MBE – an event particularly warmly welcomed throughout the Battalion. He had become one of its real characters: very large and very genial, he was a greatly respected RSM, and after retiring from the Regular Army enlisted in the TA, was commissioned, and took over C Company in 1982. He led not only it, but also the Battalion shooting team, with enormous enthusiasm, panache and conspicuous success. He originally became the captain of the team in 1976, when he was the RSM, and as the result of his dedicated and expert coaching they won the coveted China Cup for the Section Match at Bisley in 1979, the Dragon Trophy (the Major Units' Championship) in 1980, and the China Cup again two years later. In 1987, to much disappointment, he transferred back to his old regiment, the Devon & Dorsets, to become the 2IC of their new 4th Battalion when it officially came into existence on 12 October that year.

On the same day, E Company became 4 D & D's Headquarter Company, reverting to their role not only on the original formation of the Battalion in 1967, but before that as Headquarter Company of 4 Devons. At a modest parade, General Shortis presented new badges to both the Company and the Devon Band, which similarly became part of 4 D & D. E Company's conversion to a rifle company in 1969 was probably the most difficult task ever faced by any of 1 Wessex's companies – having to maintain its administrative and signals support skills for the Battalion at the same time as acquiring those of a rifle company – but, under Major Michael Anstey, Captain George Simey, Lieutenants David Pommeroy and Patrick Lambert (who quickly became known as "the tough trainer of Devon"), as well as the PSIs and the senior Volunteer NCOs, they had succeeded admirably. With some excellent other officers and NCOs, they had always been an extremely able, totally reliable, and friendly element of 1 Wessex. The Battalion's loss was undoubtedly 4 D & D's gain.

When the original Berkshire D Company left the Battalion in 1977, and B Company in Hampshire did the same in 1986, they were respectively replaced by 2 Wessex's D Company in Poole and the new B Company in Swindon. Up to now, therefore, the Battalion had retained its unique five-company orbat – but E Company was not replaced, and (bringing to reality the threat first suggested as part of the 1982 Joynson Plan)[32]the Battalion therefore reduced to four rifle companies, becoming like all the other NATO ones. Luckily, however, that did not affect the Battalion's role in 1 Infantry Brigade, and, although there seems to be no paperwork to confirm it, the assumption must be that the Commander of 1 Infantry Brigade accepted the position – possibly because at the time a change in the Brigade's own orbat was proposed which might well have needed less TA support.[33] The reduction was just one more factor in the feeling within the Battalion that it had its 'back to the wall' – and time would soon show that was indeed the case.

The perennial problems of recruiting and wastage within both the TA in general and the Battalion in particular have often been mentioned in previous Chapters – and in chronological terms two particular aspects of the subject belong in this Chapter. On a national level, by the mid-1980s vast sums of money (at least in comparison with what was made available for recruiting at unit level) were being spent by the MOD, on increasingly expensive TV advertising, glossy brochures, entertainment for 'kings of industry', and other ideas. There were two objectives, the first of which was straightforward recruiting. The second was to keep the TA in the public eye, and to stop the country as a whole continuing to believe that the TA (and the other Reserve Forces as well) had been disbanded in 1967 – in the hope that a substantial number of parents, grandparents, uncles and godfathers, remembering their own service as having been pretty (or even very) enjoyable, would 'do their bit' in persuading young men, either in their own families or with whom they otherwise came into contact, to join the Royal Naval Reserve, the Royal Marines, the TA or the Royal Auxiliary Air Force.

Despite all those efforts, however, the strength of the TA remained broadly the same, at 'subsistence level' or near it, year on year, and it gradually came to be realised that a large part of the problem lay with employers, and that it was essential to get their support. At the same time, a little over 20 years after the end of National Service, increasingly large numbers of men who were becoming company chairmen and directors, managers, and 'bosses' generally at all levels had never done it. Consequently, in that hugely important sector of society, there was little or no interest in 'the defence of the realm' or understanding of how much was to be gained from some military experience. Furthermore, the business and industrial worlds were becoming increasingly budget-driven and cost-conscious, so that employees were expected to work harder and harder, and therefore had less and less time for themselves. More and more employers were reluctant to allow employees 'time off' so that they could become, or remain, part-time sailors, soldiers or airmen. For many, it became increasingly difficult to get away early on a Friday evening for a training weekend, and in many instances employers insisted that their employees had to count the time for Camp or courses against their holiday entitlement – a complete reversal of the generally universal practice in the 1960s and 1970s. Thus families suffered, and undoubtedly a good many Volunteers were forced to give up their part-time soldiering careers.

In 1986, the Government therefore set up The National Employers' Liaison Committee, whose brief was to persuade the business and industrial worlds that service in the TA, the RNR, the Royal Marines or the RAuxAF would almost invariably made employees better employees. Every TAVRA was required to set up its own Employers' Liaison Committee, and in due course that proved to be a good way of showing at least a few important and sympathetic employers what actually happened in the TA Centres and on the training areas. The first Chairman of NELC, Sir Tommy Macpherson, a redoubtable Scot, had a real vision for the success of the idea – and, with a huge amount of effort and money being put into the scheme, it is probably fair comment that, at least during the remainder of the period covered by this book, on balance it proved its worth – but only just. It did not help that there were very few serving members of the Reserve Forces on the national Committee – and, whether justifiably or not, at ground level the whole exercise was regarded with a mixture of scepticism and, in terms of its funding, envy. Recruiting trends have always been fickle, and it is impossible to say categorically whether appreciably fewer Volunteers would have enlisted in the Battalion had the NELC organisation not existed. It is an old, but true, adage that "The best recruiter is the satisfied soldier" – and the battalions and companies, regiments and squadrons, across the whole country invariably felt that they could have made far better use of the money at their level.

Just as important as maintaining a steady flow of recruits coming in was the need to 'improve the retention rate' – i.e. to reduce the outflow of soldier Volunteers who, for one reason or another, did not want to stay in the TA. Some were those who had served for three or four years, but then decided that they had "seen it all, done it all and got the T-shirt". That was almost always a blow for their platoon and company commanders, although, in national terms, the fact that they had been pretty well trained, and possibly had specialist skills, would be of great value in the event of a major call-up of reservists for a future war. A number, however, were recent recruits who realised relatively quickly that they had simply made a mistake by joining in the first place – and unfortunately a lot of time, money and effort had been put into their initial training which was never going to be recouped.

In what was to prove a very successful way of combating wastage, Robin Pook introduced the idea of Recruit Reception & Training Teams in each of the Companies. They usually consisted of a WO2 and three or four other experienced NCOs — and they received initial enquiries, planned and ran regular selection weekends for hopeful recruits, and dealt with basic documentation; those who were selected formed small groups who got to know each other at the outset, remained at least roughly at the same stage of training, and could go together on a formal Recruit Cadre, usually at the next Camp. Although it was a somewhat slow system, it had a double advantage: on the one hand it enabled the Teams to pick those who seemed most likely to be suited to part-time soldiering, and on the other it provided a relatively structured introduction to it – which (perhaps surprisingly) had not been standard 'recruit-handling' practice in the past. It undoubtedly produced more reliable, better-trained and longer-serving Volunteers than might otherwise have been the case. During these weekends, the applicants were checked for physical fitness, aptitude and co-ordination, and given a series of academic tests:

I was sitting in the [Company] office, polishing the seat of my denims and pushing a pencil, when the following conversation took place between Sgt. Maj. Reade ("The Boss") and me. "We look like being short staffed on the Recruit Selection Weekend (RSW). Can you make it in, 'Tollers'?" "Sure Boss, I'm pretty certain I'm not working that weekend". Thus I had set myself up for my introduction to the wonders of the RSW.

Saturday morning dawns, and I find myself at the TA Centre, shepherding around a group of anxious young men in a motley selection of casual, work and army surplus clothing (except for one individual who wore a collar and tie nearly all weekend!). Meanwhile, The Boss is driving a similar group up from Bristol. Once victims and Instructors have all gathered, and the Instructors' final tasks been allocated, we can get on with the issue of kit to the recruits – rucksack, coveralls, waterproofs, mess tins, mag [= maggot = sleeping-bag] and one 24-hour ration pack,[34] the dark secrets of which would become all too horribly clear. Kit issue complete, the recruits are then whisked off for a stirring introductory speech by The Boss, and then a video about people getting extremely cold, wet, dirty and cream-crackered to really set them in the right frame of mind for the weekend. This seems about the appropriate time to introduce them to one of the fun things of soldiering – the Battle Fitness Test.

Run completed, times recorded and breath recovered, the day continues with instruction in basic weapon handling in preparation for their first shoot that afternoon, and map reading in preparation for the night navigation exercise; even lunch is used by the inimitable C/ Sgt. 'Para' Chambers to instruct the recruits in the many delights and peculiar cooking practices of the 'ratpack'.

Finally, late afternoon approaches and our pair of three-quarter-ton black and green "convertibles" head off for the woods. It is unusually fine weather for March, and The Boss is frowning and muttering to himself about the rain which he is sure he indented for.

Arriving at our base for the night, The Boss and I drive off to mark out the night navigation route. Two teams navigate around the same route, but in opposite directions, to different map references where they should be able to pick up route markers. Meanwhile Para, ably assisted by Lt. Tony Hewitt, is giving a demonstration of basha[35] building – "What, no tents!" – followed by dinner out of the above-mentioned rat packs. "I know it says bacon grill on the tin, but what actually is it?" – thoughtful pause – "Don't ask".

Route marking completed, The Boss and I head back to base. We then wait for it to get suitably dark, and send the teams off on their routes. As they both set out in opposite directions I was reasonably happy that they had got off to a good start, but I was unaware that both teams had gone in the wrong direction. Despite this initial hiccup, they got round the course in fairly reasonable times, and at no point did any of them get a sneaky ride in the back of a Rover or have any markers pointed out to them – "Honest, Boss". By some amazing fluke the night navigation exercises ended just in time for everyone to slide into a friendly local hostelry for a swift couple of pints. The recruits are fully aware that they have a physically testing day ahead, not to mention stagging[36] during the night, so most opt for an early night.

The following morning the recruits are woken up at 5 a.m. (Instructors have already been up and about for half an hour). We learn that during the night Mr. Hewitt returned from putting in an appearance at the A Company party, having stowed his pack and maggot in the front of a Rover – but he was unable to find them, and spent a cold and miserable night curled up under his basha in little more than a shirt and combat jacket.

We clear the area by 6 a.m. and drive off towards a local beauty spot. Stopping a couple of miles short of our destination, the recruits are de-bussed and run to the cliffs where Para and Mr. Hewitt have prepared ropes for some basic abseiling. Meanwhile, Mr. Hewitt cheers himself up a bit with his Peak One Stove and frying pan, soon the smell of bacon is drifting through the woods, and the sound of sizzling is blending with the knocking of woodpeckers and the groans of the injured at the bottom of the cliffs. The weather is still unseasonably warm and dry, and, although most of the recruits are very reasonably fit, the log race is obviously hard work. It's just as well to remind them that when they join their platoons they are expected to complete the same distance in full kit with weapons. At this a few jaws start to drop.

The hard work over, the recruits are given time to cool down and clean up, while in the RRTT office the writing of reports, and assessing passes and failures has started. Each recruit is only allowed two attempts at passing the RSW, after which we suggest they try elsewhere. While we prepare reports and collect in kit, the recruits are asked to write their own assessment of the weekend. We encourage them to be completely candid, although we can give a little guidance on the wording such as "The weekend was the best thing that has ever happened in my life, the RRTT were great, and I want to be just like them when I grow up".

That basically is the format for our recruits' introduction to the Territorial Army, and our chance for us to take a good hard look at them. Most give it a good try – and we can't ask for more than that![37]

A view of the process from a recruit's point of view written a year or so later by Private Goodlife, who was attracted by an A Company stand at the North Somerset Show, appears in Chapter 12.

An interesting and quite successful development of the NELC concept was Exercise Executive Stretch. The object was to boost officer recruiting – mainly for the TA, but also the other Reserve Forces – by demonstrating to both employers and middle-management employees that tremendous benefits could result from the character development and leadership training that are an inherent aspect of the soldiering life. Run two or three times a year in each District by the major units in turn, between 15 and 30 young executives from the business and commercial worlds, male and female, would come together at a training camp (more often than not, it seemed, in pretty dreadful weather), and were put through a series of 'civilianised' military activities. These were mainly variations of the traditional command tasks – from crossing a piece of water with the help of three planks of differing lengths, a leaky oil-drum and two hundred feet of extremely heavy rope in a single length, through night navigation and cooking in the field, to coping with a helicopter crash. Almost without exception the events were (at least in retrospect) hugely enjoyed by the participants, and, in some ways more importantly, many of their employers who came to watch all or part of the proceedings were greatly impressed. It does not, however, seem that any records were kept of how many of those who went through the rigours of the Exercise subsequently joined one of the Reserve Forces – but they could hardly have failed to appreciate the almost certain benefits that doing so would have given them, or to be impressed by the TA officers and NCOs, and the PSIs involved. The Battalion was responsible for running a good number of Executive Stretches, and – although they were very demanding in terms of "man-training-days" (the maximum number of days a year for which each individual in the TA could be paid) – they were greatly enjoyed by all ranks involved in running them, and did indeed occasionally produce new potential officers.

WO2 Nigel Attwood of A Company and Corporal Don Topp of C Company, two most loyal Volunteers, were both awarded the British Empire Medal in the 1988 New Year's Honours. At that time, the Attwood family had two distinguished senior soldiers – Sergeant Major Attwood was one of the original members of A Company, and his brother was the RSM of 1 Glosters. Corporal Topp had served in the TA since 1963, and earned two bars to his TEM – and the Company Notes said "He has been a tower of strength and dependability throughout his time with the Company, and we cannot think of a more worthy recipient of this honour than him."[38]

Robin Pook's third and last Annual Camp, in 1988 was NATO's

Exercise Bold Grouse in Denmark (see Chapter 11) – and so, in order to practice the Battalion in the tasks it was likely to have to face, he assembled it on Salisbury Plain for Exercise Wiltshire Pheasant:

> There have been some notable Battalion exercises during this period, but the high point must surely have been Wiltshire Pheasant. It had all the ingredients to get the adrenalin going in the Volunteers, beginning with an event which made the front page of the local paper – a very slick move out by Chinook helicopters from the football field at Dorchester. It was the first time that the boys had worn the new combat helmet, and it was declared very comfortable. There is no doubt that it is a first-class bit of kit, and it looks good as well.[39]

All the Rifle Companies were flown to the Plain. A Company were 'lifted' from RAF Innsworth, outside Gloucester, to the Training Area by four Puma helicopters, where:

> We were in fact Blue Force facing an enemy from the Royal Scots Dragoon Guards, 3 Para, 9/12 Lancers and 2 Royal Anglian, backed-up by Jaguar aircraft. A formidable foe indeed. This demanding exercise stretched all ranks to their limit. Many valuable lessons were learned[40], but it is true to say that we successfully implemented a detailed Operations Order and complete deployment/redeployment plans.[41]

Battalion HQ and HQ Company arrived considerably later than planned, giving the unlikely, albeit original, excuse that they had to "avoid the hippies and police who were on their way to the annual solstice celebrations at Stonehenge".

---

[1]   In the Battalion scrapbook.
[2]   Exercise Wessex Wherry – a build-up to Exercise Bold Guard at Camp.
[3]   *RHRJ*, November 1982.
[4]   *BB*, Summer 1989.
[5]   *BB*, Summer 1984.
[6]   16 August 1981.
[7]   *Bournemouth Evening Echo*, 25 June 1981.
[8]   Which formed the basis of his entertaining book *Soldier On! The Testament of a Tom*

(Spellmount Ltd, Tunbridge Wells,1992).

9   *BB*, Summer 1986.

10 *ibid.*, Summer 1983.

11 *ibid.*, Summer 1989.

12 *ibid.*, Summer 1980.

13 See Chapter 6.

14 *Amesbury Journal*, 11 April 1981.

15 *D & DRJ*, Jan 1981.

16 Army Ceremonial Manual Chapter 5, para 5.56.

17 As an example of the experience of the PSAOs, when he finally retired in 1989, he had completed 42 years of Army service.

18 All the material for this and the two preceding paragraphs comes from an article by Douggie McMeeken.

19 (Usually senior) members of the TA employed with TA units on a permanent basis, and generally referred to as "Nerps"

20 *Swindon Evening Advertiser*, 20 June 983.

21 *BB*, Winter 1984.

22 *RHRJ*, May 1984.

23 *BB*, Winter 1984.

24 *D&DRJ*, January 1985.

25 Henry Walton in the *Dorset Evening Echo*, 4 December 1985.

26 *D&DRJ*, Winter 1985.

27 *Ibid*, Summer 1986.

28 *RHRJ*, November 1985.

29 *Ibid*, May 1986.

30 2 April 1986.

31 *DERRJ* 1987.

32 See Chapter 8.

33 Minute of meeting between the Brigade Commander and Brigadier Starling, 6 June 1988.

34 A day's worth of packaged (and mainly tinned and dehydrated) rations, officially known as 'compo', and colloquially as a 'ratpack'.

35 A Hindi word for a rough shelter – in the Army made out of natural materials or a lightweight waterproof sheet.

36 Doing sentry duty.

37 Article by L/Cpl G Tolmie in *BB*, Summer 1990, and *Western Wessex TAVRA Newsletter* 1990. His use of the expression "The Boss" must surely be literary licence, even for the TA!

38 *D&DRJ*, Spring 1988.

39 *D&DRJ*, Autumn 1988.

40 A euphemism, often found in reports of exercises, meaning that anything from one or two small things to a great deal went mildly or seriously wrong.

41 *BB, Winter 1988.*

CHAPTER 10

OPTIONS & OTHER CHANGES: 1987–1994

[This Chapter looks at one the major consequences for the United Kingdom of the end of the Cold War and the collapse of the Warsaw Pact in 1989-1990 – undoubtedly the most momentous period for defence in the whole of Western Europe since the end of the Second World War – the complete reorganisation of the British Armed Forces under "Options for Change". 1 Wessex was only a very small element of Options for Change – but the outcome for it was complete and utter disaster. As in Chapter 8 about the first reorganisation, to avoid breaking up the narrative of the normal life of the Battalion, the history and outcome of Options for Change, as they affected 1 Wessex, are related on their own here.]

The Cold War and the Warsaw Pact, which are very briefly described towards the end of Chapter 1, had between them completely dominated European politics and defence policies from the end of the Second World War in Europe in 1945 until 1989. The former began, almost immediately after Germany's capitulation, as the result of the inability of the United States and the Soviet Union to agree on how to reconstruct post-war Europe. It developed into some 40 years of hostility and tension between them and their respective allies – and it was not until about 1986 that it slowly began to 'thaw'. Mikhail Gorbachev became the Premier of the Soviet Union in 1985, launching the reform programmes known as "perestroika" (meaning 'openness' – i.e free speech and the granting of civil rights) and "glasnost" ('restructuring' – principally the modernization of business). The Soviet Union began to realize that it could not remain isolated from the rest of the world in perpetuity, and, indeed, only two years later Gorbachev could write "For our internal progress, we need normal international relations".

The Warsaw Pact was the name given to the agreement between the Soviet Union and eight other eastern European countries (including Czechoslovakia, East Germany, Hungary and Poland) signed in Poland in 1955. It was a purely military treaty, entered into as a response to the creation of NATO in 1949 and the Allies permitting the re-militarization of West Germany in 1954, both of which were thought to pose a potential threat to those countries – and it bound its signatories to come to the aid of the others, should any one of them be the victim of foreign aggression. Although it was claimed that the Treaty was based on total equality between each nation and mutual non-interference in one another's internal affairs, it quickly became a powerful political tool which enabled the Soviet Union to control its allies, and to harness the powers of their combined armed forces.

The Cold War and the Pact became symbolized by the huge wall dividing East Berlin from West Berlin, cutting through the heart of the city, which was largely constructed by East German troops in a single night, 13 August 1961. An even more significant date in German history, however, was 9 November 1989 – when, after twenty-eight years, without any warning the Berlin Wall was opened by German Democratic Republic border police. In amazed disbelief, Berliners from both sides climbed up on, and poured through, the Wall – which had been called "the most unpleasant edifice in the world" – embracing each other, singing and dancing in the streets. As if to have a piece of German history, and a personal hand in tearing it down, some began chiseling bits away and taking them home; many started pulling it apart to create more openings, and then it was substantially destroyed by mobs.[1] East Germans immediately began flooding into West Germany, and within a few days several million people had seized the chance to see the other side of the Wall again (or, in many cases, for the first time) and their western neighbours. That astonishing demonstration of 'people-power' soon proved to be the catalyst for a series of events that completely altered the face of Europe. By July 1990, Germany had made great progress towards re-unification, with the incorporation of the German Democratic Republic (East Germany) into the Federal Republic of Germany (West Germany), and, before that formally took place on 3 October that year, East Germany had, unsurprisingly, withdrawn from the Warsaw Pact. Within another six months, Hungary had also given notice of its intention to leave, and Soviet troops were beginning to be withdrawn from there and from Czechoslovakia. At the same time, the progress of conventional arms control talks in Vienna offered the possibility of verified destruction of large quantities of Soviet military equipment, and substantial reductions in the numbers of both United States and Soviet military personnel in Europe. By 1991, the Soviet Union had lost its hold over Eastern Europe and dissolved itself.[2]

The combined result of the re-militarization of Germany in 1954, the end of the Cold War in 1989-1900 and Germany's reunification in 1990, completely altered the future prospects for Europe – and not just in defence terms – but the NATO countries fully appreciated that, sooner or later, some new major threat to peace, whether in Europe or elsewhere, would be bound to arise. In 1960, NATO had established the Allied Command Europe [ACE] to safeguard the area extending from the northern tip of Norway to the Mediterranean, and from the Atlantic coastline to the eastern border of Turkey. ACE formed the Ace Mobile Force (Land) [AMF(L)] as a small multinational force that could be sent at short notice to anywhere within ACE's area of responsibility[3], and the United Kingdom's contribution to it was UKMF(L) – of which 1 Wessex had become part in 1982.[4] Then (to jump ahead for a moment), in May 1991, there emerged from the NATO Defence Planning Committee the concept of a more substantial counter to future challenges to the alliance – the Allied Rapid Reaction Corps [ARRC], of which the AMF(L) would form part. The ARRC would provide NATO's Supreme Allied Commander Europe with a "multinational corps-sized grouping from which forward elements could be ready to deploy within 14 days (and, indeed, lead elements and recce parties at very short notice)". Its mission was "to be prepared to deploy under NATO, EU or coalition auspices to a designated area, to undertake combined and joint operations across the operational spectrum", and it was based on four different Headquarters and formations, which would "enable crisis support management options or the sustainment of ongoing operations........from deterrence and crisis management to regional conflict operations......."[5] The leadership and the main framework of the ARRC, and a brigade group that could be deployed on very short notice, would be provided by the UK.

The Cold War and Warsaw Pact had, of course, been the major *raison d'être* for the existence of a very large part of the British Army and the Royal Air Force, and to a lesser extent the Royal Navy, since the 1950s – and the Government convinced itself that there was no further need, at least in the short or medium term, to be able to counter the threat of an invasion of Western Europe, and that there could therefore be a major reduction in spending on defence. Everyone began talking about "peace dividends" – although 12 months later the Armed Forces were still wondering what the effect of those great events would be for them.

At the beginning of July 1990, the Secretary of State for Defence, The Right Honourable Tom King, therefore announced that, in view of the greatly diminished European threat, there would be a wide-ranging review of the suitability of the UK's Armed Forces for meeting the new challenges of a very volatile world, followed by their major restructuring. Intended to involve wide consultation, it was named "Options for Change" (or, as it soon became known, just "Options"), and preliminary work on it had in fact begun earlier in the year.

Before, however, relating the detailed effect of Options on the Battalion, it is necessary to go back a few years and consider what had been happening within the Prince of Wales's Division. The formation of 4 D & D in December had set the Royal Hampshires and the Duke of Edinburgh's (but, suprisingly, not the Glosters) wondering how they might have their own TA battalions again too, by means of a reorganisation and renaming of 1 and 2 Wessex. There were, however, some basic difficulties. The two battalions were spread fairly illogically across Berkshire, Gloucestershire, Hampshire and Wiltshire – and while between them they had numerically more than enough Companies for the idea to be theoretically possible, it was simply impractical, for they were not in the 'right' counties in relation to their roles; a good number of the Company TA Centres would have needed modification; and, although Brock Barracks in Reading easily accommodated Battalion Headquarters and Headquarter Company of 2 Wessex, there was no TA Centre in Hampshire big enough for those of a new 4/5 Royal Hampshires. To achieve the aim, therefore, would have needed a quite unimaginably difficult re-organisation, and substantial expense on buildings. Nevertheless, over nearly the next four years, 1 Wessex made it clear in many meetings with, and many letters to, the Director of Infantry, the Divisional Headquarters, the Colonels of the Regular Regiments and South West District that it was certainly not opposed in principle to the break-up of the Battalion in a return of 'county' battalions, provided that the new arrangements embraced the entire Battalion, and broadly speaking took effect simultaneously.

Another, almost more intractable, problem was the conflict between 'regimental interests' and operational requirements. In the very first formal discussion within the Division about TA battalions for the Glosters, the Royal Hampshires and DERR in November 1987, the general feeling was that a return to 'county' battalions was a good long-term aim, but Lieutenant General (as he was then) Sir John Waters, the Colonel of the Glosters, "was adamant that in the short term nothing should be done to harm the operational roles of the Wessex battalions", and, perhaps surprisingly, the Colonels of the other two regiments agreed.[6]

There was much discussion about the manning of 4 D & D. The TAVRA, using the Shapland Formula (which said that at any one time, in any one place in the United Kingdom, approximately 0.25% of the adult population might be expected to be in the Reserve Forces)[7], had always doubted that the population of Exeter and its surroundings was large enough to support both a Headquarter Company and a Rifle Company for 4 D & D, and experience was proving that to be correct. Furthermore, there were difficulties over its platoon locations: for example, 1 Wessex and the TAVRA had very unwillingly agreed with General Shortis in 1986 that, to give 4 D & D a presence in Dorset, they could form a Recce Platoon in Weymouth, although that was likely to affect the numbers in the C Company Platoon there – but in the event it would never actually happen. Notwithstanding the fact that E Company had already been transferred to 4 D & D, General Shortis continued to press for even more changes to 1 and 2 Wessex, not only to get over those particular problems, but generally to enhance 4 D & D. The new GOC South West District (Major General Tony Jeapes, who, whether or not by coincidence, was also a member of the D & D) was therefore asked by Headquarters United

Kingdom Land Forces to make formal recommendations for resolving their difficulties. He seemed, however, unwilling to 'toe the party line', taking a more objective and realistic view, and disagreed with the "Weymouth solution":

> Having visited C Company, 1 Wessex in Dorchester, it was stressed to me that the Company see themselves, I believe fairly, as in direct line of descent from The Dorset Regiment, and second, that Dorchester and Weymouth together are one entity. The Weymouth part of the Dorchester Company is a strong one, and were it to be removed it would damage the Company's morale and effectiveness very seriously. I cannot therefore agree to the plan to raise a Platoon of 4 D & D in Weymouth........As you know, I should personally have favoured the raising of a third battalion of The Wessex Regiment than 4 D & D, because I foresaw just the sort of problems of territorial affiliation that now faces us. Whereas it would have been acceptable to raise a company in Weston-Super-Mare (or Andover) [locations that had been earlier suggested by Western Wessex] for 3 Wessex, it makes no senses to raise a company in either place for a battalion of The Devonshire and Dorset Regiment. I propose therefore that 1 Wessex should be invited to raise a company based on Weston-Super-Mare, and that when that company is operational the Dorchester and Weymouth Company should move across to become C Company 4 D&D........I am well aware that this will cause disruption to 1 Wessex, that it is not so long ago that the Battalion lost one Company to 4 D & D, and that above all the Battalion now needs stability.[8]

and, prophetically, he said that he saw 1 Wessex's future deployment as being in East Dorset, Wiltshire, Gloucestershire and North Avon. General Mike Walsh subsequently commented to the author: "I know Colin Shortis is angry about Weymouth – the scene is set for a good row between two UK District Commanders!".[9] 1 Wessex and Western Wessex had by now privately, and (needless to say) again with extreme reluctance, come to accept that sooner or later, like E Company, C Company would also be transferred to 4 D & D. On 21 March 1988 General Jeapes held a meeting at South West District Headquarters with the Chairmen and Secretaries of the two TAVRAs, and after some very realistic discussion the main outcome was agreement that that would indeed take place when a new Rifle Company had been formed to replace it, and was 'fit for role'.[10] In July, the General accordingly put that to HQ UKLF[11] – specifically saying in his letter "I have been very impressed by the way in which the Council of The Wessex Regiment has accepted my proposal" – and in due course the Commander of the UK Field Army accepted it, and directed that it should be implemented "without delay after Ex Bold Guard [19]90".[12]

So much was going on, however, that it was difficult to see the wood for the trees. In a letter to the author in July, General Waters said "There seem to be so many wheels within wheels on this subject that I am slightly nervous about taking them [the proposals for dealing with 4 D & D's inability to recruit] at face value" – and even nine months later Major General Tony Ward-Booth, the Secretary of Eastern Wessex TAVRA, could comment on "the unseemly haste with which the chain of command is pushing through the short-term reorganisation which would result from the transfer of C Company to 4 D & D".[13] The Commander of the UKMF, not surprisingly, supported the 'operational needs first' view, and he told Brigadier Joe Starling, who visited him in June 1988, that, although an Infantryman himself and therefore well understanding the issues, from his point of view the re-establishment of County TA battalions could not be allowed to compromise the efficiency of the UKMF.

The first specific proposal for County TA battalions for the other four Regular Regiments to appear in print came from the Colonel of the Royal Hampshires, Brigadier Bob Long. In a forcefully worded paper sent to The Prince of Wales's Division,[14] he proposed that 4/5th Royal Hampshires should be re-formed from 1 Wessex's D Company in Bournemouth and Poole, and 2 Wessex's companies and platoons in Portsmouth, Winchester and Andover, Southampton, the Isle of Wight, and in Basingstoke. The rest of 2 Wessex – its platoons in Maidenhead, Newbury, Reading and Slough – would combine with the remains of 1 Wessex to form a new Glosters/DERR battalion.[15] He took a somewhat cavalier attitude to the fate of the Gloucestershire and Berkshire companies of 1 Wessex and the two Berkshire companies of 2 Wessex, saying that "If the Gloster/DERR issue presents an impasse, this should not prevent the formation of 4/5 Royal Hamps to succeed

2 Wessex". The paper was discussed at length on 9 November 1988 at the six-monthly meeting of the Colonels of the Regular Regiments, attended by the author as the Chairman of Western Wessex and the Honorary Colonel of 1 Wessex and representing the Honorary Colonel of 2 Wessex. With the Glosters, the DERR, both Wessex battalions and Western Wessex totally against the idea, however, not unsurprisingly it made no progress at that stage. Interestingly, the only minuted mention of the operational aspect at that meeting was made by General Waters, who said that "the operational requirements of the TA completely outweighed any preference of cap-badge."

A few months after that, wry smiles from some of those involved in the debate greeted the news that Brigadier Long had been appointed as the Secretary of Eastern Wessex TAVR, to succeed the hugely popular General Ward-Booth – who was a marvellous example of a Regular soldier becoming the staunchest possible supporter of every element of the TA, and The Wessex Regiment in particular. That meant, of course, that the Brigadier would have to turn from being a poacher into a gamekeeper – which he did extremely well! Indeed, at a meeting a few months earlier, he had admitted that, being entirely objective, the correct course was to leave 1 and 2 Wessex alone – but that, as the Colonel of the Royal Hampshires, he was bound to do everything in his power to secure the re-formation of their TA battalion. That was exactly the conflict of interests with which a number of other senior officers involved in the question of County TA battalions and Options found themselves burdened.

There was no doubt that the two Wessex Battalions would be able to combine in Berkshire and Wiltshire to form, and sustain, a new 4 (or 5) DERR – but that would have left A Company in Gloucester (with the Battalion's Anti-tank, Assault Pioneer and Reconaissance Platoons in Gloucester, Cheltenham and the Forest of Dean) as a 'one-off' and over-large sub-unit, extremely vulnerable to subsequent disbandment. Against that possibility, early in 1989 the TAVRA and the Glosters accordingly considered, purely between themselves, what was in many ways the very attractive possibility of its becoming a 'single' TA Company, perhaps 'W' Company, of The Gloucestershire Regiment – with a mobilisation role similar to that which it had back in the 1970s, providing a fourth rifle company for a Regular BAOR battalion, which would whenever possible be 1 Glosters. The idea was not, however, taken further at that stage.

On 10 February 1989, General Jeapes issued his instructions for the transfer of the Second Battalion's Newbury Platoon to the First and its enlargement into a Company – "to be completed in time for the 1991 training season" – and how that was achieved is described in Chapter 12. After that, however, everything went strangely quiet for over a year – at the next POW Division Colonels of Regiments' meeting in November the TA was simply not mentioned!

In May 1990, however, the Divisional Colonel produced an extremely detailed 21-page paper for the Colonels of Regiments and the two Wessex Honorary Colonels suggesting a wholesale re-structuring of the Division's TA battalions – and (somewhat surprisingly) the Yeomanry in the south-west of the Divisional area as well – to produce TA battalions for all the old Wessex Brigade regiments. The Introduction said that "The kudos of the UKMF/ NATO role for 1 Wessex, with its attendant equipment advantages, must be preserved within the new organisation" – and it proposed using the "manpower cover" currently allocated to The Royal Wessex Yeomanry and the two Wessex battalions as the basis for re-forming The Royal Wiltshire Yeomanry (although there was no explanation of how or why they came within the Division's remit), 5 Glosters, and 4/5 Royal Hampshires, all with Home Defence roles; strengthening 4 D & D; and with a new 5 DERR taking over 1 Wessex's UKMF/NATO role (established with four rifle companies and a support company). Like the earlier Royal Hampshire's and Duke of Edinburgh's idea, that simply did not 'add up', and furthermore the proposals for meeting the accommodation requirements and their cost were equally unrealistic. Even if the money could have been found, with the best will in the world, administratively, operationally and organisationally the result would have been total chaos for a long time; the reactions of the addressees of the letter (other than the author) are unknown, but can easily be guessed![16]

To return to the 'bigger picture', all the ideas about County TA battalions that had been bandied around were brought to a halt in July

1990 by the Secretary of State's announcement about the setting-up of
Options – and then, almost exactly a month later, a major international
crisis arose: on 20 August, Iraq – heavily in debt, and having failed to
achieve an increase in the price of its own oil on world markets by
demanding that Kuwait should reduce its production – invaded it.
All peaceful attempts to persuade Iraq's leader, Saddam Hussein, to
withdraw his forces and release the hostages they had taken failed
– and therefore, later that month, a coalition force, eventually drawn
from 42 different countries and numbering a total three-quarters of
a million troops, began assembling in the Gulf. Intense diplomatic
activity and the adoption of a number of United Nations' Resolutions
failed to achieve a peaceful, or indeed any, withdrawal of the Iraqi
forces, and accordingly, under the code-name Operation Desert Storm
and the authority of the United Nations, on 17 January 1991 the allied
forces began the campaign to liberate Kuwait.

The work-load which Operation Granby (the British forces'
involvement in Operation Desert Storm) imposed on the staffs of all
three Services was simply gigantic, and it was clearly going to continue
to do so for an appreciable while. In that context, there was therefore
no alternative but to put Options 'on hold'; that was done at the
end of January, and it was not until July that work on it began again.
Almost needless to say, however, during that period the 'interested
parties' to the TA debate nevertheless continued talking and thinking
about the way forward.

The ground forces moved into Kuwait on 24 February, and four
astonishing days later the aim had been achieved, with the minimum
of casualties and equipment losses; some five weeks later Iraq accepted
the terms of a United Nations' resolution banning it from any
involvement with non-conventional weapons, and a formal ceasefire
came into effect. Notwithstanding, however, that the total change in
Eastern Europe and the withdrawal of Soviet troops from their former
satellites meant that a million fewer troops would be ranged against
NATO:

> Iraq's invasion of Kuwait showed how suddenly unprovoked aggression
> can arise, but also the scope for decisive action by the international
> community.[17]

and the Gulf War therefore reinforced the need for a completely fresh look at the capability and structure of the Royal Navy, the Army and the Royal Air Force.

Options – set up under the Government's *Statement on the Defence Estimates* for 1991 – was published in July 1990, and, although it was claimed to be a purely "resource-driven exercise", it was without doubt primarily initiated on the grounds of political, and hence military, requirement, rather than financial need. No elements of the three Services and their volunteer counterparts were immune from examination, and, in most cases, change. The strength of the Regular Army would be reduced from about 156,000 to around 116,000 by the mid-1990s, which for the Infantry meant the reduction in the number of Regular battalions from 40 to 36[18]. The TA as a whole was to be cut from 75,000 to 63,000, and that would involve the disbandment or amalgamation of what was originally an unspecified number of the 33 extant battalions, but which eventually turned out to be 18, leaving only just 15. Very understandably, virtually all the proposals generated an unprecedented amount of anxiety and heat, and, not for the first time, it was sometimes difficult to see the logic of some of the ideas – for instance, the principle of 'equal misery for all' in the serious suggestion that if the strength of the Regular Army as a whole was going to be reduced by 30%, the TA should be cut by the same proportion. There were serious concerns that, in the chaos that was bound to ensue, the hierarchy and staffs of the Regular Army in Whitehall and in the UK Land Forces HQ at Wilton, many of whom had little or no in-depth knowledge of the TA, would do their best to ensure that their own particular 'empires' were favoured at the expense of many existing Volunteer units, and in particular without appreciating that "there was a critical mass for the TA at every level, below which it would cease to attract both enough and the right sort of people".[19] In the event, those worries were indeed justified – and not only in relation to 1 Wessex.

One of the first announcements made under Options was that the UKMF(L) would be disbanded in 1992 – but immediately re-formed as 1 (Mechanised) Brigade in 3 (UK) Division, and become part of the AFM(L) in its place. That cast a major shadow over the Battalion's future, but to their immense pleasure and relief, in September 1991 it was decided that, when that change took place, they would continue to be the Brigade's sole TA Infantry battalion. It could be said that, 1 Wessex having held the Stratco/UKMF role for so long, there might have been have been good grounds for giving another NATO battalion the new ARRC one – but, apart from the 'devil you know' principle, it was undoubtedly logical that the Battalion should have it.

Given the existence and strengths of the regimental system, it would have been a quite impossible task for the Ministry of Defence to decide in detail how the reduction of the size of the Army should be achieved. The Divisions of Infantry, the other Arms, and the Services were therefore all required to put forward their own recommendations – and, not surprisingly, devising solutions that pleased even the majority, let alone everyone, proved to be difficult in the extreme. As the old saying goes: "Miracles we can do at once, but the impossible takes a little longer." The Divisions were told the number of battalions they had to cut, and in the case of the Prince of Wales's Division it was three Regular ones and two TA. After an enormous amount of discussion, the Colonels of the Regiments accepted that there were no realistic alternatives to the amalgamation of the Glosters and the Duke of Edinburgh's, the Hampshires joining The Royal Sussex Regiment in forming a new regiment within the Queen's Division, and the Cheshires and the Royal Welch Fusiliers also amalgamating. In due course, the first two of those amalgamations took place (although the third never did), but at this stage no decisions were made about the TA battalions.

In an attempt to help keep the Battalion's mind on the present, rather than the future, the author, as the Honorary Colonel, wrote to every officer and warrant officer:

> I thought it might be helpful if I told you all something about the present state of play under Options for Change, and try to allay your fears for the future resulting from the many rumours which I know are going around.
>
> The Secretary of State for Defence, Tom King, has announced that the Regular Army is to be cut by some 40,000 to 116,000, and, as far as the Infantry is concerned, each Division has put forward

proposals for reducing the number of Regular battalions administered by it – apparently with the exception of the Scottish and Queen's Divisions, who have refused to do so and asked the Secretary of State to make the decisions for them. The present plan is that the new shape of the Regular Army, including details of which battalions are to be amalgamated, disbanded or retained, will be made public in a statement on 18th July.

The Chief of the Defence Staff, General Sir John Chapple, has written to all Colonels of Regiments and Honorary Colonels about the changes generally, and in his letter he said:

> "With regard to the reserves, we would envisage these statements on the size of the Army to include the broad size of the future TA, but would see the more detailed TA order of battle being addressed subsequently, with an opportunity for proper consultation. We would hope to be able to complete this by the autumn."

I can therefore categorically say that – whilst there have been, and continue to be, endless discussions, numerous proposals and countless rumours – no decisions have yet been made about the future of any specific battalions in the TA.

The Secretary of State has given the Army the opportunity to decide on the detailed regimental changes itself, rather than imposing them from above, and assurances have been given (which are supported by the CDS's remark I quote above) that we shall similarly have a considerable say as to our future in discussions with the GOC, the TAVRAs and the Prince of Wales' Division. The general view seems to be that those discussions will start in August or early September, and that the details of the new order of battle of the TA will be announced in late September or early October. It is, however, always possible that the timetable will either be shortened or lengthened.

Much, and perhaps everything, will depend, of course, on the outcome for the Regular battalions of the Prince of Wales's Division, and I am sure that the question of a return to TA battalions for Regular regiments generally will be considered again. I do not believe that we shall necessarily be against such an arrangement, and if it met with the approval of the officers and senior NCOs of the Battalion then it could well take effect. You can be assured, however, that I shall not be a party to any decisions about our future without full consultation with you all.

Nothing, however, has yet been lost! Our marvellous record, and our geographical position, must be to our advantage. Whether or not The Wessex Regiment remains in its present form, no one can say at the moment, and I can equally well assure you that anything you may hear at the present time about disbandment of Companies, reduction of Companies to Platoons, or the closure of particular TA Centres is at the moment pure speculation.

Please therefore pay as little attention to the rumours as you can, and simply get on and enjoy your soldiering – so far as the present tight financial circumstances allow! It is particularly important, of course, for you to maintain the morale of your soldiers. I shall be coming to Camp with the specific object of dealing with any questions and worries you may have, and of getting your views about the future.[20]

Although the question of re-forming County TA battalions was not part of Options, it gradually became subsumed in it, so that they ran in parallel – as General Waters had said "there were wheels within wheels", and it was often quite difficult to work out under exactly which 'head' any particular proposal came. The discussions and negotiations went on, sometimes almost on a daily basis, over almost the whole of the period covered by Chapter 12; meetings were held, and a seemingly never-ending streams of correspondence and papers flowed between the Ministry of Defence, HQ UKLF, the Prince of Wales's Division Headquarters, South West District[21] and the two TAVRAs, this way and that, for some four years. It has to be said, however, that there was not all that much consultation with the Honorary Colonels of 1 and 2 Wessex – or at least the author, as the former, who at one point he had to write to the Divisional Colonel and remind him that, since within the Division they were on the same footing as the Colonels of the Regular Regiments, they were supposed to be in the debate! In the end, though, it became obvious that there was no way in which 1 and 2 Wessex could influence the eventual outcome; they were simply pawns in a game of chess, and just had to carry on in the hope that things would turn out at least reasonably satisfactorily.

Matters then began to move extremely quickly, and on 23 July 1991, the Chief of the Defence Staff wrote to Major General Robin Grist, who had become the Colonel of The Gloucestershire Regiment at the beginning of the year, to confirm that the Regiment would indeed amalgamate with The Duke of Edinburgh's Royal Regiment. Although expected, that was, of course, a completely devastating blow, but at least the Ministry of Defence agreed that 'Amalgamation Day' could be postponed to allow the Glosters – at that time one of the few regiments in the British Army still able to do so – to celebrate their Tercentenary in 1994.

Although The Prince of Wales's Division had very reluctantly accepted that it would lose two of its nine TA battalions, no proposals had yet been made as to which ones they should be. Nevertheless, there was no denying the possibility that part of the solution would be the amalgamation of 1 and 2 Wessex. At the beginning of September, however, the Divisional Colonel told the author that 1 Wessex's future seemed secure, albeit with a reduced establishment and possibly a change of role, but that the prospects for the Second Battalion were not so good. In September, therefore, the Wessex Regimental Council met at Brock Barracks, under the chairmanship of the 2nd Battalion's new Honorary Colonel, General Sir John Learmont KCB CBE, who was shortly to become the Quartermaster-General, and as such a member of the Army Board. The author did not mention his conversation with the Divisional Colonel, but the unanimous outcome was that, if any amalgamation proposals were put forward, the Battalions would fight together – wanting to remain in being, retaining their identity, cap-badge, and titles. It was accordingly decided that both Honorary Colonels would write to General Waters, who had now become the Commander-in-Chief UKLF (as a full general) – and the author said this:

> Throughout the 24 years since its formation from the TA battalions of the old Wessex Brigade regiments, 1 Wessex has unquestionably been one of the premier TA units, and has built up its own *esprit de corps*, which, whilst obviously not comparable in time terms, is undoubtedly as strong as that enjoyed by many Regular battalions. That is equally true of 2 Wessex. The Regiment's achievements have been entirely

its own, in that it has never had a Regular 'parent' to provide the focused support of a regiment with its roots deeply implanted in a particular county. The Wessex Regiment – and 1 Wessex in particular, having had companies in Berkshire, Devon, Dorset, Gloucestershire, Hampshire and Wiltshire – is genuinely representative of the West Country, and its name is well-known and well-respected throughout both civilian and military Wessex. (It is also worth mentioning that the Wyvern of our badge dates back to the time of King Alfred!)

Given the inherent limitations on any reserve, all-volunteer army and recent constraints on the TA, 1 Wessex has maintained standards of training and administration and an operational capacity second to none, and in my view it admirably meets the sustainability criteria. Its latest strength return shows 41 + 576, or 85% of its establishment of 43 + 686. The Company in Swindon (replacing that in Winchester, which had been transferred to 2 Wessex in 1986) had a strength of over 80 within a year of its formation, soon became fully operational, and remains as well recruited – whilst the Newbury Company (formed to replace the Dorchester Company, which was taken to sustain 4 D and D in 1990) has recruited virtually from scratch to a current strength of 75 in about a year, and is well on the way to repeating Swindon's success. A further example of the Battalion's resilience is the fact that, despite having had no Company Commander or 2i/c for almost a year, through the efforts of its PSAO and the subalterns, the Gloucester Company is still at some 50% of its establishment. The Battalion's 1990 ARU concluded: "1 Wessex is a well motivated and effective TA unit...... is fit for its role..... – and its standing has, of course, long been recognised by its role in the UKMF."

For all the reasons given above, to disband 1 Wessex – and/or, indeed, 2 Wessex – now would be utterly illogical, and would show a contemptuous disregard for all the efforts of those many Territorials, particularly many long-serving officers and NCOs, who in their "twice a citizen" role have devoted a substantial proportion of their energies and lives to building the Battalion up into its present excellent state, in fulfilment of the requirements of the Ministry of Defence in 1967. At present there are no Regular regiments of which we could become the TA battalions. Whilst the prime military loyalty of the Territorial infantryman is undoubtedly to his Company, an appreciable proportion of the members of The Wessex Regiment – indeed of the TA generally – in whom the 'TA habit' is deeply engrained, looking at the chaotic state of regimental identities in the Regular Army at the present time, would have serious doubts about continuing to serve, if now required to accept a change of name, cap-badge and all that would go with that. Before my visit to 1 Wessex's Camp this year, the senior members of the WOs and Sergeants' Mess had a special meeting in order to be able to give me their collective view – which was that they unquestionably did not want The Wessex Regiment to disband. Were that to happen, for a large number of them there would simply be no other accessible TA units for them to join – and these are the people whom the TA cannot possibly risk losing.[22]

General Learmont and General Mike Walsh (as the previous Honorary Colonel) also wrote strongly advocating the retention of both Battalions; their letters were copied to other senior officers, including the Director of Infantry.

Happily, General Waters accepted the wisdom of 'no change' for 1 and 2 Wessex, and persuaded his fellow Colonels of Regiments to do likewise. The Divisional HQ therefore recommended to the Director of Infantry that, as the Royal Regiment of Wales and The Worcestershire & Sherwood Foresters each had (nearly uniquely) two TA battalions, the two to be 'lost' by the Division would be one from each regiment.[23] Taken all round, that was a very reasonable solution – and it therefore looked as though the future of both Wessex Battalions would be secure, at least for some while.

At that stage, 1 Wessex had rifle companies in Gloucester/Bristol, Swindon, Poole and Newbury; Support Company was split between Cinderford (Assault Pioneers), Gloucester (Anti-tank) and Andover (Mortars), with the Recce Platoon in Cheltenham. Thankfully unmoved since 1972, Battalion HQ and HQ Company, were still in Devizes. The relatively high hopes that nothing too awful would happen were, however, soon completely shattered by a paper from the Director of Army Reserves & Cadets, Major General Murray Naylor, in November proposing, as top of the list of unpalatable things for TA units in the Western Wessex area, that 1 Wessex should reduce to three rifle companies in Bristol, Gloucestershire and west Wiltshire, with its Battalion HQ in Bristol or Devizes, and that 2 Wessex would 'withdraw' into Berkshire and east Wiltshire, with its Battalion HQ in Devizes or Reading. That re-deployment would be achieved by 1 Wessex not only giving up D Company in Poole to 4 D & D, but both the Newbury and Swindon Companies to 2 Wessex,[24] as 'compensation' to the latter for losing its Portsmouth and Winchester Companies to become part of the TA battalion of The Princess of Wales's Royal Regiment [PWRR], which was to be formed in September 1992 from The Queen's Regiment and The Royal Hampshire Regiment.[25] The loss of Swindon would, of course, necessitate the formation of a completely new replacement Company – but there was, of course, huge relief that neither 1 nor 2 Wessex were actually to be disbanded. There was undoubtedly a 'political dimension' to those proposals, as indeed there was to the aspirations or fears of many regiments or battalions involved in the re-structuring of the TA Infantry. Notwithstanding the eminently sensible rationale behind Options, of reducing the size of our Armed Forces, there was still going to be a need for a really well-trained Reserve Army, and 1 and 2 Wessex both thought that they should be part of it.

The author then wrote to General Learmont:

> .....I would like to think that – in a reversal of the situation when we had our Regimental Council meeting in Reading, and the future of the 2nd Battalion looked distinctly grim – the 2nd Battalion will now give its full support to the 1st.[26]

but at that time little did 1 Wessex, or indeed anyone else, think that 2 Wessex would only pay lip-service to the plea, and in the end, for all practical purposes, 'take over' 1 Wessex.

Brigadier Long, who had by now actually become the Secretary of Eastern Wessex TAVRA, was strongly against re-organising 1 Wessex more than was absolutely necessary:

> 1 Wessex is especially badly affected. The proposed solution is to the advantage of 2 Wessex. It aligns them properly to their parent regular battalion. It is CO 2 Wessex's best option. He and Hon Col 2 Wessex are, however, aware of the damage that, in particular, the loss of Swindon will do to 1 Wessex.[27]

In a *cri de coeur*, the author sent this letter to General Naylor on 9 January 1992:

I had hoped that Options would be completed without my having to write a letter of protest to anyone – but most regretfully I have no alternative but to do so now, and in the strongest possible terms......

If that proposal is adopted, this Battalion will be obliged to carry out literally a complete re-organisation, from which – despite the efforts and spirit of those Territorials who will remain – we could take years to recover fully, and I have to say that it is completely unacceptable to both Battalions.....

Few people would dispute that – despite the losses of our rifle companies in Winchester some 10 years ago, and then of rifle companies in Exeter and Dorchester respectively 4 years and 1 year ago – 1 Wessex is still one of the very best Territorial infantry battalions. To expect it now, however, to accept the loss of 2 more rifle companies is not only wholly unreasonable in itself, but could well (as I explain below) put us in the position of never again being able to man a support element, and goes entirely against the principle that the Options' changes should be achieved with the least possible disturbance of existing units. It seems, I am afraid, that those responsible for this latest proposal have simply no concept at all of the extent to which a major re-organisation within a TA unit means – persuading possibly many officers and SNCOs to change locations (perhaps entailing additional travelling of 50-80 miles a trip); or of the extent to which such a change may affect their civilian jobs and domestic lives; or that it is not simply a question of directing people across the square to another part of the barracks; or of the different time scale the TA needs for organisational changes as compared with the Regular Army; or of the whole effort entailed in raising and training a successful new Company. It is my firm opinion, and that of my predecessor, Major General Mike Walsh, that the changes which are now being contemplated can only put 1 Wessex's future existence as a well motivated, recruited and trained battalion in considerable jeopardy.

The practical implications are horrendous. We would only retain 2 of our existing 5 Companies; HQ Company at Devizes would be unaffected, but Gloucester would lose its existing Platoon-and-a-half in Bristol and have to form 2 new Platoons in Gloucester;

we would probably need to raise 3 more completely new Platoons, and (on the basis of the present 'staff list') find one new Company Commander, two new Company Seconds-in-Command and 5 new Platoon Commanders, as well as numerous new SNCOs. Particularly in the present 'employment climate', the building-up of fully recruited and operationally effective new Companies would undoubtedly be a slow and laborious process, especially in TA Centres shared with non-infantry units that have more attractive roles and equipment. Irrespective of whether or not we are to keep our support weapons, on the basis of the Shapland Formula and in the light of historical recruiting factors, the new plan could not be implemented without disbanding the three Support Platoons in the Gloucester/Cheltenham area, to release the manpower for those new Rifle Platoons. Even more important than the short-term morale aspect of the giving-up of the weapons themselves would be the loss of very considerable specialist skills built up by NCOs over many years. It can only be folly to close down the Battalion's existing Support Platoons and subsequently to try to establish new ones elsewhere - and if, for demographic reasons and because of the numbers of other Reserve units 'fishing in the pool', it proved impossible to recruit sufficient numbers in North Bristol and Gloucestershire to man Support Platoons, with the result that the Battalion could never fill an ARC role, the effect on morale would be more devastating even than the existing plan. Although there are proposals for the disbandment of RE, R Signals, and RCT Squadrons in Bristol, relatively few of their members are likely to be prepared to become basic infantrymen, and certainly none of them would be prepared to travel 40 miles northwards as well; in the medium or long term those disbandments are likely to result in less pressure on the pool, but there is no realistic possibility of forming an effective second Rifle Company in Bristol in the immediately foreseeable future.

In principle, we fully support the criterion that, wherever appropriate, changes in the structure of the TA Infantry should produce common Regular and Territorial regimental or battalion boundaries – but if aligning all the TA Infantry in Hampshire with the new Queen's/ RHamps Regiment involves 1 Wessex in a total and utterly disrupting reorganisation, it is most unlikely to endear the Regular Army to the Territorials involved. A particular advantage of the present plan is that it does not pre-empt the decisions which are going to have to be made between now and 1994, depending on whether or not the

Glosters/DERR and Queens/RHamps amalgamations in fact take place.

There is one other matter which I must mention, and that is the further proposal that we should give up our Band. I understand that this is on the premise that there should be one for each TAVRA area; that Western Wessex already has the Band of 4 D and D; and that as our Band is in Eastern Wessex (where we will no longer have any sub-units) it should become either part of a unit having its headquarters in Eastern Wessex or an area band. That additional loss would be a further serious blow, and if, on reconsideration, it is accepted that 2 Wessex should retain Winchester, logic must allow that our Band is not taken from us simply because it is based in Eastern Wessex. As evidence, however, of our acceptance that Options by definition means some reductions, and of our strong regimental spirit, if the Band could retain its cap-badge, we would be more than happy for it to become The Wessex Regiment Band, serving both Battalions. To require virtually the complete re-organisation of 1 Wessex, in order to alleviate the Queens' long-standing inability to raise 2 TA Battalions in four counties simply beggars belief. I have no doubt that we are resilient enough to weather the loss of Newbury and the need to form a replacement Company in Bristol, but not (in common with all other TA NATO Battalions) the possible loss of our support weapons, and the highly prized UKMF role which we have held for many years. Adding to those, however, the loss of Swindon and the Band, the probability of never enjoying the ARC role because of the impossibility of recruiting sufficient numbers to re-form Support Platoons, and the prospect of an immense and long organisational upheaval cannot but have a devastating effect on the morale of the officers and SNCOs who are going to have to carry it out.

It is imperative to remember that we are dealing with human beings in a volunteer organisation, and not abstract concepts to produce a tidy bureaucratic solution. The continuation of those human beings' involvement with the TA depends primarily on their domestic situations and the security of their jobs. If either of those are fragile, it is not going to take much 'messing about' in their TA lives to cause them to give it up. To create such turbulence and the risk of such long-term resentment in I Wessex as the new proposals will undoubtedly do must be unthinkable.

With many apologies for such a long letter.

That plea was, of course, supported by another strong one from General Mike Walsh. In his acknowledgement of the author's letter, General Naylor (perhaps with a slight twinkle in his eye) said "your message is absolutely clear", but (definitely without one) he thought it "sad that you found it necessary to phrase some of your comments on what are still only proposals in quite such strong terms; however, we will continue to keep an open mind on the issues in question. ECAB [the Establishment Committee of the Army Board] will ultimately be asked to decide them".

As mentioned above, it had been proposed that the 2 Wessex's Company in Winchester should become part of the new PWRR TA Battalion – and the corollary of that was that if 2 Wessex did indeed lose Winchester they should take over 1 Wessex's B Company in Swindon. An alternative to that was for 2 Wessex to form a new Company to replace it in Reading. At a meeting with Colonel Tim May (the first Commanding Officer of the 2nd Battalion, a member of the Wessex Regimental Council, and who was now the Chairman of Eastern Wessex TAVRA) and the author at the beginning of January, however, General Learmont had said that if the 2nd Battalion could retain Winchester, the 1st Battalion could keep Swindon.

General Naylor wrote again to the author on 29 January 1992, breaking the news that, very sadly indeed, ECAB had decided that both Swindon and Poole should go to the 2nd Battalion. It was obvious from his letter that the General had very considerable sympathy for the task that the Battalion had accordingly been set, but he was sure that, with good leadership, it would be successfully achieved. The reasons he gave for the decision were the needs, first, to form a new, very large, Royal Engineers' Amphibious Squadron which would recruit in and around Aldershot, Camberley, Winchester and Southampton, and, second, to move the HQ Squadron of 71 Signal Regiment out of London to the Reading/Bracknell/Slough areas. The insertion of this 'wedge' into those two counties would obviously make it necessary to squeeze the Infantry both east and west.

After a 'holding reply', asking for time in which to consider the position, the author wrote on 31 March to say that the Battalion would accept the decisions, without reservation, and get down to the practicalities of making its new orbat work. He also hoped that this would be "the last time we have to raise new companies, only to have them taken away almost as soon as they are up and running!" General Naylor replied in a handwritten letter:

Dear Martin

Thank you for your letter of 31st March......I am so pleased that 1 Wessex has taken such a statesmanlike stand on the re-structuring. I can well understand and sympathise with the battalion, but the fact that they have accepted an unpalatable decision so well speaks well for them and is a good augury for the future. I wish you all well, and sincerely hope that 1 Wessex suffers no further disruption.

Yours sincerely,

Murray Naylor

The outcome of the Options re-structuring was therefore that the Battalion would indeed be reduced to just three rifle companies in, for all practical purposes, just three counties – Avon, Gloucestershire and Wiltshire. Battalion Headquarters and Headquarter Company would remain in Devizes – and A Company in Gloucestershire would have to expand to become three full companies – A Company in Gloucester, a new B Company in the Speedwell TA Centre in north Bristol (then part of Avon) to replace Swindon, and a new C Company in Cheltenham, to make good the loss of Newbury. Only the Recce and Assault Pioneer Platoons would remain where they were, in Cheltenham and Cinderford respectively; the Anti-tank Platoon would move from Gloucester to Stroud. The Battalion's connection with Hampshire was not entirely broken, as the Mortar Platoon and the Hampshire & Dorset Band would stay in Andover.

It was subsequently suggested that General Learmont, the CO of 2 Wessex and Eastern Wessex TAVRA were unaware of the engineer and signals requirements explained to the author by General Naylor – but that seems unlikely, as their final case to HQ UKLF was that "in the light of all the other TA activities that were happening in east Berkshire" it would be impossible to raise a second rifle company in Reading – and they therefore asked to be allowed to retain Winchester. It is surprising, however, that no one with any understanding of recruiting for the TA seems to have advised that the arrival of those two 'new' units, at either end of the M3 and in east Berkshire, was unlikely materially to affect recruiting for 2 Wessex in Reading and its immediate vicinity – particularly as, being specialist units, they would attract a rather different sort of recruit than would think of becoming a 'foot-slogger"; nevertheless, taking over 1 Wessex's flourishing Company in Swindon was by far the easier option. From his position as the 'winner', General Learmont could well afford, as he did, to write to the author expressing "enormous sympathy" for the Battalion's position.

At the Company HQs and, of course, even more so in Battalion HQ, the final outcome had been awaited with considerable trepidation, albeit tempered by the hope that it would not turn out to be as bad as it could be. When the announcement eventually came, however, it was, not surprisingly, greeted with understandable amazement and anger. Everyone, from the author down to recently recruited soldiers who had discovered that 1 Wessex meant something to them in emotional terms, was appalled that they should lose well-recruited and well-trained Companies to enhance two other existing major units – in the case of one of them certainly not for operational reasons – and that those Companies would have to re-role 'downwards' from being part of the Regular Army's Ace Rapid Reaction Corps to far less challenging Home Defence tasks. Equally unsurprisingly, though, once the initial shock was over, there were two clear-cut reactions. First, quite a number of the longer-serving members of B, C and D Companies realised that, in many ways, they would actually be glad to be relieved of the pressures of being in a high-profile battalion, with its exacting training standards – and that they would in fact be happy to re-role. Secondly, those who wanted to soldier on with the 'new' Battalion realised that, the 'chiefs' having (to put it mildly) had their grumble, there was nothing to be gained by their continuing to try to fight the decision – so that the only course was to accept it, and make the best of a bad job by setting-to with a will to ensure that the new battalion was trained and worked as well as 1 Wessex had – and within about a year it could be said that:

> The effects [of Options for Change] were profound and far-reaching, but are for the most part behind us: only a few ripples remain, and we are able to look to the future.[28]

Notwithstanding the resolve to make the re-deployment of the Battalion work, there was great disappointment that the 2nd Battalion had not kept (or, perhaps, had not been allowed to keep) to its promise that if it were to lose Winchester, it would form a new rifle company in Reading – which would allow the 1st Battalion to retain Swindon. That would have been a minor task in comparison with the one that faced Lieutenant Colonel Peter Cable, who had taken over as CO from Giles Brady in December 1990, and his team.

Unfortunately for him, the time of his arrival was, without question, the low point in the Battalion's history to date – and, to add to the general misery (but in fact very sensibly), it was taken out of the UKMF, albeit only temporarily, to enable it to re-structure itself without any commitments. Peter Cable therefore deserves the greatest possible credit for maintaining a thoroughly positive attitude, as well as his happy smile, throughout those difficult days. Nevertheless, things are rarely wholly bad – and before long what was probably the second most marvellous piece of news in the Battalion's history arrived in Le Marchant Barracks: that (perhaps by way of compensation for the 'messing-about') once the Battalion was pronounced fit for role again, it would become the only TA one in 1 (Mechanised) Brigade (which was simply 1 Infantry Brigade re-named), still in 3 (UK) Division. Thus it became one of only eight TA battalions in the British element of the newly-formed Allied Rapid Reaction Corps which would replace the UKMF in 1992. That the Battalion achieved that was, as it turned out, substantially due to the efforts of General Learmont at a meeting of ECAB – for which everyone was extremely grateful:

> Available for deployment anywhere within Allied Europe from Norway to Turkey, this role is prestigious and challenging, and will capitalise on the skills and experience of our specialist platoons and rifle companies gained over the years as part of the United Kingdom Mobile Force. It will also ensure we continue to be issued with the latest weapons and equipment and enable us to keep up to date with current training techniques and skills.[29]

Meanwhile, the Battalion soldiered on. Training continued as it always had done, and the extent of the struggle that had already taken place, and the one that was to begin before long, were probably not (as mentioned above) appreciated by most of the Volunteers. They simply took things as they came.

There is, however, one not very high-ranking member of every major unit in the Army who is always popularly believed to know exactly what is going on in all the corridors of power, even up to District Headquarters level – the CO's driver. This is, therefore, an appropriate point at which to pay tribute to three of those who served with the Battalion and who were known to the author. They were all Regulars, and the most junior member of the Permanent Staff. The one at this period, a great character who endeared himself to everyone in the Battalion, was the burley Lance Corporal Colin Porter of the Glosters; always cheerful, he invariably seemed to be amazingly well informed about much of what was going on around the Battalion, and sometimes outside it. He was lucky, though, in not having to drive such vast distances as his predecessors before the Battalion's area started being reduced in the late 1980s. In the early days of the Battalion, the author enjoyed the company and services of the diminutive Lance Corporal Rice of the Devon & Dorsets (who, being very much a son of Plymouth, every time they went there always insisted that the roundabout at the bottom of the hill on the A38 leading down into the city was the biggest in the world). His successor was Corporal Jones from the DERR. By that time, the staff car was the last surviving Ford Cortina in the British Army, and in constant need of repairs, sometimes minor and sometimes major. It accordingly became a challenge to the mechanics of 27 Command Workshops at Warminster to keep the beast on the road, and although the QM repeatedly asked that it should be BLR'd [declared Beyond Local Repair – and therefore scrapped] they would not do so, and it became a matter of honour for the car to be promptly returned in good working order. Whilst treasuring the Cortina as an historic artefact, and greatly appreciating the space in the back seat, which enabled him to use it as a travelling office, the CO really wanted a new car, to 'keep-up' with all the Regular, and indeed all the other Volunteer,

COs. Whenever visiting a training area Corporal Jones was therefore encouraged to drive over the roughest ground he could find and try to do some really serious and irreparable damage that would end the car's days. However, that was only achieved following a change of CO, when the new one was able to bring 'Regular clout' to the problem. Particularly in the days when the Battalion stretched from Reading to Plymouth and Cheltenham to the Isle of Wight, delivering the CO home after visiting perhaps two TA Centres in one evening, on top of having had to forgo several pints in their Clubs, it was not perhaps the best of jobs – but they nevertheless always seemed to enjoy it. They were some of the unsung heroes of life in the Battalion.

During 1992, the restructuring gradually took place, and everyone came round to accepting the new situation. The most important task, of course, was working both the new Companies and the Battalion as a whole up to the training standards that the new ARRC role with 1 Brigade would demand; that kept everyone very busy, and Chapter 12 tells how, by the early spring of 1995, it was achieved.

The next matter that now had to be addressed was the future of both the Battalions of The Wessex Regiment in regimental, as distinct from operational, terms. The amalgamation of The Gloucestershire Regiment and The Duke of Edinburgh's Royal Regiment to become The Royal Gloucestershire, Berkshire & Wiltshire Regiment [RGBW] had been announced in July 1991. At the 1992 Prince of Wales's Division Colonels of the Regiments' meeting, the author had a long conversation with the Colonel Commandant, General Sir John Wilsey, wearing his 'more important hat' as the Commander-in-Chief of UKLF. The crux of it was that the General said (in a very kindly manner, but no uncertain terms) that under Options there would be no place at all in the future for "one-off TA Infantry regiments or battalions without a Regular parent regiment" – such as The Wessex Regiment. Following that conversation, therefore, there was an ongoing discussion between Major General Robin Grist (who had recently been chosen to become the first Colonel of RGBW on their formation) and the author about the relationship between, initially, the Glosters and then RGBW on the one hand, and 1 Wessex on the other. They entirely agreed – as, indeed, by now the whole of the Infantry did – that the whole question of County TA battalions had moved on, and that it would be in the interests of all concerned for the new Regiment to have Regular, TA and Cadet components again.

In July 1993, General Grist invited Tim May (deputising for General Learmont) and the author to lunch at the DERR Regimental Headquarters in Salisbury to consider the possibility of the two Battalions becoming part of RGBW. 1 Wessex accepted that the Army had to reduce in size, but assumed, perhaps not unreasonably in view of their status as the UKMF TA battalion, that they would remain intact and with the same role, albeit with a new title. They had never taken a 'We are not prepared to change, full stop' stance, but simply wanted to retain their integrity as a complete battalion until the opportunity arose either for all the Companies to 'return' individually to their original Regular Regiments (or their successors) more or less simultaneously, or for the entire Battalion to become the TA battalion of one of them. The author therefore said that he was sure that they would definitely be in favour of the General's suggestion. Tim May was, though, considerably more cautious – making it clear that, until there was no possible chance of the 2nd Battalion surviving in its present form, they would rather stay as they were. His view was quickly confirmed by General Learmont in several letters to General Grist. Nevertheless, General Grist wrote to both Honorary Colonels[30] formally inviting both Battalions to join RGBW on its 'A[malgamation] Day'. After full consultation with the Officers and senior NCOs of the 1st Battalion, on 14 November the invitation was readily accepted,[31] but General Learmont's reply repeated exactly what Tim May had said at the Salisbury meeting. In view of that, with 1 Wessex's consent, General Grist immediately took the 'precautionary measure' of applying to the Ministry of Defence for it to be allowed to re-badge as Glosters, pending the formation of the RGBW – but, although it was not turned down, the request was put on hold until the fog cleared somewhat. At that stage, however, the question of whether 1 and 2 Wessex would both become part of RGBW, giving it two TA battalions, or whether they would amalgamate to provide one had not yet been discussed.

In 1993, the Government decided to take yet another look at the Armed Forces, and early in 1994 produced the Defence Costs Study

– the object of which was, of course, substantially to reduce the amount of public spending on defence. The TA was to become simply a general reserve for the Regular Army – although battalions could still serve as part of the ARRC on a relatively short 'roulement' [i.e. rotation] basis – but while the sizes of the Arms and Services were to be increased, the total number of TA Infantry battalions was to be reduced, yet again, from 37 to 34; anti-tank weapons and mortars would be removed from all but four battalions, which would become Fire Support Battalions, each with an anti-tank company and a mortar company.

The first 'official' mention of the possibility of amalgamation seems to have been in a letter from General Learmont to General Wilsey (who was still the Colonel Commandant of the Prince of Wales's Division) on 14 January 1994, about the Second Battalion's reluctance to accept General Grist's invitation.

Following General Grist's re-badging request, the author wrote to the Divisional Colonel[32] suggesting that, for a number of reasons, whether one or both Battalions eventually joined RGBW, "the title of 2nd Battalion [RGBW] would be the most appropriate", rather than the traditional 4th or 5th – and as he was in effect representing both Battalions, he copied the letter to General Learmont. The CO of 2 Wessex, Lieutenant Colonel Barry Paddison of the DERR, however, complained to the Divisional Colonel that the letter was in fact a request by 1 Wessex to become 2 RGBW – which was most certainly never the intention, particularly as there was no mention whatsoever in it of 1 Wessex. That was not a good prelude to the discussions that would without question have to take place between the two Battalions.

Only a few days later, on 25 July, Barry Paddison (with the express approval of General Learmont) sent an extremely detailed, 10-page, paper to the Commander of the Aldershot Area, which was part of Southern District and directly responsible for 2 Wessex. It suggested various scenarios under which the two Battalions would remain separate or amalgamate, in either case with those general reserve and possibly fire support roles; it then considered the locations, facilities and current recruited strengths of all the TA Centres of both Battalions

– but, although it claimed to be a completely impartial exercise, everything was written with a clear bias towards the Second Battalion. It then proposed three different scenarios under which a single RGBW TA battalion could be achieved 'on the ground', based on the Second Battalion, one of which – quite astonishingly, was that they should become 2 RGBW and that the First Battalion would be 3 RGBW! That proved to be the beginning of what was inevitably seen – and eventually ended – as a disastrous, total and unhappy 'takeover'.

The possibility of amalgamation was now being actively considered by everyone imaginable, and by early August General Learmont could say to the author that "it is beginning to look as if a merger of the Battalions is gaining credence within the chain of command".[33] As had, very reluctantly, been agreed by the Regiments of the Prince of Wales's Division back in October 1991, the two TA battalions of The Royal Regiment of Wales had amalgamated and one of The Worcestershire & Sherwood Forester's two had been disbanded – but the Divisional Headquarters was now told that it had to lose another one. Particularly in the light of the precedent of what had happened to The Royal Regiment of Wales, and as it would be a great deal easier than merging battalions of different regiments in the north of the Divisional area, the amalgamation of two of the same regiment was the obvious answer – and so the writing was clearly on the wall for one or other of 1 and 2 Wessex. Although General Learmont continually tried to get the brakes applied to the possibility of amalgamation, the exchanges of letters and long telephone calls started all over again, and matters frankly became emotional.

The die was finally cast in a personal letter that the Chief of the General Staff, General Sir Charles Guthrie, wrote to the author on 6 December 1994:

> You will already have heard of many of the Territorial Army restructuring measures announced in the House of Commons. I have written to the Commanding Officer to tell him how these measures affect your Battalion, and I thought you should know what I said. As you know, on 14 July this year the Secretary of State announced that the future size of the Territorial Army was to be 59,000, the reduction from the previously planned size of 63,500 being achieved

by the abolition of the Recruits Pool of 4,500. He also announced the new role of the Territorial Army as a General Reserve to the Army and explained that the Territorial Army would take on the new roles of the Nuclear, Biological and Chemical Defence Regiment and the Armoured Delivery Regiment.

That, on the face of it, such a modest reduction should cause a degree of restructuring should come as no surprise. Our Defence needs have changed. The reduced requirement for National Defence (ND), and longer readiness preparation time means that we need less infantry in the Territorial Army, and permits a higher level of cadreization than hitherto. Furthermore, there are well-identified capability gaps in our combat service support order of battle, some of which are, or are likely to become, NATO force goals. We have, therefore, altered the balance between the infantry units on the one hand and logistic units on the other. We have also taken the opportunity presented by restructuring to remove the distinction between ARRC-roled and ND-roled infantry battalions by creating General Reserve infantry battalions. Support weapons will be grouped in Fire Support battalions able to support any Territorial Army infantry battalion for training and on operations. Such a structure will allow greater operational flexibility and the maintenance of higher training standards. The capability created is entirely consistent with the new role of the Territorial Army.

Given this background, it is inevitable that some change is necessary if we are to have a Territorial Army that is relevant to the Army's operational requirements. In order to reduce the size of the Territorial Army Infantry, the Army Board decided that the two battalions of The Wessex Regiment should form a General Reserve battalion of The Royal Gloucestershire, Berkshire & Wiltshire Regiment. I realize that this may not be the news that you were hoping for but I assure you that the decision was reached after careful consideration. Failure to make this difficult decision would have led to a Territorial Army that was neither relevant nor usable to meet the Army's needs, and whose future could not be assured. It would have been exposed to continual scrutiny and review with obvious implications for effectiveness, and morale. I rely on the Commanding Officer to ensure that the soldiers understand this, and I know that he can count on your support. I have every confidence that the Battalion will overcome the difficulties of seeing through this

change. Your traditions and links with the Regular Army will be kept
alive in the new Battalion which will occupy an important place in
the Army's Order of Battle.

That was an order that, unlike those mentioned in the first paragraph
of Chapter 3, was definitely not a subject for discussion! (It is curious,
however, that the CGS said that the object of the amalgamation was
to reduce the size of the TA – but then that if it did not take place, the
result would have been to make the TA irrelevant and unusable. The
Battalion never knew that it stood in a position of such power!).

The next blow was that, notwithstanding that 1 Wessex had
support weapons (and high levels of skill in using them), they were
not to become one of the Fire Support Battalions, and therefore, as a
General Reserve Battalion, they would lose their UKMF role.

Amalgamation accepted, the most difficult question was whether
the Battalion Headquarters and Headquarter Company would be in
Le Marchant Barracks or Brock Barracks – for whichever one it was
would imply that its present occupant would in effect be 'in control'
of the new Battalion. The author, the new CO of 1 Wessex, Anthony
Lake, Western Wessex (of which Brigadier Bruce Jackman, a former
Gurkha and yet another strong convert to the TA cause was now the
Secretary), and Field Marshal Sir Roland Gibbs, the Lord Lieutenant of
Wiltshire, all tried to persuade General Wilsey (now the Commander-
in-Chief of UKLF) and his staff that Devizes was the preferable option
– but in the event ECAB decided that it should be Reading.

The real problem for 1 Wessex was that, rightly or wrongly, they
saw themselves as having been, throughout their whole existence, an
infinitely better battalion than 2 Wessex, and believed it quite unjust
that they should be subsumed into 2 Wessex. By now, everything was
going very strongly in 2 Wessex's favour, and the announcement that
Barry Paddison had been selected, as against Anthony Lake, to be
the new CO was not well received in 1 Wessex. Sadly, relationships
between the two of them had by then deteriorated badly, and in the end
there was little or nothing on which they could agree. Among other
things, Barry Paddison (in strictness quite correctly, but somewhat
unreasonably) claimed that the appointment of the Honorary Colonel
was in his gift alone, and after a number of other names had been

considered, he invited General Learmont to accept it – which he did.

Relatively early on, 1 Wessex had proposed that, if they became part of RGBW, they should be its 2nd Battalion, rather than adopting one of the traditional pre-1967 higher numbers, such as 4th Wiltshires or 5th Glosters; that, they felt, would create a greater sense of 'togetherness' between the Regular and TA Battalions. Once it was known that the amalgamation was definitely going to take place, happily that was agreed by 2 Wessex, and the official approval of that title was given by the Ministry of Defence on 14 September, just in time before the Glosters/DERR amalgamation took place on 1 October 1995.

The eventual outcome for the Battalion resulting from the take-over by 2 Wessex was a complete upheaval, the practical implications of which were horrendous and, for many Volunteers, depressing in the extreme. There would be three Rifle Companies, the existing A at Eastern Avenue in Gloucester (with a detached platoon at the Arle Road TA Centre in Cheltenham), a new B at Speedwell in north Bristol, and a new C, although where it would be was not stated at the outset. The existing A Company already had a detached platoon at Speedwell, and it would form the nucleus of the new Company there – but two more platoons and its Company HQ would have to be recruited from scratch. The existing, only three-year-old, C Company in Cheltenham, just getting into its stride, would be disbanded – although some of its Volunteers would stay there as that detachment of A Company, and the rest move to Gloucester to provide A Company's third rifle platoon. Support Company would also be disbanded; the Anti-Tank Platoon had already gone under Options; only one of the two sections of the Recce Platoon would be retained (staying in Cheltenham), and 2 Wessex's Recce Platoon, based in Brock Barracks and similarly reduced, would provide the other one. The only 'good news', insofar as there was any, was that the Assault Pioneers (technically part of Headquarter Company at Reading) would remain in Cinderford. With the Volunteers' usual and realistic approach to such matters, all that could, in due course, be weathered and made to work – but the final, stunning, blow was that 2 Wessex's Battalion HQ and Headquarter Company at Brock Barracks in Reading would become the Battalion HQ and HQ Company of 2

RGBW, and that 1 Wessex's Headquarter Company in Devizes would have to re-role as the new C Company to replace the Cheltenham one. 2 Wessex's Battalion HQ and Headquarter Company in Reading were well recruited, so there were few vacancies which could be filled by the very experienced Volunteers who were the linchpins of the 1st Battalion's administration, and its Signals, Assault Pioneer and Machine Gun Platoons. To transfer, moreover, would entail a return journey of possibly some 90 miles at least once, and probably quite often twice, a week. Even though a very high proportion of the members of the Company had part-time soldiering 'in their blood', there was a limit to their loyalty to the TA! For some, their age meant that it was not realistic to think of staying on and retraining as riflemen, and others simply did not want to trade their specialist experience and skills for life in wet ditches; a small number were, though, able to transfer to other TA units. Consequently, a significant proportion of the Company had no alternative but to apply for their discharge, and they were sadly lost to the TA for ever. To his great credit, Anthony Lake spent an immense amount of time individually interviewing every member of the Company, and trying to find them appropriate slots – but it was a most depressing task, and he only partially succeeded.

Curiously mirroring the position of the old Wessex battalions in 1967, neither 1 nor 2 Wessex had in fact been recruited up to their full strength for some while, but – even despite that and the losses from the disbanded companies and platoons – the amalgamation resulted in the new Battalion having the huge paper strength of 683 all ranks. In practice, however, the regular attenders (including trained soldiers or recruits undergoing training) numbered about 470 – but that was nevertheless in the region of 93% of the official establishment, and a very healthy way in which to begin a new life. Neither Options nor the amalgamation, however, were going to have any significant effect on the perennial problems of recruiting and retention, and 2 RGBW would have, like its predecessors, to expend much effort in maintaining that good figure.

Despite all the fears, the discussions, the papers, the proposals and the wrangling involved, none of the previous reorganisations of the

Battalion, each one fiercely fought, had in fact resulted in its end, but were weathered and eventually succeeded – and that was because the large majority of the Volunteers were determined that they would. This time, however, the odds were too heavily stacked against it, and 1 Wessex would be no more. Nearly as sad, for an appreciable number of Volunteers their TA service came to an abrupt end – but others wanted, and were able, to continue serving, without worrying too much about the name of their new unit, its cap-badge or its role. Taking an objective view, it had be a matter of great satisfaction that during the last ten of the 28 years of the Battalion's existence, the two successors of five of the original six Wessex Brigade Regular Regiments that remained in the POW Division, The Devonshire & Dorset Regiment and The Royal Gloucestershire Berkshire & Wiltshire Regiment, acquired a TA battalion again – although the manner in which the former was achieved was certainly neither fair nor impartial. The 'holding operation' mentioned in the Introduction had, as it were, succeeded, and the wheel had come full circle. What, however, might the outcome have been if the Honorary Colonel of 1 Wessex had been a serving full General?

---

[1] The official demolition of what was left of the Wall began on 13 June 1990.

[2] The material for these first three paragraphs is taken from the Report of the House of Commons Select Committee on Defence published in July 1990.

[3] During the Cold War the whole of the AMF(L) regularly exercised in northern Norway. In 1972, when the author was commanding the Battalion, he and the Training Major, Desmond Redding, spent 2 weeks as part of the team of umpires for the gigantic Exercise Arctic Express which took place north of the Arctic Circle.

[4] See the beginning of Chapter 8.

[5] See armedforces.co.uk. The ARRC was first used operationally in Bosnia-Herzegovenia between 1992 and 1997, and then in the Kosovo area of Serbia from 1995 until the present day.

[6] Minutes of Colonels of Regiments' Meeting.

[7] The Formula was 'arrived at' by Major General Peter Shapland in his 1978 review of TA recruiting and other related matters – see Chapter 8.

[8] Letter: General Jeapes to General Walsh, 29 February 1988.

[9] Letter 16 March 1988.

[10] Minutes of the meeting. The only other positive thing to emerge from this 'high-level' discussion, according to the 'Summary of action required now', was the need for the District to arrange a cleaning contract for the Shaftesbury TA Centre!

[11] Letter 21 July 1988

[12] Note of meeting at South West District, 5 January 1989

[13] Letter to the author 31 January 1989.

[14] Dated 21 October 1988.

[15] If that had happened, it would have 'pre–dated' the eventual amalgamation of the Glosters and the DERR by some 7 years.

[16] From the fact that the Divisional Colonel wrote thanking everyone for their "helpful, constructive and pragmatic comments" on the paper he had circulated in, and saying that "Rather than produce a second draft at this stage, I am going to await the various discussions as a result of Options for Change." In the event, however, a second draft of those proposals never appeared, and it would be the amalgamations of the Hampshires and the Royal Sussex (as a battalion of a newly formed 'large regiment', The Princess of Wales's Royal Regiment) and of the Glosters and the DERR that produced the eventual solution – unsatisfactory though it would be for 1 Wessex.

[17] Statement on the Defence Estimates – Britain's Defence for the 90s; HMSO 1991, Cm 1559-I.

[18] In the early 1960s there had been around 60, and periodic cuts since then had taken their toll.

[19] Letter from the Council of TAVRAs to The Rt Hon Tom King, Secretary of State for Defence, 15 May 1991.

[20] Letter 26 June 1991.

[21] A year or so later, South West and South East Districts were merged and became Southern District.

[22] Letter 27 September 1991.

[23] POW Division letter 21 October 1991.

[24] As the Battalion's Notes in the 1991 issue of the DERRJ put it: "The Phase 2 Enhancement of the TA required the Newbury Platoon of 2 Wessex [which until 1977 had been part of 1 Wessex] to become the nucleus of a new Company for 1 Wessex, who in turn would transfer their C (Dorchester) Company to 4 D & D. Thus on 1 April 1990 the Platoon in St Michael's Road [Newbury] became N Company 1 Wessex, a name it will bear until 8 December 1990, when the transfer of the Dorchester Company will allow the Newbury Company to be officially called C Company 1 Wessex. If you think that is complicated, read on."

[25] Letter 12 November 1991.

[26] Letter 11 December 1991.

[27] Letter to South East District 10 January 1992.

[28] The Back Badge, Summer 1993.

[29] The Back Badge, Winter 1992.

[30] To the author on 22 September, and General Learmont on 25 October.

[31] Letter from the author to General Grist.

[32] Letter 15 July, 1994

[33] Letter 23 August, 1994

CHAPTER 11

ANNUAL CAMPS: 1981–1994

The popular cry after it was all over was "Brill!"[1]

1981	BAOR – Ex Wessex Wald
1982	Schleswig-Holstein – Ex Bold Guard
1983	Stanford PTA
1984	Schleswig-Holstein – Ex Bold Gannet
1985	Sennybridge PTA
1986	Schleswig-Holstein – Ex Bold Guard II
1987	Sennybridge PTA
1988	Denmark (Jutland) – Ex Bold Grouse
1989	Stanford PTA
1990	Salisbury Plain PTA and Lydd & Hythe PTA
1991	Otterburn PTA
1992	Denmark – Ex Bold Grouse II
1993	Lydd & Hythe PTA
1994	Belgium – Ex Orient Express

1981

Rheinsahlen, Lüneberg Heath and Soltau, BAOR: 11 Armoured Divisions – Exercise Wessex Wald (11 – 26 October)

In October, the whole Battalion flew from Lyneham to BAOR in C130s. Rheinsahlen, our ultimate destination, welcomed us with driving rain, sub-standard accommodation and the good news that trenches were easy to dig….Although the weather for [the first week] was inclement to say the least, morale improved no end when it was discovered that digging was indeed very easy….indeed, for the first time on many exercises it was possible to occupy a position with attention to all the detail and not to have to spend 99% of the time on it.

The exercise in the second week included the defence of a wooded position, a withdrawal, the occupation of a new defensive position, and finally a Puma [helicopter] lift to an assembly area. From there, the Bn launched a 'successful' attack on well prepared positions manned by the NCO's cadre, who also thought they won. Several members of the Company became immersed in a deep bog about 100 metres from endex [the end of an exercise]. The exercise was a good one and certainly taught us that we have a lot more to do before we have mastered the 'nitty gritty' of defensive work. A near casualty was OP2 which, as a forward OP manned by the Company reported enemy APC's at 1000 metres and approaching .... 500 metres .... 100 metres .... 50 metres .... 25 metres .... silence. They were about to be posted as missing believed squashed when happily they were resurrected by the umpires. This was the first real test of Clansman [a new radio system] and it certainly makes life a lot easier from the control point of view. However, in view of the incredible cost of the system, the temptation is to spend as much time counting it as using it.[2]

The C Company Commander, Major Jeremy Lillies, persuaded the *Dorset Evening Echo* to send a reporter over to Germany for a few days, and his article gave a surprisingly good picture of a TA Camp:

Ground frost sparkled in the forest moonlight as the soldiers filed along a muddy track towards new defensive positions near a river bridge. It was just after midnight, and C and D Companies, The 1st Battalion The Wessex Regiment (Rifle Volunteers) were deep in Northern Germany, withdrawing from an ambush they had sprung on an enemy armoured advance.

C Company's Territorial Army men from Weymouth and Dorchester were at a two-week training camp at Rheinsahlen to practise their role in country where they would fight in the event of War. The exercise was a perfect illustration of what they might have to do.

It happened on the third and fourth days of my stay with them, and began when they dug deep into the forest floor to make three camouflaged positions. The first was an observation post on the edge of a wood manned by Private Ian Lawrence, Corporal Frank Ruffle and Private Mark Egglestone. Their job was to report sighting the armoured advance. One mile deeper into the forest lay D Company from Bournemouth, whose skill with camouflage made it impossible to

Exercise Crusader 80 – CO's O Group

Ready for off – Excercise Crusader 80

Lance Corporal Singleton of C Company takes a break in BAOR

Excercise Bold Guard, 1982 – Showing the German Army how it works

Platoon weapons
SA 80 Rifle; Milan Anti-tank Guided Weapon;
Light Support Weapon (LSW) & General Purpose Machine Gun (GPMG)

An unusual spot for a shave – Camp 1978 in BAOR

Corporal Lee and Sergeant Yorath wonder where they are – Camp 1978 in BAOR

"Look, General – just tell them that the decision is maybe and that's final!"

Brigadeer "Joe" Starling

"Aaaagh you've caught my tie —"

The Royal Review at Wembley, 1977

Major T M C Anstey (1971); Corporal R C Price (1979)
The Queen's Medal Winners

The China Cup, 1979

Major Mick Cook receives The Dragon Trophy from General Sir Timothy Creasey – Bisley 1980

Exercise Executive Stretch

The PSAO's picture

Is that a PSAO....?

FIBUA training on Salisbury Plain

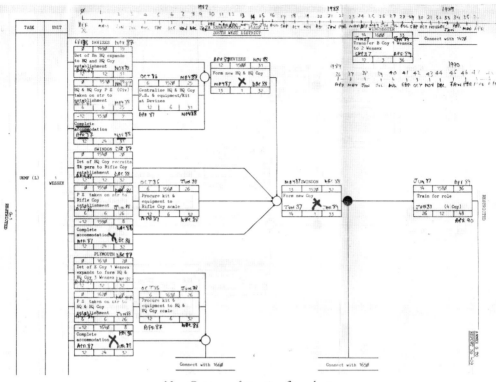

New Company formation flow chart

Recruits Cadre 1980

The last Camp – Operation Wessex Express, Arlon, Belgium, 1994

HM The Queen inspects The Royal Guard of Honour – Wilton, 30 June 1995

The Farewell Parade – Devizes, 17 September 1995

The Officers' Final Dinner – Devizes Town Hall, 30 Septemeber 1995

"Dear, oh dear!"

"Major Nick Goulding
phones home"

"There's something wrong
somewhere"

"Hey, that's my bean!"

A tailpiece or two from the Battalion scrapbook

see the rifle, machine gun and anti-tank pits from 50 feet away.

Major Jeremy Lillies, who extended his role as C Company Commander to include D Company for the two weeks, was back at the third defensive position where six tracks met. Word came through on the radio that the enemy had been seen, and as soon as they hit mines on the track a withering volley of rifle and machine gun fire smashed into them, backed up by the anti-tank support and thunderflashes. Enemy infantry, provided by men from one of the other four companies on the exercise, attacked the ambush party who screened their withdrawal with smoke canisters. They joined Major Lillies in position at his headquarters, where they were attacked twice more before pulling out late at night.

By now a heavy frost had fallen, and I had to concentrate hard on keeping-up and keeping my balance as we walked six kilometres through the forest to dig into new positions by the bridge. I managed to get a couple of hours sleep on a pile of covered rifles in the back of a Land Rover, teeth chattering, before dawn came up and the exercise finished. Major Lillies said "It went extremely well. The aim was to block the advance of enemy armour and then occupy positions for a bridge demolition guard. They did very well."

The day before this, we were orienteering and practising fighting in woods. Torrential rain fell from a leaden sky as Acting Lance Corporal Brendan Parker, Private Gordon Miners and Private Peter Holmes stepped out on the orienteering exercise. With me was Sergeant Bob Loving. Pointing to the heavily burdened soldiers from Weymouth and Dorchester, he said they would be carrying even more in the event of war. "When a modern soldier goes into battle in full marching order with equipment and ammunition he weighs more than a knight in armour." A slight mistake at a divide in the forest track cost us dearly and we ended up eighth out of nine teams, a creditable performance in difficult conditions. Lance Corporal Parker said "Where we went wrong was my fault. At checkpoint number five, we were 100 metres off, and this meant that we wasted half an hour." The afternoon was spent practising the techniques of wood-fighting, and tactical withdrawal for the exercise against enemy armour.

Before I spent a cold time in the field with C and D Companies, I interviewed storeman-driver Lance Corporal Douglas Burt, from Dorchester, as we sped to the battle area in the back of a four-ton truck. This was his last and 31st consecutive annual camp. He had time to tell me about stays in West Germany, Gibraltar and North Africa before the driver muttered a curse, slammed on the brakes, and L/Cpl Burt slid the length of the truck, still seated in his metal chair, to crash into a heap of boxes. Seated again, and with a wary eye on the road, he explained that what we had fallen against were "hayboxes" or stew containers. The contents were quickly fallen on by hungry soldiers when we arrived. When the exercise was drawing to a close, the soldiers were fed breakfast, as they would be in wartime, by supplies brought up from a prepared position. Hot tea and a bacon sandwich. Lovely!

Back at Rheinsahlen from the Soltau training area, I spoke with the 1 Wessex Adjutant, Captain Patrick Davidson-Houston, who told me that their role could soon be changing. "At the moment, we are under the command of the 4th Armoured Division whose headquarters are in Germany," he said. "From January, 1 Wessex will be coming under the control of 1 Infantry Brigade, who will be based at Tidworth in Hampshire. What this means for us is that our immediate operational headquarters, instead of being in Germany, will be in England, and communication will be easier. We could go abroad with them to Germany and possibly Denmark. We would do a similar job to the one we do now with the British Army of the Rhine. It would just be under a different organisation."

It did not seem like four days since I had flown from RAF Brize Norton to RAF Gütersloh, but time passed quickly and I had to leave. C & D Companies faced nuclear, chemical and biological warfare training and first aid training. For the latter, screaming 'injured' soldiers were provided by a casualty simulation team. After a further period of training on close-quarter battle techniques, the soldiers were allowed time off in Hamburg before they took part in an exercise as a battalion. Regular soldiers from the British Army of the Rhine were the enemy armoured reconnaissance squadron. For me the 'war' was over. I handed my kit in, climbed aboard a Land Rover and was driven to an overnight stay at Herford. From Herford I went by train across Germany the next day to Mönchengladbach, and from there to RAF Wildenrath and home to Luton Airport. England welcomed me back with a light drizzle.[3]

The Battalion's journey back to the UK proved to be somewhat difficult:

> Flexibility proved to be the great cry of Annual Camp, as ten hours before we were due to return to the UK our road party of fifty-six assorted vehicles was diverted from Bremerhaven to Zeebrugge, a difference of some three hundred and sixty miles, and timings were brought forward by seven hours! Apparently the ferry had broken down at Bremerhaven. In fact, the only vehicle not to make it back to the UK was the staff car with QM on board, which broke down fifteen miles from Soltau. Our valiant QM, having suffered breakdowns of ship and car, then boarded an aircraft at Hanover, which also broke down![4]

1982

Schleswig-Holstein: UKMF (1 Infantry Brigade) – Exercise Bold Guard (11 – 26 September)

> Our move to Schleswig-Holstein saw the whole of the Battalion (less the road party) being flown from RAF Lyneham and RAF Brize Norton in one day. On arrival at the German Air Force base at Holn, everyone was put on coaches and driven to Putlos Camp on the [German] Baltic coast. There we took advantage of the pleasant countryside, and range facilities for a week's work-up training and field firing before deploying for the exercise proper[5]

These are two reports of the fortnight, the first written by an A Company officer, and the second by Major Doug McMeeken, the OC Headquarter Company:

> Camp was particularly testing, especially for the officers and SNCOs. The first 4-5 days included a series of recces and work-up training on the nearby field firing ranges at Putlos, with the Companies operating from the area of their barns or the tented camp which was erected by the advance party. Much useful work was done in this period, which,

although hectic, was interesting and beneficial. Being so near to the sea, however, had its drawback in that the seasonal temperature changes in September brought quite a bit of fog which made shooting that much more difficult. A two-day instructional exercise followed, and that got us really switched on.

Everyone having returned from their R & R in Hamburg and other such places of architectural interest, the Company loaded its vehicles, and prepared to take its place on Exercise Bold Guard with other elements of 1 Infantry Brigade. This, for our part, involved two phases which saw us defending an assault river crossing made by 1 D & D in the very pleasant area (for some of us anyway) of an extremely helpful and generous German village. The home-made cakes and cookies continued to be provided even after we had commandeered their family bicycles in order to save getting our vehicles out of their very comfortable barns.

Phase 2 followed a period of high air activity, during which the Company were put under considerable pressure by Fighter Ground Attacks, and from the umpires who refused to let us dig where we really wanted to. After a tactical heliborne move, we changed the coloured stickers on our vehicles as well as locations and became Orange Forces, this time in the middle of a sweet-corn field. This part of the Exercise was particularly quiet for us, with most of the action happening in someone else's patch. However, we consoled ourselves with the thought that either our camouflage was too good, or that the enemy did not fancy taking us on and went for someone they might better cope with.

At 'End Ex' though, we probably moved faster than at any other time, for we were retrieved from the field, straight from our trenches on the exercise area, by helicopter, and returned to camp, given barely sufficient time to clean our boots and shave before transport arrived to take us to the airport for our flight home. Fortunately, it all seemed to happen as intended and on reflection, perhaps it was more realistic than we first thought![6]

It was a credit to the Battalion that we returned to the UK without any serious injuries to the Volunteers, and with all our vehicles in a roadworthy condition. It was a most enjoyable Annual Camp, especially for the younger Volunteers.[7]

On Thursday 23 September 1982, A Echelon [the supply base for a battalion on operations sited back from the front line] of 1 Wessex moved from the area of Itzehoe for the second phase of Exercise Bold Guard 1982. Their destination was an area some 10 km east of Neumunster, where, as Orange Forces, they were to defend against a Blue Force counter attack.

This was a 'hot' move, as no reconnaissance to find a position had been possible. First light found the Echelon in the area of the village of Scipphorst and a quick recce showed that the only possible place for us to go was a very large farm complex at Altbokhorst. There was no other place to go in, in fact we were forward of two rifle companies

The rest of the day and night of 23 September proved to be reasonably uneventful, and the routine of feeding and replenishing the Battalion went on round the clock. However, at about 0200 hrs on 24 September, events began to take a different turn. Reports were received of enemy foot and vehicle patrols in the area, and it gradually became apparent that the Echelon could possibly be in the path of one of the major enemy thrusts. After discussion, it was decided that the best policy was to lie low, not attract attention, and rely on our camouflage and cover of the buildings of the complex. We were able to follow the course of the battle closely, as the radio antenna for CS 85 had been bravely carried to the top of a 60 foot high barn.

At about 0330, one of our sentries came to the Echelon CP and reported vehicle noises, and shortly after two German Army Marder vehicles came through the barn area. Although the Echelon had no pyrotechnics save blank rifle ammunition, it was equipped with 16 66mm anti-tank weapons. The Marder vehicles, followed by umpires, therefore saw no fire, completely missed all sentries and vehicles, and stopped at the entrance to the Echelon area. They had in fact passed within six feet of two 66 mm posts on the way in, and parked within four feet of another two posts at the exit.

The Echelon Commander finally persuaded the umpires that the Echelon had not only got small arms, but anti-tank weapons, and was awarded both vehicles killed! By this time, we could hear sounds of considerable enemy activity, and were on permanent standby – the cooks were preparing breakfast in fun kit and steel helmets, with their 66mm ready to hand. At about 0600, the REME wrecker crew spotted four more Marders in a field just across the road to the west of our position. A tank-stalking party of cooks and REME was formed, and the final result awarded by the umpires was that all four vehicles were knocked out. Simultaneously, the CP at the other end of the Echelon area was attacked by a platoon–plus of Infantry, and the CP was captured. The Echelon Commander and Signals NCO prevented the attackers from seizing maps or codes with the assistance of the Regimental Medical Officer (a lady!)[8] who secured the slidex [a radio code] and other important documents where it would have been improper for even the fiercest enemy to try to recover them! At this time, the remainder of Echelon personnel mounted a spirited counter-attack, which resulted in the liberation of the Doctor and the Echelon Commander, and all the enemy being neutralised. A short break, then everyone fed, as they had not eaten for over 20 hours. The meal was rudely interrupted, for we were then obliged to deal with three tanks which were creeping up the track towards us from the east, and two more Marder vehicles which tried to turn into the Echelon area.

By now it was known that the main enemy thrust was about to come straight through our position, and all members of the Echelon were deployed in readiness. During the next hour we accounted for three more Marders and two platoons of Infantry. At the cessation of hostilities, no fewer than twenty-two Marders and two companies of Infantry were blocked off at the entrance to the east end of the Echelon area, and a final protective fire artillery strike was being called for.

On the conclusion of the exercise, the umpires were most surprised to find that we had no means of indicating weapon fire other than rifle fire, and told us we would have been credited with many more 'kills' as in many cases they had not realised that we were engaging the enemy. The total bag for the Echelon was 11 Marders, 2 Leopard tanks, a company plus of Infantry, and one very lost Hotchkiss command vehicle. It would have been considerably more if we had been able to indicate fire. The umpires were of the firm belief that we were an infantry company and not an Echelon.

For those personnel in the Echelon, whose lot it is usually to cook, fuel and resupply, never seeing action, it was a really fantastic day – and it proved to them that good camouflage, well sited positions, being alert, and knowing that the Battalion had to be looked after, even they, when stirred, can do much to change the course of the battle. We will emblazon "Altbokhorst" on our ladies, petrol cans and ammunition boxes from today for those who follow to see and remember![9]

1983

Stanford PTA (2 – 16 July)

The somewhat curiously-named Exercise Wessex Warlock was very much a 'back-to-basics' Camp, and whilst the emphasis was on the field firing of all personal and platoon weapons, the training covered a wide range of skills – NBC, Watermanship, Routine in the Field and Night Firing, AFV [Armoured Fighting Vehicle] Recognition, First Aid – and with what little 'puff' we had left, the dreaded Tickle Fitness Test (for the youngsters under 50 only). In addition, there were Potential NCOs and Signals Cadres. In the second week A Company of the Iowa National Guard and four German Reserve officers were attached to the Battalion; thick accents, thin accents and German-type English mingled well, and there were no major international incidents! The undoubted military highlights of Camp were the Annual Report on a Unit inspection, conducted by the Commander of 1 Infantry Brigade, and the Inter Platoon March & Shoot Competition – yes, all on the same day. It was extremely hot and sticky, and a very taxing competition – in fact at times the final concentration area resembling a field dressing station, with soldiers overcome by heat and exhaustion littering the ground everywhere. We are delighted to tell you that A Company's A and B teams came first and second overall, and we are the proud first winners of the Walsh Trophy, recently presented by the Honorary Colonel.[10]

Most agreed that Camp would be remembered for three things: Firstly, the excellent 10 days or so field firing on the marvellous ranges at Stanford; secondly, the Tickle Test, escaped by none, including the Bisley Team, who returned three days before the end of Camp hoping to have missed it; and thirdly, the visit of a Company of the US Iowa National Guard, most of whom spent the seven days they were with us in some sort of daze, never having seen field firing ranges, let alone used them. This was to give rise to some interesting moments. In general, it was a welcome opportunity to meet our TA counterparts from the United States, and the policy of integrating the Americans into the Platoons proved very successful.[11]

Attachments to major units of other NATO Reserve Forces, either in lieu of or in addition to, the Battalion's Camp, had become quite common – for example, Sergeants Keith Reade and John Russell (both, in due course, to become Company Sergeant Majors of A Company) would go to 212 Panzer Grenadier Battalion at Putlos on the Baltic coast of Schleswig Holstein. "They voted the trip a resounding success, including the renewal of their acquaintance with bratwürst and kartoffel salat which started on Exercise Crusader".[12] In 1989, Colour Sergeant Bob Kuczaj of the Anti Tank Platoon spent an "eye-opening" fourteen days as a 'member' of a US National Guard Company in August, and from 26 September to 5 October that year a further ten members of A and Support Companies went to stay with the 172 Panzer Grenadier Battalion in Germany.[13]

1984

Schleswig-Holstein: UKMF (1 Infantry Brigade) – Exercise Bold Gannet (13-27 September)

A Company's pre-Camp advice to its members about the R & R facilities for the middle week-end included the following description of Copenhagen:

> It boasts an important University, superb ballet and opera, four symphony orchestras, over 20 theatres, more than 40 museums ......

but, to everyone's relief, it went on to say:

> It also offers any number of jazz clubs, discos and night clubs, plus over 2,000 bars, cafes and restaurants. There are more than 100 kinds of Danish beer and fiery Aquavit that blasts the unwary through the roof......[14]

After weeks of packing, briefing and preparation the Battalion deployed on Exercise Bold Gannet to Denmark. This involved a total of 35,000 troops – 12,500 of them British and nearly 4,000 from the TA. The Battalion road party, comprising 96 vehicles, left in 3 phases. The pre-advance party, consisting of the QM in charge of six vehicles, travelled by RCT LSL [Landing Ship Logistic] from Marchwood to forestall the impending dock strike, which fortunately did not affect the move. The advance party and main body of vehicles then travelled by luxurious DFDS ferries to Esbjerg in Jutland and by road to the Finderup training area near Viborg. Meanwhile the main body of the Battalion, 424 strong, went in the comparative luxury of RAF VC1Os, to the Danish airforce base at Billund.

The Battalion then spent two days in work-up training on Finderup before crossing the Great Belt in preparation for the exercise. The exercise itself started with C Coy (Dorchester) defending a reserve bridge demolition over which the covering force of 16/5L [16th/5th Lancers] would withdraw. Meanwhile A Coy had been detached to 1 Glosters and D Coy to the 16/5L as part of the covering force. B and E Coy were frantically digging-in to conform to commander UKLF's defensive plan, and for the next 3 days the Battalion was occupied with preparing a defensive position, interspersed with patrolling against an unorthodox enemy consisting of Danish conscripts, during which time HQ Coy was busy supplying the Battalion with its required combat supplies. The main defensive battle took the usual course of NATO land battles, and resulted in a brigade counter attack to push the 'Orange' forces back. The finale of the two weeks was a full 24 hours R & R spent mostly in Copenhagen.

An uneventful recovery ensued and everybody was back in their homes by the small hours of Monday morning, ready to forget that they had been 'professionals' for 2 weeks and happy once again to be civvies until next year.[15]

Wednesday, 24 September. The plot thickened, with A Company, grubby and war hardened (sorry, 2 and 3 Platoons), being relieved by a clean, fresh-looking Company of Germans complete with Marders and go-faster stripes. They were most surprised to find that our battlefield transport consisted of a 4-tonne truck carrying twenty men with their kit. "Where are your Army [sic] Personnel Carriers?" I was asked.

"Where is your cam [camouflage] cream?" I replied.[16]

We flew from RAF Brize Norton in VC 10s, the first of which was struck by lightning when coming into land at a Danish Air Force base in Jutland. We spent three days at Finderup on work-up training – a lot of the time with two RAF Squadrons flying Chinook and Puma helicopters.

It was the Pumas who then moved most of the Company to the FTX area in Zeeland, not far from a lake called Bavelse Sø. We took our place in defensive positions alongside the other [Regular] battalions and awaited the enemy air-strike. Once in contact, the Company spent much of its time working at night, including despatching raiding parties of up to seventy-five men to search out enemy harbour areas. Some barns were made available to us for feeding and rest.

Visitors included The Lord Trefgarne (Under-Secretary of State for Defence (Army)), Lt-General Sir John Akehurst (Commander-in-Chief UKLF), Major-General BM Lane (GOC SouthWest District), Mr John Browne (MP for Winchester) and Major-General Thorsen (Director of Plans, Danish Ministry of Defence)[17]

It is worthy of note that the moves out and back were undoubtedly the best ever, very slick, with negligible delays – the only drama being a lightening strike on the aircraft as we landed in Denmark. Also worthy of note was the full 24 hours R & R that we were given, again one of the best ever and a vital ingredient in maintaining morale in a TA Company in the immediate post-Camp period........... [On the exercises] no allowance was made for the fact that we were TA, and we were deployed in exactly the same fashion as the Regular Battalions in the Brigade.[18]

1985

Sennybridge PTA (28 September –12 October)

To judge from the lack of reports of it, it would seem that this was probably the least successful Camp in the Battalion's whole history.

The whole Battalion again camped together, with the exception of the Anti-tank Platoon – who went to Warcop in Nottinghamshire, and covered themselves in glory by achieving a 92% hit rate with their Milans after an ei ght mile forced march, for the last mile of which they had to don full NBC kit. It was another 'back to basics' fortnight, with various cadres and a lot of walking over the Brecon Beacons. Numbers were badly down – no doubt because, as against a Camp in BAOR, the prospect of a cold fortnight in the rain in Wales failed to appeal – and there were only 53 all ranks from A Company, 45 from E Company, and much the same from the others. Even so, the accommodation was seriously overstretched, and most people spent most nights on the training area either training or in their sleeping bags:

> There was strong competition for the Best Basha[19] prize at an overnight bivouac site, but it was withdrawn after the Company Commander's collapsed during the night.

For Annual Camp we went to Sennybridge, and a very wet and hard-working time was had by all. The highlights of the Camp was the ARU on 3 October, conducted by Brigadier John Wilsey CBE, the Commander of 1 Brigade, and his staff. In addition, Exercise Sanyo Yetti, a trog across the Brecon Beacons was another notable highlight of the two-week camp.

Congratulations are in order to the small staff from the Company who ran the FIBUA complex for five days with the OC – the CSM David O'Connor, Sergeant Nelson Murray, Sergeant Colin Cusack, plus our two PSIs (WO2 Alan Beale D & D and Colour Sergeant "Ginger" Coleman DERR) and our TA CQMS Colour Sergeant Mick Charlesworth. This was a fun stand with lots of bangs, bullets and smoke, and the complex looked like a cross between Rorke's Drift and The Alamo, with acknowledgements to the French Foreign Legion and Camerone Day.[20]

Much more disappointing overall than the small numbers was the fact that this was B Company's last Camp as part of the Battalion. The very contrasting approaches to soldiering, and differing strengths and weaknesses of the Companies in the early days were considered in Chapter 3 – and, although the others would have been reluctant to admit it, it is almost beyond question that for most of the period since 1967 B Company had been the one against which they all judged their training standards. Characteristically, they departed on a cheerful note: "The future of B Company promises a lot of change, which we are sure will be exciting, and we look forward to the next 12 months."

1986

Schleswig Holstein: 1 Infantry Brigade's Exercise Bold Guard II (13 – 27 September)

There were, as usual, a number of work-up exercises before Camp. Exercise First Blood, designed to test command skills at all levels and consolidate individual tactical training, was based on the usual somewhat unlikely-seeming scenario – this time tensions between the Kingdoms of Netheravon and Wessex, the former having a ruthless dictator (or king?), MI Qook [alias Major Mick Cook, OC C Company], border tensions, a failed coup within the Wessex armed forces, etc, etc. From the start, after a heliborne deployment, the pace "was fast and furious, and very, very tiring – but after it ended everyone felt a sense of achievement, and more confident in their reactions under pressure."[21] That, in a few words, is all that 1 Wessex was about, and just what the new CO, Robin Pook, intended. The second major pre-Camp exercise was Wessex Wheels at the huge RCT vehicle depot at Chilwell in Nottinghamshire, involving all the drivers in the Battalion who were going to Camp, and covering every aspect of driving on the continent – singly or in convoy, with and without trailers, or camouflaged. It ended with the notorious "Tick Test", a multi-choice test on traffic signs and law, inflicted on any driver going to BAOR:

> It was made easier if the chap before you had pressed very heavily with his pen on the test sheet, so that the impressions went through to the next sheet on the pad – unless he had got it all wrong and failed.[22]

The first week was spent at Putlos, on the Baltic coast of Schleswig-Holstein, and continued the work-up process, revising anti-ambush drills, patrolling, and then a Battalion FTX. After R & R over the weekend in Hamburg – "harder for some than the rest of the fortnight" – the Exercise proper filled the second week, with an enemy drawn from one of the Regular Parachute Regiment battalions, the Royal Marines and the Dutch Marine Corps. In a hand-to-hand fight, defending a huge, 5 kilometre-long bridge over the Kiel Canal, A Company's Sergeant "Para" Chambers was said to have had to be forcibly restrained before "he killed too many Paras with his bare hands".[23] There was much flying about in helicopters, making river crossings, and the final Friday saw the whole Battalion taking part in a brigade attack on a large village – followed by the usual rush back to camp to get organised for the return to the UK the following morning:

> The consensus of opinion in the Company was mixed. To the old hands this camp had been nothing new, but the more junior soldiers learned valuable lessons and enjoyed the experience to boot![24]

The main event of the year was, of course, Exercise Bold Guard, and it was towards this that we had geared all our training. We were accompanied by our intrepid local Pressman, Harry Walton, and the exercise proved to be every bit as demanding and interesting as predicted.

The main move out was by Danish ferry and our eventual destination was the Putlos Training Area. There we spent a hectic three days of work-up training, followed by a welcome R & R weekend – a choice of Kiel or Hamburg, according to taste!

After a road move to the exercise area, we were able to prepare defensive positions in detail and dig in to await the battle for our bridge. We were fortunate to see a great deal of armour and other kit rolling back over the Bridge, until the war came to us in the form of a heliborne attack. Major Mick Cook and most of the Command Post crew were immediately declared 'dead' by the umpires; but after a spirited defence and several counter attacks later, the result was declared a draw. From the bridge, the Company moved north by road and helicopters to take part in a Brigade attack which culminated in a fine battle. Almost as the last round was fired we were on our way back – a move in record time, which went without a hitch.

This was a very full and busy two weeks in Germany with huge demands on all ranks of the Company; it was our biggest ever attendance at Camp, and it was very pleasing to record the consensus of opinion that all concerned acquitted themselves very well. We wish to record our thanks for all the hard work of WO2 Vic Williams and Sgt Burke from Exeter UOTC, and to the lads from Southampton UOTC – they all settled in to the Company to the manner born, and were a great success![25]

––––––––––

Since our last notes appeared, the main event has been E Company's participation in Exercise Bold Guard in Germany, with the UK Mobile Force, as part of 1 Brigade. Brigadier John Wilsey, the Commander of 1 Brigade, visited the Company at Exeter in the summer, prior to the exercise, to stress the importance of Bold Guard. Some 80 all ranks 'answered the call' and went out to Germany during the period 12-26 September 1986 to participate in this major NATO exercise. We worked as three platoons plus Company HQ, and hopefully we practiced our war role adequately. The Company was detached from 1 Wessex on the exercise and attached to 1 RGJ [Royal Green Jackets]. Because of a severe subaltern shortage only one platoon was commanded by an officer – 2Lt Andrew Payne with 18 Platoon, while 17 Platoon and 19 Platoon were very adequately commanded by Sgt Nelson Murray and Sgt Chris Stokes respectively.

The Company deployed to Northern Germany via the Harwich – Brunsbuttel ferry route. Unfortunately, all ranks were detained on the ship for 24 hours by the Movements Staff, resulting in their not arriving 'in theatre' till late Monday, 15 September. This meant that pre-exercise training was at a premium and after R & R in Kiel on the first Thursday, the Company then deployed with 1 RGJ to the Exercise Area. Initially the Company were in a huge forest sealing off the likely enemy approaches. This gave the platoons opportunity to practice their ability to dig trenches; these were of a very high standard, and we felt that we did very well in our 24-hour defence exercise during the brief initial training period. In addition to the Platoon Commanders already mentioned, the Company 2IC, Captain Nigel Ffitch, and the Company 2IC (Designate), Captain Roderick Newbolt-Young, affectionately known as the "Minister without Portfolio", both worked for the overall operational efficiency in no small measure. Section Commanders bore the brunt of the routine, and Cpls Terry Ryder, Mark Hutchings, Ralph Savill, Garry Watson, Richard Noble, Gordon Hyatt and Chris Chiswell made invaluable contributions.[26]

A German paper definitely approved of the way that the British Army did things:

<u>Understanding Cocktail Party at Schloss Breitenburg – Bold Guard in a Different Light – Parade in Castle Courtyard:</u>

Many misunderstandings can be avoided through personal contact; this is particularly true during a large-scale exercise such as Bold Guard – with 65,000 soldiers presently in Schleswig-Holstein. The British soldiers of the UKMF, under the command of Brigadier JFW Wilsey, solved this problem in their own, British, way. They invited their comrades from other nations participating in Bold Guard to a cocktail party at Schloss Breitenburg near Itzehoe. A neutral observer might ask whether such an occasion is suitable, a party guest would say "yes". Even the external form of the occasion was different – the British requested that guests attend in civilian clothes, the hosts were distinguishable merely by red carnations in the buttonholes of their dark blue suits. Not only the military but also civilians were invited, the latter represented by the Scheswig-Holstein Minister for Home Affairs, Karl Eduard Claussen.

To avoid the formation of German, Danish or British cliques, each host had a guest to look after. Anyone without a red carnation standing alone in the Rittersaal (Knights' Hall) of the castle was immediately engaged in conversation by one or two Englishmen; perfect organisation, and due to English being the NATO language there were no communication problems – those that did arise were solved by the immediate despatch of a liaison officer who interpreted. Over sweet, typically British, cocktails and snacks reminiscent of colonial times, conversation was both official and personal; the noise from 300 people was considerable.

Burgermeister Hornlein of Itzehoe and his colleague Hansen of Breitenburg enjoyed themselves – so too did farmer Moller from the "Hungry Wolf" who, today, at the beginning of the exercise could claim to be the man most likely to 'suffer', as the training demonstration for the guests from other NATO areas and from the Eastern Block, is taking place on his land. There were grins all round as farmer Moller told of the difficulties the British General had with German field fences. Unaware that there was electric current in the wire, he had touched one during a visit to the area and got a sizeable shock – and one of his officers was 'shocked' in a very sensitive spot!

The British soldiers wanted to know again and again how the people of Schleswig-Holstein felt about the exercise and if there would be any difficulties......Since last week British soldiers have become part of daily life in Itzehoe and the surrounding villages. In the restaurants they have tried German beer and talked to the local inhabitants. Serious problems did not arise – even when the odd soldier wandered somewhat inebriated through the town at night, no one was pestered.

<u>40 years ago</u>: Many people will be reminded of a time 40 years ago when there were British soldiers in Itzehoe. Not as friends and allies as today, but as the ruling occupation power. In the conversation in Schloss Breitenburg, the younger officers were reminded of this situation which was unfamiliar to many of them. In those days if British soldiers were at the bar counter, no German was allowed there, the counter was reserved for the occupying power. Memories of the hard and rigourous occupying power, however, do not last forever. The Allies of today are accepted, in some of the villages there were even long lasting friendship events.

<u>In the stables</u>: Otto, Count Rantzau, reminisced, and reminded Brigadier Wilsey at the cocktail party that during the Second World

War the castle served as a military hospital. This had to be cleared to make way for a British occupation command. Count Rantzau's father had to leave the castle with his family and live in a stable at the Osterhof which was also occupied. The British commander at Breitenburg asked his superior in Itzehoe to allow the Rantzau family to live in the castle library – the answer from Itzehoe was a firm "no". No Germans were allowed at Breitenburg.

In the Castle: Now the British were at the castle again, but this time as welcome guests who with their sense of style and tradition found the castle a suitable venue for their party. The lady of the house, Eike, Countess Rantzau, received Brigadier Wilsey at the door and her hospitality was rewarded with a crystal decanter and a bouquet of flowers. Brigadier Wilsey pointed out that the decanter – what else could one expect of the British? – was for sherry. Just how rank-conscious the British Army is could be seen at the two guest entrances. Both doors were flanked by soldiers in historic uniform. Home Affairs Minister Claussen, Lt Gen von Ondarza, Maj-Gen Steinkopf and Brigadier Prange from the German contingent and the NATO generals were allowed to use the main entrance, which leads through the Thorwaldsen gallery, while guests from the ranks of Lieutenant to Colonels used a side entrance. In typically British style, there were no speeches, only Brigadier Wilsey thanked the hosts at the end of the party in a short address.

"Beating Retreat": As a special present the British had planned "Beating the Retreat", the English "Zapfenstreich", whose origins date back to the 16th century. It was performed by musicians dressed in typical scarlet – the Band and Drums of the 1st Battalion The Duke of Wellington's Regiment, the 1st Battalion The Royal Hampshire Regiment and the Bugles of the 1st Battalion The Royal Green Jackets under the direction of Lt Col C G C Vyvyan, MBE, Band Sergeant Major S J Jones and Drum Major D Beer. On the floodlit castle courtyard the musicians demonstrated their various skills for more than an hour, and surprised the German guests with the fanfare "Schloss Breitenburg", the "Radetzky March" and finally "Prussia's Glory". One was reminded of 'Prussia's Glory' 40 years ago.

The cocktail party was, without doubt, the social high point of the exercise; the background was, however, very practical and it was a friendly and stylish gesture on the part of the British guests in Schleswig-Holstein to meet their hosts and partners in this way, and to present to them the spectacle of "Beating the Retreat".[27]

1987

Sennybridge PTA (30 August – 13 September)

Cadres are the training lifeblood of any battalion, and this Camp for the whole Battalion was largely based on them – they covered Junior NCOs, Junior NCOs Tactics (physically very demanding), HGV driving, signals and first aid; and among other things, helicopter training, Saxon [armoured vehicle] familiarisation, the rifle range, battle inoculation, live grenade throwing – and the dreaded TABT jabs! The fortnight ended with a two-day patrolling exercise on the Brecon Beacons, during which the GOC of South West District, Major General Tony Jeapes D & D made his first visit to the Battalion on training – and he seemed to like what he saw.

Going to Sennybridge (yet again!), however, had a numbing effect on the writers of the Company Notes for two of the Regular Regiments' Journals, for this was all they said:

Camp in 1987 was held at Sennybridge, and for once the Welsh weather was kind. A lot of the Company did courses or cadres, and enjoyed a variety of field firing and exercises – and voted it as being a first class two weeks.[28]

The exercise season culminated in our Annual Camp at Sennybridge. Despite the initial horror that the word Sennybridge usually conjurs up in people's minds, the weather was brilliant and much worthwhile training was achieved.[29]

although another had a number of striking vignettes:

The traditional Company 'Smoker' was held in the Blue Boar Inn in Brecon. It was well supported, well organised and resulted in some well-oiled soldiery. Singing was very much the order of the evening, led by Lance Corporal Stuart Cox and the other stalwarts of Bristol. However, the Senior Permanent Staff Instructor and the PSAO managed to squeeze in an oldie (Bless 'em all!) for just a brief moment before being drowned out again. Various solos followed, some unrepeatable in print but most, believe it or not, were popular in the first World War. Sergeant 'Para' Chambers assisted (?) by the SPSI and PSAO demonstrated the Chelsea Pensioners March – which puzzled some of the younger members, but made their day when the gruesome threesome concluded the parade by 'falling out' of their imaginary wheelchairs. Para Chambers performed a remarkable double act (on his own) as a man being attacked.

We were pleased to welcome the second half of "Moss Bros" to the Company in the shape of Officer Cadet Justin Moss from Bristol University OTC who came to Camp with us. Two smarter (?) Gentleman Farmers would be difficult to find. Seriously though, we hope Justin enjoyed his stay and found the change from Gunner Troop to PBI invigorating.

Well, we're now here on Camp '87 in sunny Sennybridge – well, in a tea shop in Brecon on R & R to be precise. The first week has just been spent running up and down the ranges with the SPSI and CSM in hot pursuit. The SPSI seems to have this strange habit of throwing down his beret and jumping on it during every debrief. We tend to think that this is a Regular problem but he assures us it is purely TA! Despite this everyone is working and playing hard, including Private David Curwen who went sub-aqua, complete with GPMG, on D range during his Platoon Attack.

Heard after an enjoyable Officers' Mess Guest Night, and the recovery in a Brecon Launderette watching my combats churning round in a muddy brown soup: "What, Notes for the Back Badge again, Sir? Oh very well. I'll do my best"

More worldly-wise and weary are Lance Corporals Derek Kavanagh and Andrew Marshall who completed the physically more demanding JNCO's Tactics Cadre. Finally, news of another member's activities at

Camp! Private Adrian Cooper, [also] swimming under water to the
Forming Up Point during a platoon attack and subsequently narrowly
escaping a finger amputation by Private "Adder" Smith with the aid
of a GPMG top cover, was particularly memorable! We are now all
looking forward to the thrills and spills of the NATO training year.[30]

1988

Denmark (Jutland): 1 Infantry Brigade's Exercise Bold Grouse (3 – 17 September)

The A Company Notes in the Winter 1988 edition of *The Back Badge*
included a mainly light-hearted view of the business of getting to
Camp and some of the goings-on:

As a warm-up for Exercise Bold Grouse, Exercise Wiltshire Pheasant
(bird-fanciers were not actually required) was held over the weekend
of 1 – 3 July. Its aim was to give all elements of 1 Wessex an opportunity
of working with their regular counterparts in UKMF on the activities
likely to be covered on Bold Grouse. We were in fact Blue Force
facing an enemy from the Royal Scots Dragoon Guards, 3rd Bn The
Parachute Regiment, 9th/12th Royal Lancers and 2nd Bn The Royal
Irish Rangers, all backed-up by Jaguar aircraft. A formidable foe
indeed.

Uniquely on this occasion, we were 'lifted' from RAF Innsworth,
outside Gloucester, by four Puma helicopters, to the Salisbury Plain
Training Area. This demanding part of the exercise stretched all ranks
to their limits. Many valuable lessons were learned, but it is true to
say that we successfully implemented a detailed operation order, and
completed the actual deployment and redeployment plans.

The return to Gloucester in two Chinook helicopters provided
much needed light relief. The pilots, unfamiliar with Gloucester area
and RAF Innsworth in particular, were on their second circuit of the
city in their search for the elusive sports fields when our SPSI WO2
"Dickie" Dawes from 1 Glosters decided enough was enough. Leaning
fearlessly out of the 'door', he led the pilots by shouting instructions to

them to follow the ring road, but to be careful of the traffic lights! His gesticulations and colourful language did the trick as two thoroughly irritated pilots swooped in over the sports fields, scattering football teams, families having a Sunday walk and numerous dogs to the four corners. A slightly bemused Duty Officer recorded the chaotic scene with his 'Box Brownie'. We now await the pictorial evidence with unconcealed impatience.

The ensuing build up to Bold Grouse was indeed tame by comparison, taking many hours of administrative preparation. Nominal rolls were completed and scrapped in rapid succession. Vehicles that had up to then been as good as gold suddenly became temperamental, and demanded spares which were difficult, if not impossible, to obtain. Units who were originally very keen to send men to join us kept changing their minds, while the Quartermaster at Devizes kept bombarding us with paper instructions on reams of paper. Battalion Headquarters held numerous conferences, and those of us in Eastern Avenue almost sank without trace! With Denmark beckoning so soon after block leave something just had to be done, so we got on with it. Magically the mists cleared, the nominal rolls became more accurate, the vehicles were repaired, the Quartermaster settled down and, hey presto, the Q Advance Party led by C/Sgt. Wayne Arkley left with a 4 tonne Bedford and trailer. It was all downhill after that; the three road parties left in good order on 3 September, hotly pursued in vain by a Citizen photographer who wanted to 'shoot' the move out. The drivers who had patiently waited for the 'off' were not to be denied by a mere civilian mortal. Squeezed into the short week before departure was a visit from a Danish TV producer, with camera team and public relations representative from South West District. They wanted two likely lads to interview and film at home and work in order to show the Danish public what a quaint lot we are in the TA. The lads selected were Cpl. Steve Hart and Pte. Richard Jefferies. Both gave an excellent account of themselves but Steve Hart's daughter brought the show to a halt in saying "Phew" on handing her father his boots for packing in the 'farewell' film scene! With composure fully restored, the camera team caught up with both likely lads in Denmark......

During the initial warm up period in the tented Base Camp in Denmark, everyone became 'acclimatised' in preparation for the big Exercise. The lucky Cpl. Hart continued his posing for Danish TV and was shot in a variety of situations, including a practice attack sequence. The start of the Exercise proper found the up and coming TV Star occupying a slit trench in the company of Privates Mark Stickland and Tim Colcombe of 1 Platoon. Mark and Tim could not have been more blessed in their choice of companion. His presence ensured constant supplies of hot water, tea, coffee, assorted Danish pastries and the care and attention of Family Gregers Jensen, the owners of the slit trench. Steve was even hauled out of it by the worthy Jensens to watch a Danish TV programme starring none other than – yes you've guessed it – the bold Hart. Another useful spin-off came the Company's way from the relatives of the family Jensen living some 60 kms away, who in their excitement over the Hart saga let it be known that the West German paras acting as enemy had landed in their fields. Bn HQ couldn't believe their luck!

Seriously though, all ranks agreed that relations with the Danes were absolutely fantastic – a great improvement since the last visit on Bold Gannet four years ago. To prove it:

Dear Major Stanley

We just like your people here specially the three boys we had as our own Steve, Mark and Tim. You can be proud of them, they are nice polite people as the rest of your people we have had contact with. If you during this day (after 11 am) have time for a nice cup of tea or cafe you will be welcome.

Yours

Liselolle and Benny Gregers Jensen
Kolvested

———————

This was a subaltern's view of the fornight:

I was all ready for a quiet time on Camp this year, but my hopes were shattered on meeting Captain Wallace at South Cerney whilst completing documentation. "Ah Roger, pleased to see you. Have you met the journalist from The Citizen who is going to Camp with you – see he gets looked after would you? Oh that reminds me, notes for The Back Badge are due when you return". So much for the quiet life!

We boarded the VC10 at Brize Norton, and all safely landed in Denmark. After a coach journey across Zealand to the work-up training area in Haelbaek, it was late Monday evening and time for an impromptu Company Smoker. The 'Monocled Mutineer' in the form of L/Cpl. "Spud" Murphy had set up a Kangaroo Court in the mess tent. Anyone entering – no rank exempted – was asked various questions, and depending on the response was stoned with tens or hundreds of empty beer cans. The Danish Liaison Officer was formally accepted into the Company by this dubious method. Anyway, two thousand cans or so later it was reveille, and the 21C Captain Nick Goulding took the Company around the assault course. Fortunately breakfast was served afterwards, although not too many were interested!

Work-up training began in the form of trench digging (with demonstrations by the SPSI), challenging procedures, and all the other fine points which we needed to brush up on. Then followed a 24 hour Battalion FTX, in which the Coy managed to take prisoners, and generally gave a good account of themselves. It should be noted, by the Company 2IC, that it is not a good idea to try the 'Conga' in the pitch black during a withdrawal!

After a quick wash and brush up the Coy headed off to Copenhagen for R & R. This started along the right lines with a trip around Tuborg's brewery. The trouble was that not many seem to remember how it finished!

Back to the serious business and the start of the main exercise, when A Coy redeployed to the FEBA [Forward Edge of the Battle Area]. All ranks gave 100% effort to dig in on time and prepare the Coy defensive position, for what was to be a big battle. As usual, the Orange forces took one look at us, suddenly realised they were up against A Coy "Aces" and withdrew to find a softer enemy. Credit must go to all ranks in their conduct during the exercise. Enthusiasm and keeness to do the job was solid. The move back to the UK was very much run of the mill. Most of the Coy flew back but the road party had to endure the pain of long waits at ports. Despite this all had a good Camp and the feeling of getting us to work as a team was there.[31]

and a Danish newspaper report read (literally) like this:

Hellebask: In the spring ornithologists gathers in a large crowd of people in the hills around Hellebaek breeding farm to study birds of prey passage to Norway and Sweden. But these days birdlovers have an opportunity to witness a rare visitor in this country. A bold grouse has moved into Hellebaek breeding farm. Without wings, but armed with antitankweapons, tanks and mortarguns. It is an infantrybattalion with 560 men who is staying in the breeding farm during the big NATO-exercise. The exercise with 18.000 soldiers from England, Vestgermany and Denmark is cald "Bold Grouse".

1 Wessex – 560 soldiers **is** training in the practicearea at Hellebaek. They are warming up before the fieldexercise beginds in the weekend. The spirit amoung the men is very good. We are lucky with the weather and the soldiers are looking forward for tomorrows R 8c R – rest and recreation. Many of the soldiers shall visit Tuborg. Others are visiting Copenhagen, where they can have fun in Tivoli ore Istedgade (the naughty street) if they feel like it, tells Captain Funder[32] who is liaison officer to 1 Wessex. The town of Helsingor can also expect a minor invasion of NATO-soldiers, who want to explore the country they are going to defend. Friday evening 1 Wessex leves Hellebask. The tents are taken down and the veapons shall be cleanded. But not before all 560 men has got a shower at Hovelte barracks, because there is only 3 showers at Hellebaek.

The 560 soldiers at Hellebaek breeding farm is only a small part of the total exercise force. Approximately 20.000 mainly british and german warriors takes part in "Bold Grouse". The purpose of the NATO-exercise is to strength the co-operation among the allied countries. Before the exercise is over the 17th September, bold grouse will have been eating and drinking 25 tons of food.[33]

The Recce Platoon, under WO2 Colin Snee DERR, achieved something of a distinction by being the only one in the UKMF to take all their Fox vehicles to Denmark – but, more importantly, to return with them too.

1989

Stanford PTA (Wretham Camp) (23 June – 7 July)

Stanford…..must be one of the best training areas in the UK……and, unlike Welsh Wales, it does not rain all the time.[34]

This Camp, held in the middle of a heatwave, was devoted to "low level training in all the usual subjects" – section and platoon tactics, field firing, night ambushes, assault course training, watermanship and battle inoculation, and even a confidence-building course for junior NCOs. The Battalion was joined by three officers from the German Reserve Army – "who, under the tried and tested system of 'divide and rule' (i.e. being variously attached to the Companies), thoroughly enjoyed their stay with us", as did six US National Guardsmen – and they were all were very complimentary about the British Army.

The first week was devoted to field firing, allowing us to get used to the excellent ranges. Probably without exception, every soldier enjoyed their variety and gaining the skills they required. Company Commanders were able to plan and run their training in the most imaginative and challenging ways that soldiers – not the least the Volunteers – enjoy. The second week was the culmination of the CO's training year, and brought together in a demanding patrol exercise all the skills that had been practiced in the preceding months. Only a week later, Battalion Headquarters went back to Stanford for a five-day UKMF CPX – déjà vu!

Because, in the NATO year, the UKMF exercises in October, that is when our training year starts and ends. We are therefore already in the second year of our cycle, beginning to think in earnest about staff tables, deployment and training for our exercise abroad in only 11 months time! [35]

The last five days were devoted to Exercise Wessex Aggressor – a most arduous exercise in very hot conditions. The discomfort of the heat was compounded by the new 24-hour individual ration packs – which needed so much water to make them into palatable meals that a veritable mule-train burdened with jerrycans would have been needed to satisfy most people's culinary wishes![36]

B Company suffered from "all the snakes in the area, which seemed to be taking their summer holidays everywhere that the CSM, Alan Eldridge, went."[37]

[From here on, there are increasingly few reports of the Camps in the Journals of the Regular Regiments – because, of course, the Battalion had by now contracted into just Gloucestershire, Bristol and Wiltshire, so that only two of the Regular Regiments (the Glosters and the Duke of Edinburghs) remained affiliated to it, and it was therefore only in their Journals and the TAVRA Newsletter that the activities of 1 Wessex were reported.]

1990

Salisbury Plain Training Area and Lydd & Hythe PTA (October)

Glastnost, the demise of the Wall and forthcoming German elections made the cancellation of Exercise Bold Guard [in Germany] increasingly inevitable. By mid-summer our suspicions were confirmed and Annual Camp, hitherto scheduled for Schleswig-Holstein, was re-organised. Soldiers were called up and processed through TA Centres as if going to war. The entire documentation process was practised, and by 1600 hours the following day, the Battalion was complete at Knook Camp on Salisbury Plain. The first week of Camp remained altered: the aim was simple and fundamental – to carry out such training as we would realistically conduct 7 days before deploying on operations. We concentrated, therefore upon three specific military skills – NBC, first aid and shooting. The latter tied in with our conversion to the SA80 weapon system, which we fired on the Bulford and Warminster ranges. Furthermore, this year we reserved the right to train our own recruits, and 150 young men went through our own internally run cadre, organised by Lieutenant Paul Frank. The all-up strength of those who came with us to Camp was 460, with further 40 attending courses or attachments in lieu.

The second week began with a tactical vehicle move to our new location, the Cinque Ports Training Area, at Lydd and Hythe in Kent. Here we were able to fire our new weapon system on the sophisticated electronic target ranges normally used for Northern Ireland training. The spirit of the Battalion was excellent throughout the fortnight, and there were Battalion Shows, Regimental Guest Nights, and visits by the Commander of the UK Field Army, the Commander of the UKMF and the GOC South West District. In sum, we worked hard, and had every opportunity to play hard – which we did![38]

The result of this great [Battalion] turnout meant that Headquarter Company were working flat out in their daily tasks to ensure that the administration was sound. It probably was the most realistic training we could have asked for. The move from Knook to Hythe was conducted as an operational road move, and one of the highlights was the refuel and refreshment point carried out at Crowborough Training Area. The star of this organisation was Sergeant Legg (ex Pte Legg who used to work in the QMs Department of 1 DERR as an equipment repairer). Other ex members of the Regiment who continue to give sterling service are Staff Sergeant "Brigadier" Frayling, whose culinary skills delight the Officers', Warrant Officers' and SNCOs' Messes. Sergeant Jones of the NRPS in the QM's Department, remains as smart and as conscientious as in the days he was a member of the Duke of Edinburgh's Provost Staff, and WO2 "Mitch" Mortimer still has the same passion for recounting tales of old.[39]

The high point of 1990 has been the issue of the SA80 rifle in mid-August: this has led to a mass change of attitude to shooting and range work, with everyone talking like old hands from Bisley. The first chance to fire it came at Annual Camp.....the Lydd and Hythe range package kept everyone busy.[40]

<u>1991</u>

<u>Otterburn PTA (July)</u>

Annual Camp in July took place on the Otterburn Training Area, with everyone except the administrative echelon deployed in the field for the entire two weeks. This allowed the Companies to practise and build personal and basic platoon skills. In the first phase, the Companies rotated around a series of field firing ranges which became progressively more complex and demanding. This training culminated in a realistic and exciting company battle run, with both our Mortar Platoon from Andover and the Anti Tank Platoon from Gloucester firing live in support.

During the second week, the Battalion deployed to the Kielder Forest in a counter-insurgency operation against a terrorist enemy provided by Support Company. The operation involved four days of long and hard patrolling through thick country, with full kit carried in hot and sometimes wet conditions. After clearing large areas of the Forest, the Battalion crossed the Kielder reservoir at night and assaulted the enemy training camp located in a quarry, defended by great swarms of biting flies as well as the enemy terrorists.[41]

Privates Bellamy and Goodlife (whose descriptions of their earliest days in A Company are, slightly perversely, in Chapter 12 (pages 375-377)) found the going hard in the Recruits Cadre:

Summer Camp was mentioned to me. Mmmmmm, camping, I love camping! I love camping! How wrong I was. Our cadre consisted of two weeks of getting up early, getting to bed late, getting wet and running and getting shouted at by the instructors, none of which I had encountered before. It is just the way it was all thrown at you. Still I got through it without too much trouble and not too many aches and pains and my feet were in good shape considering I only got my boots four days before camp. I was just shattered and in need of some good kip. I did come home however with a sense of achievement. With loads of stories to tell getting home was good but when I got there everybody was in bed and I had not got my key and I thought about putting up a basher in my back garden but had my girlfriend with me. So I had to knock up my mother. I went straight to bed feeling pretty cheesed off for some reason.[42]

Anyway two months later and I was off to Otterburn Training Camp for my two weeks recruit cadre. This was two weeks of constant training, instruction, tests, exercise and exams, it was very hard at times but also very enjoyable. Half way through the second week we joined our own companies and stayed with them for the final battle phase. This included a 1.5 kilometre river crossing in a rowing boat, following by a medium sized tab up to the edge of the contact point. We then waited for the go ahead to advance. When this was received, we moved forward to the enemy's quarry, and amongst all the noise, shouting and confusion, we proceeded to clear our way through their bunkers and finally secured the area. I was surprised at how exhausting this part of the battle was, also how confusing things got during the assault. I think a few of the other recruits did as well, as they ran off in the wrong direction.

At the end of the two weeks I was glad to get home and my feet up, and know that I did not have to get up at the next morning for PE. I was also very proud of surviving the two weeks, passing all the tests and exams also gaining a lot of knowledge and new experiences.[43]

1992

Denmark: 1 Infantry Brigade's Exercise Bold Grouse II (September)

When first announced, it looked as though this Camp would be very much the 'medicine as before' – a week's work on individual, platoon and company training, followed by R & R in Copenhagen over the middle weekend, and then what could have been a not very productive 5-day Brigade exercise in the second week. In the event, however, it turned out to be much more than that, particularly as there was an enormous amount of 'hardware' and activity.

It involved a battlegroup from the UKMF centred around 1 Wessex, and included attachments from 656 Squadron of the Army Air Corps with Gazelle and Lynx helicopters for reconnaissance; a Javelin air-defence detachment from 7 Regiment, The Royal Horse Artillery and Forward Observation Officers from 289 Commando B Battery RA(V); fighter-ground attacks, and a communications detachment from 55 Signal Squadron, Royal Signals. The 'friendly forces' were under the command of 1 Zetland Brigade, and included Danish and German troops with tanks and armoured personnel carriers. There was much realism and excitement, and, as always the case when, as this time, there was a great deal of activity right down to platoon level throughout the whole of an excercise, everyone felt that they had learned a lot, and that the Battalion had more than managed to hold their own against the Regular infantrymen:[44]

> During the first week, Companies and Support Platoons deployed independently to practice and develop personal skills[45] and battle procedures in preparation for the exercise. A joint training day with our Danish hosts gave the soldiers the chance to show off each others' vehicles, weapons and equipment and to compete in a series of fun sports competitions. This was rounded off with a barbecue at which the Battalion cooks produced a meal for some 1200 soldiers and helped cement the friendly relations which had been forged earlier. The event proved highly successful in advertising the TA.
>
> After a day off in celebration of our Silver Jubilee – which, among other things, was used to discover just what delights were on offer in Copenhagen – the Battalion deployed into the field in the second week alongside Danish and German troops........The exercise was fast moving and challenging and had been cleverly constructed to ensure that every soldier had a busy and eventful week. Extensive use was made of helicopters and fighter ground attack aircraft, and the tanks and armoured personnel carriers of the German and Danish armoured infantry battalions added to the realism and excitement. Exercise Bold Grouse afforded the Battalion a marvellous chance to carry out joint training with our allies on a large-scale exercise and was an excellent example of multi-national co-operation which bodes well for our future ARRC role.[46]

1993

Cinque Ports Training Area, Folkstone (July – August)

Perhaps unsurprisingly, given the turmoil that Options for Change and the related business of the revival of County TA battalions were causing, the usual scribes who reported the activities of the Battalion and the various Companies were engaged on more important matters. There were no reports of this Camp in either the *The Back Badge* or the *DERR Journal* (as explained above, by this time the only two relevant regimental journals), and the only one was in the *Western Wessex Newsletter* – and that gave a very 'bald' account of what happened;

> The Battalion's annual in-camp training this year took place at the Cinque Ports Training Area, near Folkestone. After such a big shake-up [in the organisation, layout and role] it was necessary to retrain many of the old, and train all the new, members of the Battalion. To that end the Camp was very much a cadre camp. The opportunity was taken to qualify as many recruits as possible. WO2 Reade, the Senior Sergeant Major, and his Regimental Recruiting Team took on this task and successfully trained 51 new soldiers for 1 Wessex. It was an impressive display, as WO2 Reade took the whole cadre into the field and there trained the recruits without distraction. A potential Junior NCOs' cadre was run by the Operations/Training Officer, Captain Tournay, ably assisted by full-time professionals WO2 Hussey and WO2 Ashford, amongst others. It had been some time since the Battalion had run such a cadre, and there was a need to train not only private soldiers to climb to the rank of Lance Corporal, but also to train many of those who had been promoted to provisional rank and required to be properly assessed. The cadre produced 11 new junior commanders to contribute to the leadership of the Battalion.
>
> To ensure that there was a nucleus of expertise to assist with the running of the ranges, a permanent training team was provided by 2 Brigade in Folkestone. With excellent planning by Major Tony Harveson, 13 officers and NCOs were trained in range management, thus enhancing the Battalion's ability to be self-sufficient in the conduct of its ranges and releasing many of the PSIs to other training.

A Large Goods Vehicle cadre run by the MT platoon succeeded in producing 12 more soldiers capable of driving four tonners and other related vehicles for the Battalion. This gives the Companies much more flexibility in being able to conduct their own training without being constrained by the inability to move people and supplies.

It had been 18 months since the previous Standard 2 Signals Cadre was run, and Captain Rob Hiles and WO2 (Regimental Signals WO) Gardner ran a very intensive training package. By the end of the demanding course, the Battalion had a further 20 Standard 2 signallers across the Battalion to run the various command posts vital to the Battalion's operation effectiveness. In addition a number of other cadres were run for the remainder of the Battalion – snipers, assault pioneers, recce and machine-gun sustained fire. There was a Drumhead Service on the middle Sunday; the Colours were on parade, and the Band performed, to produce a memorable service under the guidance of the padre Major Simon Wilkinson.[47]

The Battalion scrapbook contains virtually nothing about this Camp, apart from numerous photographs, and the only factual information that can be gleaned from it is that between 28 July and 1 August there were military band concerts on the imposing Leas Bandstand on the Folkstone sea-front, in the course of which the Hampshire & Dorset Band played no less than ten times, with a free evening concert in the United Reform Church adjoining the Central Station "for the benefit of all old soldiers and veterans of all regiments", the programme for which included "popular music from both World Wars". (Also playing during the same period were the Bands of The South Nottinghamshire Hussars Yeomanry and the Army Medical Services).

1994

Belgium – Exercise Orient Express I (Camp Bastin, Arlon, the Ardennes) (3 – 17 September)

Despite the fact that, short of a miracle, this would be the Battalion's last Camp, the Companies set off for Belgium in high spirits – for it would be the finale of the re-organised Battalion's efforts to be declared fit for role in April 1995, and so become part of the Allied Rapid Reaction Corps again – and, despite the weather, they all enjoyed a quite excellent fortnight:

> Wet, wet, wet: a pop group? No, just our abiding memory of Belgium – never in the field of Annual Camp has so much rain fallen on so many for so long!! The tactical lessons may fade (though I doubt it!) but the horror of those long, wet, muddy days will certainly remain.

The Battalion deployed during the period 3 – 17 September 1994 to Lagland Training Area in the south of Belgium, for its annual evaluation of tactical skills, coupled with a comprehensive training package for JNCOs and basic recruits. The programme was written around three distinct phases, in order to develop, test and exercise individual, Company and Battalion combat skills.

On completion of personal administration, zeroing[48] and briefings, we deployed for a three-day Company 'work-up' exercise. The Lagland Training Area, though small by UK standards, makes extensive use of the surrounding private land. There are of course restrictions, especially on the use of blanks and pyrotechnics, but generally the Belgian public have a greater tolerance of military training than do their counterparts in the UK.

As we deployed from our base on Monday morning, in its unremitting efforts to offer continuity, the rain was still falling. Morale, however, was high, and gone were those Monday morning blues that the Volunteers normally associate with the office, factory, hospital or building site. Here was the open road, bucketsful of fresh air and the chance to show what has been achieved in personal development and skills in the last year.

Arriving at the Company harbour area, the Platoon Commanders were briefed on the 'work-up' format and despatched to practise and reinforce SOPS [Standing Operating Procedures], OP procedures and ambush drills. The culmination of this tutorial was a surprise fire-fight in the depths of Tuesday night, during which Blue Force, yet again, emerged victorious. Lessons were learned, and in particular how difficult navigation could be during both night and day, given the lack of intensive and repetitive training in moving covertly on unfamiliar terrain.

Having won the battle, we enjoyed a non-tactical night during which we gorged ourselves on 24 hour ratpacks and slept the sleep of the contented. Being already wet and under a constant 'shower', ablutions were dispensed with except for the mandatory face scrape with one's bayonet! Rising on Wednesday morning, the weather had temporarily abated and morale was sky high. Having been called to order, the Company's enthusiasm was then directed towards success in the forthcoming Battalion Inter Platoon Competition. The contest was centred on a number of stands designed to test Platoon skills on Thursday, followed by a defensive shoot on Friday, with a conducted Battlefield Tour on Saturday. We entered two teams in what proved to be a very exacting and mentally stimulating competition. All aspects of the Infanteer's skills were covered: a 15km march with a physically demanding assault course at the end of it, various command tasks, a first aid test and a stretcher race. Most teams took two to two and a half hours to complete the course. Whilst not winning the Victor Ludorum – that was the Recce Platoon's moment of glory – "Shiny A" certainly showed the rest of the Battalion what leadership, team spirit and inspired enthusiasm can do.

The Battlefield Tour was to Sedan and Verdun in France– and it was fascinating. At Sedan in 1940, Colonel Guderian's XIX Panzer Division conducted a successful river crossing, and drove a wedge between the British and French Forces which effectively unhinged the BEF's advance into Belgium – and the results were the debacle at Dunkirk and the subsequent collapse of France. Rumours that Capt Eddie Fry was there at the time are untrue; he is just very good at telling a story. At Verdun – where the cemetery contains the remains of 130,000 unknown soldiers – we looked round one of the forts used by the French during the Great War.

Annual Camps are rarely all work and no play. The Company deployed to a local hostelry for a meal in the middle of the first week. The food was excellent and the wine flowed freely. Amid the general *bon homi* the OC was surprised with a cake and candles half way through the proceedings to mark his birthday, but had to be restrained from making a speech.

The first week ended on Sunday with the traditional drumhead service, after which preparation went ahead for the third and final phase of Camp, the Battalion Exercise. Following a loosely Bosnian scenario, we used the skills that had been practised earlier in the week, and it ended four exhausting days later with the obligatory final attack (on a most unusual Battalion objective) and then endex.

Twenty four hours R & R was granted by the CO on Friday and good use of the time was made by many in the Company. Groups went as far afield as Luxembourg and the American PX ... and came back laden with local 'fayre', carried and consumed.

In conclusion, a wet but rewarding two weeks in Belgium that built on and reinforced the year's training, bringing it all together in a realistic way on unfamiliar terrain – in the wet. On reflection, a hard but enjoyable and thoroughly worthwhile Camp. Judging by the letters received and passed down the chain of command, we have pleased, maybe even impressed, our Lords and Masters. Having survived North West Europe and the worst of its temperate conditions, we are now ready for a tropical rain forest !![49]

[Exercise Orient Express I] was the first of a series of annual deployments of TA battalions to Camp Bastin, near Arlon in the Belgian Ardennes. The Belgian Army, like our own, is undergoing a significant drop in its strength at the same time as much of it moves home from Germany. Camp Bastin and the associated Lagland training areas are being developed as a training facility for Belgian and foreign units. Unfortunately the camp is undergoing a transition from the barracks of a conscript tank regiment to becoming the Belgian School of Infantry and a training camp for visiting units. As a result, the facilities for training and the accommodation were basic, but have enormous potential. However, with the cooperation of the Belgian camp and training area staff and a liaison officer, the Battalion achieved its training objectives of running essential cadres and conducting collective training.

The move to Belgium began with the deployment of the Regular and NRPS Quartermasters, Major Philip Hall and Sergeant Mundy; driving in a small red car; they were inevitably nicknamed "Noddy" and "Bigears". Matters were complicated by the RAF switching its priorities to Rwanda. Instead of flying into Luxembourg airport, the majority of the battalion moved by coach in a 13-hour journey. The vehicle parties were not so fortunate, with some having a 24-hour journey on the route out – in part because the Belgian military police escorts refused to go faster than 35mph, even on motorways. After a swifter move back to Ostend on the journey home, hopes were dashed when a ferry accident meant that the convoy waited for four hours at the docks. Meanwhile the coach party, booked as civilians, boarded without delay and waved as they left their stranded comrades behind.

The Ardennes is an area of thick forests, wild boar and, of course, an extraordinary capability for more or less permanent rain. We quickly learnt that vivid descriptions of the consequences of such weather, by war poets and historians alike, were very true, and that we too would be subjected to showers and relentless downpours during the second week. The training area was quite small, but provided some challenging training in thick woodlands with dense, heavy, sand underfoot, making the going very slow.

The first day saw a bleary-eyed battalion tackling upgrading boards to see if they could demonstrate a high enough level of proficiency in infantry skills to merit a pay rise. This was followed by three days when the companies and support platoons conducted their own training – a valuable opportunity to revise skills and continue team building. The training was carried out on private land and in state forests. Despite some restrictions, being able to do that over 'real ground', as opposed to the artificial and often all too familiar landscapes of Sennybridge and Salisbury Plain was extremely worthwhile. This training period culminated with company and platoon smokers [parties].

Three days of battalion-organised training followed. The fighting-in-built-up-areas training package and Dien Bien Phu live firing defence range were made very realistic by the Assault Pioneer Platoon's battle simulation charges. The Battlefield Tour provoked sobering thoughts.

The battalion competition involved the assault course, a 15km march, a command task, vehicle-borne anti-ambush drills and a stretcher race. Besides this physical activity a random selection from the teams had to live fire with the 51 mm mortar and 94mm outdoor trainer, throw grenades, take part in a falling plate shoot and answer questions. After a hard fought battle, the Recce Platoon was the winning team. Any similarity between this competition and the 1992 Rawson Cup Competition in 1 Glosters in which RSM Dixon was also involved is purely coincidental!

The first week ended with a battalion drumhead service on Sunday, with the music provided by the Band of the 1st Battalion

51st Highland Volunteers, who were in Belgium to celebrate the 50th anniversary of the Liberation in 1944. The Commander Bulford Area, Brig D J Innes, then presented the padre, Major Simon Wilkinson, with his Territorial Decoration, Corporal Metcalfe with his Territorial Efficiency Medal and the Recce Platoon with the trophy for winning the battalion competition.

The scenario for the battalion exercise in the second week was a cross between Haiti, Goscigny and Uderzo as the citizens of Obelix were liberated from their tyrannical government by a multinational force. However the flanks were threatened by Obelixian infiltration throughout the neighbouring state of Asterix. An initial deployment into patrol harbours was followed by 24 hours of recce patrols, observation posts and ambushes. The Oblexian enemy, provided by the potential NCOs' cadre, the Assault Pioneer Platoon, and members of both 23 Pioneer Regiment, Royal Logistics Corps and Avon Army Cadet Force (the last looking convincingly different in borrowed Belgian uniforms!) However, their rapid redeployment led to the need to mount a heliborne operation against them on Tuesday. The Puma helicopters from 18 Squadron RAF came to give support, but the weather which was soaking the Battalion also limited their operations. This left the Recce Platoon temporarily stranded 50km ahead of the Battalion. Their natural caution led them to ignore an attempt by the Regimental Quartermaster Sergeant to contact them, even though he was nearly standing on top of them. Nevertheless enemy platoons were pinpointed, and successful company attacks were executed on Monday night with the aid of the helicopters. Tuesday saw a battalion heliborne attack on to a hill crowned by a virtually impenetrable timber yard. Meanwhile the Recce and Anti-tank Platoon, in cut-off positions, faced a new enemy when they were charged by a herd of cows! Wednesday saw a re-deployment to a line of observation posts to prevent Oblexian infiltration, followed a final dawn attack on to the imposing Montagne de Stockem.

The Catering Platoon's choice of banana custard for the meal before the night approach march proved unfortunate. However, with the last of the enemy flushed out by the Operations Officer and the RSM, the Oblexians were finally vanquished.

Meanwhile 32 potential NCOs and 40 recruits had been trained. Invaluable support was provided by the attached cadets, pioneers and others. A day and a half's rest and recreation in Belgium, Germany

and Luxembourg followed. Camp Bastin was handed over to the
3rd Battalion The Duke of Wellington's Regiment (West Riding)
(Yorkshire Volunteers) who prepared to brave the Belgian rain in
tropical combat uniform.[50]

During the fortnight, time was, of course, found for the usual jollities
– Company Smokers, and Dinners in both the WO's & Sergeants' and
the Officers' Messes. The latter's Guest Night got off to a very sparkly
start: having driven from Calais to Arlon by a somewhat curious route
– Rheims, Epernay, Saint Menehould and Verdun – and definitely
in excess of the speed limits, the Honorary Colonel arrived only 20
minutes before the photograph was due to be taken, unchanged but
with the boot of his car full of champagne. It was said that it only
lasted until the Officers' Dinner call was sounded.

After such a successful Camp, and as was generally expected, the
Battalion was indeed 're-admitted' to 1 Mechanised Brigade in 3 (UK)
Division in April 1995.

---

[1] *BB*, Winter 1992.
[2] *BB*, Winter 1981.
[3] Dorset Evening Echo 26 October 1981.
[4] *Western Wessex TAVRA Newslette*, 1981.
[5] Ibid., 1982.
[6] *BB*, Winter 1982.
[7] *Western Wessex TAVRA Newsletter*, 1982.
[8] Major Elizabeth Durant, the wife of the Adjutant, Captain Jimmy Durant DERR.
[9] *DERRJ*, Spring 1983.
[10] *BB*, Winter 1983.
[11] *D&DRJ*, January 1984.
[12] *BB*, Winter 1984.
[13] *BB*, Winter 1989.
[14] *BB*, Winter 1984.
[15] *Ibid.*
[16] 2/Lt Roger Smith in *BB*, Summer 1987.
[17] *RHRJ*, November 1984.
[18] *D&DRJ*, January 1985.
[19] See Note 28 in Chapter 9.
[20] *D&DRJ*, January 1986.
[21] *BB*, Summer 1987.

[22] *Ibid.*
[23] *Ibid.*
[24] *Ibid.*
[25] *D&DRJ*, February 1987.
[26] *Ibid.*
[27] *Norddeutsche Rundschau* 22 September 1986.
[28] *D&DRJ*, Spring 1988.
[29] *DERRJ* 1988.
[30] BB, Winter 1987.
[31] Lt Roger Smith in *BB*, Winter 1988.
[32] A Danish officer who acted as the Battalion's liaison officer. See Chapter 12.
[33] *HelsingØr Daily Newspaper*, 7 September 1988.
[34] *D&DRJ*, Autumn 1989.
[35] *Western Wessex Newsletter* No 21, 1989.
[36] BB, Winter 1989.
[37] *D&DRJ*, 1990.
[38] *Western Wessex Newsletter* No 22, 1990.
[39] *DERRJ*, 1991.
[40] *Ibid.*
[41] *Western Wessex Newsletter* No 23, 1991.
[42] BB, Winter 1991.
[43] *Ibid.*
[44] *Western Wessex Newsletter*, No.24, 1992.
[45] Perhaps the most frequently used expression of all in reporting what the Volunteers did at Annual Camps!
[46] *Western Wessex Newsletter ibid.*
[47] *Western Wessex Newsletter* No 25, 1994.
[48] Checking that weapons 'fire straight'.
[49] A Company Notes in *Western Wessex Newsletter* No 26, 1995.
[50] *The Sphinx & Dragon*, Winter 1994.

CHAPTER 12

SOLDIERING ON TO THE END: 1988–1995

The tenth Commanding Officer was Lieutenant Colonel Giles Brady. A Regular cavalryman in the 4th/7th Dragoon Guards, he had retired at a modest age to go into business – but, being unable to get the military urge out of his system, he became a Volunteer. His non-infantry background notwithstanding, he joined B Company as Second-in-Command in the spring of 1983. A quick learner of different military skills, when Major Stuart Woolles returned to his old battalion, 5 Queens, in the autumn, he succeeded him as Company Commander. In 1985 he became the Battalion Second-in-Command, was appointed to command in 1988 and took over after Camp that year. Human nature being what it is, almost every CO (and perhaps a Volunteer CO in particular!) has to make his mark in one way or another – and Giles Brady successfully did so in several.

Although TA NATO battalions had never been established with a Support Company (as distinct from a collection of 'independent' Support Platoons co-located with the Rifle Companies), he was convinced that it would be sensible to have one, so that the specialist requirements could be better managed. Back in 1978, with that in view, Bill Coppen-Gardner had reduced the then four Support Platoons in A, B, C and D Companies to two – concentrating the Anti-tanks as part of A Company and the Mortars as part of B Company – but Giles Brady felt that the logical course was now to combine them, and the Reconnaissance Platoon, into a Support Company, and he got approval to do so on 1 April 1989. Its HQ was in the excellent post-war Arle Road TA Centre in Cheltenham, which was the home of the Assault Pioneers. They were nearly the 'most moved-about' sub-unit in the Battalion. Originally formed in Gloucester, then transferred to Cheltenham in 1985, and now, under Sergeant Steve Yemm, moved to Cinderford, absorbing A Company's 4 Platoon. Sergeant Yemm was followed by Colour Sergeant (later to become WO2) Peter Blake, one of the longest-serving and most loyal members of the Battalion – of whom a local paper at around that time reported:

> One man who doesn't seem afraid of a challenge is Colonel Peter Blake of the Assault Pioneer Platoon, who is involved with the demolition of bridges and the use of explosives for battle simulations. Colonel Blake, who works at Birds Eye Walls, said "After 21 years in the TA, I am just beginning to get used to it! It is very worthwhile, as you see a different sort of life at weekends, but I think that it takes a special sort of person who will spend nights out in the open air."[1]

The new Anti-tank Platoon was at Eastern Avenue in Gloucester, but the Reconnaissance Platoon (mounted in Fox armoured recce vehicles) under Lieutenant Roger Smith remained in Arle Road – and in December 1989 they:

> ......performed outstandingly on the UKLF Recce Concentration at Castle Martin. Captain [as he had become] Roger Smith, then relatively new in post, but supported by an excellent PSI, stamped his mark early and takes a great deal of the credit for the congratulatory letters received from many quarters, including the Commander UK Field Army, our Brigade Commander and the Divisional Colonel. We consider this a major accolade for the Volunteer Army, since all the other competitors came from the Regular Army. Similarly, the Milan [Anti--tank] Platoon, which has grown in strength and numbers under the leadership of Captain Mike Idaziaszczyk (known throughout the Battalion as "3Zs"), fired their full ammunition allocation at Otterburn. They produced creditable results, despite horizontal rain and high winds.[2]

In view of all the other comings and goings, though, and much to its surprise, the Mortar Platoon remained in Andover, and:

> ....[have] had the lion's share of live firing within Support Company. They have exploited every opportunity, including giving assistance to the Regular Amy, liaison shoots with 266 OP Battery, and the testing of new ammunition types. This has been excellent practise and brought support weapon skills within the Battalion to a high pitch.[3]

Camp in 1988 was in Zealand in Denmark – the UKMF's Exercise Bold Grouse. During it, the Battalion acquired a great friend – Captain Oli Funder, a Reserve officer in the Royal Danish Army (who is briefly mentioned in a quotation in Chapter 11). He was appointed as the Liaison Officer for the fortnight, but, with his cheerful smile, wicked sense of humour and an ability to get on with absolutely everybody, he fitted in so well that he became a sort of 'Danish mascot'. He joined the Battalion again for the 1992 and 1994 Camps in Denmark, and he also came over to England on one or two occasions.

Having served, as did General Glyn Gilbert, as the "Hon Col" for six years, General Mike Walsh handed over to the author in 1989. Like General Glyn, General Mike had been a model holder of the appointment: he never interfered, but was always generous with sound advice when asked for it – and, always getting on so well with all ranks, he had thoroughly endeared himself to the Battalion.

Cutbacks in the Defence Budget for 1989 resulted in a severe restriction in the number of man-training-days across the whole TA, and hence a reduction in the number of weekends on which it was possible to train. Instead of two, or even three, a month, one became the norm – and it is a reflection of the amount of enjoyment that all ranks got out of their soldiering, and of the Battalion's high morale, that nearly everyone, but the junior ranks in particular, found it quite difficult to adjust to the slower pace of life. There is no doubt whatsoever that getting battered, bruised, cold and wet on exercises was (at least for this small section of the population) an excellent 'pick-me-up' after a week at work, and put them into a good frame of mind for Monday mornings. Without that, many of them said, life would be pretty boring! The CO, the Training Major and the Company Commanders were also very concerned that it would be difficult to maintain training standards – but the results of the annual Fit for Role inspections continued to be very satisfactory.

As is mentioned elsewhere, from time to time senior Volunteer NCOs went abroad on attachment to other military units – and in 1989 three did so. Staff Sergeant Chris Whiting (of the Medical Section) served for 17 days with 1 DERR in Hong Kong – "He was obviously kept very busy, as it has taken him a couple of months for his golf swing to get back into the groove."[4] – and then Sergeant McLurg of HQ Company went for 16 days to join a Long Range Surveillance Detachment of the US National Guard.   Finally, Corporal A J Mitchell of A Company spent a fortnight – notionally as a member of B Company, 4th Bn The Queen's Lancashire Regiment – with a Jaeger Battalion of the German Bundeswehr, and his report not only highlights many differences between the two Armies (some seeming to be quite critical), but illustrates both how well he understood 'what was going on' and the ease with which an experienced Volunteer could 'integrate' himself within another major NATO reserve battalion:

Im Oestern nich neues (All quiet on the Western front)

It all began in January when, after a course I'd applied for fell through, I suddenly found myself with a lot of surplus holiday left from the previous year. Just then a letter fluttered gently into the Platoon's in-tray, asking for volunteers for two-week exchanges with the Bundeswehr, the first in April. A quick phone call to the personnel department and I'd secured permission to carry forward my outstanding holiday beyond the usual March deadline. Then, armed only with the scant knowledge that the exchange had been set up between B Coy 4 QLR from Blackpool, and 712 Jaeger Bn in Schleswig-Holstein, I was off.

As soon as the RAF Police Corporal at Brize Norton opened his mouth, I could tell it was going to be a bad start. "Flight's delayed 'til 6 'cos the plane's knackered", he muttered reassuringly. Some seventeen hours later, I found myself being dragged out of bed in the transit accommodation at 2 am. By 3 am we were being ferried back to the terminal building – "delayed" had become "cancelled". Eventually our 12.30 pm Saturday flight was airborne at 5 am on Sunday. We touched down at Gütersloh from where a coach took us to Alanbrooke Barracks in Paderborn, home to 1 QLR. "Just in time for breakfast, lads!", the guard commander greeted us, and soon we found ourselves, almost alone, in the imaginatively named "Red Rose" tucking in to our second meal of the day. We achieved some slight notoriety in attempting to find an answer to the question "What to do on a Wet Sunday in Paderborn?" – one person even managing to blow his entire two-weeks' pay that night. Next morning, two Germans arrived in a VW van, and, after cramming ourselves and kit in the back, we began the five hour drive to No. 1 Coy 712 Jaeger Battalion in Heide.

The Germans all do fifteen months national service, with most of the basic training taking place with their unit rather than at a depot. From then until the age of thirty-five they are obliged to return every two years to perform eight days (fifteen for some of the specialists) 'Zeitdienst'. The NCOs have all done at least four years regular service, and are then liable for fifteen days' service until aged forty-five. The Officers also do fifteen days, and must serve until even older. Those liable for fifteen days service report in first, and have a few days grace in which to brush up on their own training, as well as preparing for the arrival of the mass of the Battalion. The majority of those in 712 Bn had done their national service as either Infantry or Panzer-Grenadiers, but there were sizeable numbers of ex-paras, tankies and gunners – and there were even two who had previously served as Guided Missile Operators.

The first morning we were shown a couple of safety films, a sort of German equivalent of "It could be you!". We then watched as the crews began to familiarise themselves with the 20mm Feldkanone-2 which, it appeared, was the only integral support weapon the Battalion possessed – no mortars or Milan here.

At this point the German CO decided it was better to divide and rule – with only two of us having even a little German, it would be easier to explain things to us in ones and twos, rather than a large group. So most of us were attached in twos and threes to the four Rifle Companies, which were located all across Schleswig-Holstein. After another, thankfully shorter, road move I found myself with No 4 Company at the Freiherr Von Fitsch Barracks just outside Itzehoe. Here again, we were split up, one to a Platoon, and I was given a room with StabsUnteroffizier Ralf Reiber from Hamburg. Like a number of the Germans I met he spoke impeccable English, and did his best to improve my small stock of German throughout the rest of my stay.

Over the next couple of days, the Officers and NCOs prepared for the reception of the rest of the Company, under the watchful eyes of the Regular Training Staff, a HauptFeldwebel (Colour Sergeant or WO2) for each Platoon. Among other things, the Platoon Commander, Sergeant and Section Commanders between them laid out a defensive position (for later use in a Company warm-up exercise), spitlocking trenches and marking out a track plan as well as drawing up their local counter attack plans. We were told about the duties of a sentry and challenge procedure.

On the whole, their Platoons seemed well equipped – with full-sized spades, shovels, picks, axes and saws at Section level, to help speed up their defensive preparations. As for weaponry they were equipped on a similar scale to us, with an MG3 and 84mm MAW per Section, but in addition each Section boasted an SF Kit, two-sets of telescopic sights for their Heckler Koch G3 Rifles and a 40mm Grenade Launcher. Once the radios, stores, weapons and ancillaries were loaded, the individual Platoons dispersed to various local farms, where, after concealing the vehicles amongst the outbuildings, we made ourselves comfortable in a hay-filled barn, and settled down to await the arrival of the rest of the Reservists the next day.

One vehicle and an NCO from each Platoon returned to Seeth to collect the reservists in a shuttle service around the Company's locations. Gradually they appeared, usually in groups of two to four, some in civvies clutching kit bags, others in their one set of uniform, their webbing slung on one shoulder. They sported an interesting variety of haircuts, beards, stubble and earrings. One or two looked as if they'd only just exchanged their uniforms for a set of greasy leathers and an 850cc BMW. Attitudes seemed to range from those who obviously did not want to be there, to others who seemed to look forward to a break from the wife and kids, and to seeing old friends again. As they arrived, those not already in uniform changed and personal weapons and ancillaries were issued. Eventually the Platoon mounted up and began to move in convoy back to Itzehoe. Incidentally, the German authorities take this mobilisation very seriously and, so I was told, the Police and Customs are warned weeks in advance of these exercises, to prevent any Reservists either staying at home or skipping the country.

The next three days were devoted to warm-up training, since it was two years since any of these soldiers had handled weapons, acted as sentries or, indeed, carried out any other kind of military duty. Weapon training covered 84mm MAW handling and the MG3 in both light and SF roles. The SMG seemed quite robust, with an excellent optic sight, but light in comparison to our own SF Kit – needing, I later discovered, to be well weighted with sandbags when firing. The training also briefly covered the 40mm grenade launcher, though this weapon seemed to be carried only by Section and Platoon Commanders. The one area in which they were definitely worse off than us was night vision devices.

I don't think I will ever moan about the size of the IWS [an individual night sight] again! The Germans were equipped with an infra-red sight with a lamp the size of a car headlight mounted on a Heckler & Koch G3, and attached by a thick cable to a battery about the size of a PRC351 battery, making the sight almost useless except in a defensive position.

One complete day was spent on the ranges, which were immaculately kept and run with German efficiency. The G3 shoot was six rounds at 100m and six at 250m, all fired prone supported at a target similar to a figure twelve. The sharpshooters fired with telescopic sights at the same targets at a mix of 270m and 300m. The MG3 turned out to be quite awkward to fire in the light role, which was done at 25m against a landscape target, but very easy to use in the SF role, again fired at only 25m but used to traverse a number of representative targets both horizontally and vertically. The MG3 has an extremely rapid rate of fire which took most of the light role shoot to get used to. The only other weapon fired was the 9mm P1 pistol, five rounds standing at a 'figure eleven' type target on a witness screen. The troops moved from shoot to shoot until they had completed them all. Surprisingly there were no Normal Safety Precautions, declarations or weapon cleaning carried out.

The NBC training was fairly brief – a quick stroll round a gas chamber to check that everyone's respirator functioned OK; perhaps this was just as well as they only get issued with NBC suits in wartime. The other thing which seemed to have gone by the board was fitness training, there being no attempt to assess the general condition of the Reservists.

The actual exercise began with an early morning move to the Battalion RV in a Company convoy. The Germans brought only weapons and CEFO, but the British had been warned that we would not return to Itzehoe and so had to bring all our kit on the transport. Driving through Itzehoe we passed another barracks just in time to see an armed German Patrol exit the front gate, all wearing flashing orange lights strapped to the top of their helmets. The weather was now quite bitter, and by the time we reached the RV near Hohne Airfield forbiddingly overcast. At Hohne a number of senior Officers made speeches. Afterwards we were told that we should go back to our Platoons and that we would be picked up "sometime later" in the exercise. On returning to 2 Platoon I found that the Platoon Sergeant,

OberFeldwebel Wolfgang Uhleman, had them drawn up in three ranks and, after a short speech, he presented me with a green Jaeger beret by way of a memento.

As the 2 Platoon Commander was also the Company 2I/C, and in charge of the Company's road move, it was left to ObFw Uhleman to take Platoon HQ forward to recce and site the defensive position. Here we were joined by another of our training staff, HauptFeldwebel Beilke. The position was just to the North of the bridge over the Kiel Canal at Rendsberg, and a narrow, sunken lane led away towards a number of farms. Once the position was sited to the Company Commander's satisfaction, and the rest of the Platoon had arrived and started to dig, I went forward with the Platoon Sergeant and four others some two km along the sunken lane. Like most other moves this was done by vehicle, which was then left some 300m back behind a bend where an OP was established. As dusk drew in we were visited by a Lieutenant Colonel, one of the umpires, and heard that we would be subjected to a heliborne attack next morning. This seemed to be confirmed shortly afterwards by the arrival of a Flakpanzer Gephard [an anti-aircraft tank] with an attendant Unimog Ammo Carrier. The night, bitter cold and wet, was spent stagging on and off in pairs.

After dawn, the umpire returned accompanied by a film crew with a video. Within the hour the distant thud of rotorblades filled the air and four UHlOls appeared. They eventually landed some 500–600m from the Gephard which withdrew after engaging them. One of the helicopters passed some 50m directly over the OP, who opened fire on it after its take-off. Being unsighted, the Platoon Sergeant took his OP forward to try and observe where the enemy had landed and in which direction they were moving. After springing a snap ambush, we rapidly withdrew out of sight and returned at high speed to the Platoon position. After another half hour the German Paras started probing down the sunken lane. The rest of the morning was spent fending them off, their attempts to infiltrate the position being met with flanking fire from the two Sections and also two 20m Feldkanone. With the exercise almost over, the ubiquitous VW van arrived, having already collected half the other British Volunteers from neighbouring Companies, and it was time to say farewell to my German hosts.

When everyone was accounted for, we were driven to a large barracks in Schleswig to shower and change, and spend our last night. Inevitably it rained for the rest of the time, limiting any exploration to a few bars. It was a Thursday morning when we began the journey home, starting with a three to four hour drive down to Hanover, from where we were to fly back to Luton. Air travel seemed to be unlucky for us. This time it was Britannia Airways having trouble with their aircraft, it being some three hours late arriving. Air traffic control added another half an hour delay, and so it was a pleasant surprise when we landed in Luton to find a driver from A Company still waiting to take me back to Gloucestershire.

Who says that life in the TA is dull?!⁵

———————

1990 was as busy a year for the Battalion as any. First, there were two major changes in the hierarchy, Major E D Brown taking over from Mike Cornwell as the Training Major and Lieutenant Colonel P J Cable became the CO. Both Glosters, Ed Brown was a big, cheerful officer who always had the attitude that all things were possible, and that they would be fun – while Peter Cable was, somewhat unusually, both an 'officers' officer' and a 'soldiers' officer'; with a quiet confidence, he soon empathised with the Volunteer ethos, and 'ran the ship' with a light touch. An excellent sportsman and an extremely active soldier, he was a graduate of the Army Staff College at Sandhurst, and had skilfully managed to avoid having more than one strictly 'desk' job. He had trained Junior Soldiers, and was 'much-travelled', having served in Northern Ireland, Canada, BAOR, Zimbabwe, and with the British Military Advisory and Training Team in Nigeria – the last, no doubt, excellent preparation for commanding a West Country TA battalion.

In June, the Battalion had a very successful ARU, which concluded:

1 Wessex is a well motivated and effective TA unit......is fit for its role......and its standing has, of course, long been recognised by its role in the UKMF.

and at the end of July there was UKMF's Exercise Druids Drake on the Plain. All the Companies were flown there from their TA Centres in a mix of Chinook and Puma helicopters, and 12 hours later the whole Battalion was fully dug-in. The exercise was hot, challenging and at times very fast moving – but the Battalion had no difficulty in 'keeping up' with the three Regular battalions, one of which, 2 RRF, made the last full-scale attack early on the Sunday morning.

For a host of reasons – of which financial cuts, *glasnost* and "green issues" were just the main ones – MOD decreed that a number of the major, largely Regular, units making up the UKMF would not take part in that year's NATO Exercise Bold Guard, which would have been Camp for the Battalion. The Commander of the UKMF, Brigadier J G Williams OBE, accordingly decided that the only Infantry battalion in the single battle group going to Denmark would be 1 Wessex. Whether it was Giles Brady's persuasive manner and positive approach, or the Battalion's continuing excellent state of training, (or both), that persuaded him was never revealed, but that was another great boost to morale. Only a few months later, however, the Exercise was completely cancelled, and at (as by now seemed quite normal) very short notice, a substitute Camp was arranged. Its dual location could hardly have been more disappointing or less glamorous – Knook Camp on the Plain (now terribly run-down compared with its very smart condition for the Presentation of Colours in 1973) for the first week, and the second week in the tented camp at Dibgate, near Folkstone and training on the Hythe & Lydd ranges. Nevertheless, the commitment of the Volunteers was such that over 450 attended. In the meanwhile, however, between the 'going' and the 'not going' the Battalion's spirits were lifted even further by its becoming the first TA unit to be issued with the new SA80 rifle in place of the by then distinctly out-of-date Self Loading Rifle. Every Volunteer had to be retrained, and so the week on the ranges actually proved to be another morale-raiser, and its timing could not have been better.

To fill the gap in the Battalion's orbat that would be created by the forthcoming transfer of C Company to 4 D & D at the end of the year, a new Company was formed in Newbury:

> The Newbury Company has also been an interesting challenge. The GOC's remit was to form a "viable" Company between April and December 1990. The existing Platoon of our Second Battalion, from which it was to be formed, stood in April at 23 all ranks. In January, we selected and placed the PSAO, Captain Richard Nicholson MBE; at

the same time, a project team was formed, which included him and key staff from battalion headquarters, the Quartermaster [Captain Colin Burnett, R Hamps[6]] and Captain Jim Mitchell, who [as the PSAO there] had played such a key role in creating the new B Company in Swindon. This became a 'Think Tank' responsible for devising the necessary strategies for marketing, recruiting and public relations, as well as solving the essential problems of bricks, mortar and stores. A great deal of the credit for the success and growth of the Company goes not only to the highly charismatic Richard Nicholson, but also to Captain Bill Quarterman, the 2I/C, who performed outstandingly as the Company Commander for most of the Company's first six months. Lieutenants Chris Challis, Frank Moran and Paul Frank line up in front of the Platoons.[7]

Tucked away in St Michael's Road, Newbury is the Territorial Army Centre that up until 31 March 1990 was the home of 11 Platoon of D Company 2 Wessex. Under Phase 2 of the enhancement of the TA, this Platoon was to become the nucleus of a new Company for 1 Wessex. Thus on 1 April 1990 the Platoon became N Company 1 Wessex, a name it will bear until 8 December 1990, when the transfer of C Company in Dorchester to 4 D & D will allow the Newbury Company to be officially called C Company. If you think that is complicated read on.

Lt Bill Quarterman was promoted to Captain, and given the task of increasing the strength of the platoon to a target figure of 60 all ranks by September 1990. To assist him, he has a newly-arrived and diligent PSAO by the name of Capt Richard ("Mad Nick") Nicholson MBE, late RCT. WO2 Tadhunter moved across from HQ Company to start the ball rolling, and he was soon joined by WO2 McCleod, returning to UK from the bright lights of Hong Kong.

Needless to say, a Platoon that becomes a Company overnight has a distinct lack of NCOs or indeed soldiers. On the first training night under 1 Wessex colours Sergeant Major McCleod had the grand total of seven men on parade. However the permanent staff of the PSAO, the two PSIs and the Company Storeman (who incidentally is also the TA Company Sergeant Major) and an ex SASC QMSI [Small Arms School Corps, Quartermaster Sergeant Instructor] WO2 Patey, worked extremely hard to bring in the stores equipment, vehicle and weapons that the Company needed.

Recruiting then became the priority, and the Company Headquarters concentrated their message on the fact that the Company were in a Battalion which had a NATO role in the UKMF. With the issue of SA80 imminent and the possibility of Exercise Bold Guard '90 being held in Schleswig-Holstein, the Company attended fetes and displays in the local area, as well as embarking on a substantial press campaign. The response to the latter was tremendous and, coupled with the well-tried recruiting aid of satisfied soldiers bringing in friends, the number steadily improved. By June attendance was regularly averaging 22.

The next objective was to prepare for the UKMF FTX which was to take place on SPTA [Salisbury Plain Training Area] towards the end of July. A full strength platoon was assembled, and flown in by helicopter to a reserve demolition objective which became the focal point of our defensive position for the weekend. All members of the Company thoroughly enjoyed their initial UKMF exercise and gave very good accounts of themselves.

August saw the first change in the permanent staff, with WO2 Tadhunter returning to 1 DERR as we welcomed C/Sgt (Dickie) Vincent as the QPSI – whose first task was to survive an inspection some three days after joining.[8]

The Company in fact went to Camp with 40 Volunteers, and by the end of the year its strength had grown to 5 officers and 80 other ranks – a remarkable achievement. Bill Quarterman was followed into the Company Commander's chair by Major Tim Shapland.[9]

C Company in Dorset left the Battalion in December 1990, with and extremely well-executed Rebadging Parade at Dorchester. Their moving 'farewell message' so well reflected the positive attitude of Volunteers to a change of cap-badge or unit:

Finally, on 8 December, with great sadness, we will have to say farewell to our Wessex regimental family, and our own 1st Battalion of it. We have worn the Wessex Wyvern with great pride for nearly a quarter of a century, and have grown with the Battalion as it has attained the premier position that it holds today.

However, we look to the future with our Devon and Dorset family

with a great deal of confidence. We feel sure that we will quickly find
our feet in the 4th Battalion, and very much hope that we can help to
build it into an even stronger and more effective organisation than it
already is.

In the changing times, no one can tell exactly what the future will
hold, but, as always, we will try, to whatever family we might belong,
to produce and maintain a strong, well-trained and happy Company
who will, we know, give of their best in all things. We are indeed most
fortunate that the Volunteer in Dorset is in the enviable position
of being held in high regard, and it is our aim to maintain our high
standards and build on them, so that they may long continue.[10]

Notwithstanding that the Battalion's future was so uncertain,
recruiting could not be allowed to stop. By now, however, recruits no
longer went away to a Regular Army depot for their initial training,
and they learned the basic crafts of soldiering in their Companies and
with the Regimental Recruit Training Team. The nucleus of the Team
was four extremely experienced members of A Company – all of whom
had joined the old TA in the 1960s – WO2 Keith Reade, Sergeant
John Nelmes, Sergeant Jim Beeley, and WO2 (as he later became)
"Para" (few people ever knew his Christian name) Chambers, who:

..... is in fine fettle working hard alongside WO2 Reade in the RRTT.
"Or-right, Guv?" When he is not being a busy Colour Sergeant, he
works at a place opposite the TA Centre and is often seen struggling
out of the back of a red van, sack on back, with a black and white cat
in tow. Since he and WO2 Reade took over the reins of the RRTT,
many a weekend is spent with recruits in remote corners of the British
Isles for "character-building" adventure training. Many a finger-nail
mark has been seen on the side of an exposed, windswept cliff-face
after a particularly "hard sell" to the recruits about the virtues of
climbing difficult mountains in arduous conditions.[11]

The Companies were always on the lookout for local events that
would be likely to attract a reasonable number of young men between
18 and 24, some of whom might possibly be interested in joining the
TA. A good example was a 'campaign' based on the North Somerset
Show during the May Bank Holiday weekend in 1991; considerable
effort went into publicising the TA stand: many thousands of

programmes contained a 'flyer', and "600 or so posters were mailed, and sellotaped or superglued to "anything that did not move" in and around south Bristol. Although, as with so much recruiting publicity, it was impossible specifically to target potential recruits, it was certainly a way of letting people in general know that the TA was alive and well. Nine days after the Show, an Open Evening was held at the Speedwell TA Centre – to which 15 people (including a World War 1 veteran and two 10-year-old boys) turned up. Interestingly, of the 12 who expressed genuine interest, seven were deemed to be potential recruits, and five of them were actually accepted. Although two could not get time off work, astonishingly the other three – attested, medically approved and kitted-out – went to Camp at Otterburn exactly 26 days later. This account of the experience by one of them is typical of the attitude of many recruits who joined the Battalion and quickly found that life in the TA was both fun and worthwhile:

I started attending the TA Centre regularly from September 1990, and have continued to do so up to now. The reasons for initially joining were varied, I enjoyed shooting, thought the job would be interesting, and the main reason at the time was to get myself back into shape, after three years of Insurance work 90% of which is sat down. My fitness had declined considerably so I thought I needed to do something where fitness is essential, and in this job it certainly is.

Before I could do any of the training weekends available, I had to pass a medical examination in Gloucester, followed a couple of weeks later by an RSW [Recruit Selection Weekend]. This weekend is designed to test fitness, confidence and character, and also lets you know if this is really what you want, and gives you a good guide as to how fit you really are. After completing this and still thinking this is what I want, I was able to go on a training weekend with some other new recruits. It was the beginning of February, and a bit cold on Salisbury Plain to say the least. All the same, the weekend went well, and we came back knowing a lot more than when we started (as well as being frozen solid).

The next weekend I went on was the Battalion skill at arms meeting. This weekend involved a lot of shooting, followed by a big competition, and therefore I should have had a great time. However, due to unforeseen circumstances I twisted my ankle, and ended up spending all the competition day doing "light duties" like washing up – yuk! I learned from the experience not to get injured again if it is at all possible......

[Here followed his description of going to the 1991 Camp at Otterburn, which can be found in Chapter 11].

.....The last training weekend I have been on to date was last week, when we were acting enemy for the 24th Airborne Brigade. This was a good weekend as we were flying in Chinook and Puma helicopters, and the final assault on the village was done following a helicopter approach and landing. The actual battle was in a FIBUA village [for training in Fighting in Built-Up Areas], and lasted some hours before we were finally beaten (as all good enemy must be).

The End.

Pte P J Bellamy[12]

as was this by a later one, Private Goodlife:

Monday 3 June 1991 – an Open Evening at A Company 1st Battalion Wessex Regiment, TA Centre. That is what the leaflet I was given by the Sergeant on the stand at the North Somerset Show read. We chatted for about 5-10 minutes about the TA and Army life, which until a year ago had not interested me at all. The Open Evening went well and I had a short think about what I had seen. Looking at the advantages and not being able to find any disadvantages I agreed to join the Regiment. From then on Monday night was TA night. The next Monday we all turned up, that is me and four other lads that had been to the Open Evening. All of us turned up in Civvies sticking out like a sore thumb. We had our medicals and got to know a few of the lads.....

.....Now Monday nights with all my kit and having passed the recruits cadre I feel much more part of the Company. The weekend of 3 and 4 August, we were acting enemy for the regulars. They chucked my name down – I did not get any say – but did not mind. I was away the weekend before including the Monday so I did not find out times and places until the Friday just before dinner when I got a phone call at work. Be at the TA Centre at 2030 hours tonight was the message. All a bit quick but ready to go and what a weekend – really enjoyable, flying around in Chinooks and Pumas. I had never been up in a helicopter before so I found it bloody magic and totally the opposite to one lad who was holding on for dear life with his eyes closed. I got back to the TA Centre late again. I am always the last one left waiting for my lift because everyone lives closer but my lift has to come 20 miles. I am on Block Leave now and Monday nights are back to the usual. However, all my kit is hung up waiting to go again.[13]

Becoming a young officer in the TA was, very properly, appreciably more serious than that – for, on top of the hands-on learning during Company and Battalion training, there were selection boards, and physically and mentally exhausting courses to be attended. 2nd Lieutenant Lawrence Brennan made light of them:

The change from being an 'other rank' to a Platoon Commander with 1 Wessex has been incredibly smooth. In April 1994 I was still a private soldier in the Recce Platoon, but at a the end of the month I was posted to C Company in Cheltenham as an officer cadet. In June I was in the middle of the Fast Track course at Sandhurst, followed by the commissioning course. At the end of July I had passed out of Sandhurst and returned to my platoon at the TA Centre in Cheltenham.

I had originally arrived in Cheltenham as a student in October 1992, having passed RCB the previous July, and was advised to go to Oxford UOTC. Unfortunately, it was not an arrangement which suited me, as the travel between the two towns was difficult and irregular. However, they wisely advised me about 1 Wessex and the following week I appeared, still with an Oxford UOTC cap badge (much to the contempt of Sgt Chamberlain) at the Recce Platoon's training night. Working with the platoon was very different from anything I had done before. It had just been re-roled from Fox to Land Rover, so I missed that kind of vehicle and started to learn about the new role at the same time as everybody else.

There is more responsibility for a private soldier in a support platoon than in a rifle platoon, and I enjoyed weekends – moving around in vehicles, working at night, securing LODs [Lines of Defence] and creating a QRF team. All that was to end when Major Durant (then 2IC) collared me and started the commissioning process, saying

"There is no point holding you back, Lawrence, particularly if you are going to join the Regulars later". Words which I believe even he has regretted saying!

Back with C Company in Cheltenham, I prepared for RMA Sandhurst under the careful eye of Major Quarterman and the guidance of CSM WO2 Wood (himself soon to be commissioned as well). Exercise Fast Track is an educational yet intensive three-week course. I would advise anyone that the initial relaxed and slow weekend is not a fair representation of the following weeks at that great establishment. In fact, at the end of the three weeks there was a church service at which, needless to say, most of us chose to remain kneeling throughout, much to the horror of our colour sergeants at the back of the chapel. It is an educational course, designed to get those if us who needed revision on working in a rifle platoon up to speed, rather than an assessment course. That began, in earnest, on the third weekend of July. When the course had finished, just like most people who leave RMAS, I slept for a few days before returning to Cheltenham.

The Company had been preparing for summer camp in Belgium for some time. In September we left, as a battalion, for Arlon in Belgium. Fitting into the Officers' Mess was never a problem with people who were so welcoming and hospitable. What was to be the most challenging aspect of life as a subaltern was to follow: earning respect as an individual rather than as purely a commissioned man. The transformation from a private soldier to a commission has been smooth, although fast, and that is a tribute to the people who serve in 1 Wessex. As a 'sucker for punishment', I will be returning for more RMAS training in the autumn as a Regular officer cadet.[14]

––––––––––––

The Ministry of Defence's management of its financial affairs having improved since 1990, the planned 1992 Camp in Denmark on the UKMF's Exercise Bold Grouse II actually took place. As is evident from the report of it in Chapter 11, it was a great success. Before that, a composite Platoon of 25 members of the Battalion joined 1 Glosters at Fort Lewis, Washington State in America for a fortnight of training on 'high-tech' ranges, realistic field firing exercises, and adventure training in the mountains. There was time for everyone to see a bit of

America, and some even managed to get to Canada.

As related in Chapter 10, the outcome of Options for the Battalion was that it would withdraw into just Bristol, Gloucestershire and Wiltshire (although the Mortar Platoon and the Band would stay in Andover). The enormous challenge faced by the Battalion in 1992 was therefore the formation of yet two more new Companies – B in Bristol and C in Cheltenham. Recruiting was, without question, the first priority, and the efforts put into it yielded very good results.

Major Phillip Hatton had been a regular officer in the Royal Hampshire Regiment, and (among many other things) trained Infantry NCOs on the equivalent of a six week-long Outward Bound Management Development Course in Wales. When he came out of the Army, he became a Manager in the National Health Service and joined the TA. Although not written until some two years later, in this quite excellent article – which very perceptively sets out the whole 'TA ethos' – he reflected on the challenge of establishing and training the new B Company:

> It would be encouraging to think that there is a set formula to raising, recruiting and retaining the manpower for a viable TA unit. If there was, we could all simply plug in, and carry on with devoting all our efforts to meaningful training. The reality is, however, different. Like designing a successful business, the secret of attracting people to the TA remains elusive. Sometimes it seems to happen for no reason at all, at other times, despite stringent recruiting efforts on the part of everyone, allied to costly and comprehensive PR campaigns, nothing moves. In writing this article my aim is to highlight what I believe to be some important factors towards creating the conditions for success. Please re-read that last sentence. Please note the hedging that is going on. I do not believe there is or ever will be a magic formula. I can simply highlight what worked for us. If it works for you – great, if it doesn't – oh well, there's always that Signals Unit down the road.
>
> When the Company was formed in July 1992, the whole Battalion moved further west along the M4 into the Gloucester-Cheltenham-Bristol-Devizes area. Existing Companies were lost wholesale into the 4th (Volunteer) Battalion The Devonshire and Dorset Regiment and our own Regiment's second battalion. The Battalion had effectively

to start again. Consequently, A Company was split in half and the old 2 and 3 Platoons became the nucleus of B Company. This may seem like a head start – two Rifle Platoons after all is a substantial group of men. However, those acquainted with the TA will not be surprised to hear that this actually translated into no more than 25 men in total. Putting this in bayonet strength, we had around 18 soldiers on the ground. The TA Centre was at Speedwell in north Bristol, where a RCT Ambulance Squadron was being disbanded. They had very few Volunteers who wanted to move into an Infantry Company – but those that did were welcomed, and provided the essential personnel to undertake the administrative tasks of feeding, pay, REME support and medical cover. Interestingly we did not get a single RCT driver, although the administrative staff in many cases were HGV trained. It was an inauspicious and depressing start. In July 1994, however, the Company attested its 100th member. We now [September 1994] have a strength of 80 trained soldiers plus a recruit Platoon that averages 30. Annual Camp attendance is expected to be 70 men and women, and training nights routinely see 60 on parade. Why did things change?

It would be a lie to claim that this is the result of a finely judged two year plan. At most times there was no strategy at all beyond the occasional PR surge funded by the local TAVRA. It happened through a combination of circumstances – some planned, some lucky, some inexplicable. It would also be nice to think that this rise was accompanied by some ongoing quality audits aimed at establishing why people joined and left. Again this was not the case. As always we relied on the old standby of Officer and NCO hearsay – sometimes reliable, sometimes not – but definitely not measurable.

1 Wessex is a little over 25 years old, but it has no formal Regular unit links. It has no distinctive coloured beret, no hundreds of years of tradition, no county to call its own. It may be heresy to say, but the name is of no interest to the overwhelming number of recruits. Once in, however, it becomes a slightly different story, but even then the identity of minor importance. We are B (City of Bristol) Company, 1st Battalion The Wessex Regiment (Rifle Volunteers). How about that for a name? Has a certain ring to it, doesn't it? But the identity is the people, not the name. The recruit is joining a gang – he or she must like them and they, most definitely, must like him or her in return.

The recruit is joining a vision of the Army that he has picked up from a wide variety of media. From realistic awareness to vague comprehension (nearly always the latter it must be said) we get the recruit who is looking for the excitement implied and inherent in the advertising. He is not looking for 1 Wessex, but almost without exception he is the Infantry type. The age range, educational standards and social backgrounds of TA and Regular Infantry soldiers are remarkably similar yet the latter are defined only after the filtering process of the Recruiting Offices. Once in the TA he is, therefore, among people whom he understands and with whom he has much in common. His identity is accordingly these people. The fact that his gang is called B Company is a very secondary consideration.

The identity of the unit is the hard core of attenders and we must recognise this. Commanders shudder at the thought of having to take into account the likes and dislikes of this parallel group of power brokers, but you ignore them at your peril. Private Jones may be a troublemaker and a hopeless soldier, but if his presence guarantees that of five or six other souls are you going to sack him? It requires a level of tolerance and understanding to which most military men will find it hard to reconcile themselves. It certainly requires better man managers. The TA vision of the Army accepts the concept of discipline, but only as it relates to more extreme offences. This is the core of the volunteer ethos. Regular soldiers do things because ultimately they have to. TA soldiers do things because they want to. My experience in establishing a Company identity would be to set high standards for a unit, but to interpret them sensibly – and always, always remember the men who keep the others turning up – they are the unit, not you or the Permanent Staff.

We have always seemed to have a steady trickle of recruits. About two or three new faces each week turn up. If 25% make it through to being Phase 2 trained then this alone represents an annual intake of around 35 men. Not bad, but not enough and, in reality, only just enough to cover turnover of existing numbers anyway. Regular surges are necessary. To do this we have found the Bring a Friend night to be remarkably useful. Easy and simple to run, these sessions invariably bring in about a dozen or so interested parties. Each successive one shows a greater return as numbers steadily grow. Alongside this is the more formal recruiting night. Our last effort drew in over one hundred visitors of whom a very high proportion subsequently came back. Train these and then have a Bring a Friend night.

What brought our recruits in is less certain, as many of them find it hard to single out any single factor. National background campaigns undoubtedly help. The TV advert of "What are you doing this weekend" (Answer: "Getting wet through on Sennybridge") most certainly has an appeal which helps to create an image. But it was the local press that really did the trick, and I believe careful positioning of adverts (on the TV listings page) was crucial. I do not think anyone will forget the never-ending stream of people turning up at the TA Centre on that evening – certainly the RRTT will not. The role of RRTT is clearly important. We have the most enthusiastic and committed team one can imagine, but they must be supported by a training cycle that is fast without being simply going through the motions. However, it is only in the Platoons that training really takes off. Can we really call a soldier trained after Phase 2 recruit training at the Infantry Training Battalion, Strensall has been completed? Of course not. He is simply acquainted with military life at this stage. It is the camaraderie of the Platoon that will keep him in the TA, so get him there as quickly as possible. Accept the shortcomings of a fast training cycle and aim for the long haul in building the reliable soldier. To do that, you need to see him for at least 2 years to create the conditions that will get him to stay, not fully train him.

For the established soldier, we must train realistically and frequently. The TA is a habit for most people, so make it meaningful. Yet another weekend of dossing in the back of a 4 tonner prior to going to the Company bar does not qualify. Our experience is that the weekends planned along the lines of any Regular Army sub-unit training are remembered and appreciated. I would stress that this applies to Company level training. Whilst the need for Battalion weekends is appreciated, these are rarely well attended, despite the Red Weekend imposition (which requires 100% turnout), and are generally speaking not enjoyed. We have found that the old adage of giving the TA soldier something different every thirty minutes does not work. Giving them the chance to do something properly does.

Much of this article may seem to be a statement of the obvious. There is nothing worse than the smug pontificating of someone who has achieved something but without knowing how or why. We have no doubt that there will be lean times ahead, and that not every weekend will draw the numbers we would hope for. If we have learnt anything it is that recruiting in the TA is the long haul. It happened for us, and I hope that whatever Options brings that it happens for you.[15]

Two physically demanding events towards the end of 1993 showed how well, after only a year's existence, his Company was doing:

The Pill Regatta Fun in August was the brainchild of Corporal Stuart Cox, of the Company's Signals Detachment, who for a number of years had been wanting to arrange something that would link his local community, the village of Pill, with his exploits in the Territorial Army. As 1993 was the 350th Anniversary of the first siege of Bristol, Corporal Cox devised an event which not only provided publicity for B Company, but raised £200 for charity. It involved two teams of 8 men from 4 and 5 Platoons pulling two replica cannons (made by Corporal Cox) from the centre of Bristol along an arduous 9.5 mile route to the slipway at Shirehampton. Along the way, members of the local Army Cadet Force unit made the collection. When the two teams arrived at Shirehampton, and after the obligatory refreshment stop, they formed the finale to this year's Pill Regatta by racing each other (and the cannons) across the Avonmouth estuary to Pill. This part of the event proved to be quite spectacular, as Corporal Cox and Lieutenant Mark Garratt stage-managed a show of smoke, light and sound as the two teams crossed the river. Without doubt the show was well received by the general public. The event – which was started by the Lord Mayor of Bristol, Councillor John Shannon – gained considerable publicity on BBC Radio Bristol, an article on Galaxy Radio, a piece on HTV West, and a number of articles and photographs in the local press, including the Bristol Evening Post and the Western Daily Press.

B Company's involvement in this year's Cambrian Patrol was not conceived until after Annual Camp, and the team had only 5 weeks in which to get ready. It would have been a tall order for any Regular unit to prepare for the elitist British Army Patrolling Competition, but the Volunteers decided to go for it. Under the guidance of their SPSI WO2, Dave Ashford, they set about a training programme which was to fill two evenings a week and every weekend for those 5 weeks, which undoubtedly showed the commitment that the keen Volunteer can truly give. On 29 October the team, consisting of Lieutenantt Garratt, Corporal Weston, Lance Corporal Smith and Privates Begley, Belcher, Bracey, Demery and Slade, were packed and ready to go. None of them had taken part in the event before, so there was an element of the "fear of the unknown" as they travelled up to Brecon.

Not surprisingly, it proved to be arduous, with rough terrain, little sleep, heavy kit, and miles of tabbing. Fortunately there was no rain. However, the whole team completed the event and gained a creditable (though disappointing to the team) certificate for the wall of the TA Centre.[16]

The new C Company was based (with the Recce Platoon) at the Arle Road TA Centre in Cheltenham, and formed from one of the platoons of A Company. The Company Commander was Major Bill Quarterman, and 1 Glosters provided the first PSIs, WO2 Stapley and C/Sgt Bourne. Recruiting began immediately after Camp in 1992, and by the late spring of 1993 37 new members had been enlisted. A detached Platoon was soon started in Tewkesbury, a quite sizeable former market town in which there had been no TA presence since 1967, and which was thus a largely untapped recruiting area.

A major event to celebrate the Battalion's 25th anniversary took place in the former Hopton Barracks at Devizes (on the opposite side of the main road from Le Marchant Barracks) on 12 & 13 September 1992 – "The Wessex Tattoo". After a near 'saturation' publicity campaign, spreading far away from Devizes, the public were welcomed to the Barracks, for a modest entrance fee, between 10 and 5 on both days. The opening ceremony was performed by the 1 Wessex (Hampshire & Dorset) Band, the Band and Drums of 1 DERR, and the Band of the 3rd Bn The Royal Regiment of Wales. Thereafter, the many attractions included The Parachute Regiment's free-fall team, the Red Devils; 'Napoleonic' and 'modern' battles, the first involving 120 Volunteers in period uniform, and the second intended to show some of the skills needed by the modern-day TA; an obedience demonstration by MOD Police Dogs, and The Royal Signals' White Helmets Motorcycle Display Team; the 'firing' by 266 Battery RA from Bristol of "three large guns used in the Napoleonic wars" and a World

War II 25 pounder. A Military Marquee held stalls for model soldiers, military books and war-gaming, as well as an exhibition of a number of items from the DERR Regimental Museum in Salisbury. It was not, however, an entirely military event, as there were also a considerable number of 'house and garden' and other trade stands, a craft show, and a sports and leisure show. Unfortunately, poor weather meant that the number of visitors was appreciably smaller than had been hoped – but, although the event lost money, it was agreed that it nevertheless attracted good publicity for both the Battalion and the TA.

The Commanding Officers changed for the last time in the early autumn of 1993. The first one, John Sellars was a member of The Duke of Edinburgh's Royal Regiment, and, very 'tidily', Peter Cable handed over to another, Lieutenant Colonel Anthony Lake. By any standards, Peter Cable had done an extremely good job in the normal business of raising training skills, maintaining numbers, and generally keeping the Battalion in the forefront of the TA Infantry. On top of that, however, he had cheerfully and realistically borne the brunt of the never-ceasing and worrying flow of ideas and proposals about the future of the Battalion – and the award of the OBE was a very proper and popular recognition of all that he had done. His next posting was designed to widen even further his experience of soldiering – as an Instructor at the Canadian Army Staff College.

Anthony Lake found himself with the dreadful task of arranging and negotiating the details of 1 Wessex's side of the amalgamation with 2 Wessex – which can be found in Chapter 10 – and that undoubtedly took up much more of his time than actually running the Battalion. He was very lucky, therefore, that the ever-cheerful Paul Dutton of the Glosters, who had been the Adjutant in the early 1980s, returned in 1994 to be the last Training Major; needless to say, he was thoroughly well-versed in the idiosyncrasies of the TA, and he had the highest regard for the Volunteers. The final senior management team was completed by the extremely efficient Adjutant, Captain Huw Morgan-Owen of The Royal Regiment of Wales (another of the very rare 'infiltrations by outsiders'!), and the effervescent RSM, Tony Dixon, another Gloster for whom life was meant for living and no problem was unsolvable.

On 13 November 1993, the eve of Remembrance Sunday, the Battalion provided the TA Contingent at The British Legion's Festival of Remembrance in the Royal Albert Hall – and WO2 Poole, the Senior PSI in Gloucester, organised it all:

Early in October the Regimental Sergeant Major summoned me to Battalion Headquarters in Devizes. I drove there from Gloucester, wondering if this was to be the end of my Army career, and at the same time trying to remember if I had upset the Commanding Officer in some way. Luckily I had not, and he told me that 1 Wessex had been invited to provide a contingent of 1 Officer and 12 other ranks to participate in the Muster at the Royal Festival of Remembrance in the Royal Albert Hall; due to the fact that I had participated in this parade with 1 Glosters the previous year it seemed that I was deemed to be the ideal candidate to prepare the 1 Wessex contingent and travel with them to London.

On arriving back in Gloucester I rushed to my pamphlet library, located my drill manual, picked up my pace-stick and whilst reading through the different types of drill movements involved in the parade, I polished my pace-stick like it had never been polished before, telling myself that I could, either way, be famous after this parade.

Volunteers were invited from all over the Battalion, and eventually the RSM sent me a list of who would be representing it on this, for the Volunteers, once in a lifetime occasion. By this time pieces of information were making their way towards me from HQ London District, telling me where I was to report, and when, and a number of administrative tasks which had to be carried out before leaving for London. Weekly rehearsals took place in a Primary School in Gloucester, the stairway in the school being the only one we would find that resembled the stairs at the Royal Albert Hall. The whole of the contingent worked extremely hard, and soon the drill movements started to look like drill movements. Uniforms were tailored. Boots were bulled. Brass was polished and a general sense of pride in bearing and turnout was reached by every member of the team. In the meantime accommodation and transport were booked, and we were ready to hit the lights of London.

Friday the 12th November arrived and the minibus was loaded with all the equipment we needed to see us through our lonely mission.

We set off for Hounslow, which was to be our place of residence for the next night, and changed into working uniform ready for our first rehearsal at the Royal Albert Hall at 1900hrs. Into the centre of London we raced, trying to reach the Royal Albert Hall in time, and found that we were the only ones there. I started to wonder if I had got the date right when the RSM of London District arrived and I duly introduced myself, looking up at the 6' 8" giant in front of me wondering if he had snow on the top of his head.

The other TA units started to arrive and the rehearsal began. I stood to the side as people fell down the stairs, tripped one another up and lost the step. The RSM had a fit about anything and everyone that moved – so I closed my eyes and said to myself that it would be all right on the night. When we got back to Hounslow, I informed my team of my displeasure, but put it down to the fact that everyone was nervous and reminded them that they were the selected few.

The next morning we handed back our accommodation, loaded the minibus and again set off into the centre of London for a full dress rehearsal. Everyone changed and inspected, the rehearsal began and I sat to one side waiting for our contingent to enter the arena. Then those famous words "The Territorial Army" came out over the microphone, the band played, and I again closed my eyes, praying for it to go right. Like a squad of Guardsmen, they marched down the stairs, across the area and up the stairs in front of the band, and stood in front of their respective seats. There they were as proud as punch, and I knew they had got it together.

After completing two performances that day we climbed into the minibus for the return trip to Gloucester. Every member of the team was silent and I knew they had all been deeply affected by the occasion. To watch the event on TV is emotional enough, but to participate is certainly one of the most moving experiences anyone could possibly have, and it will be a long time before the members of my team forget their parade at the Royal Albert Hall.[17]

The major event at the beginning of 1994 was the Battalion's experience, as part of 1 Mechanised Brigade, of high intensity warfare during Exercise First Crusade, the largest armoured exercise to take place on Salisbury Plain for many years. In the course of it, the GOC of the 3rd (United Kingdom) Armoured Division, Major General Hugh Pike DSO, MBE visited the Battalion, and, in what might well have been a unique little ceremony, presented both Regimental Medical Officers, Major Nigel Salisbury and Major Liz Madigan, with their Territorial Decorations, as well as several Territorial Efficiency Medals.

In July, an assorted, but relatively experienced, 19 members of the Battalion, drawn from several Companies, went to Canada for six week to join The Royal Welsh Fusiliers for their Battle Group's Exercise Pond Jump West on the huge Fort Wainwright training area in Alberta. The programme was the usual routine for working over there – acclimatisation and build-up training, followed by adventure training and a battle run:

> The adventure training package took place in the Rockies. The heat of the Alberta plain was replaced by clouds, rain and the chill of the mountains. The four and a half day package included ice climbing, canoeing, white water rafting, mountain biking, hiking and glacial walking….. Bears were commonplace and had a nasty habit of turning up at the campsite in search of food.
>
> We all returned to Wainwright safely, and in time to have a day's build-up before embarking on the company battle run – which turned out to be the highlight of Pond Jump West. Two operations stand out. The first was a live firing platoon attack on a Soviet style trench system protected by many obstacles. A successful breach of the wire obstacles was achieved by using bangalore torpedoes. Once the break-in was achieved, my lead section, Cpl Chesters and his aptly named Devil Dogs, soon had a firm foothold allowing the rest of the platoon to clear the system using grenades on all the positions leading off the main communications trench. A counter attack on the objective was only partially repulsed with 94mm light anti-tank weapons, and we were ordered to withdraw to a helicopter landing site with all our casualties. Following that, the company assault on Artillery Hill overlooking the border lake was preceded by an 8km night infiltration to a line of departure with artillery, Milan anti-tank guided weapons, sustained fire machine guns and our platoon in fire support. The remainder of the company, under Major Kilvert-Jones, carried out a lake-crossing, and proceeded to assault their objectives. Major Kilvert-Jones was killed off after trying to walk on water, but miraculously came back to

life later to lead a successful assault on what turned out to be a very big hill.

That was followed by the Battle Group exercise, and last, but certainly not least, R & R in Edmonton. The verdict was that "the whole experience was really quite incredible, and everybody thoroughly enjoyed themselves".[18]

Annual Camp in September 1994 was the Battalion's last. Exercise Orient Express I in Belgium was intended to ensure that 1 Wessex would be declared fit for its prestigious and challenging new role as part of the Allied Rapid Reaction Corps. It involved all the aspects of the TA 'going to war' on the continent – the mobilization drills, and the transporting of 55 vehicles and mountains of equipment and stores across the North Sea – and some very tough training for the whole of the fortnight. It was good to use new training areas – often on 'private' land – and, among other achievements, 32 potential NCOs and 40 recruits were qualified. Two, as-seen-on-the-ground, reports are in Chapter 11.

The planning and running of the practical part of the Lieutenant to Captain Promotion Examinations for TA officers was something normally undertaken by a Regular brigade headquarters with the help of a Regular battalion. Being asked to do one was therefore probably a unique accolade for the Battalion. It was held within a few weeks after the return from Camp, on Roundway Down, the scene of a Civil War battle in 1643, north of Devizes – and history repeated itself as the 42 candidates had to plan a company attack on the same ground. It was a ten-hour day, and involved 25 examiners – all from within the Battalion, and all of whom naturally had to be fully briefed on their tasks. Paul Dutton, who had been given the task of planning virtually everything and then controlling the day, "worked his fingertips to the bone" writing instructions and scenarios – and in typical TA fashion, the use of the land was negotiated by the Operations Officer, Captain Robin Tournay, a Land Agent in real life, who "just happened" to know its owner. The weather turned out to be definitely inappropriate for that sort of event, for, on the Sunday, early morning fog made it virtually impossible to see any of the objectives, and then a strong wind threatened to blow away not only all the maps and papers but the examiners' tents too. Not unexpectedly, the candidates perpetrated a number of dreadful howlers, but by and large the standard of knowledge was high, and passes were awarded to most of them – although not, somewhat embarrassingly for him, to a Regular subaltern who came for a 'trial run'. In addition to the examiners, a considerable number of Volunteers from right across the Battalion were involved, and high praise was received from the Regular Army.

It was very sensibly decided to carry on a full programme of activities and training right up to the Regulars' block leave in August 1995 – 'business as usual' – to maintain everyone's interest and skills, and minimise the wastage that the uncertainty and disruption would inevitably cause. Over the 1994/95 winter, and right into the summer, therefore, everything continued with almost more than the customary vigour – and a tremendous amount was achieved. As for 'activities', in January a team from Headquarter Company did well in the Tough Guy Challenge at a previously unheard-of training area, the Tettenhall Horse Sanctuary, near Wolverhampton – a "punishing multi-terrain" run of approximately 13 miles (perhaps better titled Tough Guy & Girl Challenge, as mixed bathing arrangements were apparently available at the finish); and later in the same month the Company also won the South West District TA Orienteering Championships for the seventh time in ten years. Over 50 members of the Battalion participated in the Ypres Marches (raising £1,400 for local charities); there was a canoeing expedition for the Recce Platoon, under Captain David Crozier, to the south of France; and there were inshore and offshore sailing weekends around the Solent, as well as hill walking in Wales; finally a group of Volunteers from HQ Company spent a week-end renovating the badge of The Wiltshire Regiment, one of the eight of World War I British and Commonwealth Army formations and units which still remained visible – there were originally over 30 – carved on a chalk hillside at Fovant, between Salisbury and Shaftesbury.

On the 'serious' side, both Battalion and the Company Headquarters were put to test on the battle-group trainer at Warminster – after which the directing staff commented that the Battalion's procedures were better than those of some Regular battalions that went through their hands; over the late autumn of 1994 and into the early spring of 1995, the RSM, Tony Dixon, and then he and the Training Major together, organised a progressive and demanding programme of field firing:

> The Battalion's package.....saw a progression from the range work at Camp, through platoon attacks in October and November, to a demanding company group attack with 81mm mortar support in February at Sennybridge. (There, the TA Quartermaster, Capt Richard Butt, and his team erected a 12ft by 12ft tent to feed the Battalion. This was immediately christened 'Dick's Big Top'. However, when it became clear that he had sited it on the edge of a marsh it was renamed 'Dick's Poolside Diner'). The culmination of this training was Exercise Bold Wyvern, a battalion live-firing attack near Imber in March, watched by the new Brigade Commander – who, at the end, gave the marvellous news that the Battalion had been declared Fit For Role. The Exercise proved that the Battalion was indeed fit for its role in the Allied Rapid Reaction Corps, and that the recruiting and training programmes with that aim had been successful.[19]

Although Bold Wyvern would have been a 'good way to finish', the hard work did not end there:

> 1 Wessex ran an Executive Stretch over the weekend 24/25 April. Although the CO had done one before, much of the regular element of the management team had changed and, after the recent restructuring of the Battalion, a fair proportion of the TA element was new too. It was, therefore, not only the executives who approached the weekend with a degree of trepidation!
>
> Rather than have a series of isolated stands, an attempt was made to produce a theme which ran as a thread throughout the weekend. Finding one that was relevant and unmilitary without being farcical proved difficult. In the event a degree of all three crept in, and it was to the credit of the participants that they entered into the spirit of the weekend with such gusto.
>
> After kit issue, an initial brief and a quick introduction to map reading on the Friday evening, participants were presented with their first challenge, an abseil from the top floor. Despite the height and darkness, there were no refusals, and a few additional volunteers (including the Western Wessex TAVRA Secretary), but some did manage to come down head-first.

Arriving on Salisbury Plain in the early hours of Saturday morning, the executives had their first experience of a night navex, most finding it somewhat more difficult than the classroom theory had suggested. Not many found time for more than a few hours sleep in dubiously weatherproof bashas before being awoken at first light by the Royal Navy Sea King helicopter which flew them to a classic Army breakfast in the field. After a "battle picture" brief, groups were given the opportunity to select items of kit, some useful some not, which they felt might prove useful in the trials ahead. For the staff "in the know", it proved challenging to keep a straight face watching a group arguing over the merits of extra ration packs against radio sets.

Set off on a course around the wonders of the Salisbury Plain Training Area, the groups visited stands which tested their powers of communication, leadership, initiative, memory, team-work and, when confronted with "Benny", the deaf mute driver to take them on the longest leg of the circuit or "Hawkeye" the blind helicopter pilot, their powers of patience.

By Saturday evening, exhausted through lack of sleep and physical exercise, preparations and recces for the inevitable river crossing with a self-built bridge began. To their credit, all completed the task early on Sunday morning, helped near the end by the adrenalin buzz from the hovering Sea King waiting to take the luckless executives to their final hurdle, the run and assault course.

The executives were unanimous in their appreciation of the exercise (but only after they had returned to Devizes, showered and were wrapping themselves around a pint of Wadworth's 6X!). However, from the Battalion's viewpoint the Exercise was very rewarding to run. It was different from the normal training weekend, but more importantly an insight into the qualities present in every individual. We, in the Army, pride ourselves on strength of character, leadership, determination, initiative and so on. As a result we develop the feeling that we have a monopoly of such attributes – but Executive Stretch proves that we do not. They are latent in everyone – well, most people to some degree or another. It is merely that we, in our daily lives, have the chance to exercise and develop them for which we should be very grateful. Running Exercise Executive Stretch was challenging and worthwhile for those who took part, but it was equally fulfilling for those who ran it.[20]

After that there were the notorious Battle Run at the Nuclear,

Biological and Chemical Defence Centre at Porton Down on the edge of Salisbury Plain; practicing fighting-in-built-up-areas at Longmoor, near Aldershot; Company weekends on the Plain, and then the last of the 'wars' against 2 Wessex.

In addition to all that, before the final Farewell Parade in Devizes, there was one last high-profile event – the provision of a Royal Guard of Honour for H M The Queen when she visited Headquarters, Land Command at Erskine Barracks, Wilton on 30 June. An enormous amount of practice was put in, with a full dress rehearsal five days earlier. The Guard was commanded by Major Bill Quarterman, and the Ensign for the Queen's Colour was Lieutenant Mark Garrett. Unfortunately, although there are a few photographs, no paperwork other than local newspaper reports about the occasion seems to have survived, and exactly who the NCOs of the Colour Party, the second subaltern, and the senior NCOs of the two half-Guards were remains a mystery. There was, no doubt, what is specified in an amazingly vague manner in Queen's Regulations as "a sufficiency of other ranks"[21] – although, as the parade was on a Thursday, some employers were unwilling to give "sufficient" Volunteers in the Battalion the day off (or those who would like to have taken part lived too far away to make it practical); the numbers were therefore made up with 23 from the Second Battalion and 15 from 5RGJ. To judge from the photographs, Her Majesty found no fault with the Guard!

Everyone, from Anthony Lake downwards, was determined that 1 Wessex would end its life as it had lived it: professionally, cheerfully and with great style. The Farewell Parade on 17 September would mark its passing, celebrate its achievements, and publicise its transition to 2 RGBW. Like the Presentation of Colours 22 years before, it was not to be a simple affair, and, as several of the PSIs who acted as drill instructors were heard to comment during the rehearsals, the drill was ambitious:

> As well as the usual elements of inspection, march past and so on, there was to be a drumhead service and a ceremony to pass the Liberty of Devizes from 1 Wessex to the RGBW. It was decided to parade in No 2 Dress – no mean feat given that most TA soldiers are not issued with it. The administration was also ambitious. Families, friends,

former members of the Battalion and civic dignitaries from across the three counties and Bristol were invited. Three spectator stands were acquired and erected; everyone attending was to be catered for at lunch – there were so many of them that five separate places in the town centre had to be used, and cooks and staff had to be arranged for all of them; and finally, the Battalion had to be ferried from Le Marchant into the town.

Work started, uniforms were ordered and tailors were busy. Major Phil Hall, the Quartermaster, and his team worked at full stretch. PSIs, as acting Drill Instructors throughout the Battalion, and led by the RSM, were practising every drill night, and (as is always the case) he took personal charge of the Colour Party's drill. There was a full rehearsal weekend early in September – and the morning devoted to sword drill for the officers was particularly memorable: WO2 Walker, a PSI from 1 RGBW, who took it, had obviously been specially selected by the RSM for his patience and ability to keep a straight face.

The Battalion Orderly Room, particularly the TA Chief Clerk, WO2 Stoddart, were submerged in a welter of paperwork: invitations, tickets, car passes, orders of service, menus and a splendid souvenir programme – all of which, it seemed, had to be approved in draft by everyone! The Town Council was particularly helpful. Not only had it agreed to transfer the Liberty to the RGBW (the first civic honour to be granted to it), but it sponsored the day, gave the use of its premises, and its parks department transformed the Market Square and the stands into a colourful arena. The Royal Wessex Yeomanry and the Royal Wiltshire Yeomanry Squadrons of the Royal Yeomanry provided sterling workers who, on the day, erected the stands, received guests, ran the car parking and much else. The former RQMS "McGilly" Gillingham, a builder, was brought in – you never retired from 1 Wessex! – to calm Major Hall's fears about the erection of the stands, which were a cross between a Meccano set and a Rubik's cube; at one point, the Quartermaster was heard to declare that the pieces left unused in the box were obviously spare! On the final rehearsal, the REME displayed their usual versatility: Lance Corporal Badman had made a set of rests to keep the Colours firmly on the Drums, and when they needed to be removed for the photographs, he produced a screwdriver from one of his No. 2 Dress Uniform pockets. The huge Battalion photograph – getting everyone 'sized', and the cooks in their 'whites' placed with mathematical accuracy in different places in the rows – took forever! The cooks, under the always indefatigable TA Quartermaster, Capt Richard Butt and WO2 AJ Smith, were working flat out.

On the day, the Battalion fell in and marched-on behind the 1 Wessex (Hampshire & Dorset) Band, to the marches of the TA Battalions of the old county Regiments from which The Wessex Regiment had been formed in 1967 – and it was with relief that they found that the dimensions of the parade area in the Market Square matched those marked out on the square at Le Marchant for the rehearsals by the RSM. On parade were four Guards – each made up of a Guard Commander, three other officers and 60 NCOs and soldiers – the Colour Party, and the Band. There was a quite marvellous turn-out of families and friends, former members of the Battalion, and many distinguished guests, who included the Lords Lieutenant of Wiltshire and Gloucestershire, Field Marshal Sir Roland Gibbs and Mr Henry Elwes; General Wilsey, the C-in-C Land Command; the GOC of 4 Division; Lieutenant General Sir Maurice Johnson (who would become the next Lord Lieutenant of Wiltshire); Generals Mike Walsh and Robin Grist; The Reverend Victor Dobbin, the Chaplain General and Brigadier Joe Starling; and Brigadiers John Patrick (145 (Home Counties) Brigade), BC Plummer (1 Mechanised Brigade) and Christopher Wolverson (43 (Wessex) Brigade), and the Secretary of the Wessex Reserve Forces & Cadets Association, Brigadier Bruce Jackman – almost all with their wives. A large crowd of the people of the town gathered, there were two television crews, and photographers everywhere; Major Mark Boden, the parade 2IC on the right flank, nearly removed the ear of a particularly keen one who leapt forward to get a better view during the general salute.

A procession of the The Mayor of Devizes, Councillor IRP Hopkins with his acolytes, Town Councillors and the VIP guests followed the Battalion into the Square. The author, as the Honorary Colonel, accompanied the Mayor on his inspection; the Drums having been piled and the Colours placed on them, the Battalion's Padre, The Reverend Simon Wilkinson, took the short but fitting Service, with the Chaplin General giving an address; the Mayor presented General Grist with the Liberty scroll; and there was then a Fly Past by helicopters from 666 Squadron, Army Air Corps (Volunteers). From the moment that the CO asked the Mayor for permission to march the Battalion off parade for the last time, not only were there few dry eyes in the spectators' stands, but a good many Volunteers had more than lumps in their throats too. When the Band began the Regimental March, *The Farmer's Boy*, all the spectators, so it seemed, joined in with the words – in many ways the most moving moment of the whole parade. The Battalion halted outside the Town Hall, where the Colours were marched inside to *Auld Lang Syne*. Everyone, including everyone on parade, then dispersed to the various lunches.[22]

On the following day, Part One Orders consisted of just two messages – from the Honorary Colonel and the CO:

> My warmest congratulations and thanks to everyone who was involved for making our final Parade yesterday such a splendid occasion. Nobody can have watched it without being most impressed, and our principal guests and the former members were not only full of praise for the excellent drill and turnout, but deeply moved by the marvellous sense of pride in the Battalion which came over so strongly. The organisation of the day was superb, and in every respect the Battalion showed itself off supremely well. The Farmers Boy is unlikely ever to be sung like that again!
>
> The 28 years of our existence and our parting, could not have been celebrated more fittingly or in better style. It now remains for all those who will become part of The 2nd (Volunteer) Battalion, The Royal Gloucestershire, Berkshire and Wiltshire Regiment to make it, as I believe we have been, the best Battalion in the TA – and all of us who are not coming with you wish it and you the very best of good fortune.

————————

> I wish to record my deepest thanks to all of you who, on or off the Farewell Parade, gave your best to leave firmly with all those who watched it the clear message that 1 Wessex departs, as it has so often performed in all its previous roles and tasks, with the highest professional standards achievable by the Army. No one present in Devizes Market Place on Sunday will ever forget the greatness of 1 Wessex and nor should they. Thank you for making it so.

Finally and properly, there were splendid and memorable Dinners

of the Officers' and WOs & Sergeants' Messes – and it is believed
that total decorum was maintained throughout both of them. The
Warrant Officers' and Sergeants' Mess held theirs in the Devizes Corn
Exchange on 2 September. The Officers' one was in the Devizes Town
Hall on 30 September, the very last day of the Battalion's existence;
the Honorary Colonel and his predecessor, with 108 Volunteer and
Permanent Staff officers, past and present, attended the latter, with
the RSM, Tony Dixon, as their only guest. The repeated playings of
The Farmer's Boy were acclaimed as the best ever, and the marching
out of the Colours for the last time at midnight was one of the most
poignant moments that anyone there had ever experienced.

On 6 October 1995, the two Battalions of The Wessex Regiment
formally amalgamated and became the 2nd (Volunteer) Battalion The
Royal Gloucestershire, Berkshire & Wiltshire Regiment.[23]

To adapt a remark once made by a B Company soldier:
"1 Wessex – good, wa'n'it?!"[24]

---

[1] From a cutting in a newspaper lacking any form of identification.
[2] *Western Wessex Newsletter* 1990.
[3] *Ibid.*
[4] *DERRJ*, 1990.
[5] BB, Winter 1989.
[6] On his appointment in October 1987 he 'received' 10 jobs: Quartermaster, Regimental
     Messing Officer, Unit Equipment Manager, Unit Safety Officer, Unit Project Officer,
     HASN Officer, COSHH Officer, Unit Road Safety Officer, OC REME Section and
     OC Catering Platoon!
[7] *Western Wessex Newsletter* 1990.
[8] *DERRJ* 1991.
[9] Tim Shapland's father, Major General Peter Shapland, it will be remembered, had been
     responsible for one of the very early papers on the 'bringing up to date' of the pre-1967
     TA – and it was very appropriate that there should have been a Shapland, as it were, at
     the end of 1 Wessex's lifetime as well as at its beginning.
[10] *D&DRJ*, Autumn 1990.
[11] BB, Summer 1990.
[12] *Ibid*, Winter 1991.

[13] *Ibid.*

[14] unknown.

[15] *Western Wessex Newsletter, 1995.*

[16] *Western Wessex Newsletter, 1994.*

[17] It consisted of Lieutenant Mark Garrett, WO2 Poole, WO2 Munday, Colour Sergeant Kuszak, Sergeants Yemm and Vizor, Corporal Kavanagh, W/Corporal Penfold, Lance Corporals Ball, Edgar and Hill, and Privates Attwood, Gale, Gorman and Newman.

[18] Adapted from an article by 2/Lieutenant R M A Kirkup in *S & D*, Winter 1994.

[19] *S&D*, Summer 1995.

[20] *Western Wessex Newsletter, 1994.*

[21] Chapter 8, para 8.038.

[22] Slightly adapted from an article in *S & D*, Winter1995.

[23] In yet another reorganization of the TA in 1999, however, 2 RGBW and other TA battalions in the South of England were split between two new regiments, The Rifle Volunteers (which 'absorbed' the former 1 Wessex elements) and The Royal Rifle Volunteers (with took in the former 2 Wessex elements). The final, ironic, twist in the story was that in February 2007 all the Regular regiments involved in the story of 1 Wessex – D & D, RGBW (as it were, representing its predecessors, the Glosters, the Berkshires and the Wiltshires) and The Light Infantry – joined together to become the 1st Battalion The Rifles, a new large Regular regiment in The Light Division. The Rifle Volunteers became the 6th Battalion The Rifles, and The Royal Rifle Volunteers its 7th Battalion.

[24] See Report on the 1977 Camp in Chapter 7.

APPENDIX 1

THE FARMER'S BOY

The sun had set beyond yon hill,
Across yon dreary moor,
When weary and lame a lad there came,
up to the farmer's door,
"Can you tell oi were oi might find
some one who'll me employ
To plow and sow and reap and mow
and be a farmer's boy – and be a farmer's boy?"

"My father's left my mother with
ten children large and small,
and what is worse for my mother dear
I'm the largest of them all.
Though little I am I'll labour hard,
if I could find employ,
To plow and sow and reap and mow
and be a farmer's boy – and be a farmer's boy"

The farmer's wife cried, "Try the lad –
let him no longer seek,
"Yes father dear", the daughter cried
as tears rolled down her cheeks,
"For those who seek tis hard to find
labour or employ,
Don't let him go but make him stay
and be a farmer's boy – and be a farmer's boy".

The farmer's boy grew up a man,
the dear old couple died,
they left the lad the farm they had
and their daughter for his bride,
The lad that was, the farm now has,
and he often thinks with joy,
And he bless'd the day he came that way,
to be a farmer's boy – to be a farmer's boy.

———————

APPENDIX 2 - Part 1

SENIOR OFFICER & NCO APPOINTMENTS 1967-1995

(TA Officers are shown with ranks at end of their service)

Honorary Colonels

Colonel J W Weld OBE TD JP   1967-1970
(Late The Dorset Regiment; HM Lord Lieutenant of Dorset)
Colonel W Q Roberts OBE DSO* MVO TD JP DL   1970-1975
(Late The Somerset Light Infantry & The Dorset Regiment)
Major General G C A Gilbert CB MC   1975-1981
(Late The Parachute Regiment)
Major General M J H Walsh CB CBE DSO DL   1981-1989
(Late The Parachute Regiment)
Colonel M S Lee-Browne CBE TD* DL MA   1989-1995
(Late The Wessex Regiment)

Commanding Officers

Lieutenant Colonel J A Sellars MBE, DERR   1967-1968
Lieutenant Colonel P R B Freeland, D & D   1968-1970
Lieutenant Colonel M S Lee-Browne OBE TD, Wessex   1970-1973
Lieutenant Colonel L C Tremellen, DERR   1973-1976
Lieutenant Colonel W E C Coppen-Gardner MC, R Hamps   1976-1978
Lieutenant Colonel J G T Southwood, R Hamps   1978-1981
Lieutenant Colonel T B Dutton OBE Bsc, Glosters   1981-1983
Lieutenant Colonel P B Goddard, Light Infantry   1983-1986
Lieutenant Colonel R J Pook, D & D   1986-1988
Colonel G E Brady, Wessex   1988-1990
Lieutenant Colonel P J Cable OBE, Glosters   1990-1993
Lieutenant Colonel A P B Lake, DERR   1993-1995

Seconds-in-Command

Major G E Fulford
Lieutenant Colonel (Brevet) J D Roberts TD**
Major P J M Whiteman TD*
Lieutenant Colonel (Brevet) A F Ravenhill OBE TD*
Lieutenant Colonel (Brevet) F W Fifield TD*
Lieutenant Colonel A M Grazebrook TD*
Major M S OF Cook TD
Lieutenant Colonel S A Durant TD (previously Adjt, 2IC HQ Coy & OC B Coy, Swindon)
Major I J G Cunningham
Colonel M J Boden TD LLB

Adjutants

Captain E G Churcher, R Hamps
Captain N J Sutton, DERR
Captain R J Shrimpton, R Hamps
Captain M M A Tulloch, WFR
Captain J G Dewar, R Hamps
Captain S W J Saunders, DERR
Captain P W L Hughes, R Hamps
Captain P E O'R-B Davidson- Houston, DERR
Captain R P Dutton, Glosters
Captain J D Wort BSc, DERR (later OC B Coy, Swindon)
Captain J M C Rylands, DERR
Captain G E Woodcock, Glosters (later OC A Coy)

Training Majors

Major R R Jury, D & D	1967-1968
Major M M A Gilmore, Glosters	1968-1969
Major R M C Wilson, DERR	1969-1970
Major J D Redding, DERR	1970-1972
Major R A F Jarman, Glosters	1972-1975
Major C P Aylin, DERR	1975-1977
Major P M Baxter, DERR	1977-1979
Majpr R D Turrall, D & D	1979-1981
Major N P H Woodward, R Hamps	1981
Lieutenant Colonel P Bradley MBE, DERR	1981-1983
Major H Doodson, R Hamps	1986-1987
Major R Fenning-Mills, Staffords	1987-1988
Major M J Cornwell OBE, DERR	1989-1991
Major E D Brown, Glosters	1991-1992
Major S J Oxlade, Glosters	1992-1993
Major M E Nurick, Glosters	1993-1994
Major R P Dutton, Glosters	1994-1995

Quartermasters 1 (Regular)

Lieutenant Colonel P E Allen, DERR
Major J W Smythe BEM, Glosters
Major J J Price, DERR
Major T Lewis, WFR
Major J Ryan, RRW
Major R S Pollard, D & D
Major C Burnett, R Hamps
Major W R Stafford MBE, DERR
Major P Goss, Glosters
Major G E Thomas MBE, R Hamps (later PSAO B Coy, Winchester)
Major R W Coleman MBE, R Hamps
Major P H Hall MBE, Glosters

Adjutants (continued)

Captain J O'Brien, Cheshire
Captain J H Morgan-Owen, RRW

Assistant Adjutants

Captain G(ill) E Sharpe (also IO)
Captain K(aren) Walcroft

Regimental Medical Officers

Major P W Tucker MBE TD* MB BS LRCP MRCS, RAMC (1967-1982); Civilian MO (1983-1995)
Major E A Madigan (Mrs Durant) TD MB BS LRCP MCRS, RAMC
Major N S Salisbury TD MB BS LRCP; RAMC

Regimental Administrative Officers

Captain J F Foreman
Lieutenant Colonel M J Cornwell OBE, DERR

Chaplains (all RAChD)

Captain The Reverend J F Parkinson TD
Captain Monseigneur E Peach (RC)
Captain Monseigneur M P Reid (RC)
Major The Reverend S J Wilkinson TD BA
Major The Reverend A Woods

Paymasters, etc

Major J G Greatrix, RAPC
Major P G Marriott, RAPC
Major B C Staig TD (previously D Company)
Captain A F Rogers MBE, RAPC
Lieutenant G Shapley
WO2 Lloyd (Personal/Finance Clerk)
Sergeant Kerr (Personel/Finance Clerk)

Quartermasters 2 (TA)
Captain L K J Courtenay
Major J J Loftus MBE TD (also A Coy Arms Storeman)
Captain F G Sheppard MBE TEM*
Captain R H Butt TD

Regimental Sergeant Majors
WO1 W I Sutherland, D&D   1967-1968
WO1 R E Bryant, R Hamps   1968-1970
WO1 E Ellis, D&D   1970-1971
WO1 M J W Chappell, Glosters   1971-1974
WO1 J H Wheeler MM (also Queen's Medal), R Hamps 1974-1976
WO1 M S O'F Cook, D&D   1976-1978
WO1 P Goss, Glosters   1978-1980
WO1 D Wiggins, DERR   1981-1982
WO1 M W Gibson, R Hamps   1982-1983
WO1 P J Mullins MBE, DERR   1983-1985
WO1 Long, DERR   1985-1986
WO1 A P Morgan, D&D (later PSAO, D Coy, Poole)   1986-1987
WO2 N Minty LS&GCM, DERR   1987-1988
WO1 P Andrews, R Hamps   1989-1991
WO1 J L Clay, R Hamps   1991-1993
WO1 A R Dixon, Glosters   1993-1995

Bandmasters
WO1 R Alberry (Hants & Dorset Band)
WO1 ("Dippie") Dyer (Devon Band)
WO1 R Hibbs (Devon Band)
WO1 A W Johnson (Hants & Dorset Band)
WO1 E F ("Nobby") Knowles MSM TEM* (Devon Band)

TA Public Information Officer/Unit Press Officer
Captain M F Glynn
Captain S(ally) P Coulthard

Regimental Quartermaster Sergeants (Chief Clerks TA)
WO2 Burton TEM
WO2 A J Eldridge TEM
WO2 Mortimer TEM
WO2 H Mower TEM*
WO2 ("McGillycuddy") Gillingham TEM
WO2 A W C Mundy (NRPS) TEM*

Chief Clerks & Orderly Room C/Sgts (Regular & TA)
WO2 P Barrett BEM
C/Sergeant A D Breen, Glosters
WO2 B P Crowther TEM
WO2 Ficke, DERR
WO2 P Habgood, DERR
WO2 M Hooley TEM
C/Sergeant J Lindsay
WO2 G Maddox TEM*
WO2 M Merchant, Glosters
WO2 M A Needs TEM*
WO2 C M Nicholson, DERR
WO2 B D Pickford, Glosters
WO2 B R Stoddart TEM
WO2 B W Taylor, R Hamps
WO2 V R Townley, Glosters
C/Sergeant M Wright BEM, late Royal Military Police (NRPS)

Bandmasters (continued)

WO1 J Parrott LS&GCM MSM TEM* (Hants & Dorset Band)

WO1 J Quayle (Devon Band)

Lieutenant WN M Rogerson MBE (Director of Music Hants & Dorset Band)

Lieutenant W Roe (Director of Music - Hants & Dorset Band)

Senior Band NCOs

Sergeant GD Hart TEM (Devon Band)

WO2 Hennin TEM (H&D B)

WO2 M Smith TEM (H&D B)

S/Sergeant Smith TEM (H&D B)

Sergeant Strange TEM (H&D B)

Sergant Thompson TEM (H&D B)

Drum Majors

WO2 D Beer TEM

WO2 G W Kerswill TEM*

WO2 W Morris

WO2 M J Munday TEM*

WO2 Thornton

WO2 P Veal

CO's Drivers

L/Cpl D Rice, D&D

L/Cpl Jones, DERR

L/Cpl Tucker, DERR

L/Cpl Atkins, RHamps

L/Cpl P Watts

L/Cpl D Middleton, RGBW

L/Cpl C E Porter, Glosters

APPENDIX 2 - Part 2
SENIOR COMPANY APPOINTMENTS

1. Wherever possible, Company Commanders, PSAOs, CSMs and SPSIs are listed in date order – but all other names are given in alphabetical order.
2. Volunteers promoted within their Companies, but who did not move to another, are shown in their most senior known rank held there. Where a Volunteer served in more than one capacity or Company, their names are generally given in their last known appointment.
3. Support Platoon PSIs, although latterly in HQ Company, are, as far as possible, shown with the Rifle Company by which their Platoon was administered.

A Company - Gloucester, Bristol & Cheltenham (1967 - 1995)
(All PSIs Glosters unless otherwise shown)

Company Commanders

Major M S Lee-Browne TD (later Bn 2IC, CO & Hon Col)
Major P J M Whiteman TD*
Major D C Ryan TD (previously IO)
Major A M Grazebrook TD* (later OC HQ Coy & Bn 2IC)
Major R D O'Neill TD (also OC HQ Coy)
Major P J Stanley TD* (prev. C Coy, Dorchester)
Major P I W Pay
Major G E C Woodcock (previously Adjutant)
Major W J C Quarterman (also C Coy, Cheltenham & Newbury)

Seconds-in Command & Support Platoon Commanders

Captain J C Cook (later 2IC HQ Coy)
Captain D J Crozier (Recce Pl)
Lieutenant J A Fletcher
Captain D R Gardner
Captain M S Garrett (later B Coy, Bristol)
Captain N W S Goulding (later C Coy, Newbury)
Captain S C R Griffiths (Recce Pl)

Company Sergeant Majors

WO2 R J Keitley TEM*
WO2 D J Pack TEM*
WO2 H W Marriott TEM*
WO2 K M Reade MBE TEM* (later OC RRTT)
WO2 D A Mears TEM**
WO2 M Yorath TEM
WO2 N Attwood BEM TEM*
WO2 L D Garton TEM (also HQ Coy)
WO2 R D Heatley TEM (later OC HQ Coy)
WO2 J Russell TEM*
WO2 R W Kuczaj TEM (previously Anti-tank Pl, HQ Coy)

Warrant Officers

WO2 P R Blake TEM (Asslt Pnr Pl)
WO2 "Para" Chambers

Permanent Staff Administrative Officers

Captain R Wallace MBE, late RTR
Captain R Mawdesley BEM, late REME
Captain E W Fry, late Glosters (later C Coy, Cheltenham) NRPS

SPSI WO2s

WO2 M J W Chappell
WO2 J Alderman, R Hamps
WO2 B J Murphy
WO2 P J Garland
WO2 K F Fisher
WO2 J Price
WO2 J W Hyde LS&GCM (Second tour)
WO2 R B Wright
WO2 I J Davies
WO2 A R Dixon (later RSM)
WO2 B A D Phillips
WO2 N A Poole
WO2 M Cornock

2ICs & Sp Pl Commanders (continued)
Captain JE Hunt
Captain M ("3 Zs") Idaziaszczyk (Anti-Tank Pl; later 2IC C Coy, Cheltenham)
Captain P J James (Mortar Pl)
Captain R N Lawrence (later OC B Coy, Swindon)
Captain R G Lawson-Lee BA (Recce Pl)
Captain P Mayne
Captain M J Rollin (Anti-tank Pl)
Major R Smith (Recce Pl)
Captain D Tucker (LI)

Subalterns
Lieutenant J C Adby (also B Coy, Bristol)
2nd Lieutenant P Black
2nd Lieutenant L A J Brennan (later C Coy, Cheltenham)
2nd Lieutenant R N Blunt
2nd Lieutenant M Cassidy
2nd Lieutenant M Duff
Lieutenant G Fox
Lieutenant A Hadfield
Lieutenant R C S Hall
Lieutenant T F Hand
2nd Lieutenant A J S Henry
Lieutenant R N Hungerford
Lieutenant P R Jarrett
Lieutenant R Kirkup (also MG Pl & B Coy, Bristol)
2nd Lieutenant T Laney (also E Coy)
Lieutenant P J Lintott
Lieutenant A J E McElwee

Colour Sergeants
C/Sgt K C Clarke
C/Sgt T Clapham TEM* (also Mortar Platoon)
C/Sgt F George
C/Sgt P L Jefferies TEM* (Anti-tank Pl)
C/Sgt G E Reynolds (NRPS)
C/Sgt A C Taylor TEM (MT)
C/Sgt M Vizor TEM

Sergeants
Sergeant T Barfoot
Sergeant J T Beeley TEM (RRTT)
Sergeant Begley
Sergeant G Connelly
Sergeant Cooper
Sergeant D Cross
Sergeant J Dale
Sergeant A Derrick (later B Coy, Bristol)
Sergeant J Evans
Sergeant S Harding (Anti-tank Pl)
Sergeant D Harvey (Anti-tank Pl)
Sergeant B Homer (later B Coy, Bristol)
Sergeant Kavanagh
Sergeant J Lee
Sergeant Marshall
Sergeant M Miller
Sergeant B Murphy (later B Coy, Bristol)
Sergeant J Nelnes TEM
Sergeant Skenlar (Anti-tank Pl)
Sergeant R D Smith (RRTT)
Sergeant K Wiltshire

SPSIs (continued)
WO2 M R Dawes BEM
WO2 R V Evans
WO2 J P Hussey (also C Coy, Cheltenham)
WO2 C M Smee (Recce Pl & C Coy, Chelt)

PSI Colour Sergeants*
C/Sergeant W H Arkley
C/Sergeant G D Bloor (also HQ Coy)
C/Sergeant T W Boon (2 tours)
C/Sergeant P W Bourne (Recce Pl & C Coy, Chelt)
C/Sergeant R S Bramley
C/Sergeant D C Fenwick
C/Sergeant S Fogg (WO2 on leaving)
C/Sergeant R A C Francis
C/Sergeant C Gleeson
C/Sergeant A J Harris
C/Sergeant Heavens
C/Sergeant J Hewitt LS&GCM, RWF
C/Sergeant W Hunt, D&D
C/Sergeant N Kilburn (Anti-tank Platoon)
C/Sergeant P Lewis, R Hamps
C/Sergeant H Maber
C/Sergeant I Matthews
C/Sergeant E McCue
C/Sergeant D J McPherson
C/Sergeant Metcalfe, DERR
C/Sergeant M D Morgan (also B Coy, Bristol)
C/Sergeant W F Murphy
C/Sergeant M J Osowieki
C/Sergeant M J O'Reilly (QPSI)

Subalterns (continued)
2nd Lieutenant D Mayne
Lieutenant J(onathan) Moss (also Swindon)
Lieutenant J(ustin) Moss (ditto)
Lieutenant R J Poole
Lieutenant S J Ramsay (later B Coy, Bristol)
Lieutenant M D Taylor
2nd Lieutenant P Tiernay
2nd Lieutenant D Van Eden
Lieutenant G A B Walters
Lieutenant R Whittard (later B Coy, Bristol)
Lieutenant R Wood
Lieutenant R C Zajko

Attached NCOs
Staff Sergeant D Hatton TEM***, RAPC/AGC
    (later HQ Coy)
Staff Sergeant J Deuten TEM, ACC
Corporal "Nobby" Hall TEM**, ACC
Corporal "Jock" Nelson TEM, ACC
C/Sergeant G E Reynolds (NRPS)

PSI Colour Sergents (continued)
C/Sergeant S J Pepper (QPSI)
C/Sergeant C R Porter (Recce Pl PSI)
C/Sergeant R Slade, R Hamps
C/Sergeant F R Standlick
C/Sergeant C S D Stevens
C/Sergeant R W Vale
C/Sergeant A Walker
C/Sergeant G W Wardle
C/Sergeant D Way
C/Sergeant White
C/Sergeant J W Wilcox

PSI Sergeants
Sergeant G Barnes (Recce Platoon PSI)
    (also C Coy, Cheltenham)
Sergeant Chamberlain (Recce Platoon)
Sergeant G Connelly
Sergeant I R Galley
Sergeant P Lewis, R Hamps
Sergeant R C Masters, R Hamps
Sergeant I M Walker

* (The large number of PSI Colour Sergeants was due to the fact that over the years many of the Support Platoons were part of, or administered by, the Company.

B Company - Winchester, Basingstoke & Isle of Wight (1967 - 1986)
(All PSIs R Hamps unless otherwise shown)

Company Commanders

Major J D Roberts TD** (also Bn 2IC)
Major M A R Oakley TD* (also OC HQ Coy)
Major F W Fifield TD* (also Bn 2IC)
Major I P B Taylor TD** (also Bn Mortar Offr)
Major P M Booth TD
Major S E Wooles (also 5 Queens)
Major G E Brady TD (later Bn 2IC & CO)
Major A C Cundy BEM TD/TEM

Seconds-in Command & Captains

Captain H R Astin (Mortar Pl; also C Coy)
Captain Chapman
Major W F Conroy
Captain P J James (Mortar Pl)
Captain J Loveys Jervoise
Captain Maxwell
Captain T J Oxborough (Mortar Pl, also
   D Coy, Bournemouth)
Captain A R C Peel
Captain T Shapland (also C Coy, Newbury)
Captain H W Steadman
Captain F R Thomas TD
Captain S M L A Slater (also D Coy, Reading)
Captain H E A Wedderburn (also Ops Officer)

Subalterns

Lieutenant C A Bullied
Lieutenant J E Burgess

Company Sergeant Majors

WO2 R D Witt TEM
WO2 J Bamber TEM
WO2 B A Fitzpatrick TEM
WO2 M J Blow TEM
WO2 M McManus TEM
WO2 R J Hoare TEM
WO2 Smith TEM

Colour Sergeants

C/Sergeant A Campbell
C/Sergeant W F Crisp
C/Sergeant B Ewington
C/Sergeant C M D Feist
C/Sergeant M Heigho
C/Sergeant T Hoare BEM, (Mortar Pl)
C/Sergeant I P Knight TEM (Mortar Pl)
C/Sergeant Lane
C/Sergeant J Sansom (Mortar Platoon)
C/Sergeant K W Turner
C/Sergeant W Verney
C/Sergeant J Wrixon (later Caretaker, Newburgh Hse)

Sergeants

Sergeant Brown (Mortar Pl)
Sergeant A Campbell
Sergeant R A Corbett
Sergeant J Desmond (Signals Pl)
Sergeant C M D Feist

Permanent Staff Administrative Officer

Captain G S Thomas MBE, late R Hamps
   (previously QM)

SPSI WO2s

WO2 "Benny" Goodman
WO2 P J Hamlyn, D & D (previously C Coy)
WO2 M A Horder
WO2 B J Lane
WO2 N P Jesty
WO2 H W Perkins
WO2 B W Plastow
WO2 M R F Powers
WO2 M Rose
WO2 R R Smith

PSI Colour Sergeants

C/Sergeant M J Allen
C/Sergeant D M Carpenter (Mortar Platoon)
C/Sergeant P J Copping
C/Sergeant B E Edwards
C/Sergeant B Ewington
C/Sergeant P A Lancey (QPSI)
C/Sergeant B Lane
C/Sergeant J ("Jack") Lemmon
C/Sergeant P A Lewis
C/Sergeant R C Masters (Also A Coy)

Subalterns (continued)
Lieutenant R C Dugalby
2nd Lieutenant G Farrell
Lieutenant N W S Goulding (later OC C Coy)
Lieutenant T P Lowden
Lieutenant D M Nisbett
Lieutenant R A H Nunneley
Lieutenant P I W Pay (later OC A Coy)
2nd Lieutenant Peach
Lieutenant N S Pope
2nd Lieutenant J P Turner
2nd Lieutenant Scott
2nd Lieutenant T Simpson

Sergeants (continued)
Sergeant P Green
Sergeant R J Hoare
Sergeant Huxam TEM
Sergeant D C Lacey
Sergeant Lloyd
Sergeant Machin
Sergeant J A Randall
Sergeant Smith (Mortar Pl)
Sergeant Verney
Sergeant J Vorley (Mortar Pl)
Sergeant C F Whent
Sergeant B White
Sergeant J Wrey

Attached SNCOs
S/Sergeant Hill TEM, RAPC
Sergeant Goddard, ACC

PSI Colour Sergeants (continued)
C/Sergeant K H Price
C/Sergeant P L Reeves
C/Sergeant S C Sanders
C/Sergeant D E ("Spud") Taylor
C/Sergeant G Townesend
C/Sergeant West
C/Sergeant M M Wilson (QPSI)

PSI Sergeants
Sergeant M E H Allen
Sergeant J W Beal
Sergeant D Bryant
Sergeant Cannings
Sergeant M E H Clarke
Sergeant W Constantine
Sergeant A Crawley
Sergeant R Curtis
Sergeant B E Edwards
Sergeant M Navarro (Mortar Pl)
Sergeant S Tucker, D&D
Sergeant P Tuckwell (Signals Platoon)

B Company - Swindon (1986 -1992)
(All PSIs DERR unless otherwise shown)

Company Commanders
Major P M Booth (also HQ Coy)
A/Major J Mitchell (otherwise PSAO)
Major R N Lawrence
Lieutenant Colonel S A Durant (previously Adjt,
   OC RRTT & later Bn 2IC)
Major J C Wort BSc (previously Adjutant)

Seconds in Command
Captain N T Barrett (also IO)
Captain M A J Cornish
Captain M Thomas (also Anti-tank Pl)
Captain R A Wannell

Permanent Staff Administrative Officer
Captain J Mitchell, late 9/12 Lancers
   (also Coy Comd)

Subalterns
Lieutenant E R C Broderstad
Lieutenant D J Gillingham
2nd Lieutenant P N Hall
Lieutenant B Lai
2nd Lieutenant McEwen
Lieutenant J(onathan) Moss
Lieutenant J(ustin) Moss
Lieutenant M Thomas
2nd Lieutenant Q M Wilkins

Company Sergeant Majors
WO2 A Eldridge
WO2 S Gray

PSIs
WO2 P R M Andrews, R Hamps (later RSM)
WO2 C Chapman,
WO2 J Clay, R Hamps (later RSM)
WO2 I Tait
C/Sergeant R Irving
C/Sergeant R H Povey (QPSI)
C/Sergeant J Williams (QPSI)

Colour Sergeants - none known

Sergeants
Sergeant P Fell
Sergeant A Humphries
Sergeant J Phillips
Sergeant N Runnalls

B (City of Bristol) Company (1992 - 1995)
(Both PSIs Glosters)

Company Commander
Major P J Hatton BA MBA (previously Ops Officer)

Seconds in Command
Captain M S Garrett (previously A Coy)
Captain M Idaziasczyk (also Anti-tank Pl & 2I/C A Coy)
Captain F P Moran

Subalterns
Lieutenant J C Adby (previously A Coy)
2nd Lieutenant N O Crewe-Reade
Lieutenant R Kirkup (previously A Coy & Machine Gun Pl)
Lieutenant S J Ramsay (previously A Coy)
Lieutenant R Whittard (previously A Coy)

Company Sergeant Major
WO2 N Attwood BEM TEM (previously A Coy)

Colour Sergeant
C/Sergeant Marks

Sergeants
Sergeant A Derrick (previously A Coy)
Sergeant B Homer (previously A Coy)
Sergeant G Kerr, RAPC /AGC
Sergeant B Murphy (previously A Coy)
Sergeant Nelmes (RRTT - previously A Coy)
Sergeant E J Ryan
Sergeant S Western (acted as C/Sergeant?)

Permanent Staff Administrative Officer
Captain P E C O'Brien, late RCT

PSIs
WO2 D M Ashford (SPSI)
C/Sgt M D Morgan (QPSI)

C Company - Dorchester, Poole & Weymouth (1967 - 1990)
(All PSIs D & D unless otherwise shown)

Company Commanders
Major M W Evans TD
Colonel P-J A Robson TD MA LLB
Major J N Speakman MBE TD (also HQ Coy)
Major J Ives (late D&D)
Major J C Lillies, late D&D
Major M S O' F Cook MBE TD (late D&D)
Lieutenant Colonel M C Faussett TD
(later CO 4 D&D)

Seconds-in-Command & Captains
Captain H R Astin
Captain G A Coveyduck
Captain S C O Davidson-Houston
Captain C Finegan
Captain T K Jeanes TD
Captain P J King
Captain J Malloch
Captain D K F McIver TD (Anti-tank & IO)
Lieutenant Colonel I T Mereweather TD
(later CO 6 Rifles)
Captain L E Thornton-Grimes
Captain I R Upshall

Subalterns
Lieutenant J J Falkner
Lieutenant C H R Fookes

Company Sergeant Majors
WO2 K W G Gover TEM*
WO2 T W Price TEM*
WO2 M Gould TEM*
WO2 P J Hendrick (late D&D)
WO2 K J Chivers TEM**
WO2 A P H Janes (former PSI)
WO2 R C Price TEM* (also Queen's Medal)

Colour Sergeants
C/Sgt P Breeze
C/Sgt T Denty TEM
C/Sergeant R R Fraser TEM
C/Sgt R H T Riglar TEM (later Sgts' Mess Caterer)
C/Sergeant T J Webb TEM

Sergeants
Sergeant H J Baker
Sergeant W Bastable
Sergeant H A G Boggust TEM
Sergeant D W Burt TEM*
Sergeant P I M Camp TEM*
Sergeant Dewland
Sergeant T R Harris
Sergeant T Harvey

Permanent Staff Administrative Officer
Captain G D McMeeken MBE, late 9/12 Lancers
(also OC D Coy Poole & OC HQ Coy)

SPSI WO2s
WO2 P Carpenter LS&GCM
WO2 R A Crocker
WO2 A Dunn
WO2 P J Hamlyn (also B Company,'
WO2 M Hunt
WO2 A P H Janes
WO2 M Knight
WO2 P L Lambert
WO2 G F Riley QGM
WO2 J W Wright

PSI Colour Sergeants
C/Sergeant M Clarke, R Hamps
C/Sergeant P Copping, R Hamps
C/Sergeant P Hodge
C/Sergeant W Hunt (2 'tours')
C/Sergeant C Jeffery
C/Sergeant S Keane
C/Sergeant K H Latham
C/Sergeant P Sheppard
C/Sergeant N Stannard

Subalterns (continued)
Lieutenant R Gillam (also D Coy, Bournemouth)
Lieutenant D M A Hill
Lieutenant L R Keir
Lieutenant W R A Kirke
Lieutenant A J L Mew
2nd Lieutenant M K H Ostocke
Lieutenant C R F Petchey
Lieutenant P R Sanguinetti
Lieuenant D Waller
2nd Lieutenant H J D Webster
2nd Lieutenant R J Williams

Sergeants (continued)
Sergeant R Hodges
Sergeant D S Jefferies TEM
Sergeant J R Laurence
Sergeant R J Loving TEM
Sergeant B A Northam
Sergeant Perrin
Sergeant G Ring
Sergeant F Ruffle
Sergeant N V Smith TEM (also D Coy)
Sergeant A Vater
Sergeant L Webb
Sergeant T Webb
Sergeant R Wills
Sergeant D Woods

Attached SNCOs
Sergeant Blake, REME
Sergeant M Clayton TEM, REME
Sergeant S Cooper, ACC
Sergeant A W Dennis TEM*, RAMC
Sergeant G Galpin TEM***, RAPC
Sergeant Hider, RAMC

PSI Colour Sergeants (continued)
C/Sergeant N J Ryder
C/Sergeant G Williams
C/Sergeant Wright

PSI Sergeants
Sergeant Clements
Sergeant B Colley BEM (later E Coy)
Sergeant G Deans
Sergeant P Sheppard (later E Coy)
Sergeant J Wibberley

C Company - Newbury (1990 - 1992)
(All PSIs DERR)

Company Commanders
Major W J C Quarterman
Major T C A Shapland (prev. B Coy,
  Winchester, Mortar Pl)
Major N W S Goulding (prev. A Coy)

Permanent Staff Administrative Officer
Captain R L ("Mad Nick") Nicholson MBE,
  (late RCT - also PSAO HQ Coy, Devizes)

Company Sergeant Majors
WO2 Patey (late QMSI, SASC, and
  later Coy Storeman)
WO2 J Lewis

Captains
Captain H G Bolton
Captain C J Challis
Captain F P Moran (also B Coy, Bristol)

PSIs
WO2 R Tadhunter (SPSI - also HQ Coy)
WO2 P W McLeod (SPSI)
WO2 S P Traveller (SPSI)
C/Sergeant S J Probetts (QPSI)
C/Sergeant R Vincent (QPSI)

Subalterns
Lieutenant R A H Berry (also HQ Coy)
Lieutenant P Frank

Colour Sergeant
C/Sergeant B G Mackriell

Sergeants
Sergeant Cross
Sergeant P J Holmes

C Company - Cheltenham (1992 - 1995)
(All PSIs Glosters)

Company Commander
Major W J C Quarterman

Second-in-Command
Captain M Idaziasczyk (also A Coy & Anti-tank Pl)

Permanent Staff Administrative Officer
Captain E W Fry, late RGBW (previously A Coy)

Subalterns
2/Lieutenant L A J Brennan (previously A Coy)
Lieutenant R W G Soult (previously, A Coy)

WO2s
WO2 P G Wood (CSM) (late Pl Commander C Coy Chelt & 2IC A Coy)
WO2 C M Snee (RRTT, also Recce Pl)

PSIs
WO2 M Cornock (SPSI prev. SPSI A Coy)
WO2 J P Hussey (SPSI)
WO2 C M Stapley (SPSI)
C/Sergeant P W Bourne (QPSI)
C/Sergeant W F Chapman (NRPS)
C/Sergeant Cooper
C/Sergeant C R Porter (SPSI - Recce Platoon)
Sergeant G Barnes (Recce Platoon)

Note: Unfortunately there are no extant records of the names of any TA SNCOs

D Company - Reading & Swindon (1967 - 1977)
(All PSIs DERR)

Company Commanders
Major D J Heavens TD
Lieutenant Colonel A F Ravenhill OBE TD**
Major D G Hallett
Major B W Jarvis
Captain P G T Morgan
Major M J Baggs TD

Company Sergeant Majors
WO2 P A Reader TEM
WO2 R Jerome TEM

PSI WO2s
WO2 K Szmelter
WO2 D A Puffett (later civilian storeman)
WO2 E ("Tiger") Head, R Hamps
WO2 E A Kimberley MBE, R Hamps
WO2 R E Povey
WO2 W G Wright (also HQ Coy, Exeter)
WO2 A Hobbs
WO2 N Minty LS&GCM
WO2 H Perkins

Seconds-in Command & Captains
Captain B A Carte TD
Captain J B Leese
Captain P E Q Long
Captain B C Staig TD (also Bn Paymaster)
Captain T P Wild

Colour Sergeants
C/Sergeant G Brown (also B Coy)
C/Sergeant Rhodes TEM

PSI Colour Sergeants
C/Sergeant A A C Beck
C/Sergeant R J Guppy
C/Sergeant C D L Metcalfe
C/Sergeant G Mills
C/Sgt T Watton
C/Sgt A Whitfield

PSI Sergeants
Sergeant A C Chaffey
Sergeant T Freelove
Sergeant E J Martin

Attached NCOs
WO2 Hing TEM ACC
Sergeant Roberts TEM ACC

Subalterns
Lieutenant E W H Bryan
Lieutenant M J Campbell-Rickets
2nd Lieutenant J Falkner
Lieutenant D M Fuller
Lieutenant D P Heath
Lieutenant R Howman
Lieutenant B K Hudson
2nd Lieutenant S E T Mostyn
Lieutenant J E H Roberts
Lieutenant S M L A Slater (also B Coy, Winch)
2nd Lieutenant J C Walton
Lieutenant P Wilde

Sergeants
Sergeant H A T Cossey TEM*
Sergeant Day
Sergeant P Fitgerald
Sergeant D Jagger
Sergeant W Morris (later Drum Major)
Sergeant D Murphy
Sergeant Roberts
Sergeant Rowe

D Company - Bournemouth & Poole (1977 - 1992)
(All PSIs D & D unless shown otherwise)

Company Commanders
Major M J Baggs TD
Major M J A Bond JP
Major J Stanley (ex-Royal Marines)
Major H J N Kent BSc

Permanent Staff Administrative Officers
Captain G R Burt MC, late The Parachute Regiment
Captain A P Morgan, late D & D (former RSM)

Company Sergeant Majors
WO2 B Worthy
WO2 S J Houghton

Second-in-Command
Captain M J Baggs
Captain G D McMeeken MBE, late 9/12 Lancers
(also PSAO C Coy, Dorchester & OC HQ C Coy)

PSIs
WO2 D Federick, DERR
WO2 N Haynes, DERR
WO2 A Hobbs
WO2 N Minty LS&GCM, DERR (later RSM)
WO2 A J Rogers
C/Sergeant D Beale
C/Sergeant B T Convery LS&GCM
(also C Coy, Dorchester)

Subalterns
Lieutenant S Bielecki PhD
Lieutenant R Brown BA
Lieutenant E Bryan
Lieutenant R G Hiles (also HQ Coy)
Lieutenant T P Jenkins (later RSO)
Lieutenant H Jennings
Lieutenant P G Metcalfe
Lieutenant M W Sorge
Lieutenant G Summers
Lieutenant J D Temple
Lieutenant T Weale
2nd Lieutenant G J W Wilson

Note: There is no record of the names of any of the TA SNCOs in this Company.

HQ Company - Exeter & Barnstaple (1967 - 1969)
E Company - Exeter & Barnstaple (1969 - 1987)
(All PSIs D & D unless shown otherwise)

Company Commanders
Major T M C Anstey TD (also Queen's Medal)
Major C A Rimmer TD
Major P V B George TD
Major C H Parnham TD

Seconds in Command & Captains
Captain L J K Courtenay (MTO)
Captain S C O Davidson-Houston
Captain N A Ffitch
Captain P R Evens
Captain D P Heath
Captain G Newsum (Training Officer)
Captain R Newbolt-Young
Captain R N R Owen
Captain G R S Simey TD (also RSO)
Captain B M Willis
Captain R H B Wood

Company Sergeant Majors
WO2 Beer TEM
WO2 L Butler
WO2 A Budge BEM TEM
WO2 D B Gigg (previously PSI)
WO2 D G O'Connor TEM
WO2 F G Smale TEM

Permanent Staff Administrative Officer
Captain J A Barrow MBE, late DERR

Intelligence Officers
Lieutenant G Boucher
2nd Lieutenant P J James
Lieutenant H D Pomeroy

Subalterns
2nd Lieutenant M J W Doherty
2nd Lieutenant S Goad
2nd Lieutenant S Green
Lieutenant T J L Hunt
2nd Lieutenant T L Keene
2nd Lieutenant R A Kelly
Lieutenant P J Lambert
2nd Lieutenant T Laney
2nd Lieutenant M Mawbey-Adamson
Lieutenan T McCarthy
2nd Lieutenant D Michaelis (Asst RSO)
Lieutenant M K H Ostocke
2nd Lieutenant A Payne
Lieutenant D Pommeroy
Lieutenant S J Poulson
2nd Lieutenant R Young

Colour Sergeants
C/Sergeant D Bate-Jones TEM* (Officers' Mess Sgt)
C/Sergeant M J Charlesworth
C/Sergeant D Diggle TEM* (reverted to Pay Sgt)
C/Sergeant M J Charlesworth
C/Sergeant Toulcher TEM
C/Sergeant Vodden TEM

Sergeants
Sergeant G Body
Sergeant D T Bradford
Sergeant T Carman
Sergeant C Cusack
Sergent A Ellicott
Sergeant D Evers
Sergeant P J Ford TEM*
Sergeant A Helm
Sergeant Lewis
Sergeant A Midson BEM TEM* (NT)
Sergeant Mitchell
Sergeant T Murphy
Sergeant J N Murray
Sergeant C Stokes
Sergeant N Tout BEM TEM*
Sergeant Triggs (Corps of Drums)

SPSI WO2s
WO2 A J Beale
WO2 K Crawford
WO2 J W Fowler
WO2 D B Gigg
WO2 C Madders
WO2 J Westlake

PSI Colour Sergeants
C/Sergeant M Butler
C/Sergeant J B Coleman, DERR
C/Sergeant R B Colls
C/Sergeant B Convery
C/Sergeant Gordon
C/Sergeant G Hendrick
C/Sergeant S Keane
C/Sergeant E A Millard (QPSI)
C/Sergeant T Murphy
C/Sergeant N Stannard
C/Sergeant E Skinner, DERR
C/Sergeant T H Thornton, DERR
C/Sergeant Walker, Glosters
C/Sergeant Wright

PSI Sergeants
Sergeant Carnegie
Sergeant Crawley
Sergeant P Fallon
Sergeant B Foster, DERR
Sergeant C Horn LS&GCM
Sergeant M Kerr
Sergeant P Murphy
Sergeant P Sheppard
Sergeant J Thorner (Signals Platoon)
Sergeant J Wibberley (later C Coy, Dorset)
Sergeant W Wilkinson
Sergeant R Wise (MT)
Sergeant W Young

Attached personnel
WO2 Roberts, ACC TEM*
S/Sergeant Moore, ACC TEM
Sergeant Bradford, RAPC

HQ Company (Trowbridge 1970-1973 & Devizes 1973-1995)
(All PSIs DERR unless shown otherwise)

Company Commanders
Major J N Speakman MBE TD (prev. C Coy, Dorchester)
Major P L Jacques TD
Major M A R Oakley TD (also OC B Coy, Winchester)
Lieutenant Colonel A M Grazebrook TD* (also OC A Coy & Bn 2IC)
Major A S P Cook JP (also RSO)
Lieutenant Colonel (ACF) R D O'Neill TD (previously OC A Coy)
Major P M Booth (also B Coy, Swindon)
Major B Thomas
Major R D Heatley TD (prev. A Coy & CSM HQ Coy)
Major M J Boden
Major R G Hiles TD (previously RSO)

Support Company & RRTT Commanders
Major M R Ashman TD
Captain E J Borup (OC Support Coy, prev. Mortar Pl)
Major S A Durant (OC RRTT prev. Adjutant, HQ Coy; B Coy, Swindon & later Bn 2IC)
Major P J Hudson (OC Support Coy)
Major J Tristram TD (OC RRTT)
Major A P Williams (OC Support Coy)

Permanent Staff Administrative Officers
Captain J F Foreman (NRPS)
Captain R L ("Mad Nick") Nicholson MBE, late RCT (also C Coy, Newbury)

Seconds-in-Command & Specialist Platoons
Captain H R Astin (Mortar Pl & C Coy)
Lieutenant R A H Berry (MTO)
Captain C P J Challis (Recce Pl)
Captain J C Cook (also A Coy)
Captain M Cornish (RSO)
Lieutenant P James (Mortar Pl)
Captain T P Jenkins (RSO, also D Coy, Poole)
Captain C R M Kewish (RSO)
Captain J B Leece
Captain B Lai (RSO)
Captain F P Moran (Mor Pl, also B Coy, Bristol)
Lieutenant N M Rogerson MBE (MTO, prev. H&D Band)
Captain P J Simpson (IO & RSO)
Captain M Thomas (Anti-tank Pl)
Captain R A Wannell (Asst RSO)

Operations Officers
Major P J Hatton (later B Coy, Bristol)
Captain R J D R Owen
Major R N A J Tournay

Intelligence Officers
Captain N T Barrett (also B Coy, Swindon)
WO2 A C Cundy BEM (later OC B Coy, Winchr.)
Capain D C Ryan (also Bn A/T Offr & OC A Coy)
Captain G E Sharpe

Sergeants
Sergeant Anderson (Signals Pl)
Sergeant Batchelor (Signals Pl)
Sergeant R Bryant (Weapon Training)
Sergeant D C Chamberlain (Recce Fl)
Sergeant Clarke
Sergeant M Davidson (Signals Pl)
Sergeant H Dunn (MT Pl)
Sergeant C Fielding
Sergeant G S Gordon (Asslt Pioneer Pl)
Sergeant Gray (SF Pl)
Sergeant "Taffy" John (MG Pl & Provost Staff)
Sergeant P Legge (Orderly Room)
Sergeant Lindsay (Intelligence Sect)
Sergeant J Long
Sergeant R Mitchell (MT Pl)
Sergeant Neate (QM's Dept)
Sergeant Palfrey (Signals Pl)
Sergeant Parkyn
Sergeant J A Olphert (MG Pl)
Sergeant Prescott (QM's Dept)
Sergeant Robertson TEM
Sergeant Smith (Orderly Room)
Sergeant Steele
Sergeant P D Uglow
Sergeant P Utteridge
Sergeant Witts (QM's Dept)

Company Sergeant Majors
WO2 G V Crawley TEM*
WO2 R D Heatley TEM
WO2 Lavery
WO2 W Morris (also D Coy & Drum Major)
WO2 "Mitch" Mortimer (also RRTT)
WO2 C V Stone TEM (formerly MT Pl)
WO2 Townsend TEM (formerly Provost Section)
WO2 J Nicholls (prev. Int Section & Asst RSO)

SPSI WO2s
WO2 D Fedrick (also D Coy, Bournemouth)
WO2 Gardner LS&GCM, AGSM (Signals Pl)
WO2 K Hack, R Hamps
WO2 A Jones, Glosters
WO2 W H Sherman
WO2 R Tadhunter DERR
WO2 I Tate, R Hamps
WO2 R J Walker

PSI (Specialist) Warrant Officers
WO2 Gardner
WO2 P Lloyd
WO2 K Price MSM, R Hamps (Signals Pl)
WO2 C Snee DERR (Recce Platoon PSI)

Warrant Officers (TA)
WO2 S R Beacham (MT Pl)
WO2 Fell (RRTT)
WO2 D W Lobb (Mor Pl)
WO2 K M Reade, MBE TEM** (previously A Coy)
WO2 C V Stone (MT Pl)

Colour Sergeants
C/Sergeant Clark
C/Sergeant Colyer (Sgts' Mess Caterer)
C/Sergeant M D Currey, (NRPS)
C/Sergeant M Dallard (MT, Provost Section & HQ Pl)
C/Sergeant Elsen
C/Sergeant N W Fishwick TEM (MT Pl)
C/Sergeant Hill
C/Sergeant R W Kuczak (later CSM A Coy)
C/Sergeant D Mackintosh (Signals Pl)
C/Sergeant McClurg (MT Pl)
C/Sergeant McCormack (CQMS)
C/Sergeant B Ramm
C/Sergeant R Ritson (Signals Pl)
C/Sergeant Robbins TEM
C/Sergeant Stevens
C/Sergeant C Stone (MT PSI)
C/Sergeant Tuckwell (Signals Pl)
C/Sergeant R Stockley TEM* (QM's Dept)
C/Sergeant J L Viveash TEM*

Attached NCOs
S/Sergeant Ball, REME (MT Pl)
Sergeant R Cocker, REME (MT)
S/Sergeant "Brigadier" Frayling, ACC/RLC (Catering Pl)
S/Sergeant D Hatton TEM****, RAPC/AGC (Pay Section & previously A Coy)
WO2 Lloyd, AGC (Pay Section) TEM
S/Sergeant King, ACC (Catering Pl)
S/Sergeant McCready (Medical Section)
WO2 Parsons TEM, RAPC (Pay Sect)
WO2 Roberts TEM, ACC (Catering Pl)
S/Sergeant P Robinson TEM, REME (Armourer)
WO2 A J Smith TEM, ACC (Catering Pl)
S/Sergeant C Whiting, RAMC (Medical Section)

PSI Colour Sergeants
C/Sergeant K Batty
C/Sergeant M Clarke
C/Sergeant K Foy (Signals PSI)
C/Sergeant D R Head
C/Sergeant J Lindsey
C/Sergeant M Kerr
C/Sergeant "Moc" McGuire (Signals Pl)
C/Sergeant R C Rossiter, Glosters
C/Sergeant J Samson (Mortar PSI)
C/Sergeant W Sherman (Signals PSI)
C/Sergeant B Smith

PSI Sergeants

Sergeant W Apperley, RGBW (Signals Pl)
Sergeant K Batty
Sergeant F Bird
Sergeant A D Breenn, Glosters (Signals Pl.)
Sergeant M Browne (MT Pl)
Sergeant R Crocker (MT Pl)
Sergeant J Dobie (MT Pl)
Sergeant T Evans (QPSI)
Sergeant P Fennell (Signals Pl)
Sergeant C Fielding (Signals Pl)
Sergeant C Gleeson, Glosters (QPSI)
Sergeant Jones (NRPS - QM's Dept)
Sergeant P Legg (MT)
Sergeant A B Linker, Glosters

PSI Sergeants (continued)

C/Sergeant M Wright BEM TEM
Sergeant "Titch" Little (Mortar Pl)
Sergeant Martin
Sergeant D McPherson (Q PSI)
Sergeant N D Moore, Glosters
Sergeant Sheppard, D&D (MTP1)
Sergeant D Thatcher, R Hamps
Sergeant P Utteridge (MT Pl)
Sergeant J J Walsh, Glosters
Sergeant D Watts (MT Pl)
Sergeant Wise, DERR (MT Pl)
Sergeant D Young (Anti-tank Pl)
Sergeant Zawadski ("Sgt Z"), DERR
    (Signals Pl; then TA, D Coy)

PSI Colour Sergeants (continued)

C/Sergeant S E Smith, Glosters (Mortar Pl)
C/Sergeant Ward
C/Sergeant A Whitfield

APPENDIX 3

1st Battalion The Wessex Regiment (Rifle Volunteers)

Appointments – September 1995

Battalion Headquarters
Commanding Officer: Lt Col A P B Lake, RGBW
Second in Command: Major M J Boden TD
Adjutant: Captain J H Morgan-Owen, RRW
Training Major: Major R P Dutton, RGBW
Operations Officer: Major R N A J Tournay
Chaplain: Major The Reverend S J Wilkinson TD
Regimental Administrative Officer: Captain M J Cornwell OBE
Assistant Adjutant: Captain G E Sharpe
Regimental Sergeant Major: WO1 A R Dixon, RGBW
Chief Clerk: WO2 P B Crowther

A Company (Gloucester)
Major W J C Quarterman
Captain J Cooke
Lt S C A Griffith
Lt R M A Kirkup
Lt R C Zajko
2/Lieutenant M Cassidy
WO2 R W Kuczaj
Permanent Staff
Major R Mawdesley, BEM
   (PSAO)
WO2 M Cornock RGBW

B (City of Bristol) Company
Major P J Hatton
Captain M S Garrett
Lieutenant J C Adby
Lieutenant S J Ramsey
2/Lieutenant N O Crewe-Read
WO2 N Attwood BEM
Permanent Staff
Capt P E C O'Brien, (PSAO)
WO2 D M Ashford RGBW

C Company (Cheltenham)
Major W J C Quarterman
Captain M Idziaszcyk
Lieutenant R W G Soult
Lieutenant P G Wood
2/Lieutenant L A J Brennan
Permanent Staff
Captain E W Fry (PSAO)
WO2 Snee
C/Sgt Cooper RGBW

Support Company
Captain E J Borup
Captain F P Moran (Mortar)
Captain M Thomas (A/Tk)
Captain C P Challis (Recce)
WO2 P R Blake (Assault Pioneer)
Permanent Staff
C/Sgt Morris
C/Sgt Smith
C/Sgt Young

Headquarter Company

Major R G Hiles
Major N S Salisbury (RMO)
Major E A Madigan (RMO)
Captain R H Butt (QM TA)
Captain K Walcroft (2IC)
WO2 A J Eldridge (RQMS TA)
WO2 M J Munday (Drum Major)

Captain T P Jenkins (RSO)
Captain N T Barrett (IO)
Lieutenantt D Gardner (MT)
2/Lieutenant D Rogers (M/Gun)
WO1 A W Johnson (Bandmaster)
WO2 K M Reade (Senior Sgt Major)
WO2 B R Stoddart (Chief Clerk TA)

Permanent Staff
Major P H Hall MBE, (QM)
Captain R L Nicholson MBE (PSAO)
WO2 A W C Munday (RQMS)
WO2 Walker
Sgt Apperley

APPENDIX 4

THE LAYING UP OF THE COLOURS

As 1 Wessex had no Regular 'parent' regiment, the task of deciding where the Colours should be laid up fell to the last Honorary Colonel and Commanding Officer. For them to be in the cathedral or regimental museum in one of the counties forming the Battalion's area would in effect have favoured the Company there as against the others – and although Battalion Headquarters and Headquarter Company had been in Devizes for 23 years, there had in practice been virtually no connection with its Parish Church.

The School of Infantry at Warminster (later known as the Combined Arms Training Centre (CATC)) had been the 'spiritual home' of 1 Wessex throughout almost the whole of its existence, and the Battalion strongly identified itself with its ethos, as taught to large numbers of Volunteer officers and NCOs who attended courses there. After consultation, therefore, with a representative number of officers who had served for long periods and those former 1 Wessex officers serving in 2 RGBW, it was agreed that the Colours would be laid up in The Hythe Mess at the CATC. That was therefore done on 17 May 1998, as magical a day as that on which they were presented – in the presence of the Director of Infantry, Brigadier The Hon S H R H Monro, and some 60 former Honorary Colonels, Officers and SNCOs, many with their wives. Unfortunately, there was not enough room to allow everyone who wanted to attend, but a good contingent came from the original C Company in Dorset, and all the other 'original' counties were represented. About 20 members who had served in the Battalion during the first six years of its existence were distinguishable by their green (rather than the later blue) Wessex Volunteers' ties.

After a brief introduction by the Honorary Colonel, the Laying Up was carried out in a short service taken by Simon Wilkinson (by then the padre of 2 RGBW, as well as the Honorary Chaplain to the RGBW Regimental Association) – assisted in characteristic fashion by Father Michael Reid, one of the padres who had been on parade back in June 1973, and who had come over from County Cork for the occasion; he never changed, for during the lunch that followed, he was overheard giving tips for the next meeting at Uttoxeter.

At that time, some 2,700 Infantry officers, both Regular and TA, went on courses at Warminster and lived in The Hythe Mess each year, broadly speaking at least twice in their careers and, as the Colours were on the staircase leading up to the anteroom and the dining-room, they would have been be seen by students, let alone other visitors, on something over 150,000 occasions a year. They have served, and will continue to serve, as a fitting memorial to a fine TA Battalion.

———————————

NB: The CATC has readily agreed that former members of 1 Wessex, and indeed anyone else who is interested, may see the Colours on reasonably short notice – security considerations, of course, permitting. Appointments to do so can be made by telephoning the Mess Manager on 01985-222464. Evidence of identity incorporating a photograph will be needed to gain admission at the security barrier. Over the past 10 years, however, the use of The Hythe Mess has substantially decreased, and the security arrangements are likely to become increasingly stringent. Notwithstanding, therefore, the earlier reservations about the suitability of Devizes, consideration is currently (2009) being given to moving the Colours to a Church in or near Devizes.

APPENDIX 5

SHOOTING

Competition shooting had played a big part in the activities of the old TA for many years – particularly in 43 Division. It attracted two sorts of Territorials – some took it very seriously, and did lots of other soldiering as well; others preferred it to being in the field on wet weekends, and did little else but lie on the ranges on the sunny ones. For the latter, it was like belonging to a civilian rifle club, but getting paid to do so.

There have always been doubts as to the truth of the view that, as the protagonists of competition shooting claimed, the skills of a good shooting team 'rubbed-off' on the companies to which the members of the team belonged, and thus increased the standard of marksmanship generally in the unit. The truth is probably that, while in some cases it did, in the large majority it did not.

Because of the TA's lack of a proper role, however, nobody seemed to realise that one day the ability to shoot very straight would save lives. Nevertheless, within unit and sub-unit teams, a tremendous amount of good camaraderie was engendered, and the heightened morale which resulted made many of their members obvious candidates for transfer to the TAVR. Indeed, in 1967, good young shots were almost guaranteed a place somewhere in the new TA, and a good many 'old sweats' managed to find their way in too.[1] When the Territorial Army Skill at Arms Meeting [TASAAM – very understandably, it never became the TAVRSAAM!] was revived at Bisley – the shrine of competition shooting throughout the world – in 1968, it attracted many entries. From then on, a relatively small number of units – not just the Infantry battalions, but of the Arms and Services as well – took shooting very seriously, invariably sent a team, and between them, almost in turn, as it were, consistently took the first half dozen or so places in most of the competitions. Some of them built up a very strong shooting tradition which was maintained for many years, despite the inevitable retirements of the senior members of their team, and they seemed to have relatively little difficulty in recruiting young soldiers.

The fact that in 1967 the TA was given a proper mobilisation role, rather than being just a general reserve, meant that competition shooting had to modernise itself. The Territorial Army Rifle Association [TARA], which organised the Bisley meeting, as well as many Non-Central Matches (shot on a unit's local range), had been run for a good many years on a real 'one-horse' basis by a retired TA officer, who had a long-standing Bisley connection. He was an accountant with an office in central London, and in practice much of the work was done by his Indian assistant. More importantly, however, most, if not all, of the competitions dated back to the pre-war days. It was time for another change.

From the outset, 1 Wessex was very much involved in that 'sharpening-up' process. It was represented on the Council of TARA from 1968, by Michael Anstey until his retirement from the TA in 1973, and by the author, who was its Chairman between 1975 and 1980. They were both in the forefront of the movement to get away from static 'gravel-belly' shooting, very largely at fixed targets – "Ten rounds at the target in front, in your own time, carry on" – to battle-shooting-type competitions involving not only rapid and snap, but much fire and movement as well. Several NATO battalions presented TARA with trophies for the new-style competitions, which – after they had been approved by the Small Arms School Corps [SASC – the Regular Army's shooting experts) – were shot for the first time at the 1969 TASAAM – The Highland Volunteers' Quaich (for the Moving Target Match), The Parachute Regiment Cup (for a two-mile run, with a difficult shoot when you got there), The Yorkshire Volunteers' Cup (for the Converted Gallery Range Match), and The Wessex Volunteers Cup.

The last was a fire-and-movement shoot of very considerable complexity, which was dreamed up, recollection has it, in the course of some jolly drinks and much laughter after training on a drill night somewhere. It involved so many targets – small, circular snap targets appearing for a few seconds at different points along the butts, those sinister full-length targets with a picture of a very aggressive soldier (No 8s) and standard 4' and 6' square targets for the team's LMG to score on – that after its first year, when chaos was not far away, the SASC, whose members supervise the butts and firing points at Bisley, refused point-blank (although, in view of the innovative idea, somewhat reluctantly) to direct it again until it was made a lot simpler. That first year, the Battalion only managed to come second, and the rules were changed for 1970; that notwithstanding, the Battalion team were again only the runners-up, and in 1971 they were not even placed. The shoot in fact still proved too complicated to run in the butts, so it was agreed that they should be changed a second time, for the 1972 TASAAM – and, whilst the intention was not, of course, to enable the Battalion to secure a win, it succeeded beyond all reasonable expectations, by taking the first and third places.

The first post-1967 TASAAM, in 1969, when the Battalion team largely came from A Company, was notable as the year when Captain Jim Loftus (the TA Quartermaster) and the author competed in the Volongdis GPMG competition in one of the heaviest downpours Bisley had experienced for many years, and as the first time that the Battalion did well in the Section Match for the most coveted of all the 'single competition' trophies, the vast China Cup – so big that it needs eight people to lift it. Furthermore, three members of the 14 or so strong team got into the TAVR 50 – an excellent start to many years of successful shooting.

The Battalion produced two winners of HM The Queen's Medal for the TA. Captain George Simey, the RSO and a solicitor in 'real life', came third in 1970 (also winning the Officers Cup and shooting for the TA in the Inter-Services Match – despite the fact that, so he said, he had not found the time to do any pre-Bisley practice. The following year, 1971, he was 'pipped' by his own Company Commander, Michael Anstey (another solicitor), who won both the Queen's Medal and the Officers' Cup, came seventh in the TA Service Rifle Championship, and was also a member of the TA team for various Inter Services competitions. Then in 1979 – which was by far the Battalion team's best year yet – Corporal Robin Price of C Company (the son of its CSM, WO2 Tom Price) won it with a score that was an astonishing 44 points ahead of his nearest rival – one of the biggest winning margins for a good many years).

In 1973, because of the Colour Presentation Parade, the Battalion did not send a team to Bisley, but its own Skill at Arms Meeting was held there over a week-end in the autumn. None of the long-serving civilian range staff could remember a major unit having done that before, and the very attractive setting of the ranges, with trees and clubhouses in profusion, was very different from those ranges normally used by the Battalion, such as Bulford, Pilning on the River Severn, Willsworthy on Dartmoor, Longmoor in Hampshire and Sydling St Nicholas in Dorset (where the old 43rd Division SAAM used to be held). A different Company for once, D, proved very successful, winning the GPMG Match and the Falling Plates competition, and coming second in both the GPMG (SF) Match and the Section Match.

One of the 'powers behind the throne' in the early days was Staff Sergeant Peter Cracknell – the Battalion's REME Armourer, responsible for supervising the Arms Storemen in (during his time) the Battalion's 13 TA Centres, and ensuring that every weapon in their armouries was properly maintained. A Regular before joining 4th/5th Royal Hampshires, he was one of those people whose somewhat laconic approach belied a warm heart; he was supremely good at his job, and with his sheer professionalism he made an enormous contribution to shooting, both with the team and generally throughout the Battalion. The award of the British Empire Medal to him in 1973 said all that needed to be said about his long and outstanding service.

Three successive COs between 1976 and 1981 gave shooting much encouragement. Colin Tremellen (1974–1976), Bill Coppen-Gardner (1976–1978) and John Southwood (1978–1981) were all members of "If you can't shoot.....' school in the old Army saying that "There are only three sorts of soldiers........" mentioned in Chapter 6, believing that shooting skills are an absolute essential for the trained Infantryman. They were determined to improve the skills of everyone in the Battalion, and it can be said without contradiction that, although 1974 to 1977 were lean years in terms of results at SAAMs, throughout that period there was a definite improvement in the individual Annual Range Classification results [the shooting qualification for getting one's Bounty] right across the Companies – and their support for the Battalion team was such that between

1978 and 1985 the Battalion team went from strength to strength, becoming one of the 'magic circle' of regular winners at both the South West District SAAM and Bisley.

It is, of course, a commonplace that, however much the Commanding Officer of any unit, Regular or TA, wants his battalion or regiment to become, or remain, an excellent 'shooting one' (or, indeed, good at any 'sporting' activity), whether or not that is so depends almost entirely on there being at least one really keen officer or SNCO, prepared to spend hours and hours coaching the team. At TASAAMs, of course, they were everywhere; everyone who had been there more than a few years knew many of them well, if only by sight. If, however, a unit was without one its chances of finishing up in the prize lists were fairly slim. From the late 1970s until 1990, 1 Wessex had one in particular, and there were a number of excellent individual 'shotists' who did very well from the beginning; the building-up of a good team, though, took a few years. The early records are incomplete, but it seems that it was not until about 1975 that the Battalion began to dominate the South West District SAAM, and have really successful visits to Bisley. John Roberts and the author trained the Battalion team from 1969, but the really successful team captain and coach arrived in 1976. He was the RSM, WO1 MSO'F Cook of the D & D, and his practical skills were shown the following year when he won the PSIs' Cup – as had his predecessor, WO1 JH Wheeler, in 1975. As mentioned in Chapter 9, after finishing his tour as the RSM, Mick Cook became a Volunteer with C Company, and although he rose to become its Company Commander he continued to train both the Company and Battalion teams.

The combined enthusiasm of John Southwood and Mick Cook began to pay off handsomely. The Bisley team had a good year in 1978, but 1979 and 1980 proved to be the most successful years ever. First of all, at the 1979 South West District combined Regular and TA SAAM, in addition to the Battalion's entry in the Major Unit Championship, every Company had a team in the Minor Units Championship – and there were therefore more members of 1 Wessex taking part than from any other Regular or TA unit. The Battalion and C Company teams both came second in their respective Championships. Then, at Bisley, apart from Corporal Price's winning of the Queen's Medal, the team surpassed itself by not only collecting the Jubilee Cup for the Sub-Machine Gun Match, coming second in the Highland Volunteers' Quaich for the Moving Target Match and third in the Rifle Aggregate (the total of all the team's scores in the individual rifle competitions) – but, best of all, they also won the China Cup for the Section Match.

In 1980 they at last won the Wessex Volunteers Cup again, it having eluded its original donor for eight years – but considerably more exciting of all was the capture of the ultimate Bisley 'pot' – The Dragon Trophy for the best-performing major unit.[2] The team was WO2 Pat Hendrick, Sergeants Price (as he had become) and Ken Chivers, Private P Maple – all of of C Company – Lance Corporal M Daden and Private R Warren of E Company, and Private I Edwards of HQ Company; the team captain was, of course, Mick Cook and Plate 24 shows how pleased he was.

1980 was the pinnacle of the Battalion's achievement at Bisley – but there were also extremely satisfactory visits between 1982 and 1985, when the team won a total of 9 cups for the major competitions, and there were very good performances by individuals, including a number of young soldiers,

In the first four years of the return of TA smallbore (0.22) competition shooting, A and E Companies were often to the fore in the TA Smallbore Company Team Match for The Duke of Norfolk's Cup – the former were the runners-up out of 59 teams in 1972 (the team being WO2 Keitley, Sergeants Clapham, Mears and Marriott, Lance Corporal Garton and Private Binding). The undisputed champions, however, were C Company, who, in 1976 and every year except for two between 1982 and 1989, won either The Duke of Norfolk or the other major Army team competition, the National Heckler-Koch. On the individual front, two members of E Company, Colour Sergeant Dirk Bate-Jones, the long-serving and very popular member of the Battalion who ran the Officers' Mess, and Corporal Peter Evens (before he was commissioned), shot for the TA in the 1974 Inter-Services Small-Bore Match, personally coming respectively third and thirteenth.

As will be seen in the table below, C Company completely dominated the South West District Regular and TA SAAM Minor

Units Championship between 1975 and 1986. Until 1977 and his retirement after 26 years' TA service, the team was trained by WO2 Tom Price – and his work was amply rewarded by their first three consecutive wins. Even without him, though, they continued their inexorable progress through the competition, winning it every year from 1979 until 1986 – 10 times out of 12. They often produced higher scores than Regular units practising for Bisley, and they consistently encouraged young shots: in the 1979 District SAAM, Lance Corporals Dade of E Company and Ferguson of C Company were respectively the winner and runner-up in Class B (junior ranks with between two and five years' service) of the TA Individual Championship, and the following year, apart from Corporal Ruffle ands Lance Corporal Camp, the team consisted entirely of private soldiers: Anderson, Broadbent, Camp, Clarke, Gough and Parsons – a remarkable achievement. The team also shot consistently well in the TARA Non-Central Matches year after year.

As is mentioned several times in preceding Chapters, from the early 1980s life in the Battalion became busier and busier. More often than not, Camps in Schleswig Holstein and Denmark, for which there had to be lengthy preparation and frequent large 'warm-up' exercises, took place in September, so there was less and less time for the other 'fringe activities', including competition shooting practice. Indeed, it was sometimes very difficult for the Companies to squeeze a weekend for classification shooting into their year's programme. Consequently, the last year that the Battalion sent a team to Bisley was 1991 – and in only two of the five previous ones did they bring any silver back with them. One can never, though, do everything in life, and it was almost inevitable that the increase in the battalion's efficiency as part of UKMF(L) had to be 'paid for' with less success in other activities. That state of affairs was mirrored in most of the NATO Infantry battalions, and year by year more and more units of, in particular, the Royal Signals and the Royal Logistic Corps became the well-known names on the Common, and took away a high proportion of the prizes. The fact that in earlier years 1 Wessex had played a major part in TA competition shooting is, however, a cause for much pride.

SHOOTING ACHIEVEMENTS

South West District Skill at Arms Meeting

1975–1977	Minor Unit Champions: C Company
1979	Major Unit Competition: 2nd
	Minor Unit Competition: C Company: 2nd
1980–1986	Major Unit Champions
1980–1982	Minor Unit Champions: C Company[3]
1982	Champion Shot: WO2 Hendrick
1983–1986	Minor Unit Champions: C Company
1986	Major Unit Championship: 2nd
1988	Major Infantry Units Champions
	TA (South of England) GPMG (SF) Match: Winners

TA Skill at Arms Meetings (TASAAM) at Bisley

1969	HM The Queen's Medal: L/Corporal Stevens (A) in the Top 20
	National Rifle Association [NRA] Kinnaird Cup (Rifle): Sergeant D A Mears, Winner
	Hamilton Leigh Cup (Falling Plates Match): Winners
	China Cup (Section Match): 3rd
	Wessex Volunteers Cup: 2nd
1970	HM The Queen's Medal: Captain G R S Simey, 3rd; three team members in the TA Top 20
	Officers' Cup: Captain Simey, Winner
	Hamilton Leigh Cup: 1st & 2nd (i.e. both finalists)
	Wessex Volunteers Cup: 2nd
1971	HM The Queen's Medal & Officers' Cup: Major T M C Anstey, Winner; also 7th in TA Individual Championship
	China Cup (Section Match): 2nd (lost on tie re-shoot)
1972	Young Soldiers' Prize: Private Cooper (A), Winner
	NRA Kinnaird Cup: Corporal Stainer (C), Winner
	China Cup: 5th
	Dragon Trophy (Major Units Championship): 5th
	Wessex Volunteers Cup: Winners & 3rd
1974	Sitting Cups (TARA & NRA): Private A Lee (A), Winner
1975	PSIs' Match: WO1 J H Wheeler, Winner

1976   Converted Gallery Range Match: 3rd
              Team Rifle Match: 4th
              Yorkshire Volunteers Cup (Moving Target Match): 3rd
1977 (50)[4] PSIs' Match: WO2 M S O'F Cook, Winner
              Electric Target Range [ETR] Match: L/Corporal Daden, Winner
1978 (73)   Dragon Trophy: 9th
              Yorkshire Volunteers Cup: Winners
              Wessex Volunteers Cup: 2nd
1979   HM The Queen's Medal: Corporal R C Price, Winner
              China Cup: Winners
              Converted Gallery Range Match: 4th
              ETR Match: 8th
              SMG Match: Winners
              Team Rifle Aggregate Match: 3rd
              Yorkshire Volunteers Cup: 2nd
1980   Dragon Trophy (Major Unit Championship): Winners
              China Cup: 2nd
              ETR Match: Winners
              NRA Daily Telegraph Cup (Rifle team): Winners
              SMG Match: Winners
              Snap Shooting Match: Winners
              Wessex Volunteers Cup: Winners
              Volongdis Cup (GPMG Match): Winners
1981   3 members of the team in the TA Top 20 for HM The Queen's
                 Medal
1982 (32)   HM The Queen's Medal & TA Top 20: Sgt R C Price, 3rd;
                 Sgt Chivers, 13th; & L/Cpl R V Turner, 19th
              Mullens Trophy (Individual): Sgt K Chivers, 2nd; WO2 C P
                 Henrick, 9th;
              Secretary of State for War's Cup: Corporal I R Upshall &
                 Private Jessop tied for 4th place
              Army Rifle Association [ARA] Cup: Winners
              China Cup: Winners
              Dragon Trophy: 5th
              ETR Match: winners
              Mullens Trophy (Rifle team): Winners
              Quartet Cup (Rifle team): Winners
              TARA Cup (Rifle team): Winners

1983 (63)   HM The Queen's Medal: Sergeant Price, 20th
               Wessex Regiment Cup: 6th

1984 (60)   HM The Queen's Medal & TA 50: Private Bull, 10th & Best
               Trained Soldier; WO2 Hendrick, 13th; C/Sergeant Chivers,
               19th
               ARA Cup: Winners
               Dragon Trophy: 3rd
               Highland Volunteers Quaich (Rifle team): 2nd; (Individual):
               C/Sergeant Chivers Winner
               NRA Imperial Tobacco Trophy (Rifle): Private Bull, Winner
               Standing Match (Rifle): Private Bull, Winner
               Wessex Regiment Cup: 2nd
               Yorkshire Volunteers Cup (Rifle team): 2nd

1985 (60)   HM The Queen's Medal & TA 50: Private Lee, 16th & Best
               Trained Soldier, 2nd
               NRA Imperial Tobacco Trophy: Private Bull, Winner
               China Cup: 2nd
               Dragon Trophy: 6th
               Highland Volunteers Quaich (Team): Winners; (Individual):
               Private Bull, tied 3rd
               GPMG(SF) Match: Winners
               Moving Target Match: Winners
               Wessex Regiment Cup: 6th
               Yorkshire Volunteers Cup: 7th

1986 (51)   China Cup: 41st (!)
               Dragon Trophy: 42nd (!)
               GPMG(SF) Match: Medalists

1987 (52)   NBC Match: Winners
               GPMG Match: 2nd
               Yorkshire Volunteers Cup: 3rd

1988 (57)   HM The Queen's Medal & TA 50: Private D Coward, 26th
               China Cup: 2nd
               GPMG Match: winners
               NBC Match: 3rd

1989 (56)   HM The Queen's Medal & TA 50: Colour Sergeant R C
               Price, 22nd
               Highland Volunteers Quaich (Team): 4th; (Individual):
               Colour Sergeant Price, Winner

1990   Dragon Trophy: 11th

[1991–1995 No teams at Bisley]

Smallbore Competitions

1969	TAVR Smallbore Team Competition (Duke of Norfolk's Cup): A Company 1st in Stage 1 & 4th in Stage 2
1971	Duke of Norfolk's Cup: Battalion teams 5th, 7th & 15th (ex 52)
1972	Duke of Norfolk's Cup: A Company 2nd ex 64 teams
1974	C/Sgt D Bate-Jones & Cpl P Evens members of the TA team in the Inter Services Smallbore Match
1975	TAVR Smallbore Individual Match: C/Sgt D Bate-Jones, Winner
1976	National Small Bore Association Match: C Company 6/72 TAVR Smallbore Individual Match: C/Sgt D Bate-Jones, Winner
1982	Duke of Norfolk's Cup: C Company, Winners
1983	Duke of Norfolk's Cup: C Company, Winners
1987	National Heckler-Koch Conversion (Shooting) Competition: C Company, Winners
1987–1988	Army Smallbore Winter League (Div 3): HQ Coy PSIs, Winners
1988	National Heckler-Koch Competition: C Company, Winners
1989	National Heckler-Koch Competition: C Company, Winners

---

[1] For example, a number of members of the former Royal Green Jackets TA battalions' shooting teams, unable to get into the new NATO-roled 5 RGJ joined an RAOC Mobile Bath Unit – which, contrary to what its title implied, won a large number Bisley trophies and prizes for a good many years.

[2] The Dragon Trophy is the aggregate of the scores in the China Cup, Highland Volunteers' Quaich, Wessex Regiment Cup, Mullens Trophy, Yorkshire Volunteers' Cup, Volongdis & SMG Match.

[3] "A distinct feeling of inevitability creeps into the proceedings" *D&DRJ*, July1983.

[4] The total number of competing teams.

APPENDIX 6

OTHER MAJOR BATTALION ACHIEVEMENTS: 1980-1995

1980	SW District Section Competition: 2nd, 3rd & 4th
1982	1 Infantry Brigade Medium Anti-tank Weapon Concentration: L/Cpls Hyatt & Cusack (E Company) winners
	SW District Section Competition: C Company winners
	SW District Unit Cookery Competitions: winners
1983	SW District Section Competition: C Company winners
	SW District Unit Cookery Competition: winners
1984-1986	1 Infantry Brigade TA Line Laying Champions
1986	SW District TA Orienteering Champions: HQ Company
	UKLF TA Orienteering Finalists: HQ Company
	Regular & TA Infantry Major Units Orienteering: HQ Company 3rd
1987	SW District TA Orienteering Champions: HQ Company
	UKLF TA Orienteering finalists
1988	UKMF Orienteering champions
	SW District Orienteering champions
	Prince of Wales' Division (Regular & TA) Sailing Regatta: 3rd
	Infantry Sailing Regatta: winners
	Army Sailing Regatta: 8th
1989	SW District TA Orienteering champions: HQ Company
	Regular & TA Minor Units Orienteering Competition: HQ Company 4th
1990-1994	[No extant information about competition successes]

APPENDIX 7

THE COUNCIL OF TAVR ASSOCIATIONS
1967 — 2001

CHAIRMEN

Major The Duke of Norfolk KG PC GCVO CBE TD
1956-1969
Colonel The Lord Clydesmuir KT CB MBE TD
1969-1973
Major General Lord Michael Fitzalan Howard GCVO CB CBE MC DL
1973-1981
Lieutenant General Sir Peter Hudson KCB CBE DL
1981-1990
General Sir John Akehurst KCB CBE
1990-1995
General Sir Edward Jones KCB CBE
1995-2000

SECRETARIES

Brigadier A C Tyler CBE MC DL
1967-1972
Brigadier B T V Cowey DSO OBE DL
1973-1975
Major General W Bate CB OBE DL
1975-1985
Major General M Matthews CB DL
1986-1993
Major General W A Evans CB DL
1993-2001

INDEX

NB: "*passim*" means "many times"; "*et seq*" means "and after this"; "*et seq passim*" means "many times after this".